RENT-A-GIRLFRIEND

VOLUME **9**

REIJI MIYAJIMA

CONTENTS

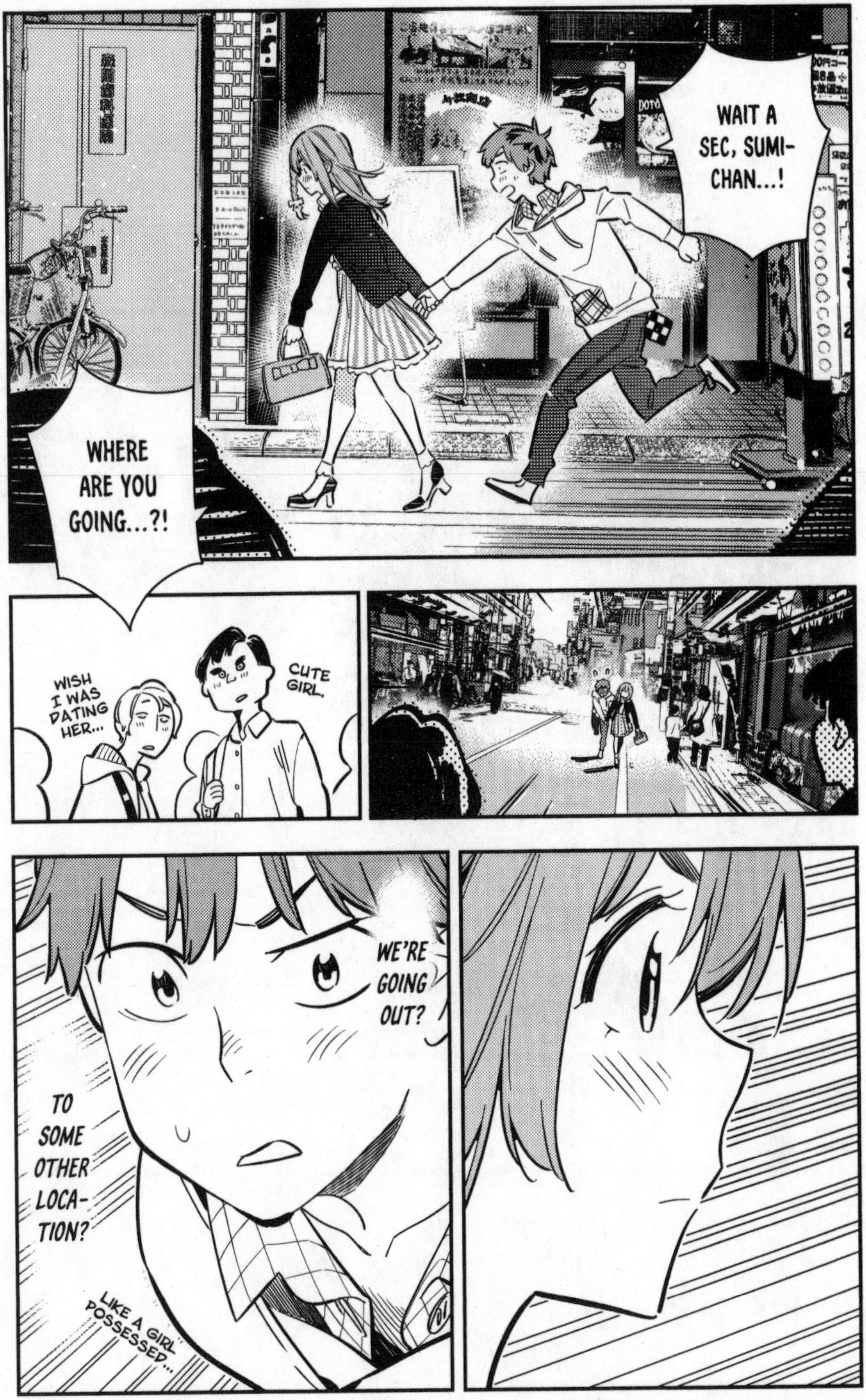
WAIT A SEC, SUMI-CHAN...!
WHERE ARE YOU GOING...?!
CUTE GIRL.
WISH I WAS DATING HER...
WE'RE GOING OUT?
TO SOME OTHER LOCA-TION?
LIKE A GIRL POSSESSED...

RATING 68 THE BIRTHDAY AND MY GIRLFRIEND 3

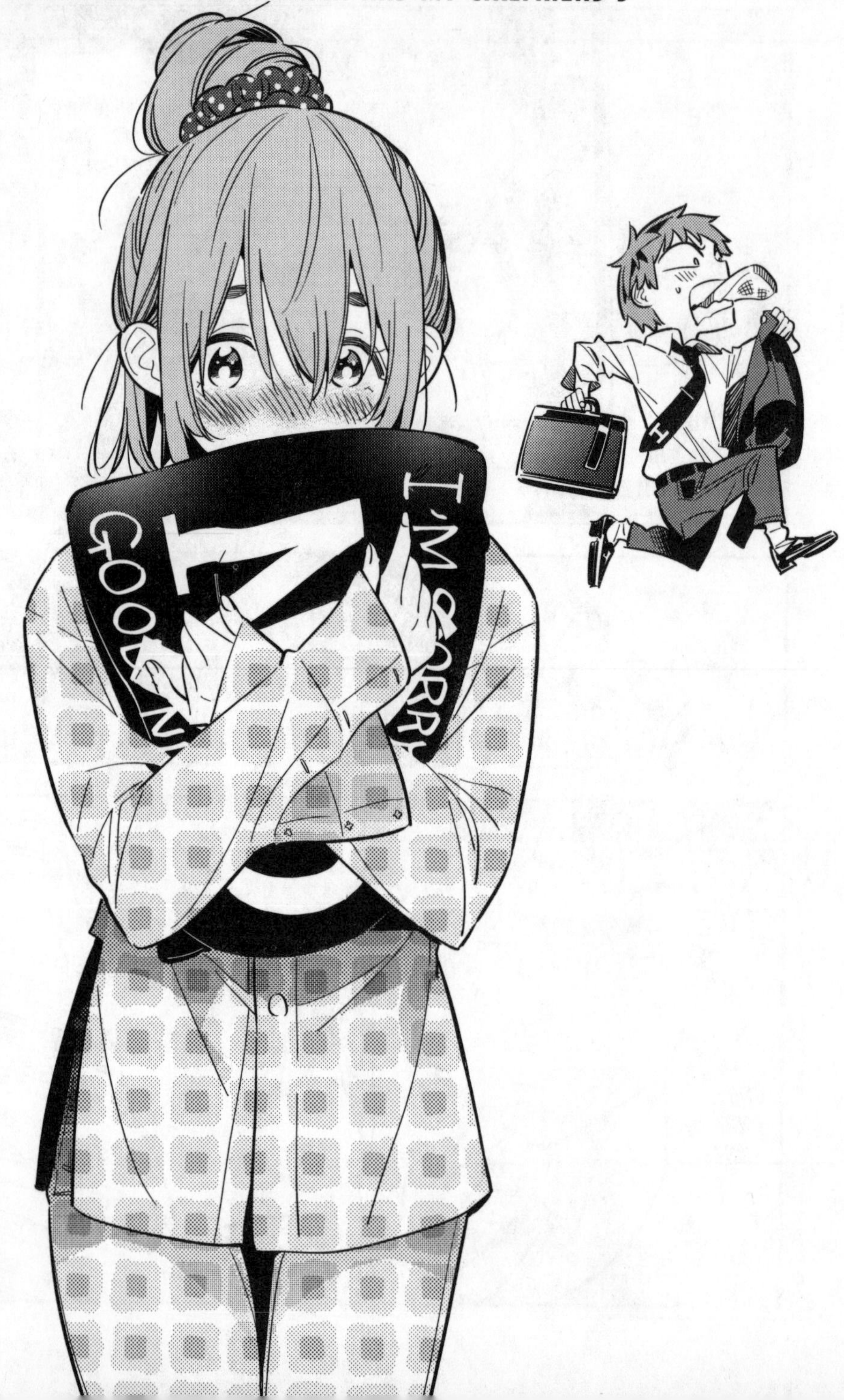

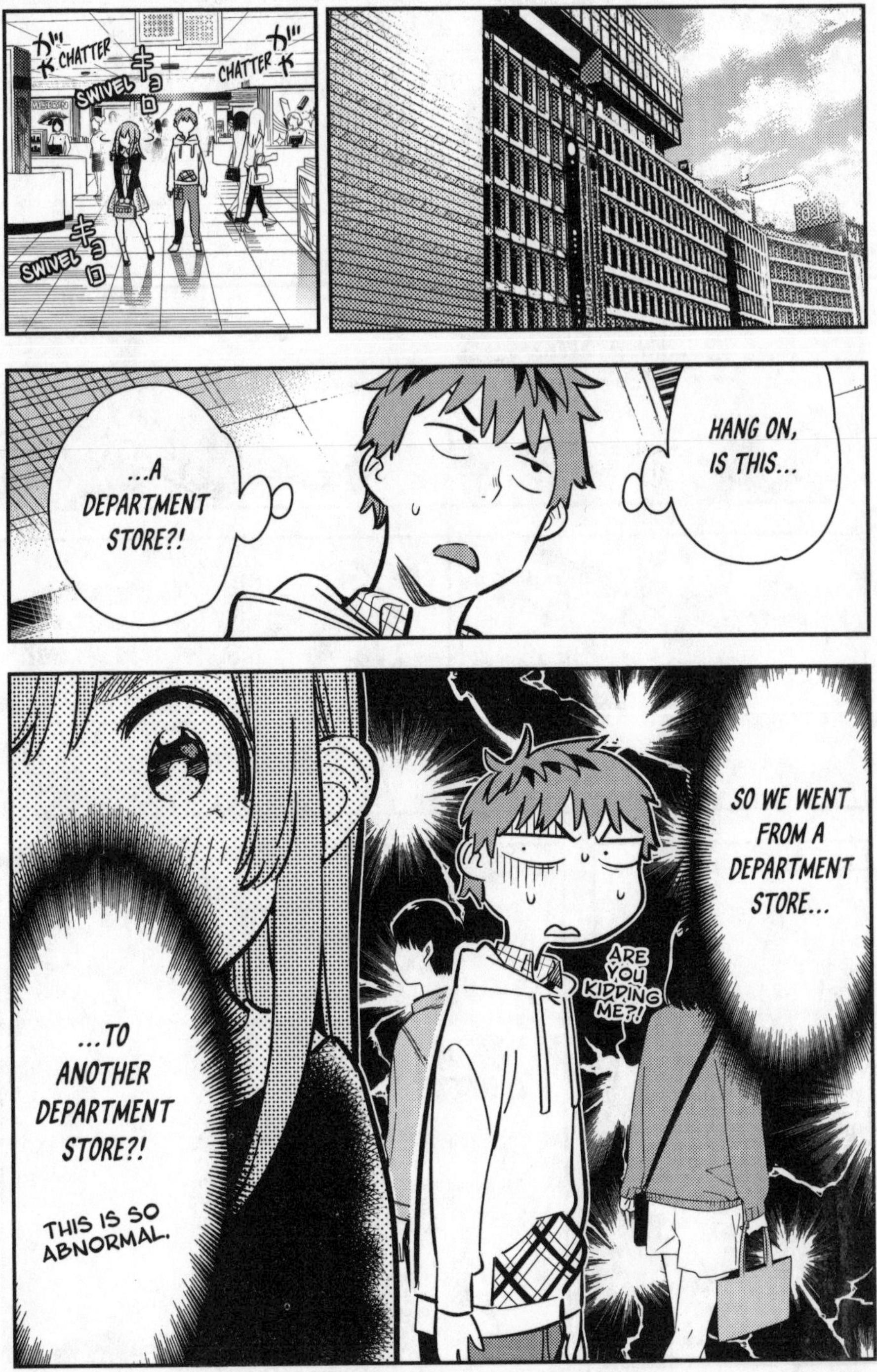
CHATTER ガヤ
ガヤ CHATTER
キョロ SWIVEL
キョロ SWIVEL
HANG ON, IS THIS...
...A DEPARTMENT STORE?!
SO WE WENT FROM A DEPARTMENT STORE...
ARE YOU KIDDING ME?!
...TO ANOTHER DEPARTMENT STORE?!
THIS IS SO ABNORMAL.

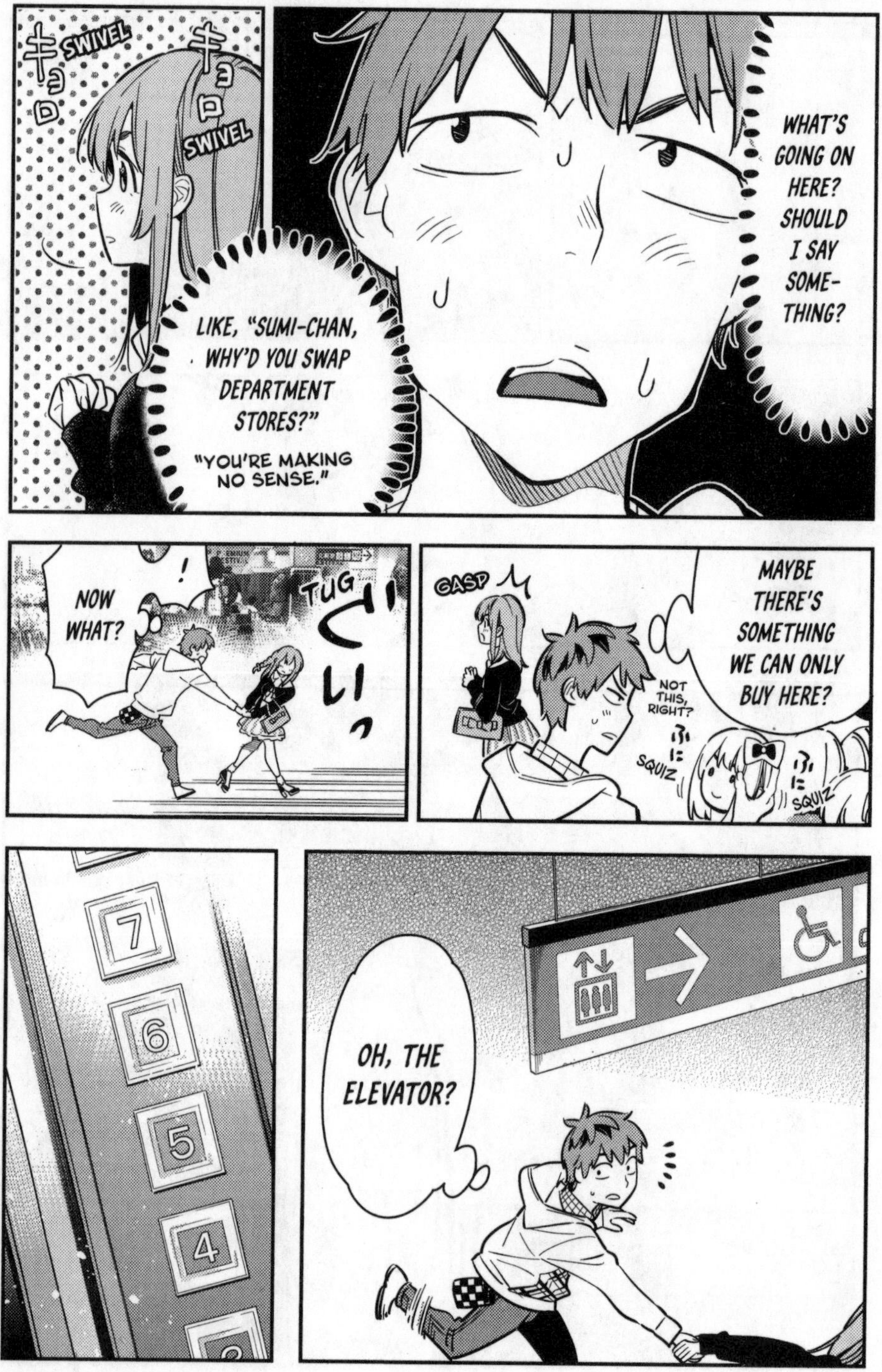
WHAT'S GOING ON HERE? SHOULD I SAY SOME-THING?
LIKE, "SUMI-CHAN, WHY'D YOU SWAP DEPARTMENT STORES?"
"YOU'RE MAKING NO SENSE."
キョロ SWIVEL
キョロ SWIVEL
MAYBE THERE'S SOMETHING WE CAN ONLY BUY HERE?
GASP
NOT THIS, RIGHT?
ふに SQUIZ
ふに SQUIZ
TUG ぐいっ
!
NOW WHAT?
OH, THE ELEVATOR?

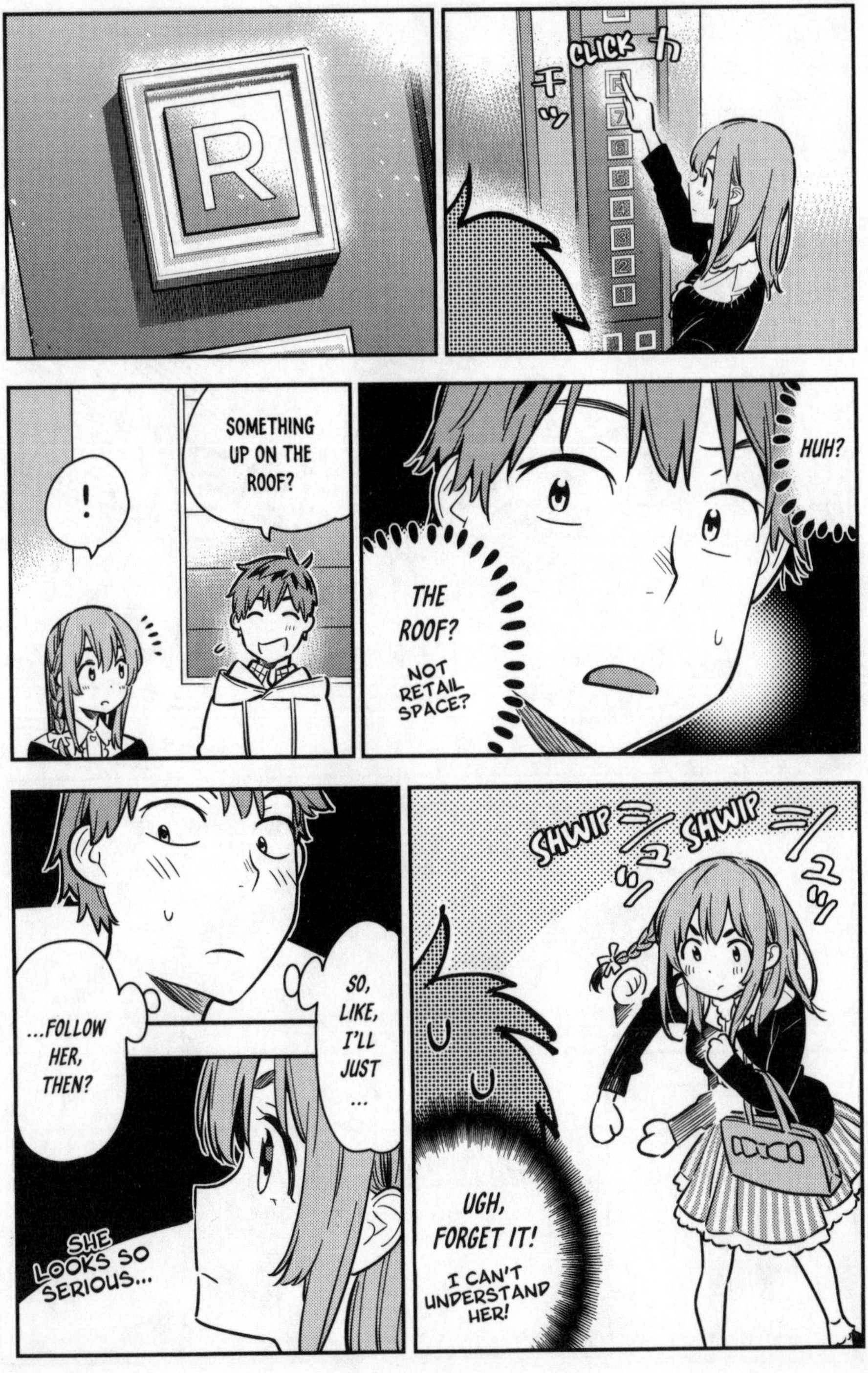
CLICK カチッ
R
HUH?
THE ROOF?
NOT RETAIL SPACE?
SOMETHING UP ON THE ROOF?
!
SHWIP シュッ SHWIP シュッ
UGH, FORGET IT!
I CAN'T UNDERSTAND HER!
SO, LIKE, I'LL JUST ...
...FOLLOW HER, THEN?
SHE LOOKS SO SERIOUS...

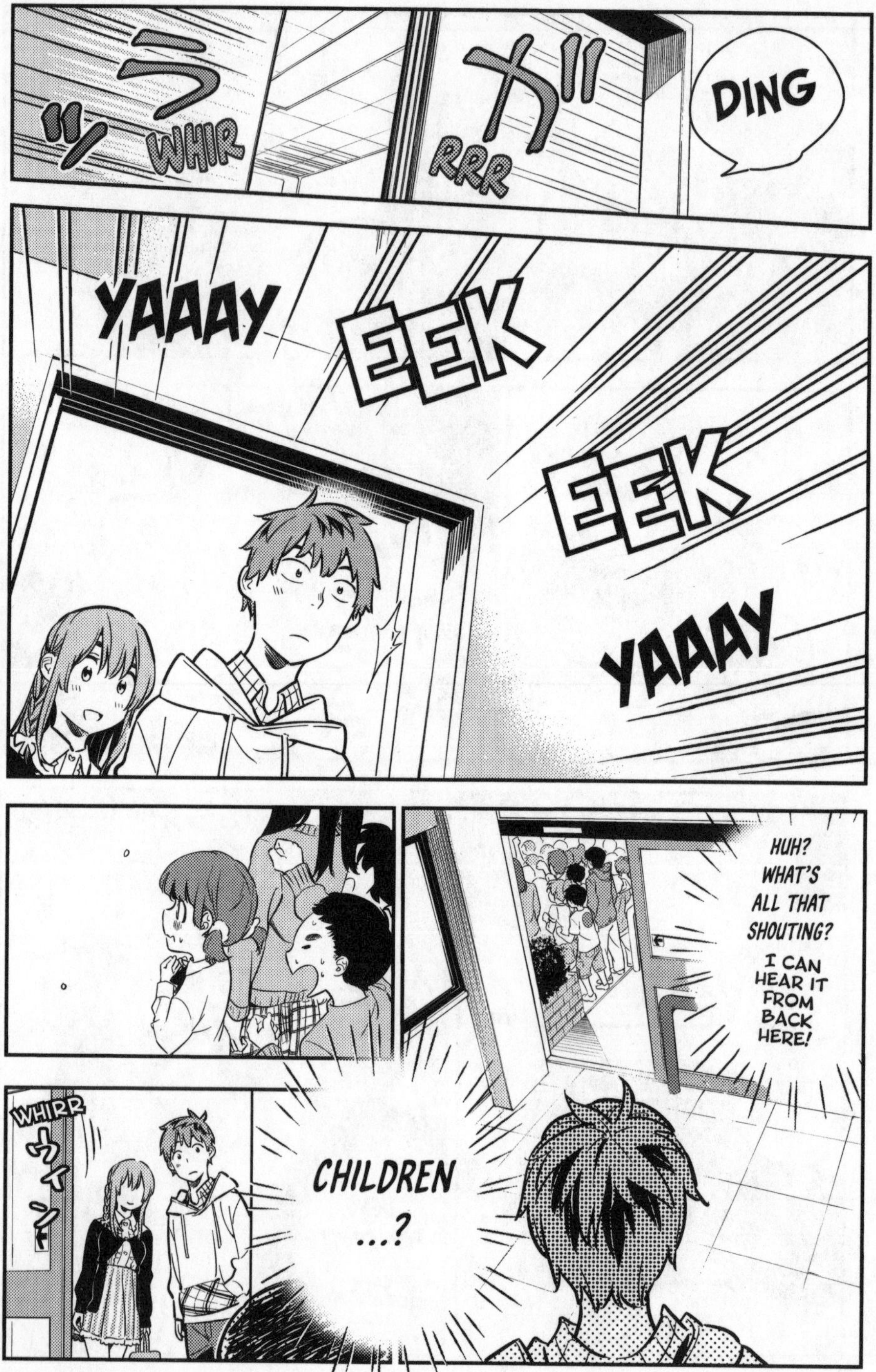
DING
RRR
WHIR
EEK
YAAAY
EEK
YAAAY
HUH? WHAT'S ALL THAT SHOUTING?
I CAN HEAR IT FROM BACK HERE!
CHILDREN ...?
WHIRR

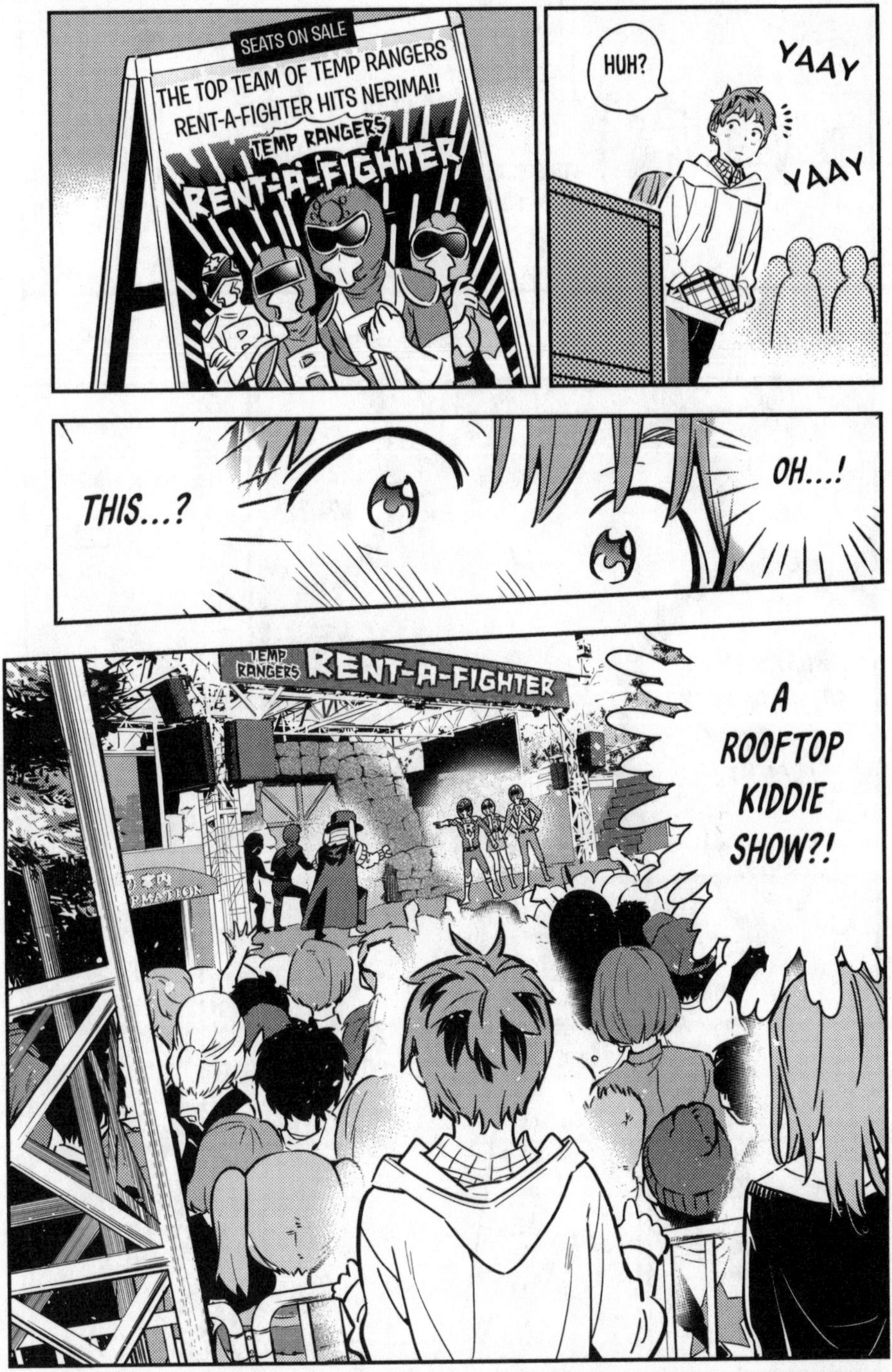
HUH?
YAAY
YAAY
SEATS ON SALE
THE TOP TEAM OF TEMP RANGERS
RENT-A-FIGHTER HITS NERIMA!!
TEMP RANGERS
RENT-A-FIGHTER
OH...!
THIS...?
A ROOFTOP KIDDIE SHOW?!
TEMP RANGERS RENT-A-FIGHTER

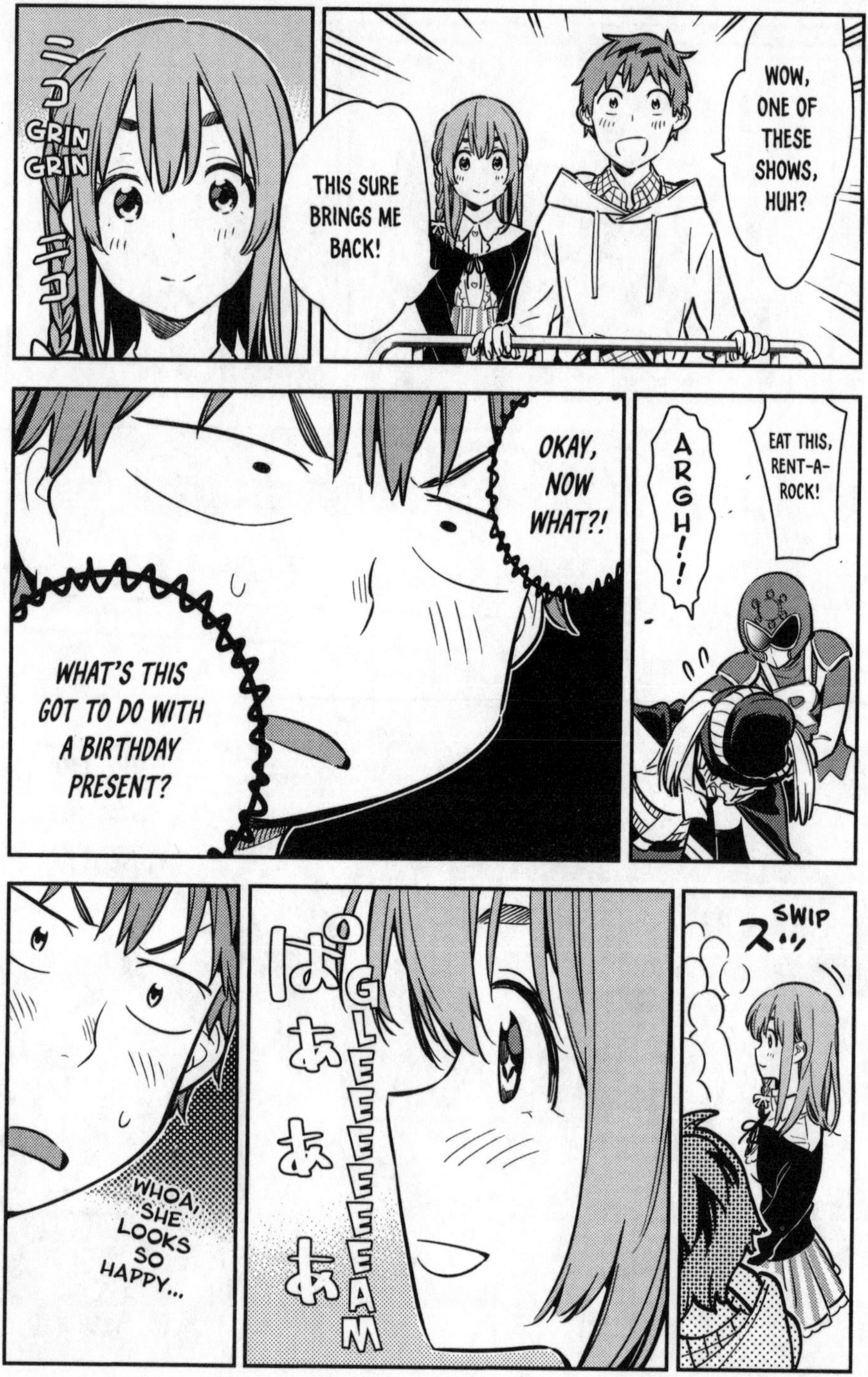
WOW, ONE OF THESE SHOWS, HUH?
THIS SURE BRINGS ME BACK!
ニコ GRIN GRIN ニコ
EAT THIS, RENT-A-ROCK!
ARGH!!
OKAY, NOW WHAT?!
WHAT'S THIS GOT TO DO WITH A BIRTHDAY PRESENT?
スッ SWIP
ぱあああ GLEEEEEEAM
WHOA, SHE LOOKS SO HAPPY...

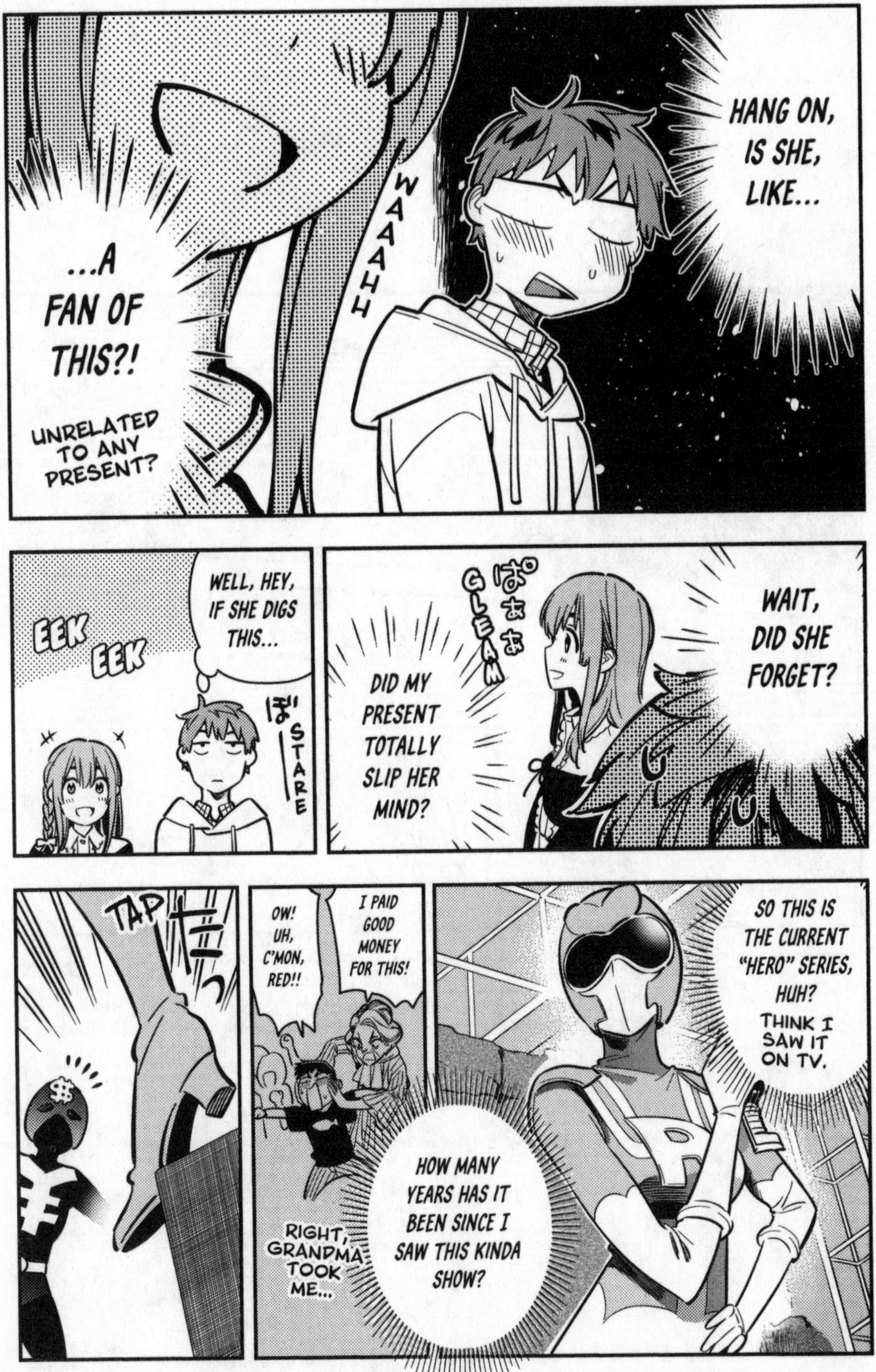
HANG ON, IS SHE, LIKE...
WAAAAHH
...A FAN OF THIS?!
UNRELATED TO ANY PRESENT?
WAIT, DID SHE FORGET?
ぱぁぁ GLEAM
DID MY PRESENT TOTALLY SLIP HER MIND?
WELL, HEY, IF SHE DIGS THIS...
ぼー STARE
EEK EEK
SO THIS IS THE CURRENT "HERO" SERIES, HUH?
THINK I SAW IT ON TV.
HOW MANY YEARS HAS IT BEEN SINCE I SAW THIS KINDA SHOW?
I PAID GOOD MONEY FOR THIS!
OW! UH, C'MON, RED!!
RIGHT, GRANDMA TOOK ME...
TAP

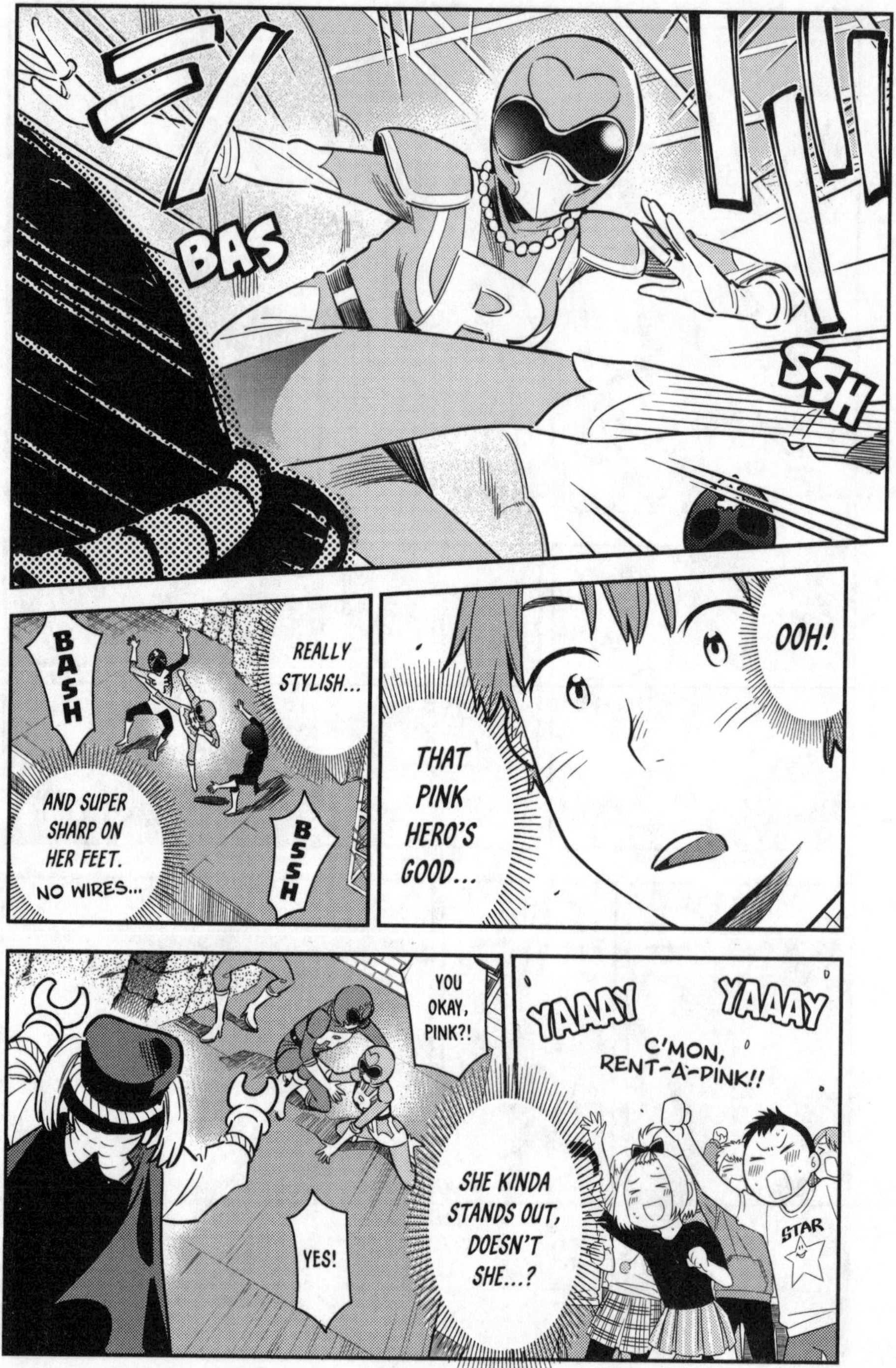
BAS
SSH
OOH!
THAT PINK HERO'S GOOD...
REALLY STYLISH...
AND SUPER SHARP ON HER FEET. NO WIRES...
BASH
BSSH
YAAAY
YAAAY
C'MON, RENT-A-PINK!!
SHE KINDA STANDS OUT, DOESN'T SHE...?
STAR
YOU OKAY, PINK?!
YES!

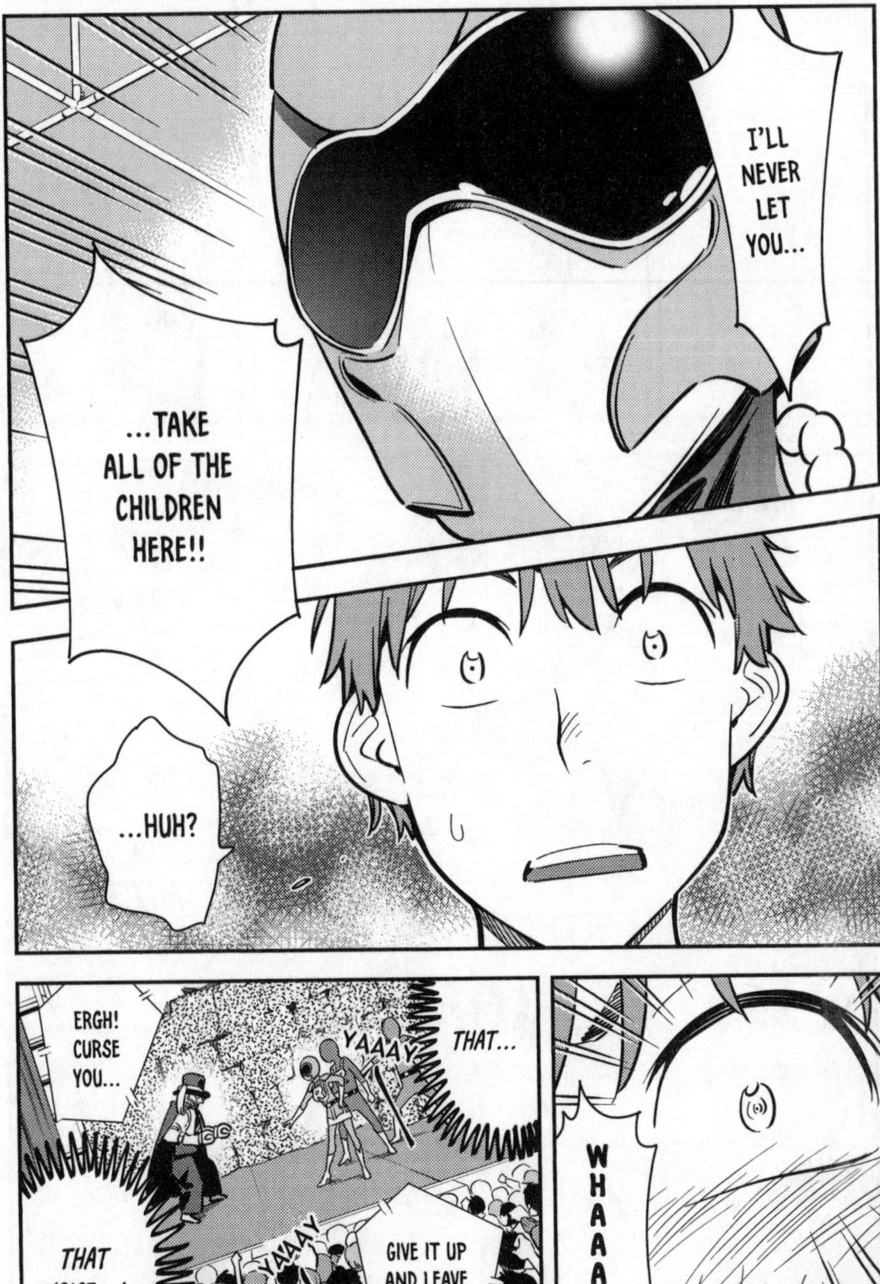
I'LL NEVER LET YOU...
...TAKE ALL OF THE CHILDREN HERE!!
...HUH?
WHAAAA?!
THAT...
YAAAY
ERGH! CURSE YOU...
GIVE IT UP AND LEAVE NOW!
YAAAY
THAT VOICE...!

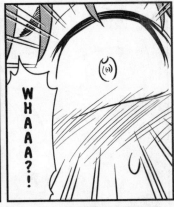

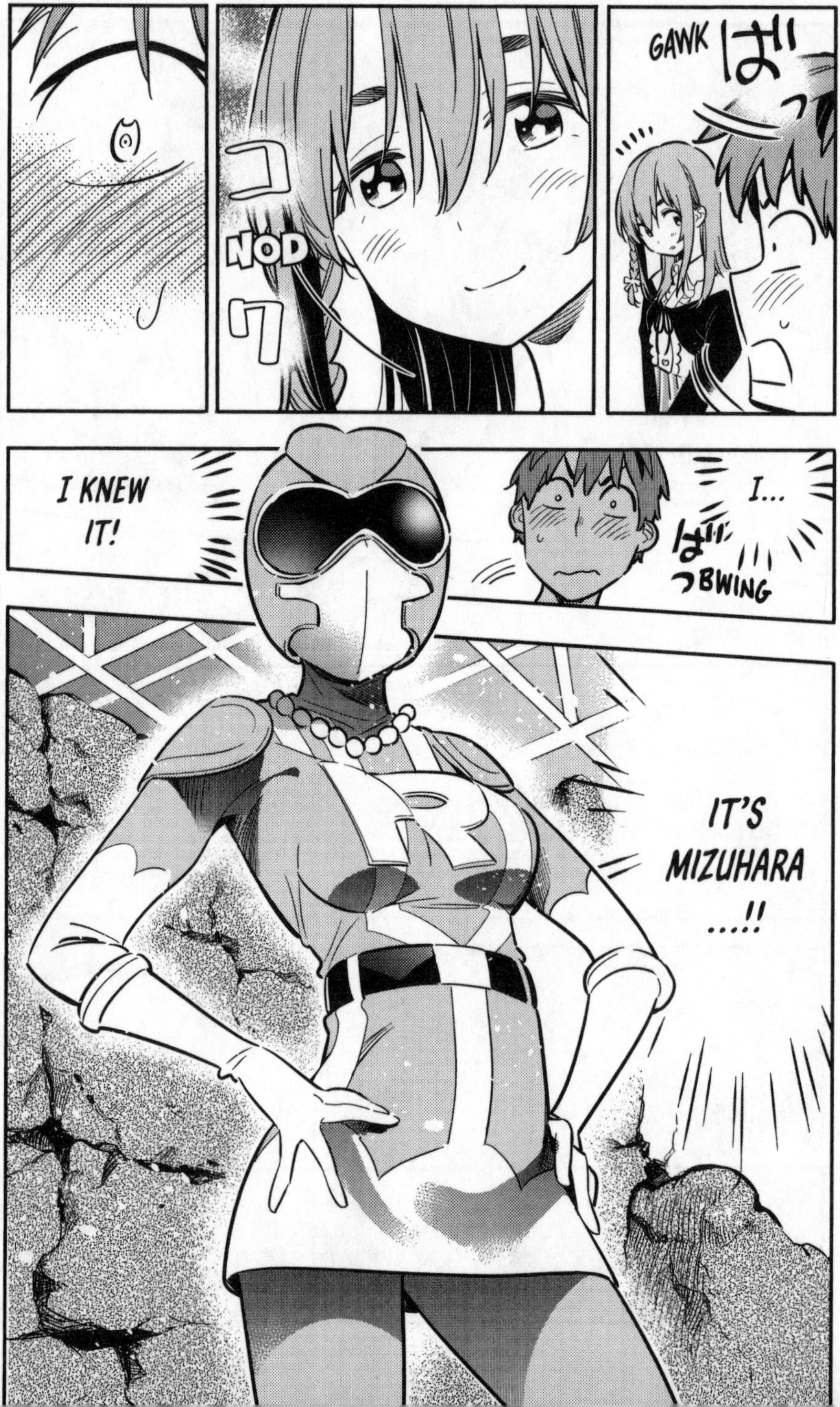
GAWK
ばっ
コク
NOD
I...
ばっ
BWING
I KNEW IT!
IT'S MIZUHARA ...!!

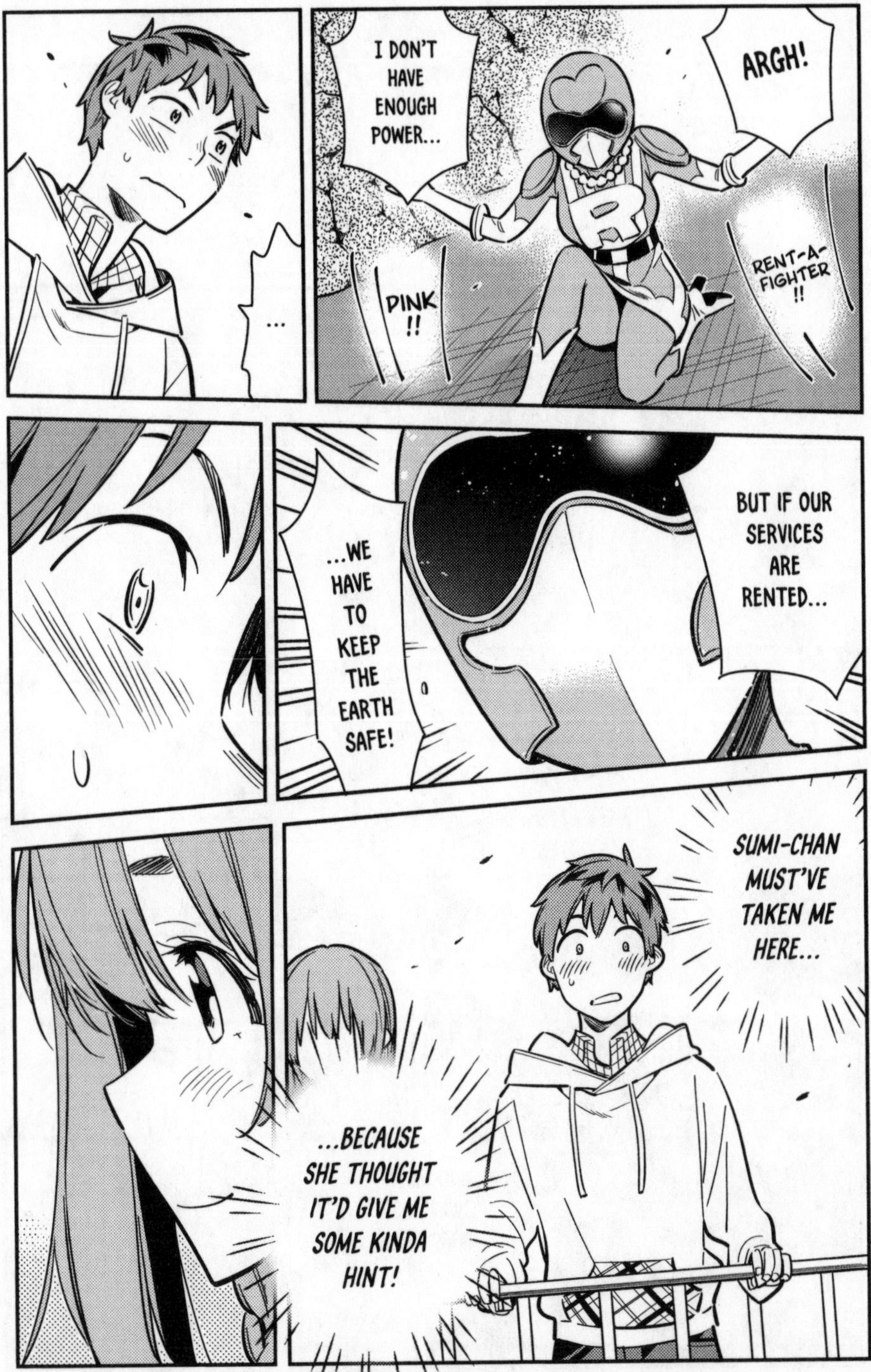
ARGH!
I DON'T HAVE ENOUGH POWER...
RENT-A-FIGHTER !!
PINK !!
...
BUT IF OUR SERVICES ARE RENTED...
...WE HAVE TO KEEP THE EARTH SAFE!
SUMI-CHAN MUST'VE TAKEN ME HERE...
...BECAUSE SHE THOUGHT IT'D GIVE ME SOME KINDA HINT!

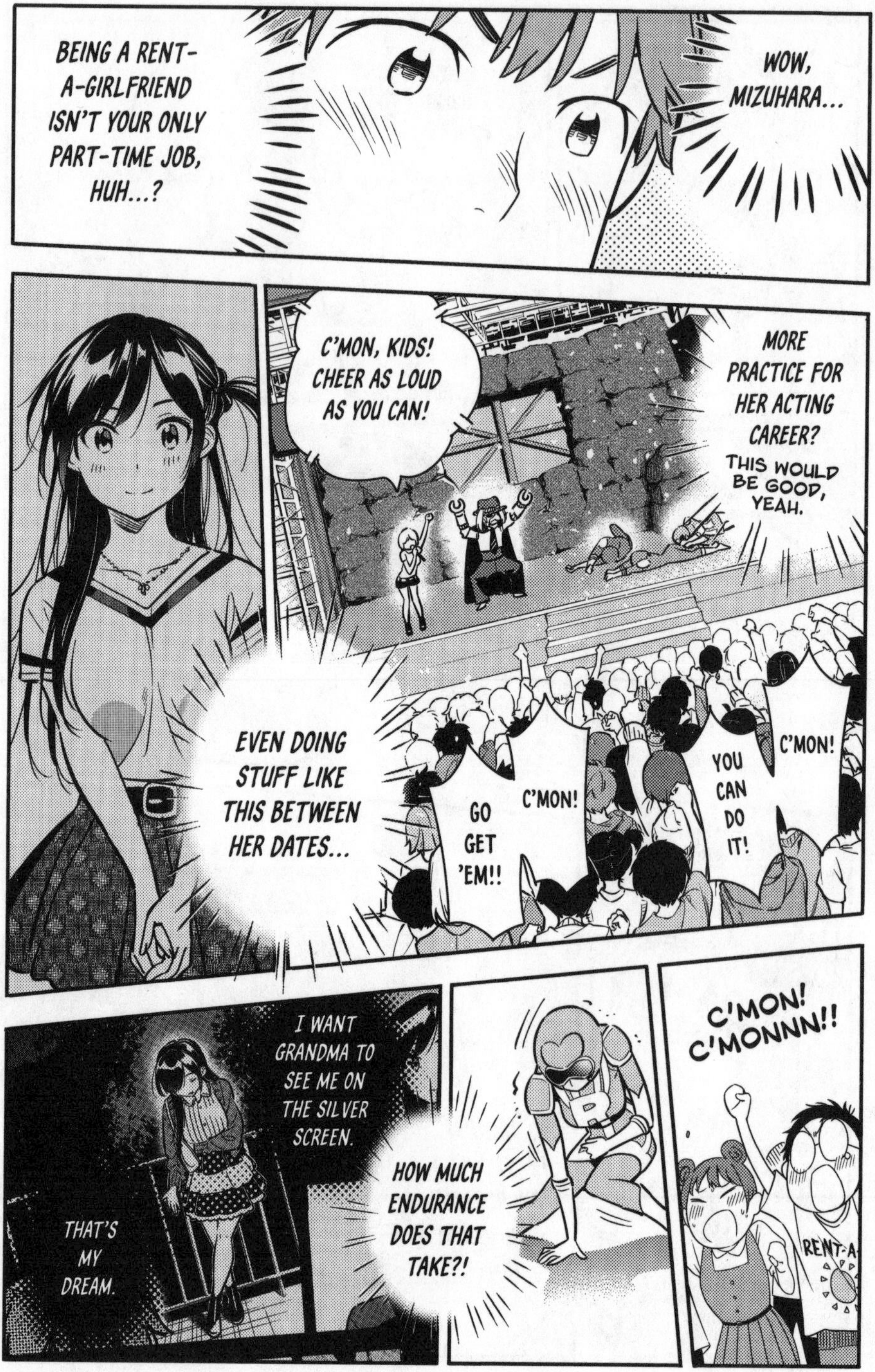
WOW, MIZUHARA...
BEING A RENT-A-GIRLFRIEND ISN'T YOUR ONLY PART-TIME JOB, HUH...?
MORE PRACTICE FOR HER ACTING CAREER?
THIS WOULD BE GOOD, YEAH.
C'MON, KIDS! CHEER AS LOUD AS YOU CAN!
C'MON!
YOU CAN DO IT!
C'MON!
GO GET 'EM!!
EVEN DOING STUFF LIKE THIS BETWEEN HER DATES...
C'MON! C'MONNN!!
RENT-A
HOW MUCH ENDURANCE DOES THAT TAKE?!
I WANT GRANDMA TO SEE ME ON THE SILVER SCREEN.
THAT'S MY DREAM.

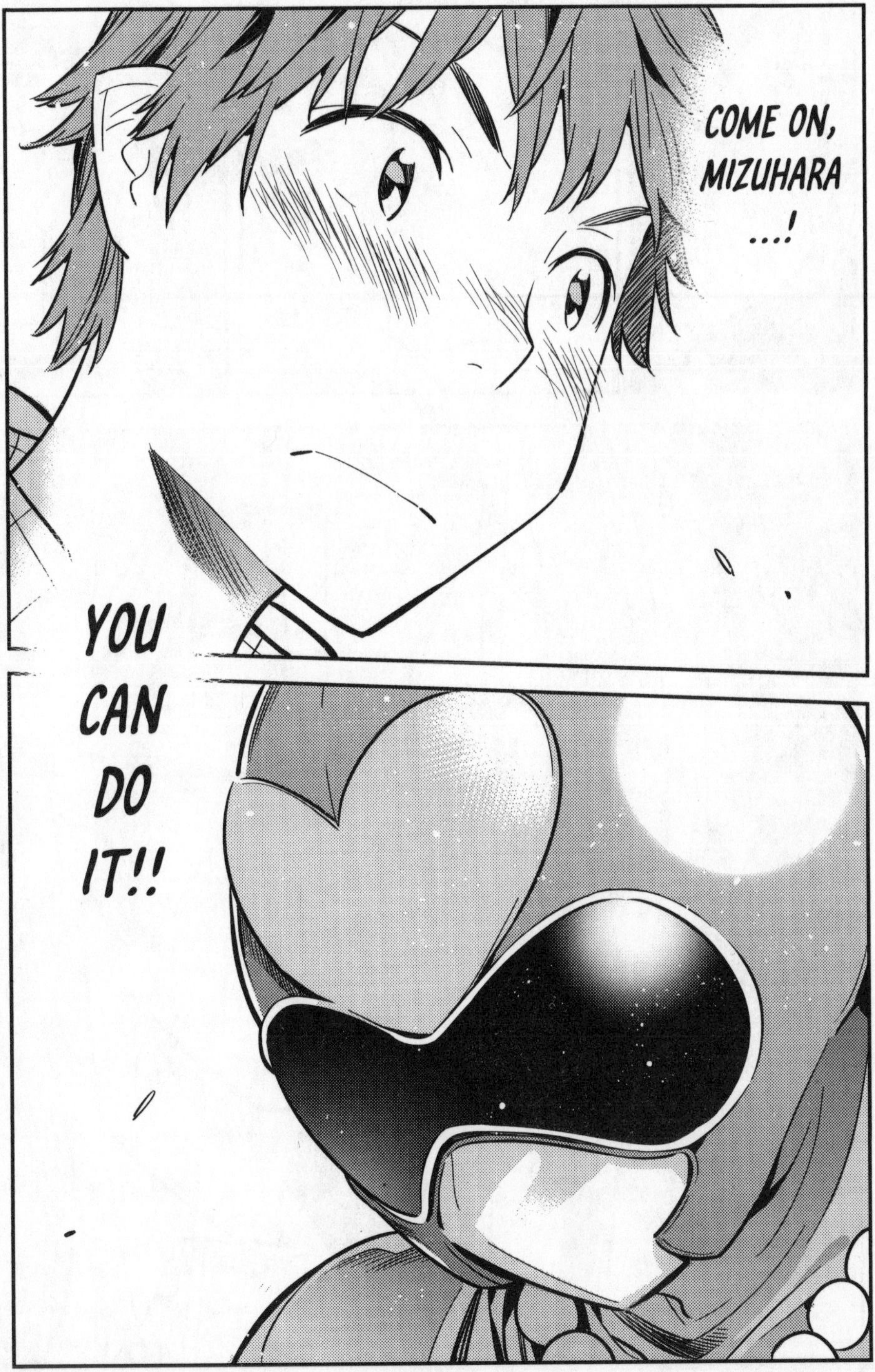
COME ON, MIZUHARA ...!
YOU CAN DO IT!!

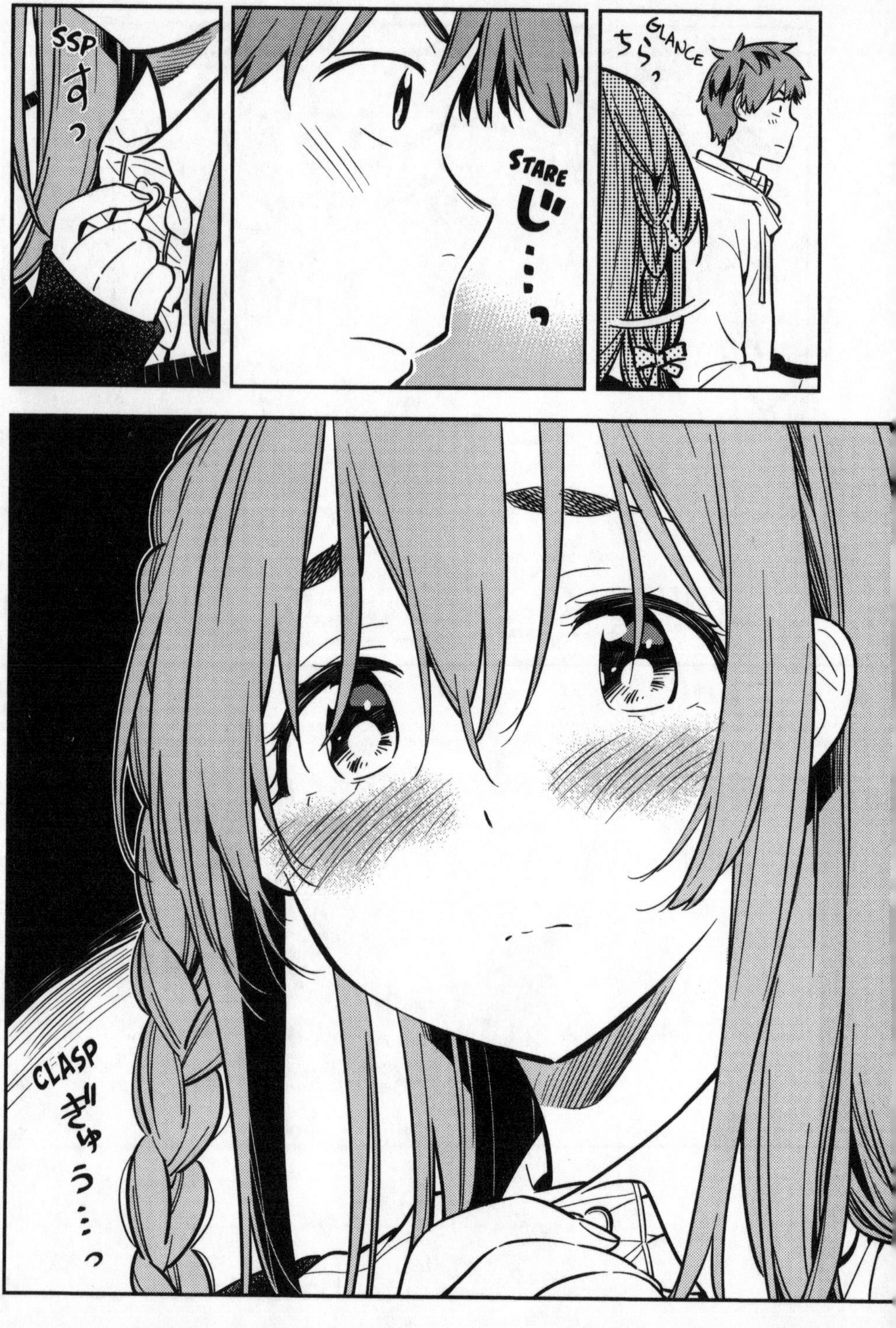
GLANCE
ちら,
STARE
じ…っ
SSP
すっ
CLASP
ぎゅう…っ

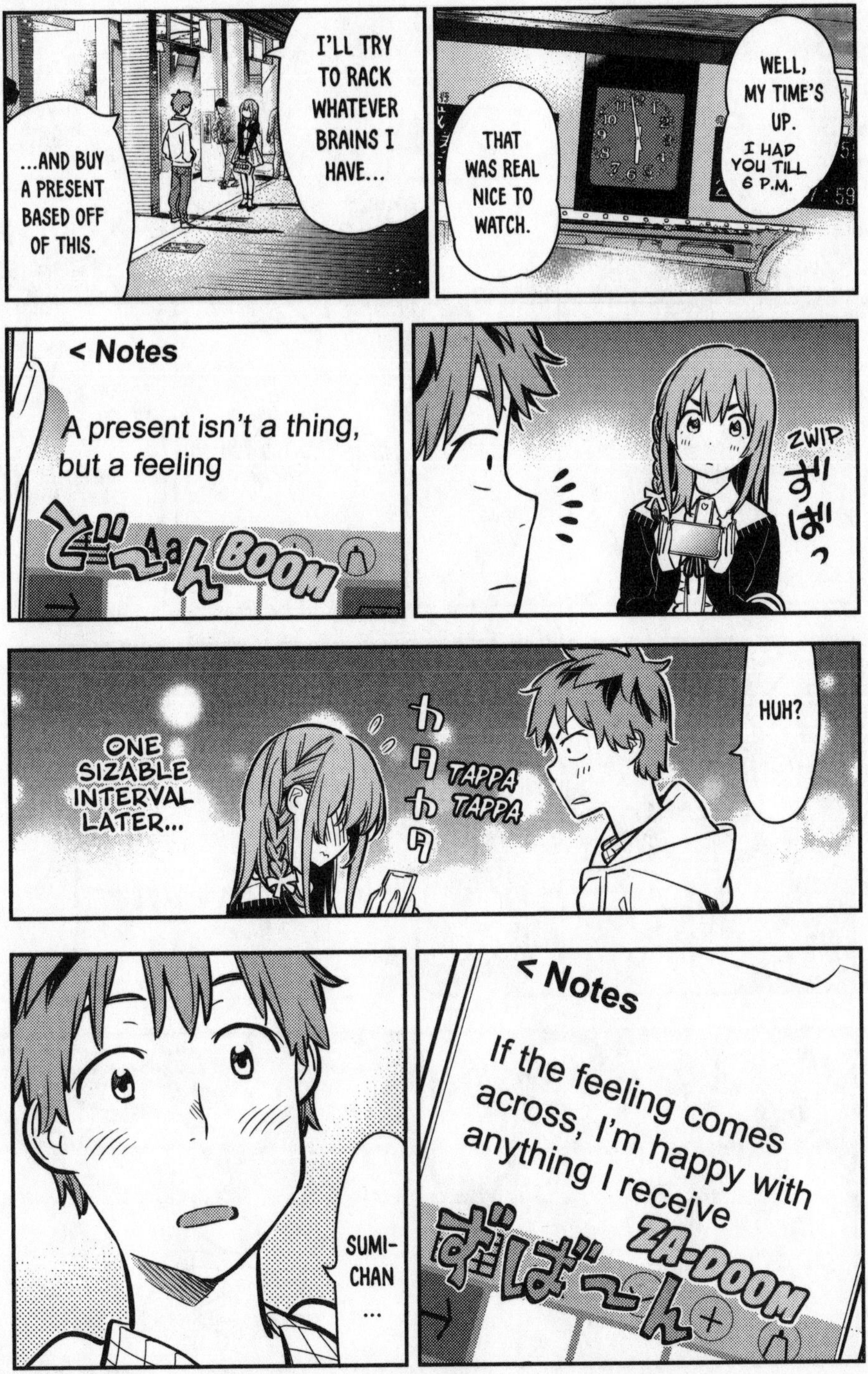
WELL, MY TIME'S UP.
I HAD YOU TILL 6 P.M.
THAT WAS REAL NICE TO WATCH.
I'LL TRY TO RACK WHATEVER BRAINS I HAVE...
...AND BUY A PRESENT BASED OFF OF THIS.
ZWIP
ずぼっ
< Notes
A present isn't a thing, but a feeling
ど〜ん
BOOM
HUH?
カタカタ
TAPPA TAPPA
ONE SIZABLE INTERVAL LATER...
< Notes
If the feeling comes across, I'm happy with anything I receive
ずば〜ん
ZA-DOOM
SUMI-CHAN ...

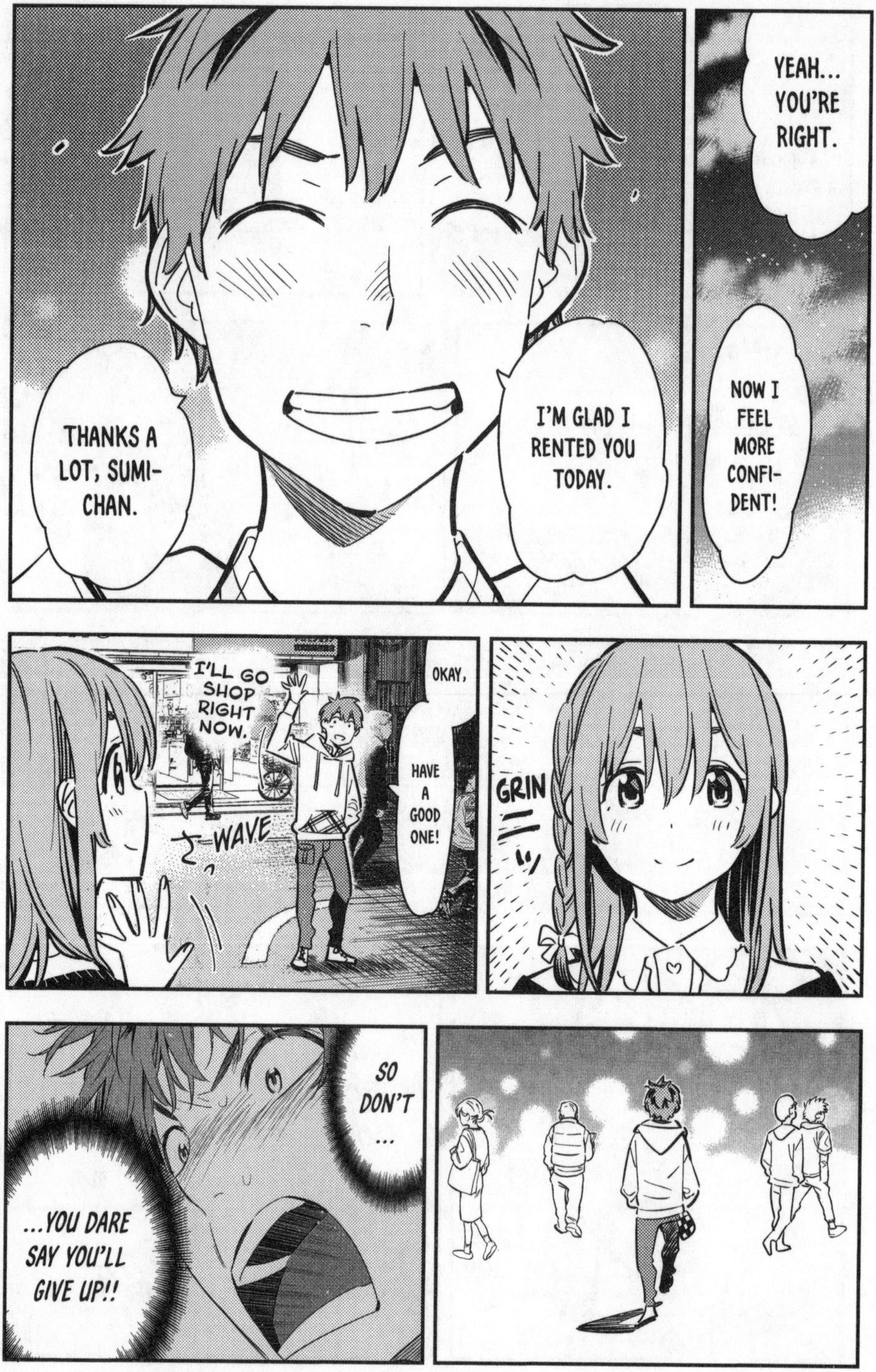
YEAH... YOU'RE RIGHT.
NOW I FEEL MORE CONFI-DENT!
I'M GLAD I RENTED YOU TODAY.
THANKS A LOT, SUMI-CHAN.
GRIN
OKAY,
I'LL GO SHOP RIGHT NOW.
HAVE A GOOD ONE!
WAVE
SO DON'T ...
...YOU DARE SAY YOU'LL GIVE UP!!

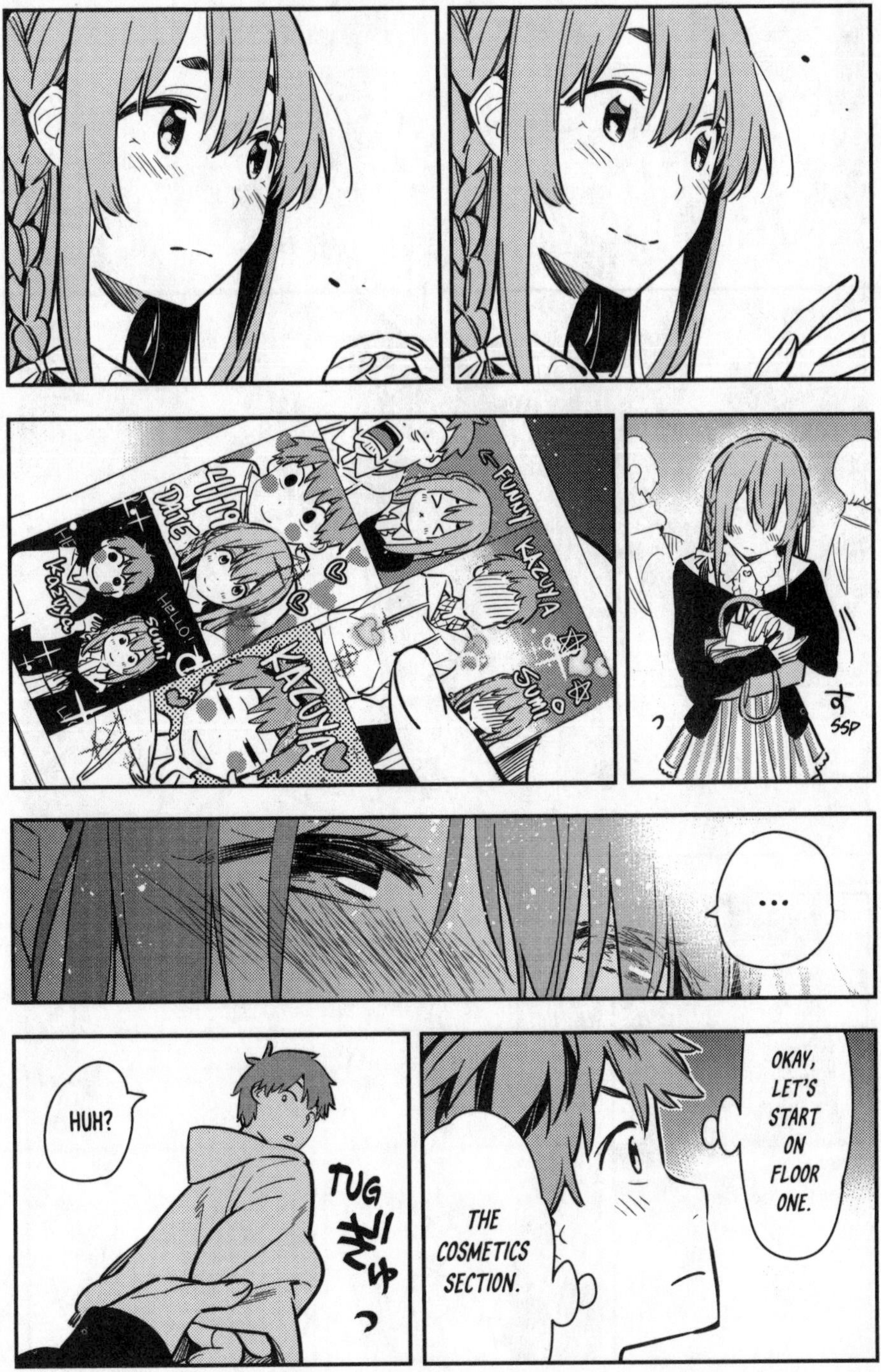
す
SSP
←FUNNY
KAZUYA
SUMI
KAZUYA
4th DATE
HELLO!
SUMI
KAZUYA
...
OKAY, LET'S START ON FLOOR ONE.
THE COSMETICS SECTION.
HUH?
TUG
ぎゅっ

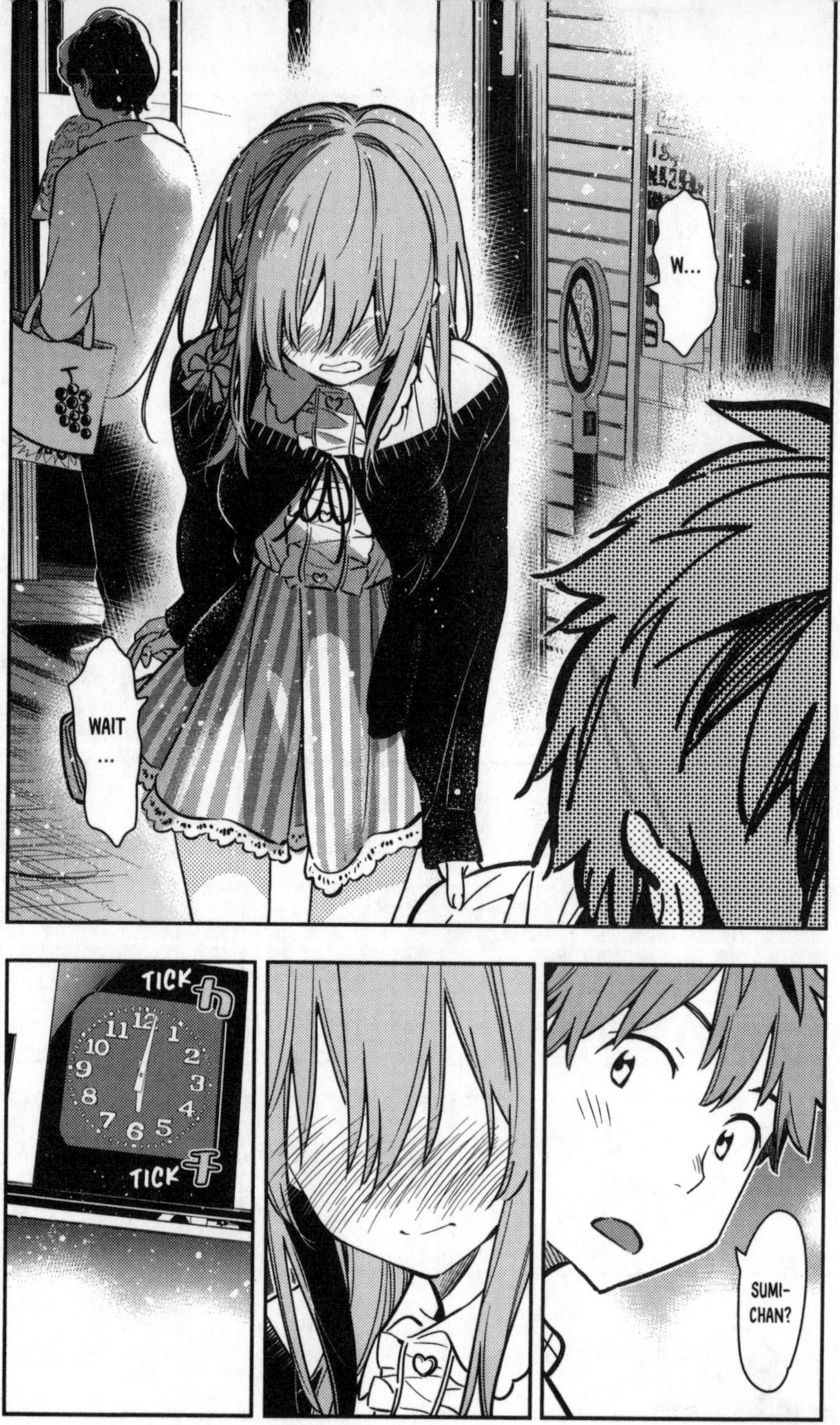
W...
WAIT ...
SUMI-CHAN?
TICK カ
TICK チ

RATING 69 THE BIRTHDAY AND MY GIRLFRIEND 4

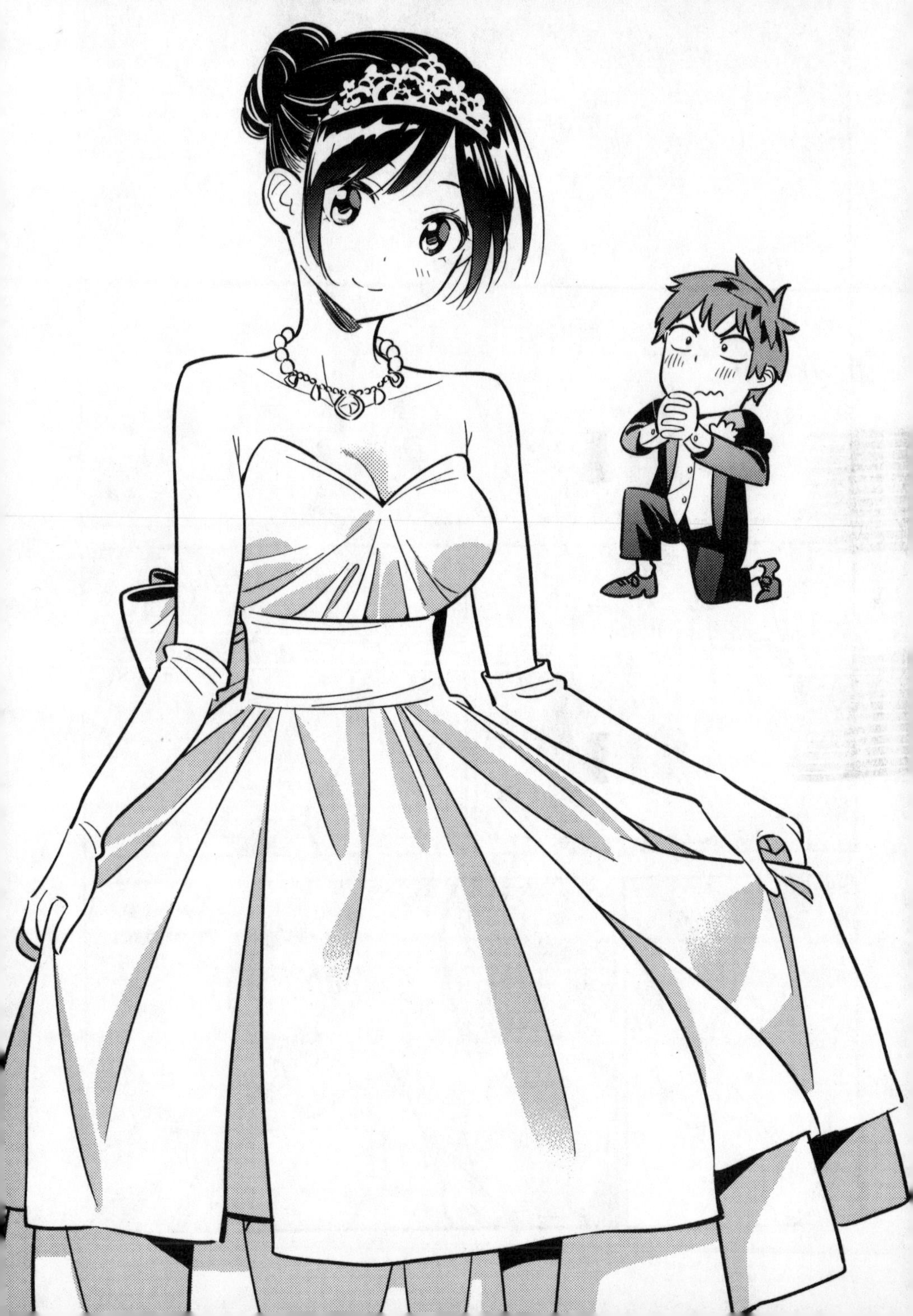

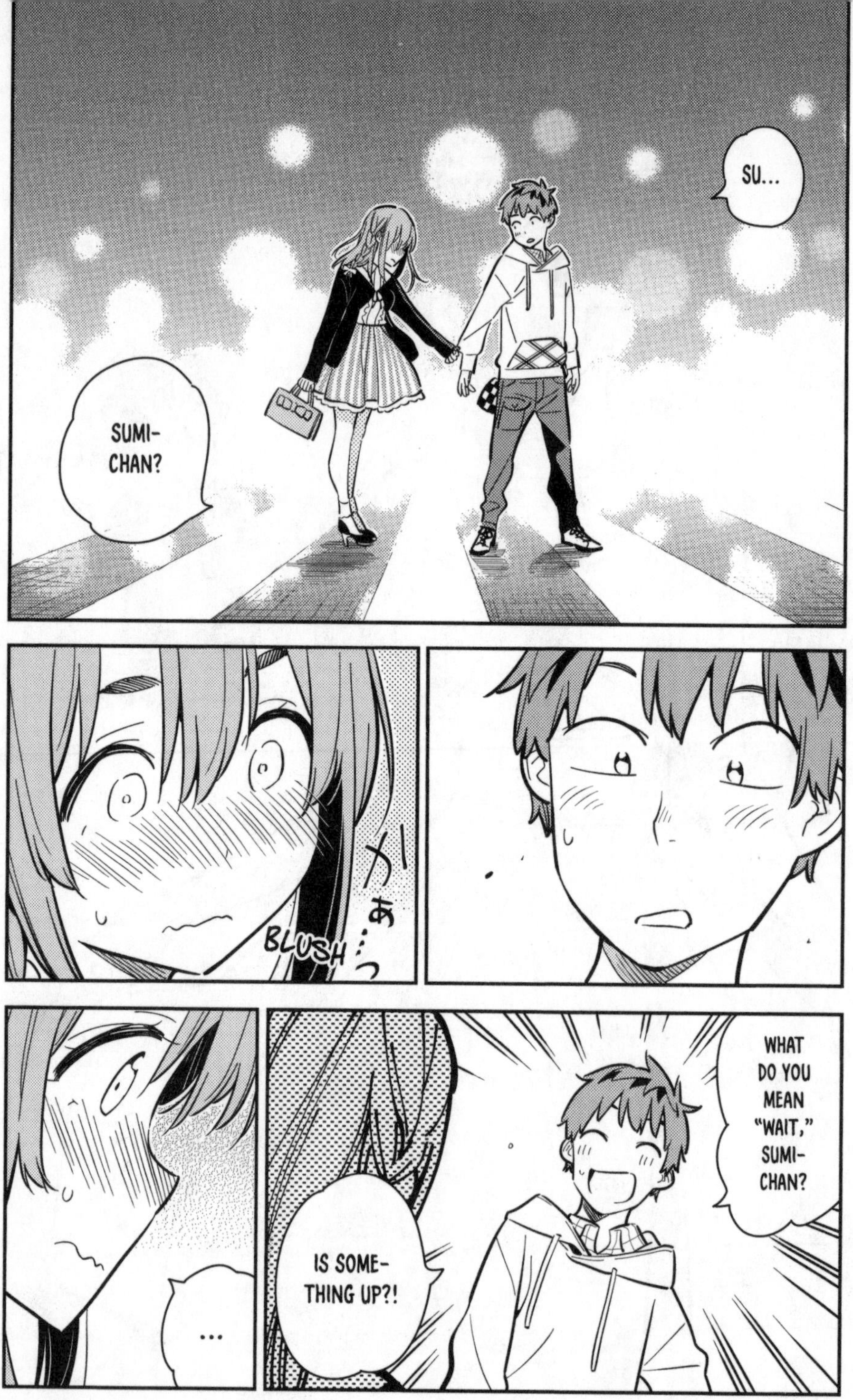
SU...
SUMI-CHAN?
かあ…っ
BLUSH
WHAT DO YOU MEAN "WAIT," SUMI-CHAN?
IS SOME-THING UP?!
...

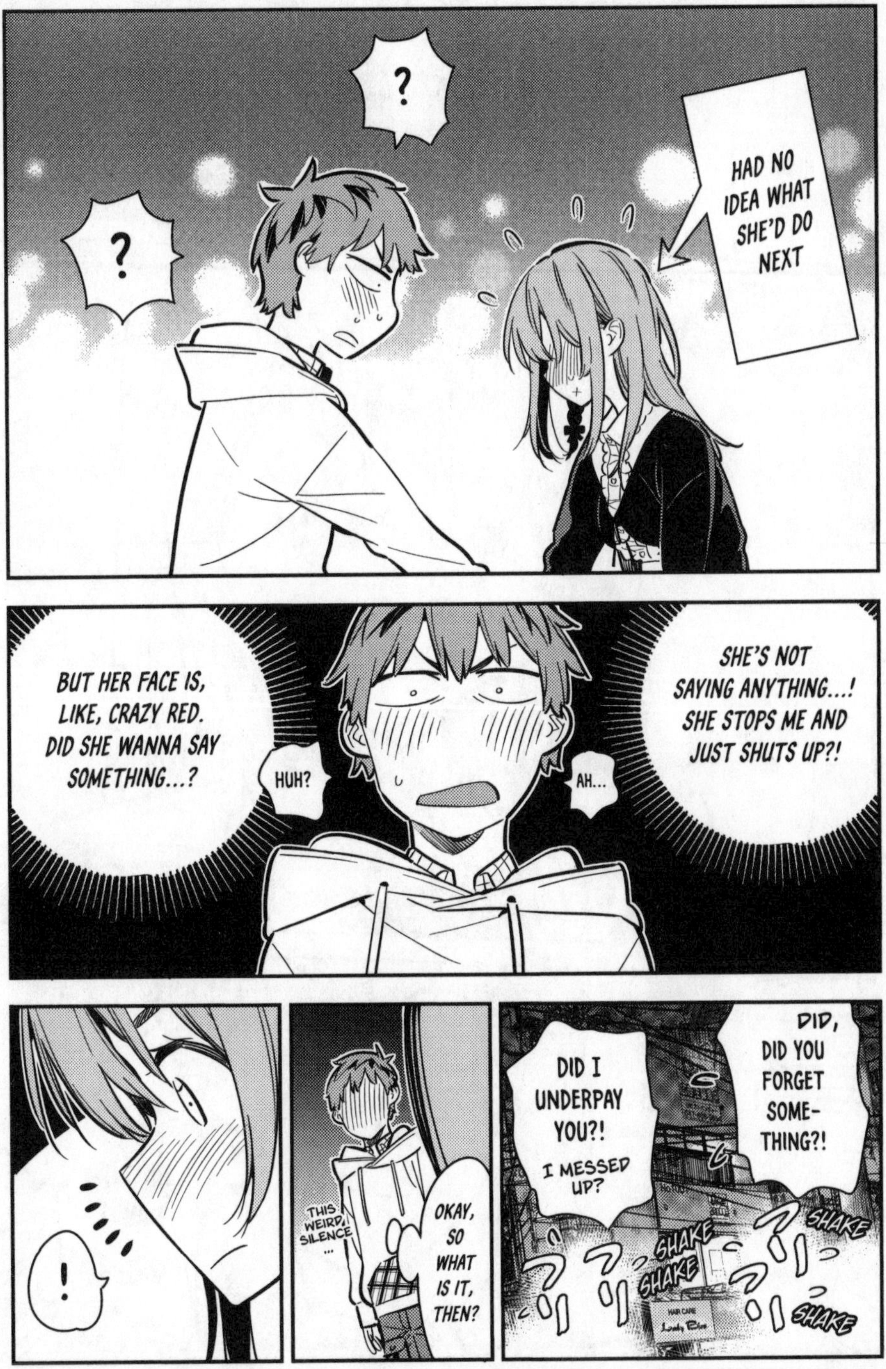
HAD NO IDEA WHAT SHE'D DO NEXT
?
?
SHE'S NOT SAYING ANYTHING...! SHE STOPS ME AND JUST SHUTS UP?!
AH...
HUH?
BUT HER FACE IS, LIKE, CRAZY RED. DID SHE WANNA SAY SOMETHING...?
DID, DID YOU FORGET SOMETHING?!
DID I UNDERPAY YOU?!
I MESSED UP?
SHAKE
SHAKE
SHAKE
SHAKE
HAIR CARE
OKAY, SO WHAT IS IT, THEN?
THIS WEIRD SILENCE ...
!

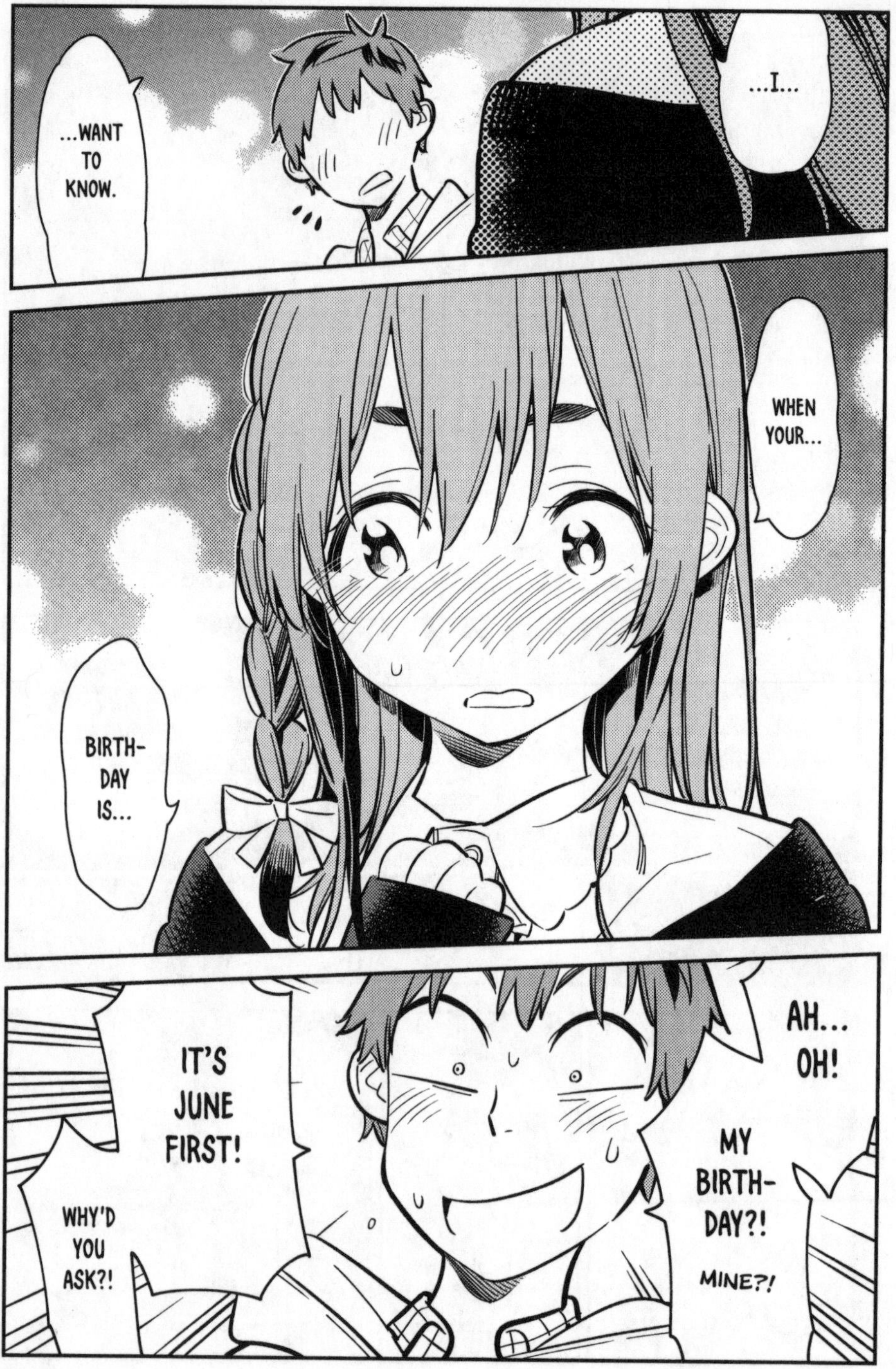
...I...
...WANT TO KNOW.
WHEN YOUR...
BIRTH-DAY IS...
AH... OH!
MY BIRTH-DAY?!
MINE?!
IT'S JUNE FIRST!
WHY'D YOU ASK?!

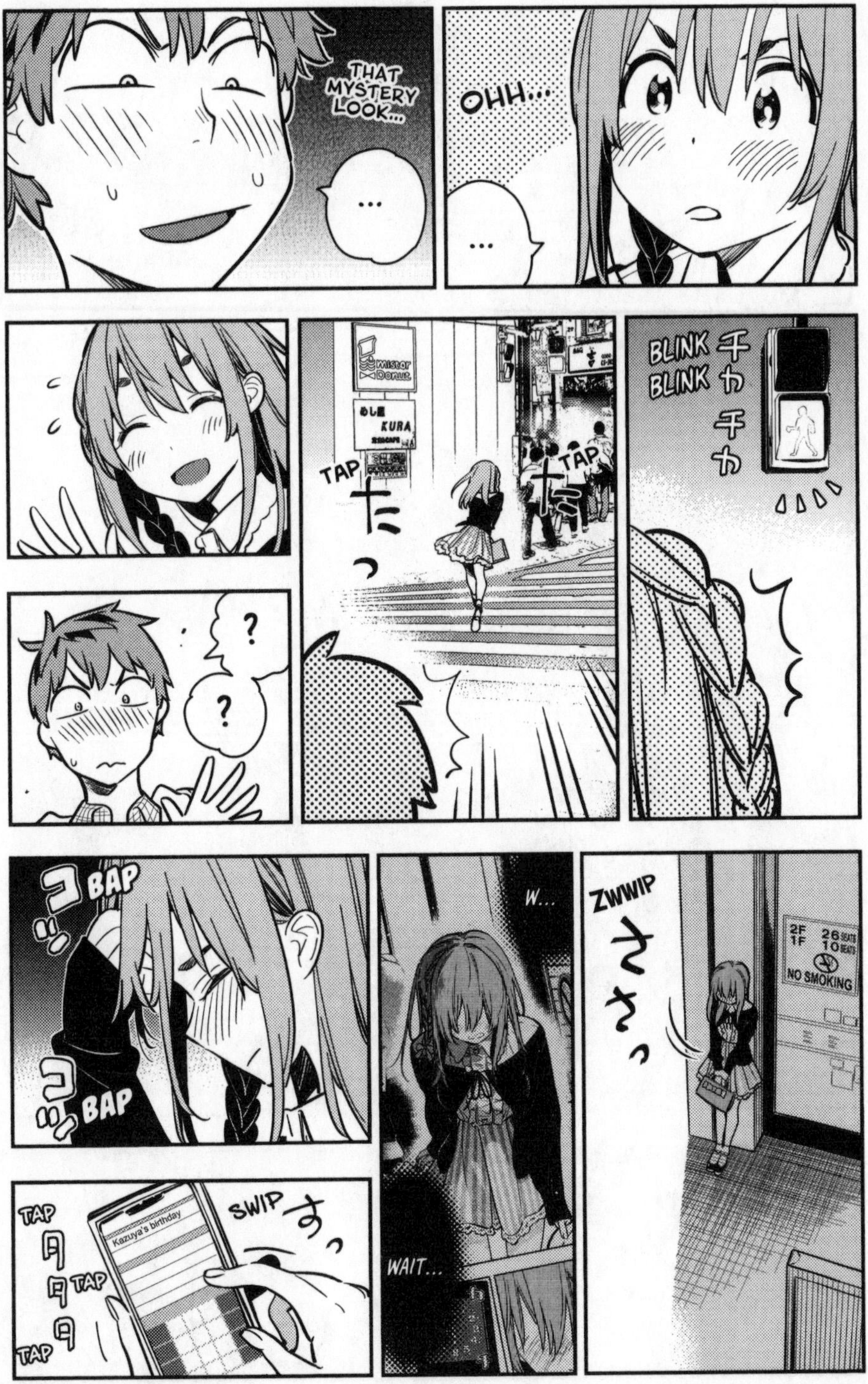
OHH...
...
THAT MYSTERY LOOK...
...
BLINK BLINK
チカチカ
TAP
たっ
TAP
?
?
ZWWIP
さっ
2F 26 SEATS
1F 10 SEATS
NO SMOKING
W...
WAIT...
BAP
コッ
BAP
コッ
SWIP
すっ
Kazuya's birthday
TAP
タタタ
TAP
TAP

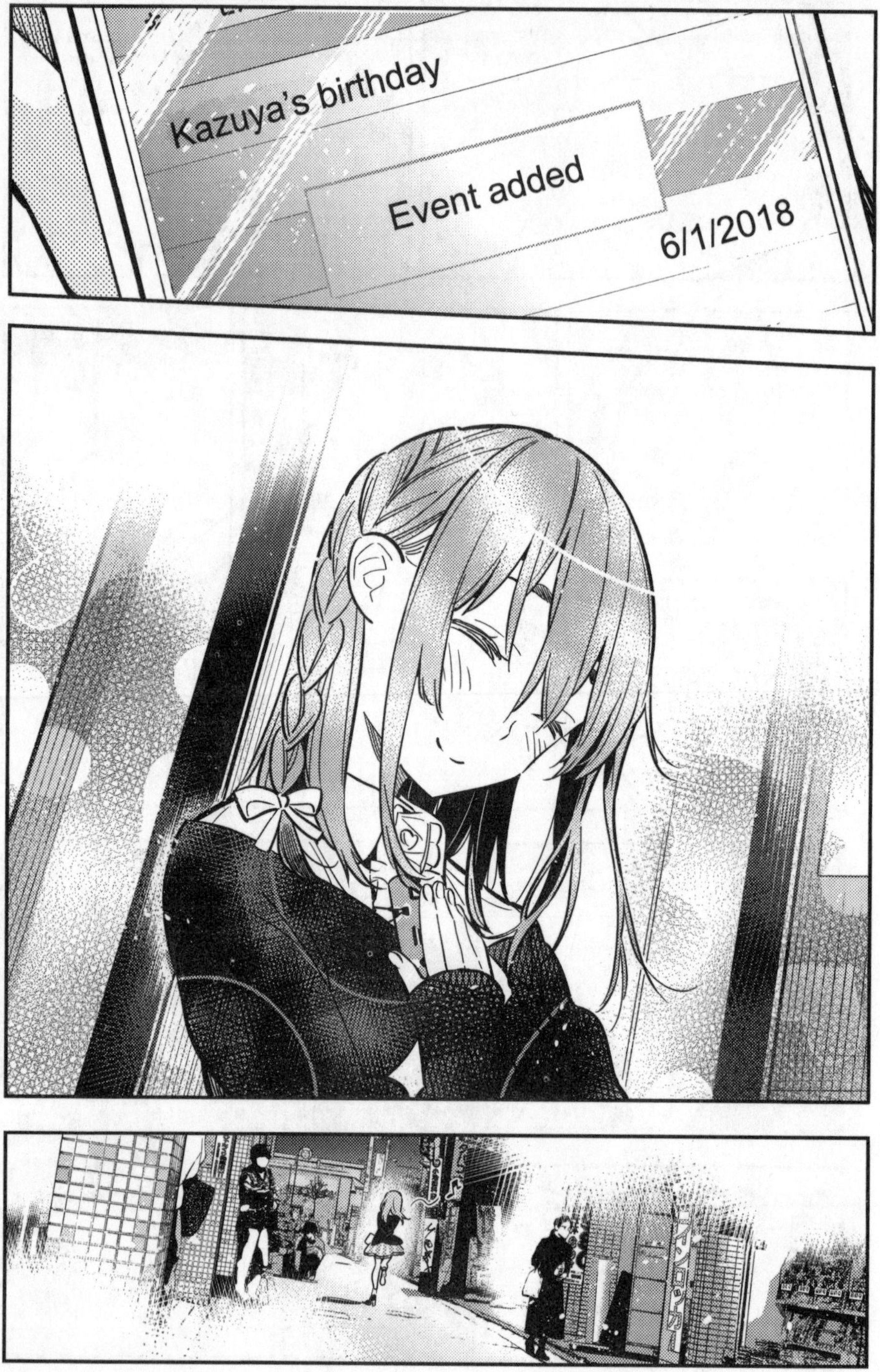
Kazuya's birthday
Event added
6/1/2018

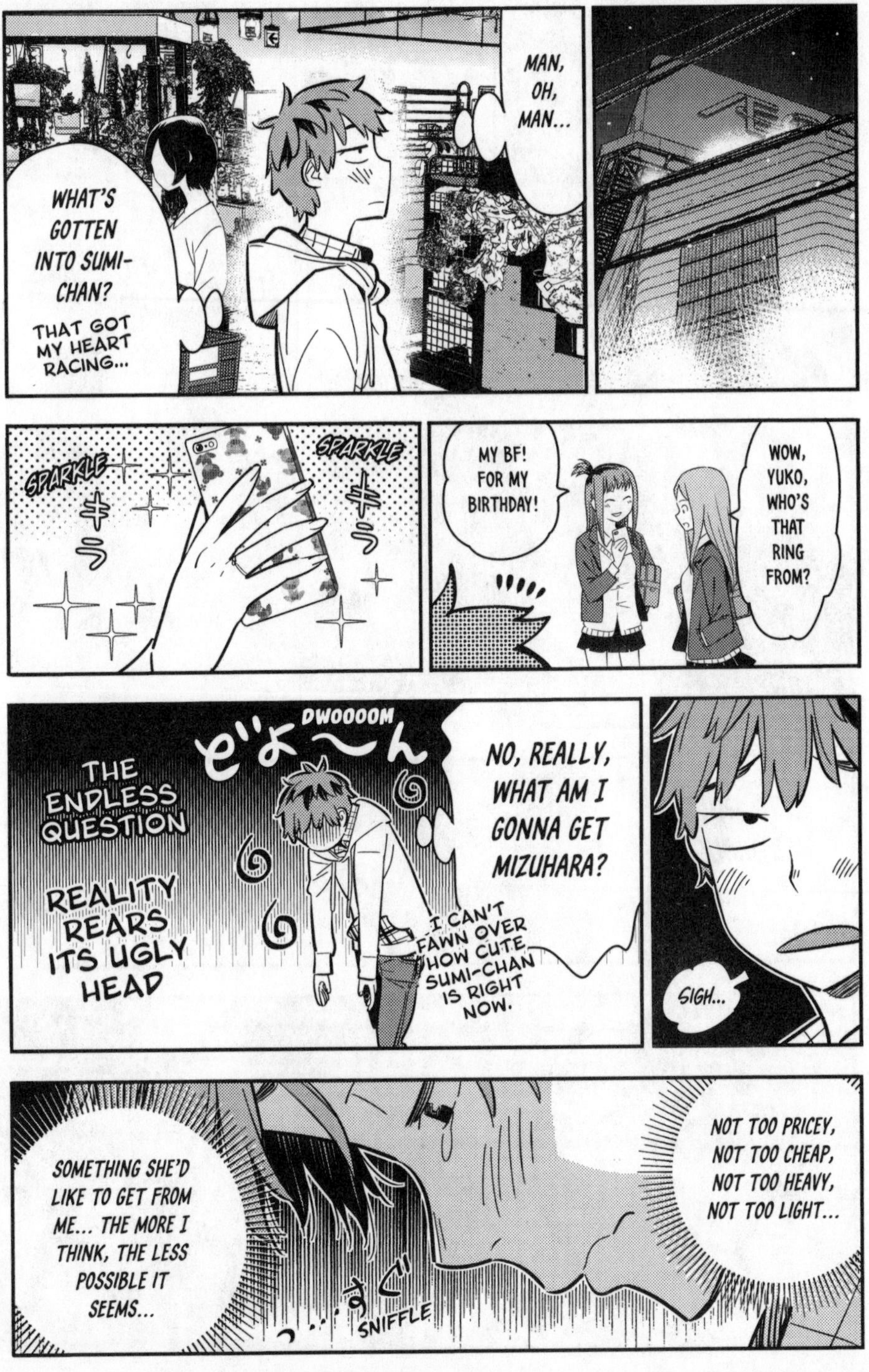
MAN, OH, MAN...
WHAT'S GOTTEN INTO SUMI-CHAN?
THAT GOT MY HEART RACING...
WOW, YUKO, WHO'S THAT RING FROM?
MY BF! FOR MY BIRTHDAY!
SPARKLE
キラ
SPARKLE
キラ
SIGH...
NO, REALLY, WHAT AM I GONNA GET MIZUHARA?
I CAN'T FAWN OVER HOW CUTE SUMI-CHAN IS RIGHT NOW.
DWOOOOM
どよ〜ん
THE ENDLESS QUESTION
REALITY REARS ITS UGLY HEAD
NOT TOO PRICEY, NOT TOO CHEAP, NOT TOO HEAVY, NOT TOO LIGHT...
SOMETHING SHE'D LIKE TO GET FROM ME... THE MORE I THINK, THE LESS POSSIBLE IT SEEMS...
SNIFFLE

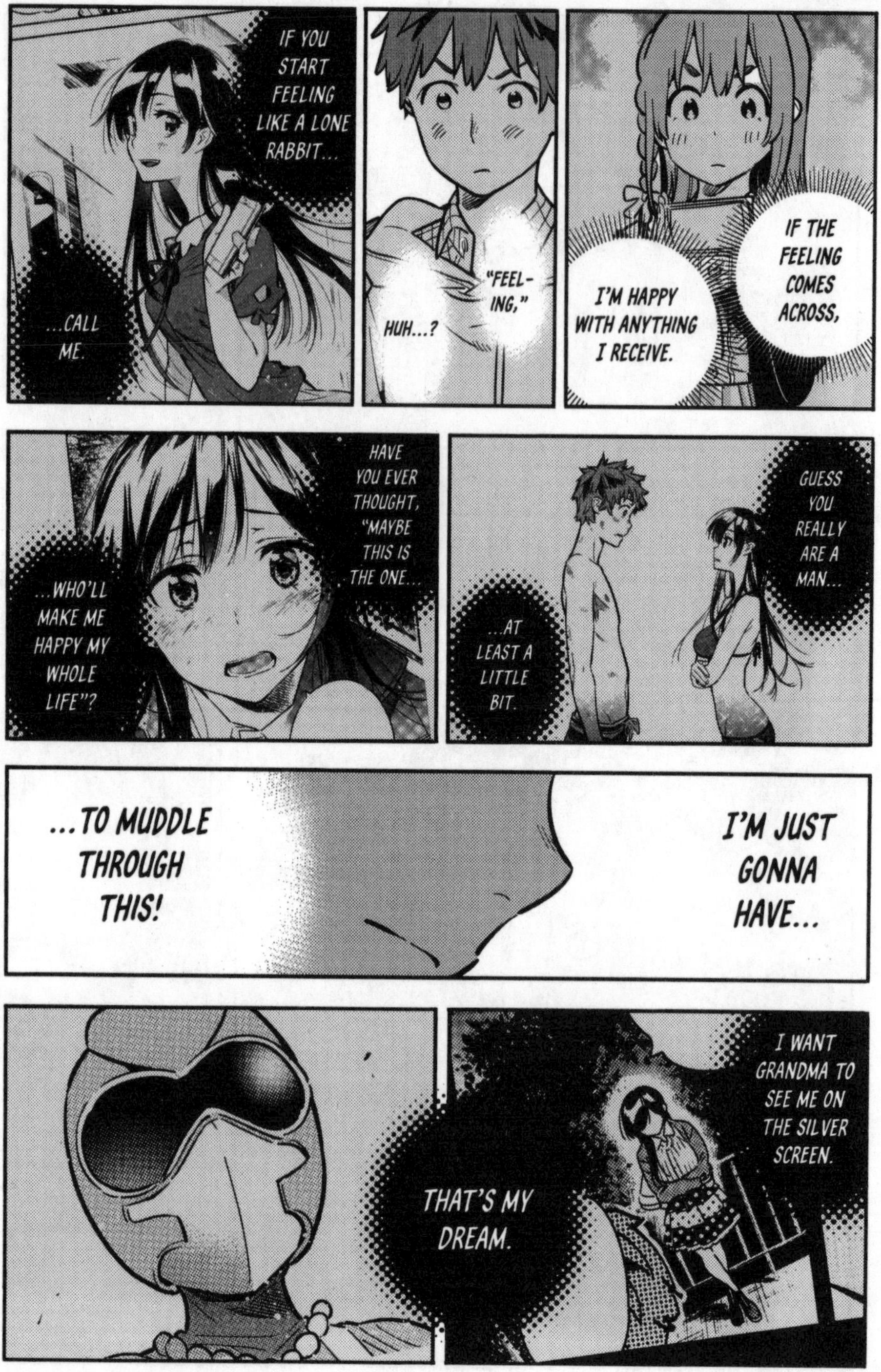
IF THE FEELING COMES ACROSS,
I'M HAPPY WITH ANYTHING I RECEIVE.
“FEEL-ING,”
HUH...?
IF YOU START FEELING LIKE A LONE RABBIT...
...CALL ME.
GUESS YOU REALLY ARE A MAN...
...AT LEAST A LITTLE BIT.
HAVE YOU EVER THOUGHT, “MAYBE THIS IS THE ONE...
...WHO'LL MAKE ME HAPPY MY WHOLE LIFE”?
I'M JUST GONNA HAVE...
...TO MUDDLE THROUGH THIS!
I WANT GRANDMA TO SEE ME ON THE SILVER SCREEN.
THAT'S MY DREAM.

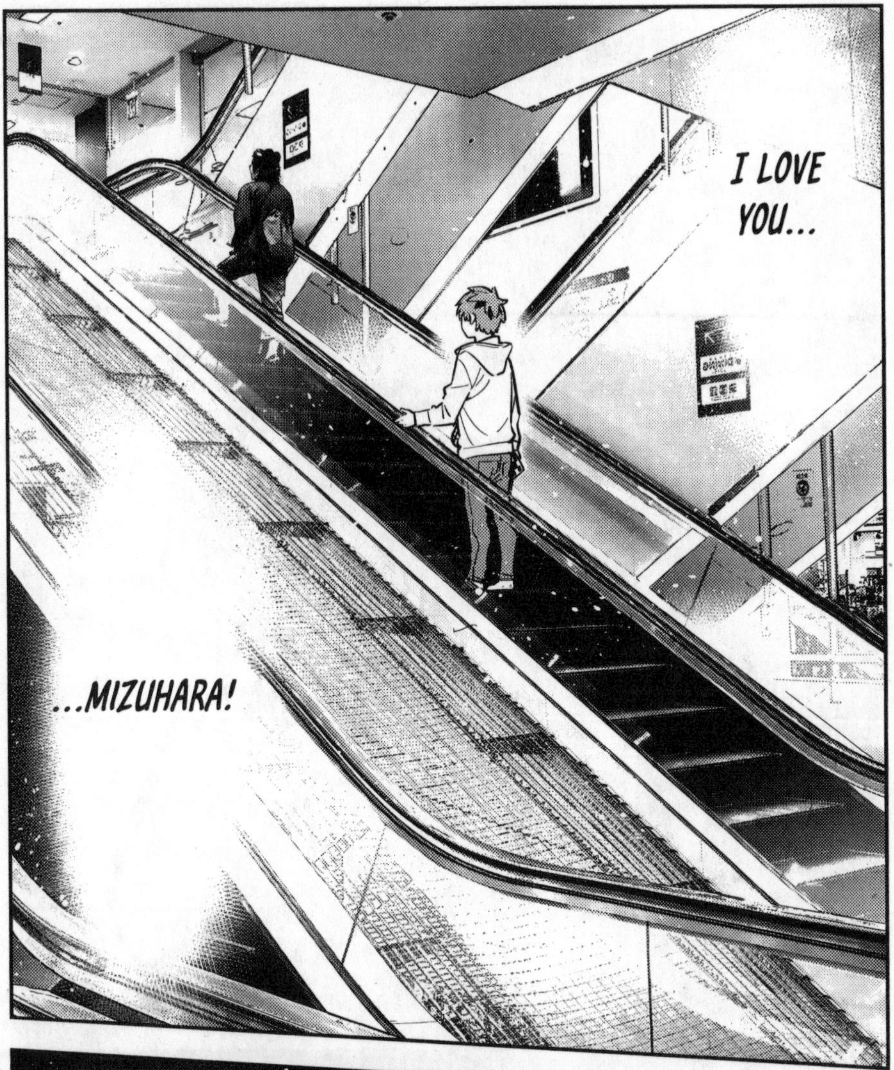
I LOVE YOU...
...MIZUHARA!
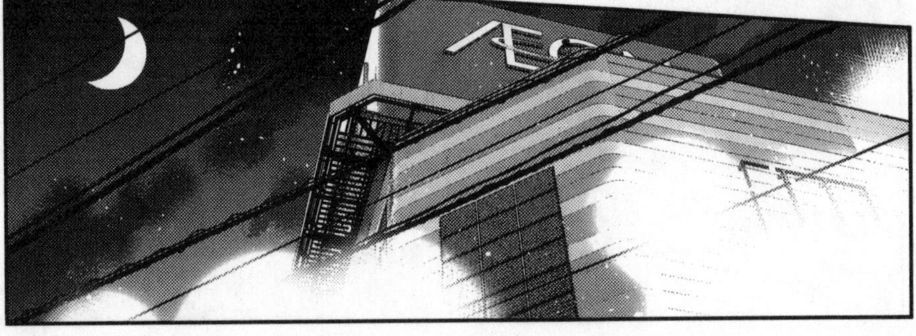

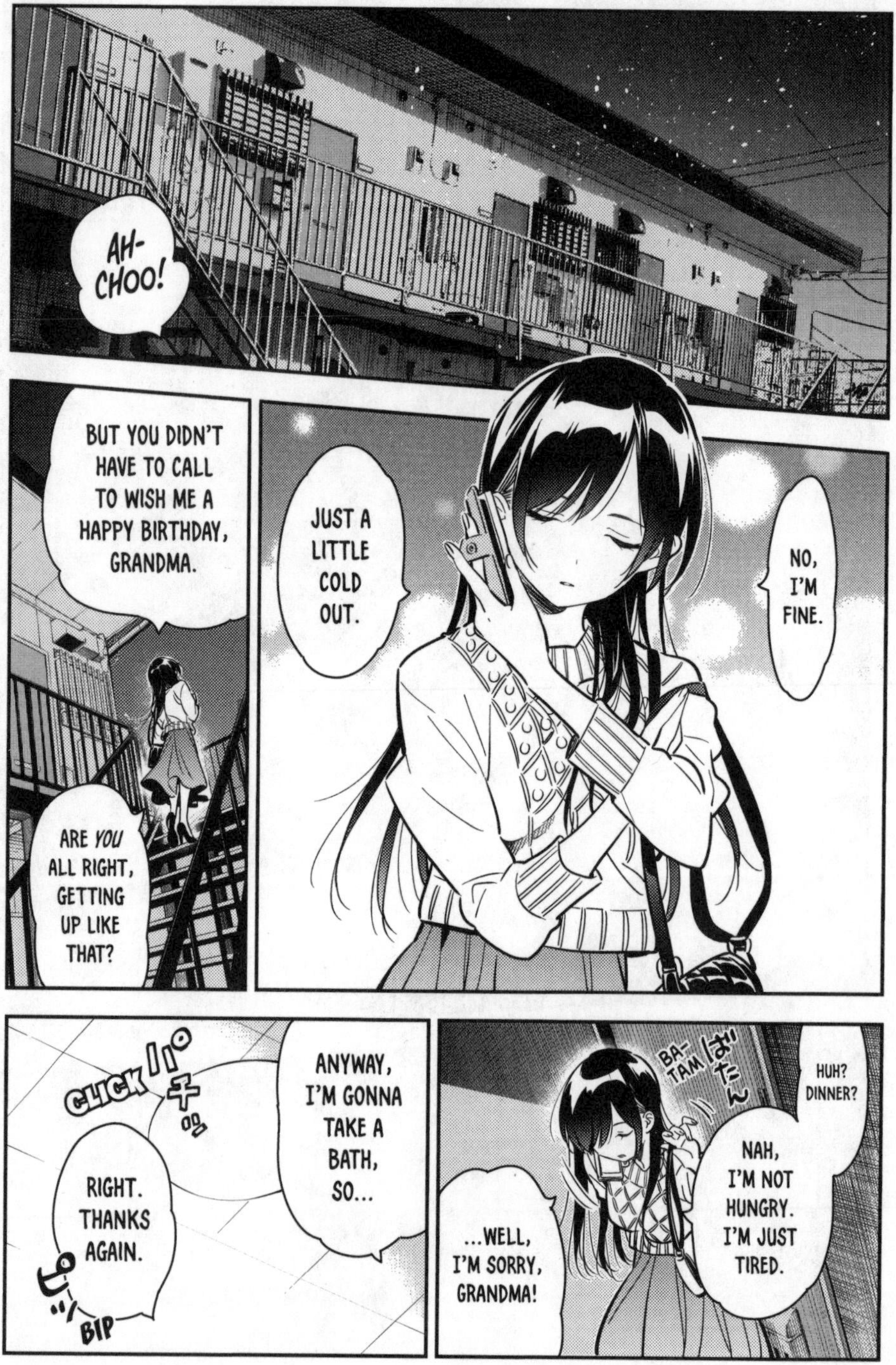
AH-CHOO!
NO, I'M FINE.
JUST A LITTLE COLD OUT.
BUT YOU DIDN'T HAVE TO CALL TO WISH ME A HAPPY BIRTHDAY, GRANDMA.
ARE *YOU* ALL RIGHT, GETTING UP LIKE THAT?
BA-TAM ぱたん
HUH? DINNER?
NAH, I'M NOT HUNGRY. I'M JUST TIRED.
...WELL, I'M SORRY, GRANDMA!
ANYWAY, I'M GONNA TAKE A BATH, SO...
CLICK パチ
RIGHT. THANKS AGAIN.
ピッ BIP

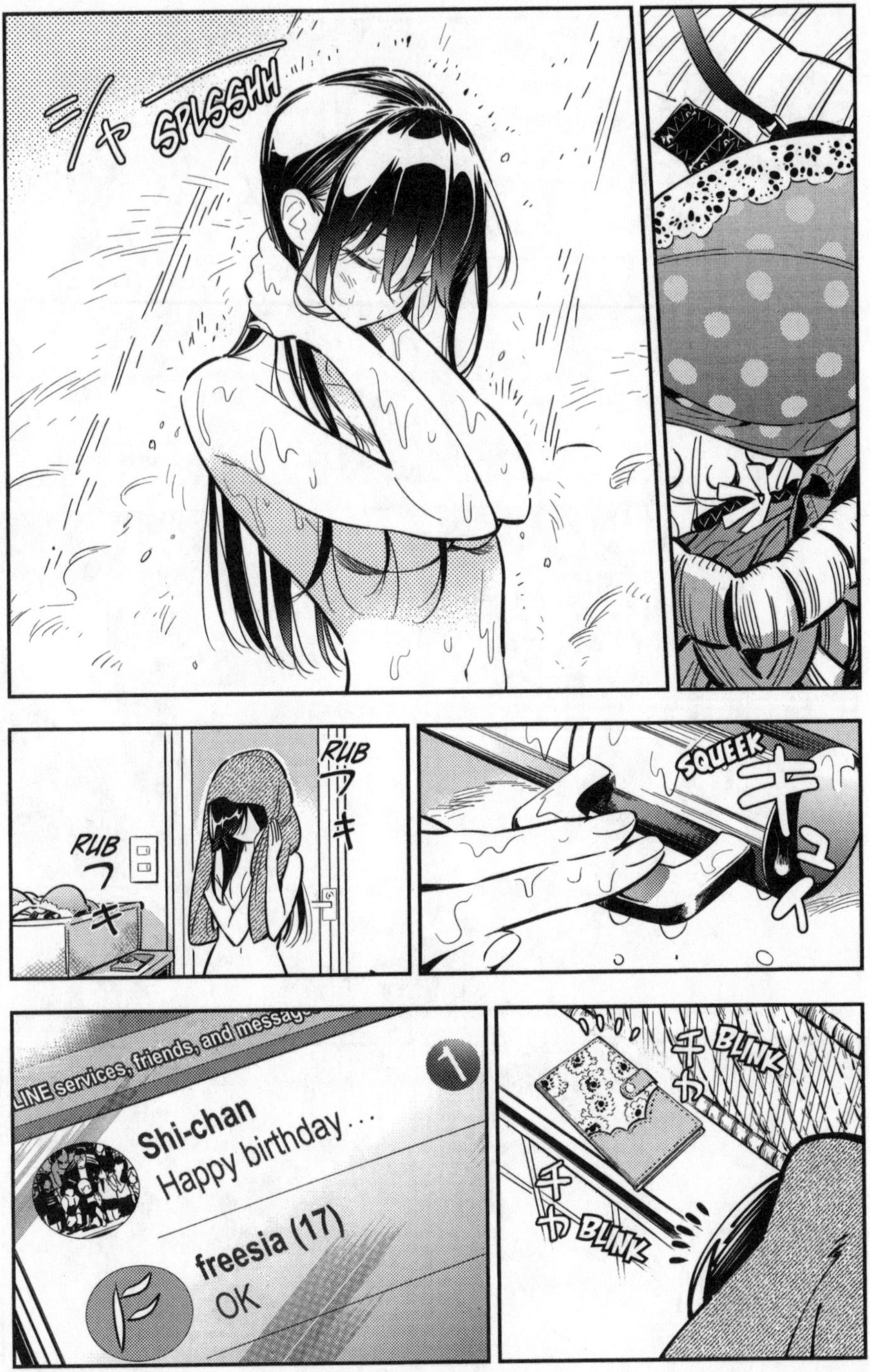

シャ
SPLSSHH
SQUEEK
キュイ
RUB
フキ
RUB
フキ
チカ
BLINK
チカ
BLINK
LINE services, friends, and
1
Shi-chan
Happy birthday…
freesia (17)
OK

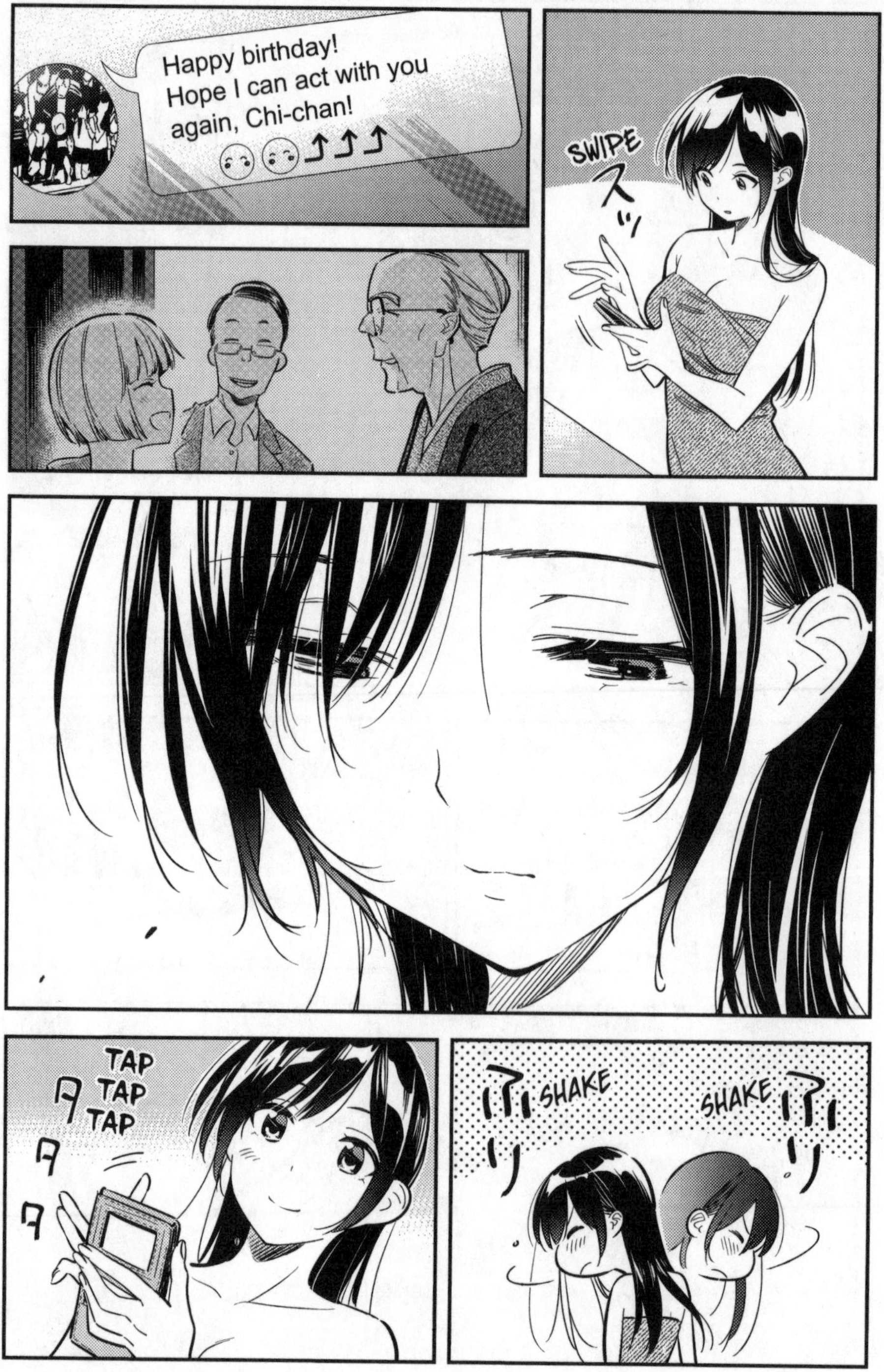
SWIPE
スッ
Happy birthday!
Hope I can act with you again, Chi-chan!
SHAKE
SHAKE
TAP
TAP
TAP
タ
タ
タ

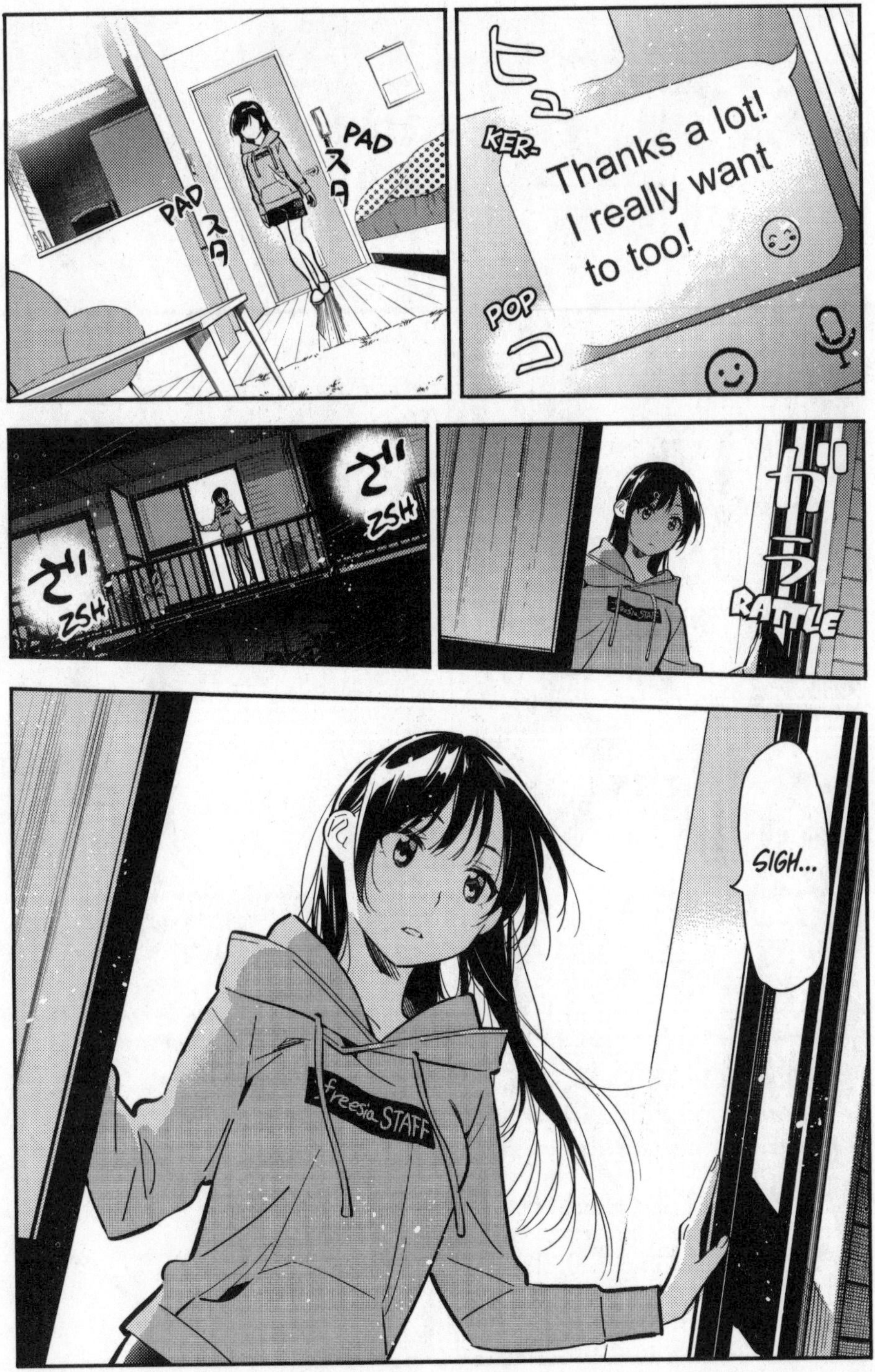
ヒュ
KER-
Thanks a lot! I really want to too!
POP
コ
PAD
スタ
PAD
スタ
ガラ
RATTLE
freesia STAFF
ざ
ZSH
ざ
ZSH
SIGH...
freesia STAFF

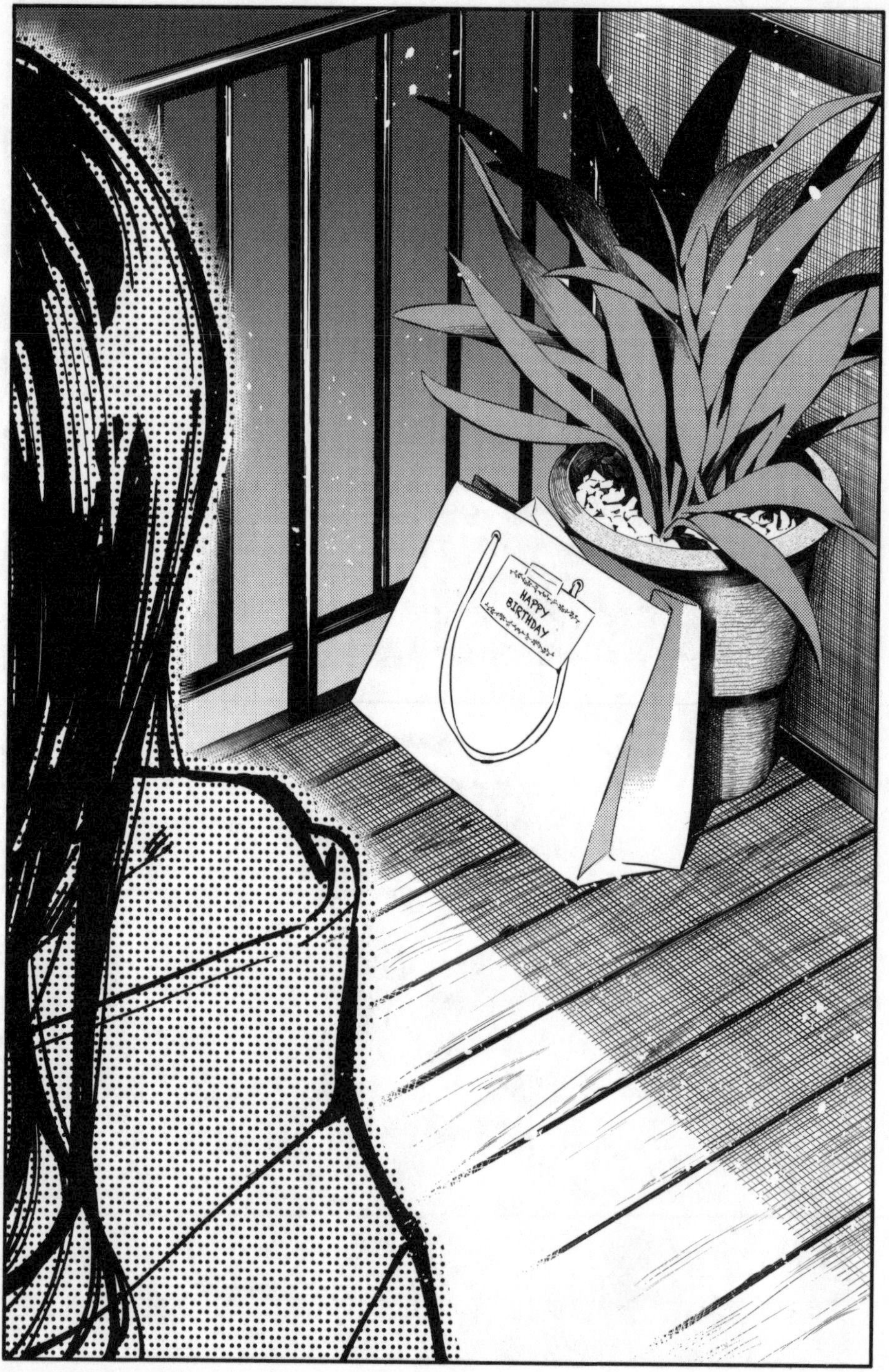
HAPPY BIRTHDAY

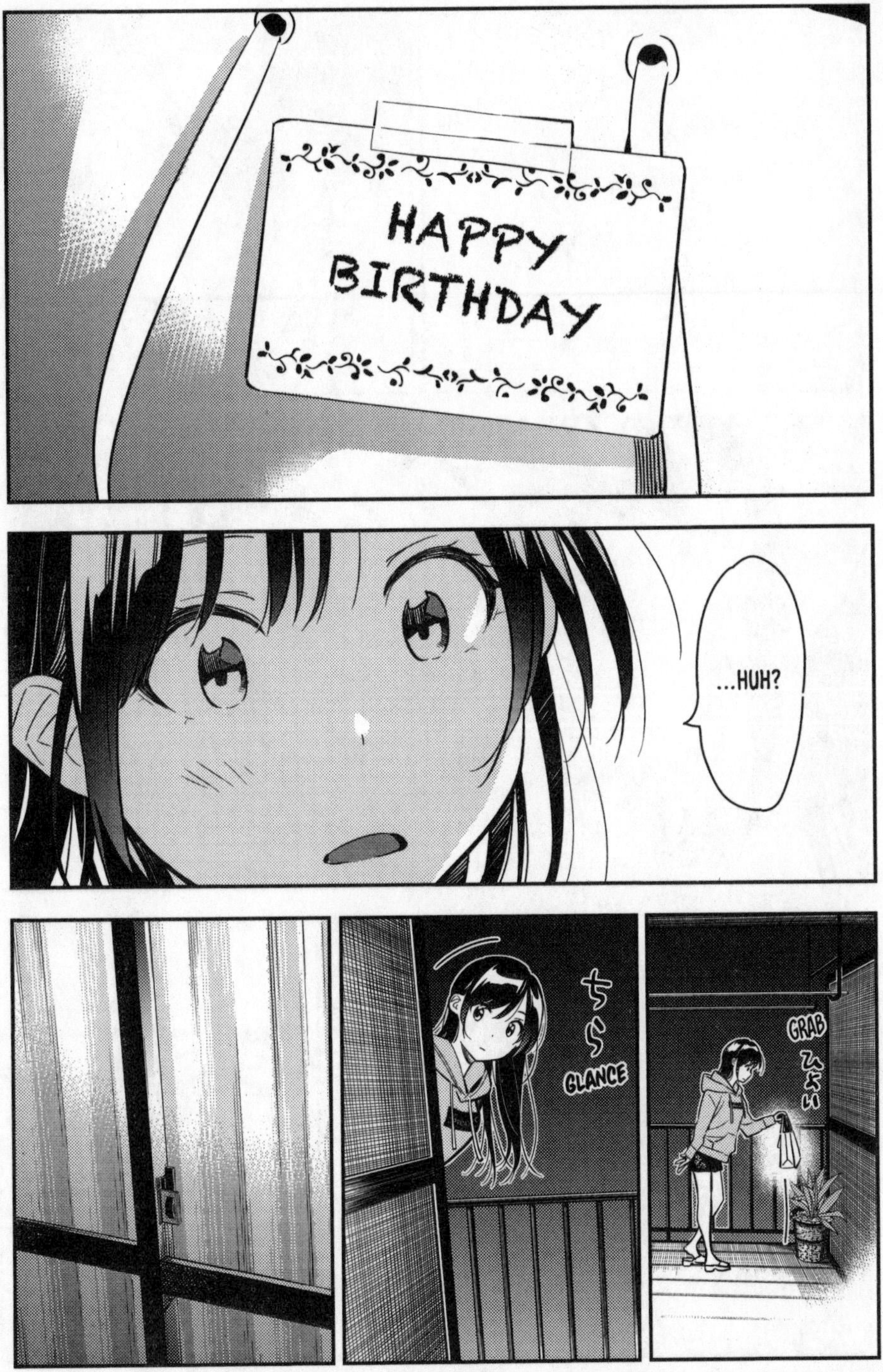
HAPPY BIRTHDAY
...HUH?
GRAB
ひょい
ちら
GLANCE

HAPPY
BIRTHDAY

RUSTLE

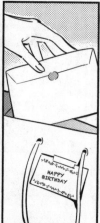

HAPPY
BIRTHDAY

PLINK

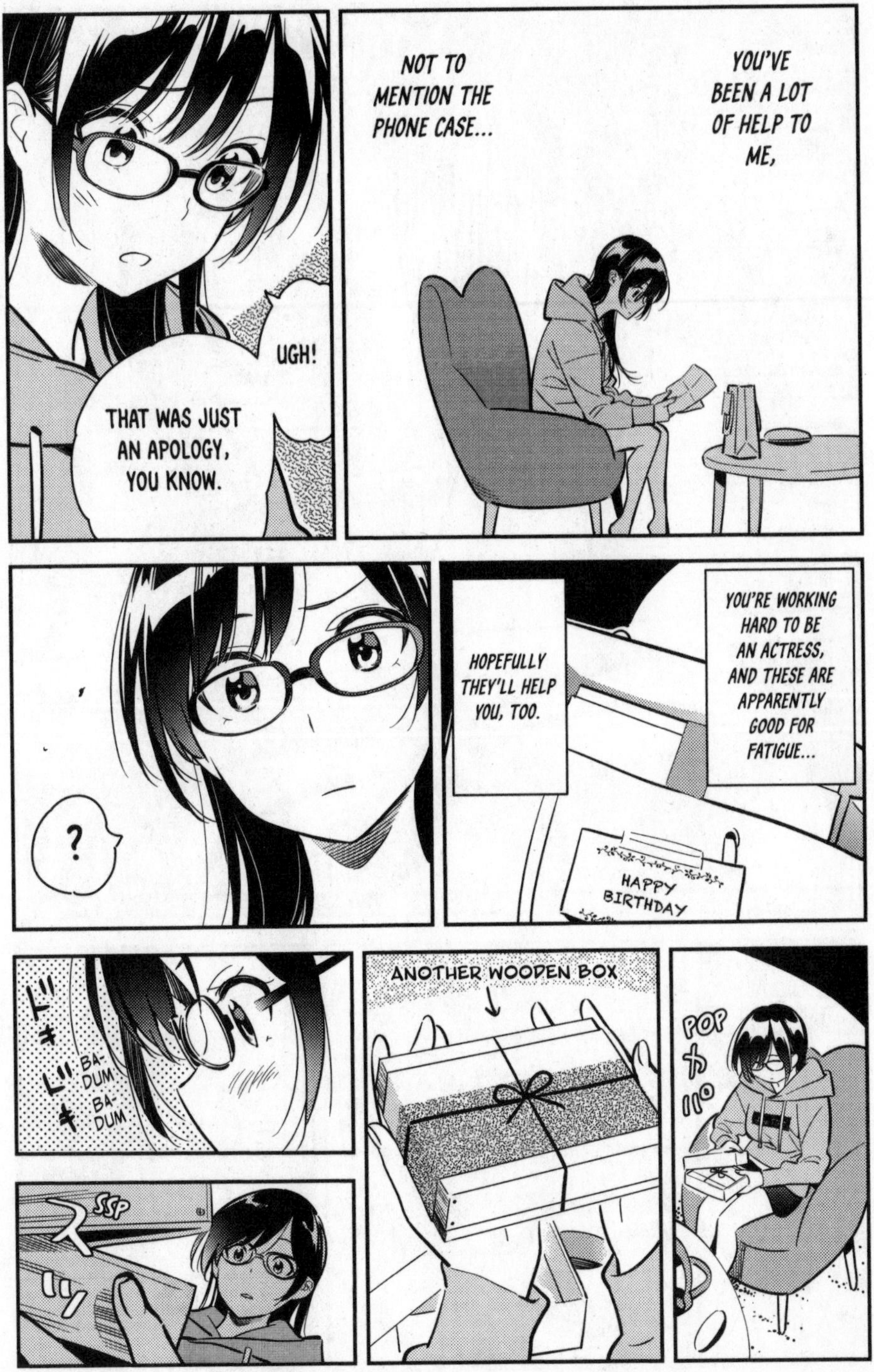
YOU'VE BEEN A LOT OF HELP TO ME,
NOT TO MENTION THE PHONE CASE...
UGH!
THAT WAS JUST AN APOLOGY, YOU KNOW.
YOU'RE WORKING HARD TO BE AN ACTRESS, AND THESE ARE APPARENTLY GOOD FOR FATIGUE...
HOPEFULLY THEY'LL HELP YOU, TOO.
HAPPY BIRTHDAY
?
POP
カパ
ANOTHER WOODEN BOX
ドキドキ
BA-DUM BA-DUM
スッ
SSP

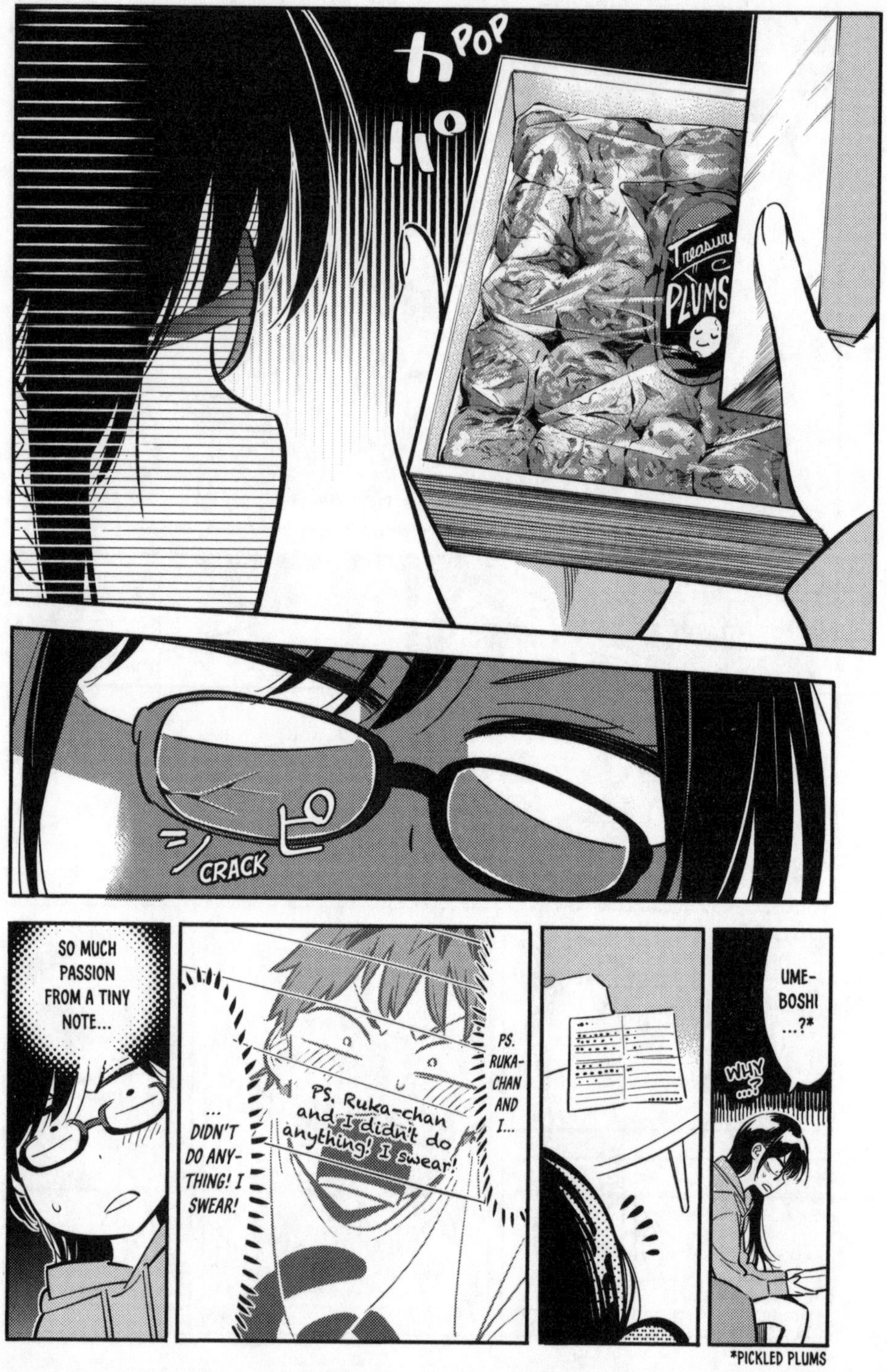
POP
CRACK
UME-BOSHI ...?*
WHY ...?
PS. RUKA-CHAN AND I...
PS. Ruka-chan and I didn't do anything! I swear!
... DIDN'T DO ANY-THING! I SWEAR!
SO MUCH PASSION FROM A TINY NOTE...

*PICKLED PLUMS

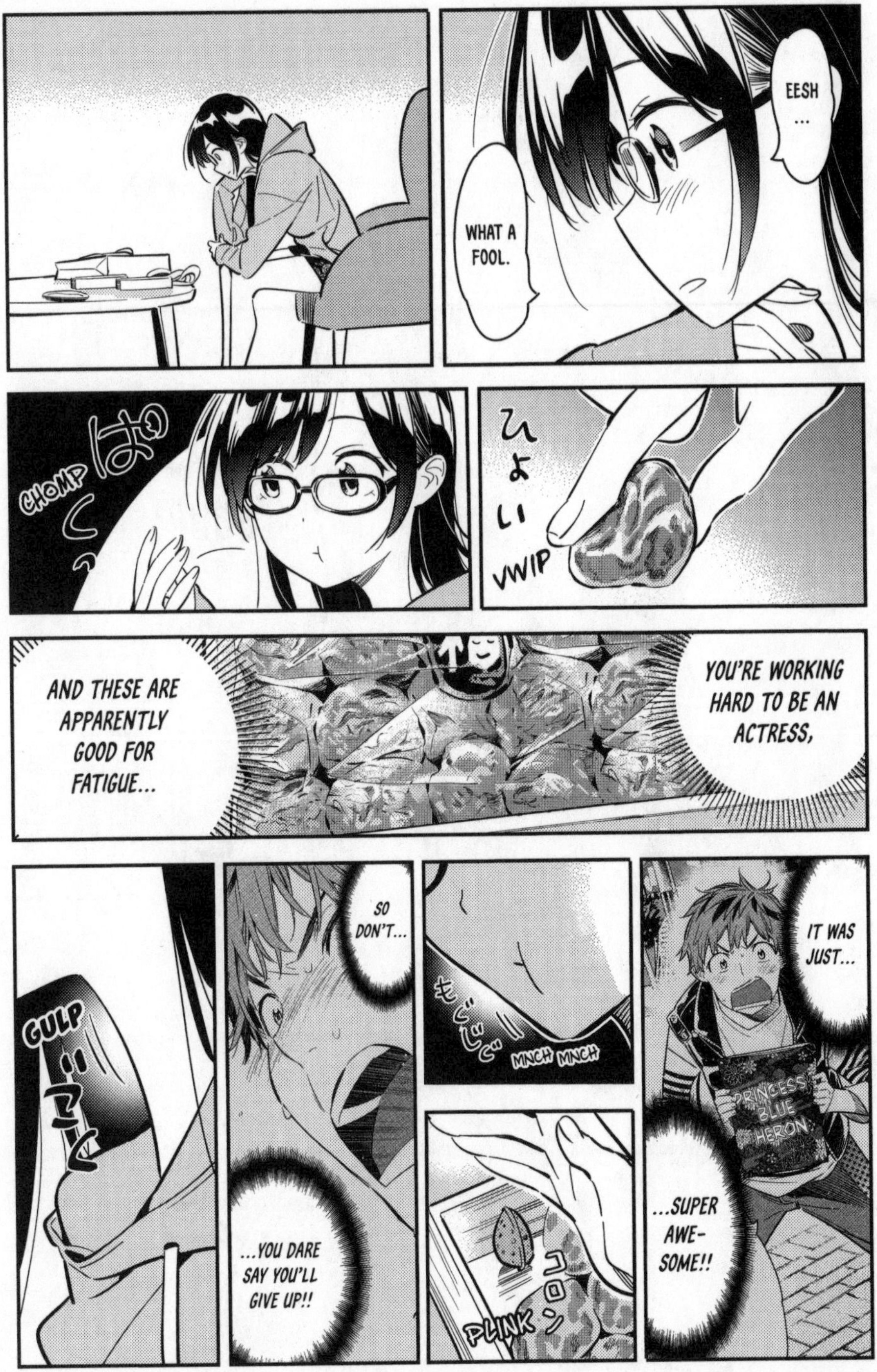
EESH ...
WHAT A FOOL.
ひょい
VWIP
ぱくっ
CHOMP
YOU'RE WORKING HARD TO BE AN ACTRESS,
AND THESE ARE APPARENTLY GOOD FOR FATIGUE...
IT WAS JUST...
...SUPER AWE-SOME!!
PRINCESS BLUE HERON
MNCH MNCH
コロン
PLINK
SO DON'T...
...YOU DARE SAY YOU'LL GIVE UP!!
ごくっ
GULP

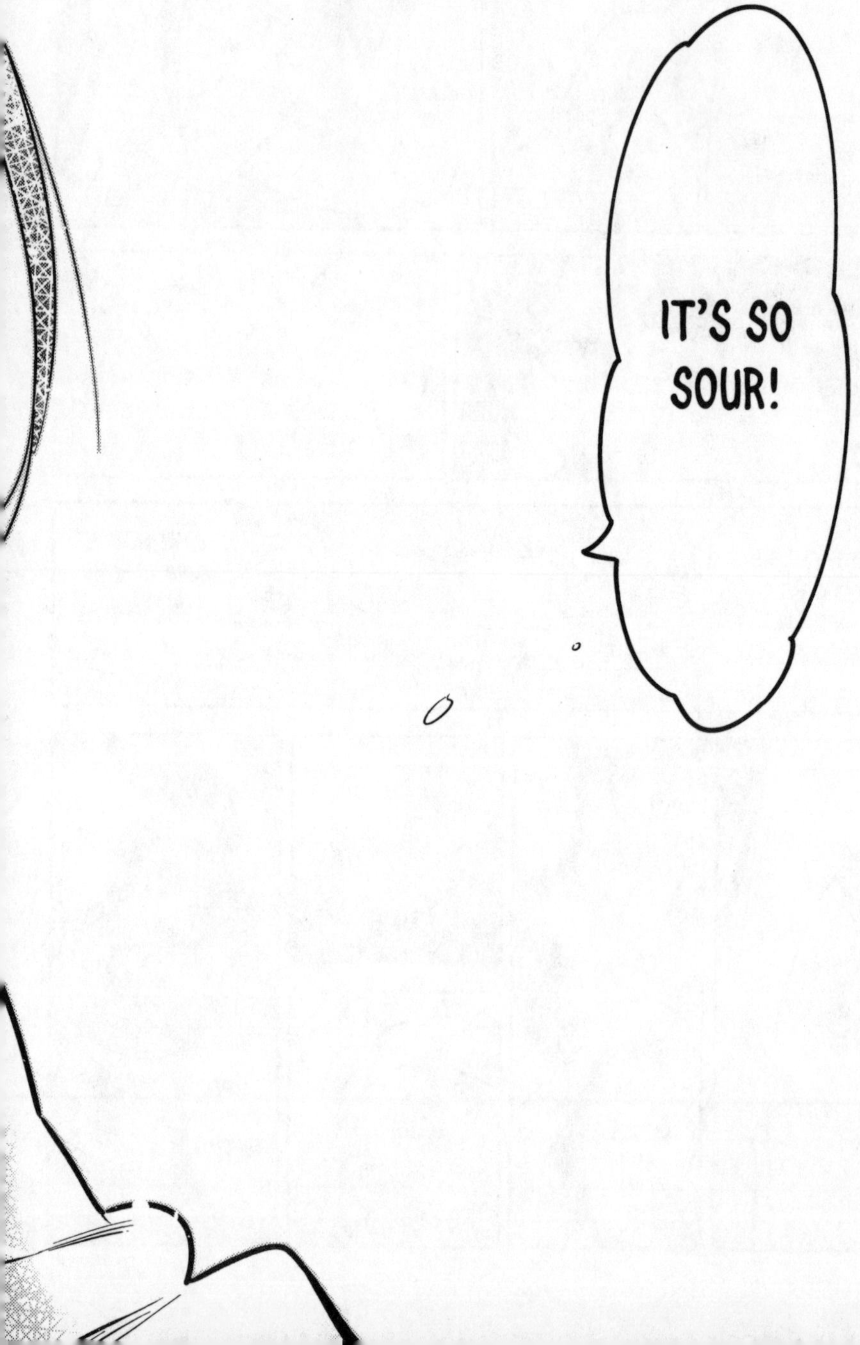
IT'S SO SOUR!

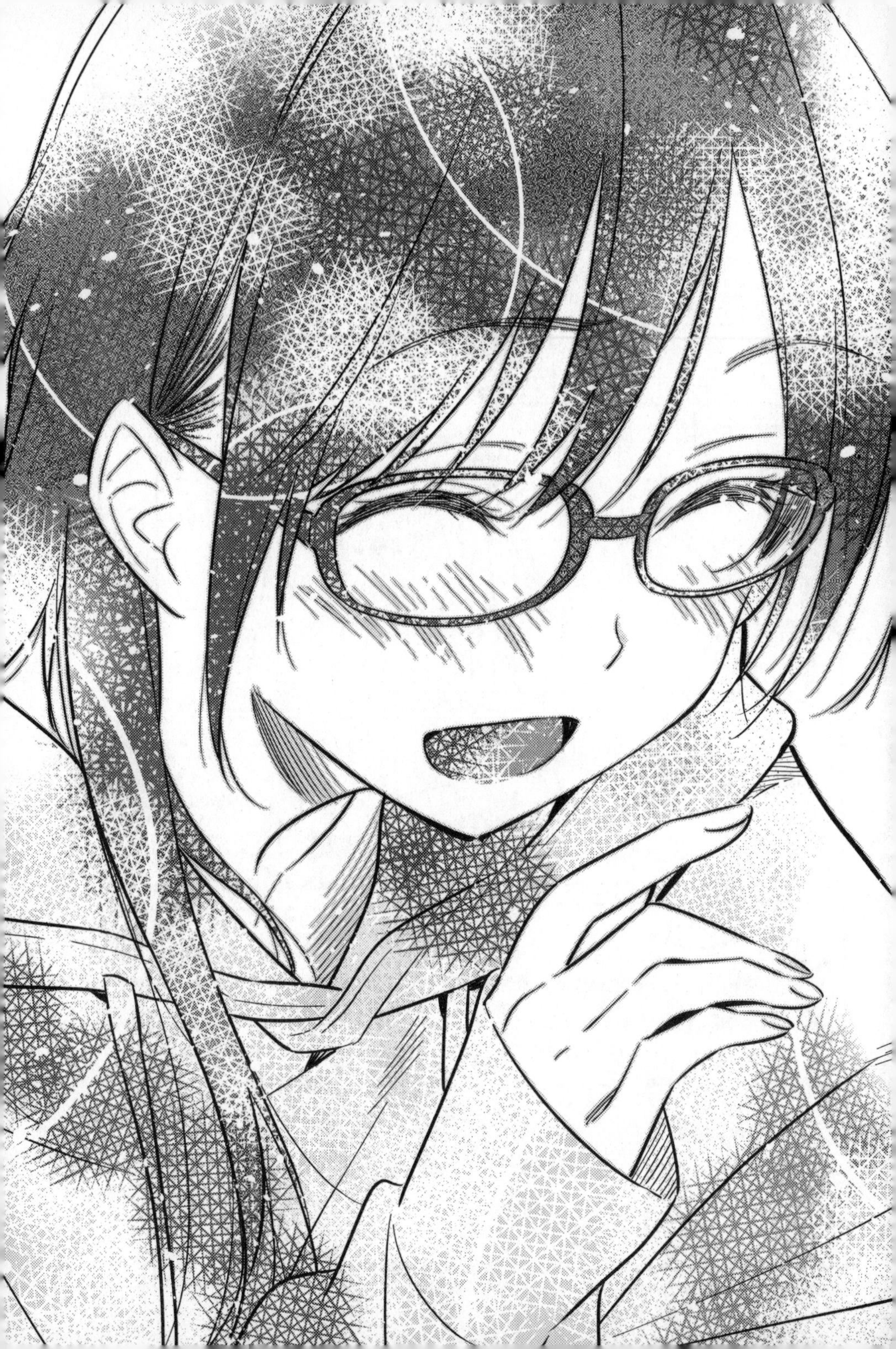

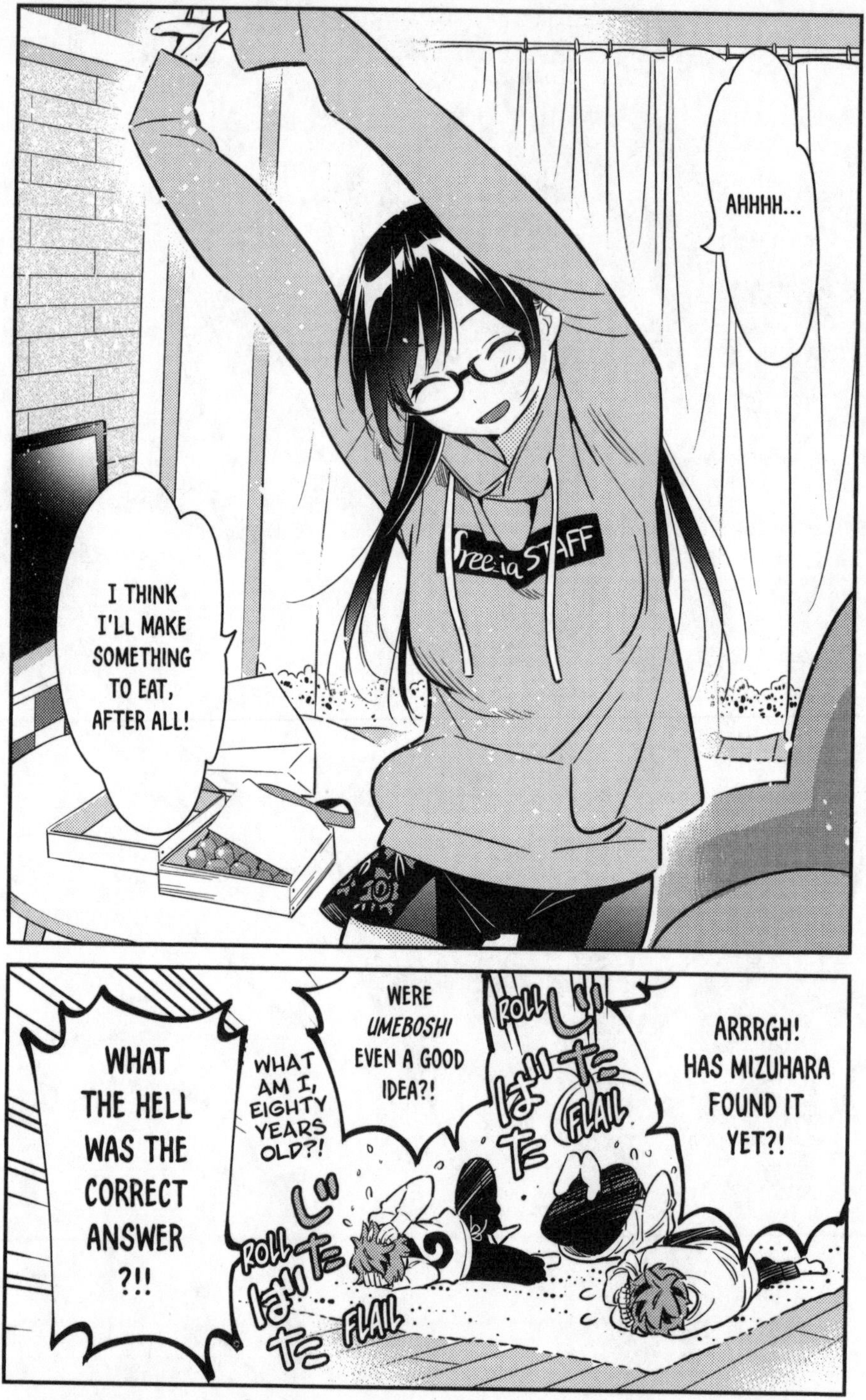
AHHHH...
I THINK I'LL MAKE SOMETHING TO EAT, AFTER ALL!
free:ia STAFF
ARRRGH! HAS MIZUHARA FOUND IT YET?!
じた ROLL
ばた FLAIL
WERE UMEBOSHI EVEN A GOOD IDEA?!
WHAT AM I, EIGHTY YEARS OLD?!
じた ROLL
ばた FLAIL
WHAT THE HELL WAS THE CORRECT ANSWER?!!

RATING 70 ALCOHOL AND MY GIRLFRIEND 1

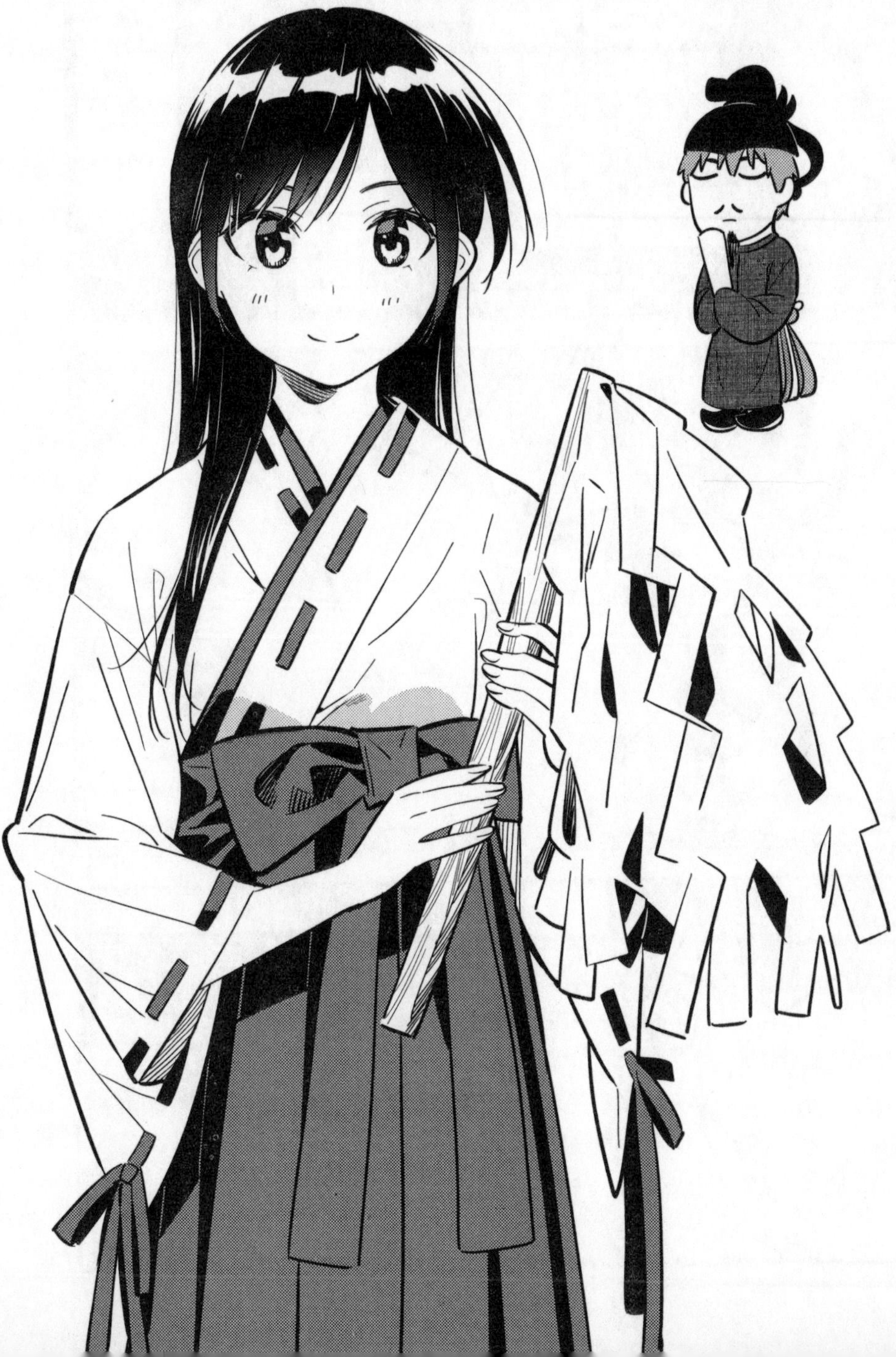

STAAARE

THE MORNING AFTER MIZUHARA'S BIRTHDAY...

AND HER PRESENT.

STAAARE

IT...
IT'S GONE
...!

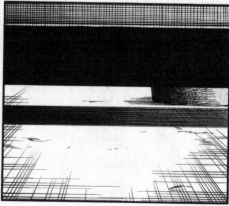

BOLT
UPRIGHT

BA-DUM

KA-TAM

RATTLE

!

BWING

...

STIFFF!!

MI...
MIZUHARA
...!!

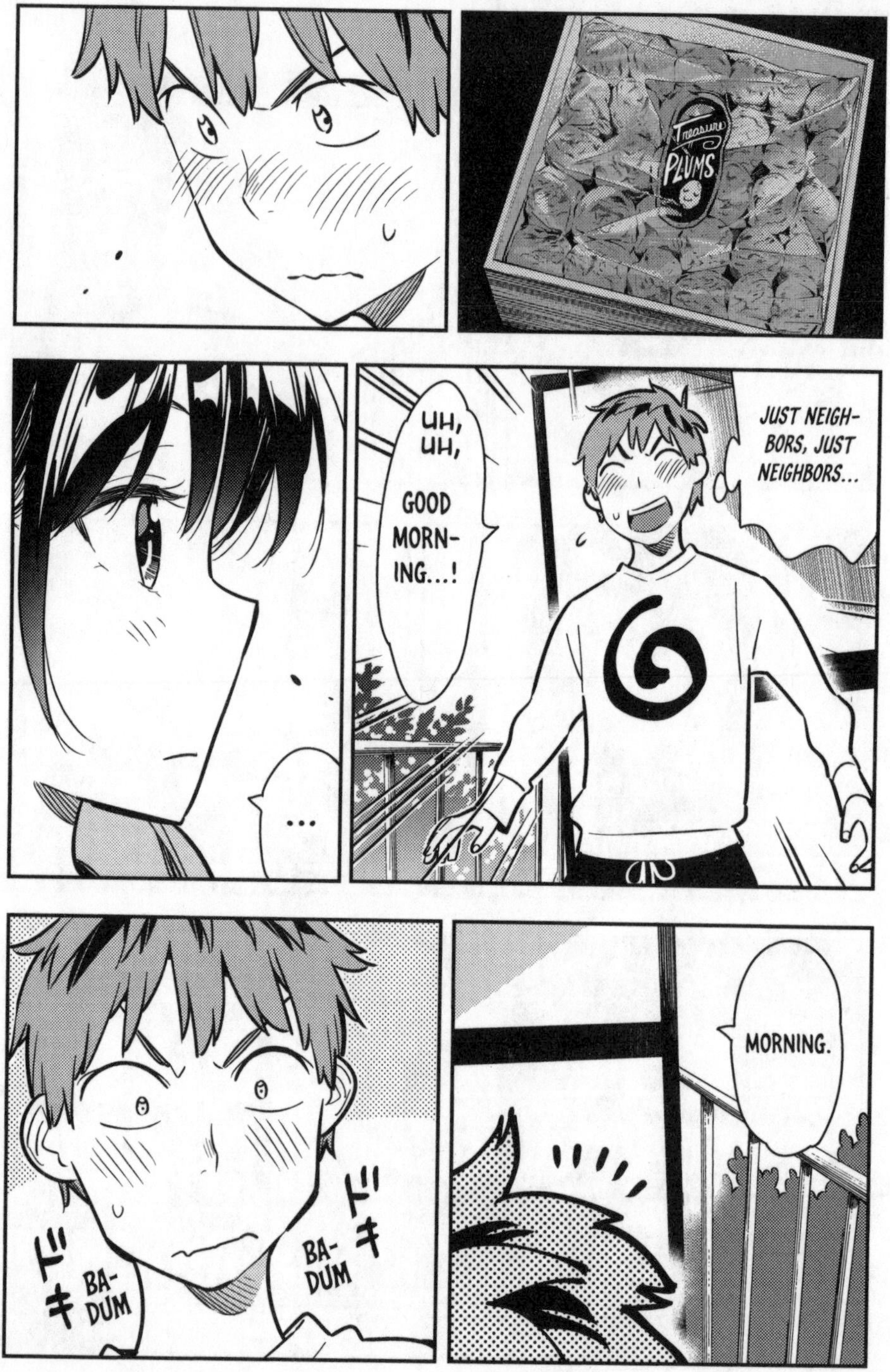
Treasure PLUMS
JUST NEIGH-BORS, JUST NEIGHBORS...
UH, UH, GOOD MORN-ING...!
...
MORNING.
ドキ BA-DUM
ドキ BA-DUM

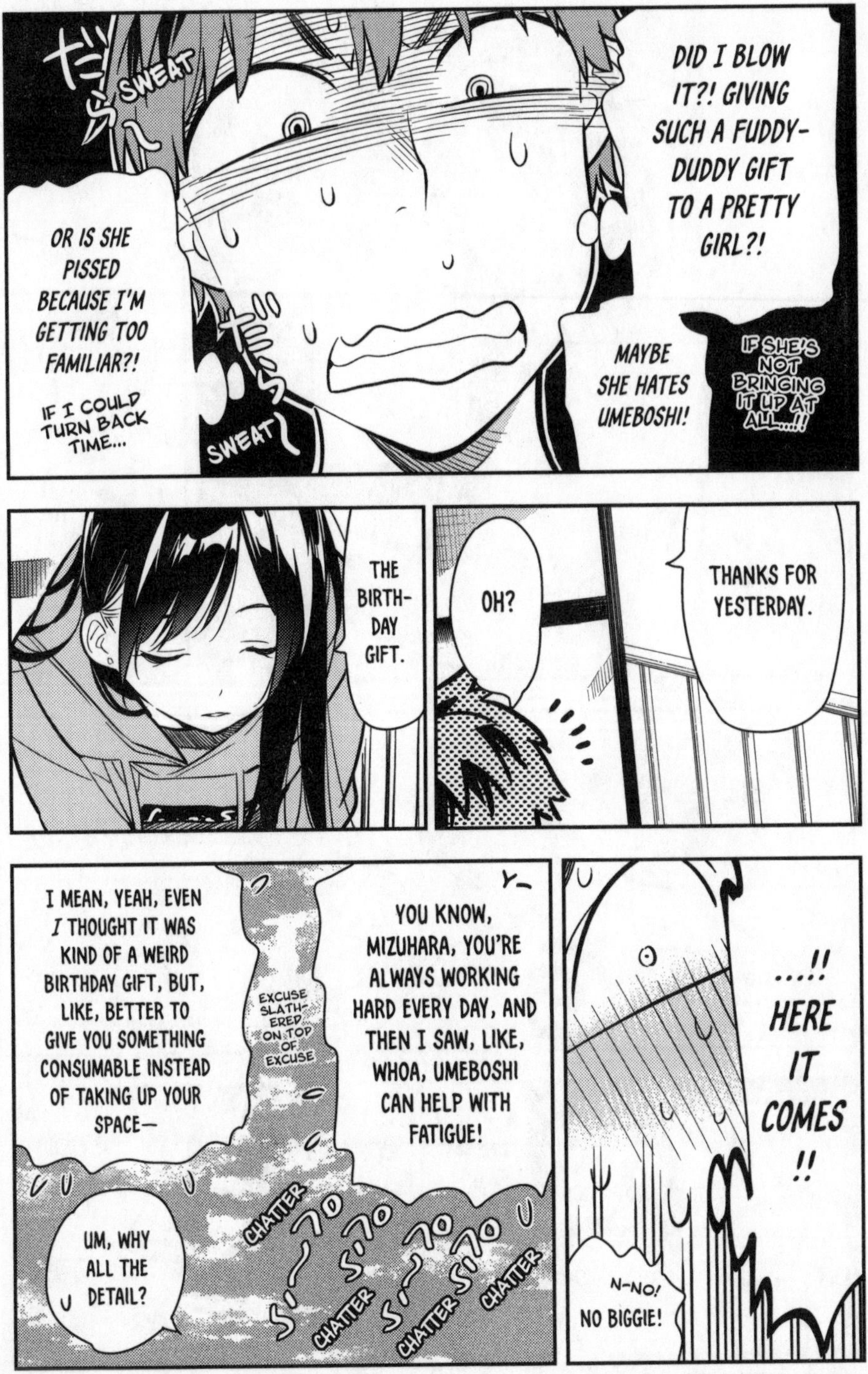
DID I BLOW IT?! GIVING SUCH A FUDDY-DUDDY GIFT TO A PRETTY GIRL?!
IF SHE'S NOT BRINGING IT UP AT ALL...!!
MAYBE SHE HATES UMEBOSHI!
SWEAT
OR IS SHE PISSED BECAUSE I'M GETTING TOO FAMILIAR?!
IF I COULD TURN BACK TIME...
SWEAT
THANKS FOR YESTERDAY.
OH?
THE BIRTH-DAY GIFT.
...!! HERE IT COMES!!
N-NO! NO BIGGIE!
YOU KNOW, MIZUHARA, YOU'RE ALWAYS WORKING HARD EVERY DAY, AND THEN I SAW, LIKE, WHOA, UMEBOSHI CAN HELP WITH FATIGUE!
EXCUSE SLATHERED ON TOP OF EXCUSE
I MEAN, YEAH, EVEN *I* THOUGHT IT WAS KIND OF A WEIRD BIRTHDAY GIFT, BUT, LIKE, BETTER TO GIVE YOU SOMETHING CONSUMABLE INSTEAD OF TAKING UP YOUR SPACE—
CHATTER
CHATTER
CHATTER
CHATTER
UM, WHY ALL THE DETAIL?

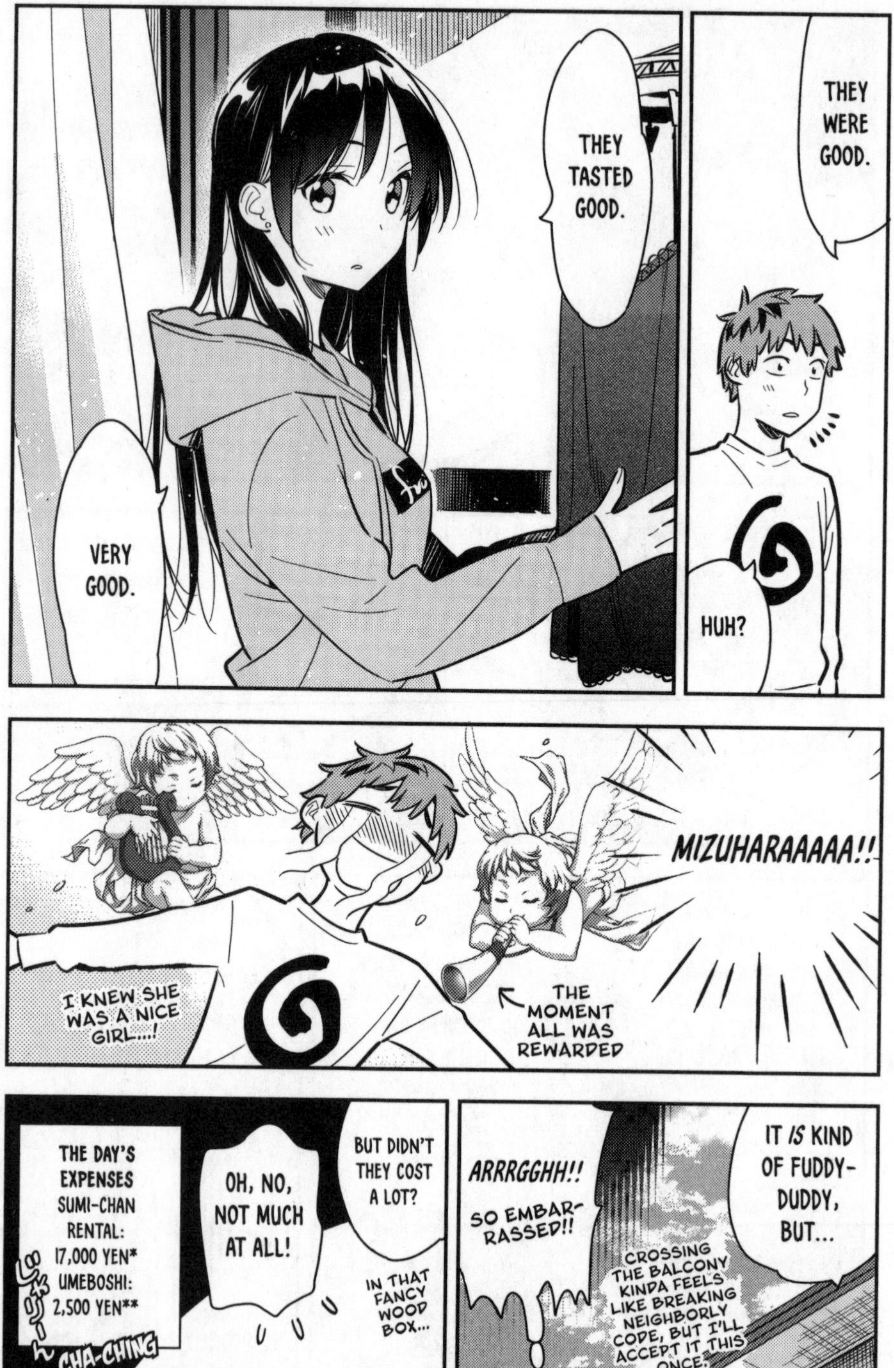
THEY WERE GOOD.
HUH?
THEY TASTED GOOD.
VERY GOOD.
MIZUHARAAAAA!!
THE MOMENT ALL WAS REWARDED
I KNEW SHE WAS A NICE GIRL...!
IT *IS* KIND OF FUDDY-DUDDY, BUT...
CROSSING THE BALCONY KINDA FEELS LIKE BREAKING NEIGHBORLY CODE, BUT I'LL ACCEPT IT THIS ONCE.
ARRRGGHH!!
SO EMBARRASSED!!
BUT DIDN'T THEY COST A LOT?
IN THAT FANCY WOOD BOX...
OH, NO, NOT MUCH AT ALL!
THE DAY'S EXPENSES
SUMI-CHAN RENTAL: 17,000 YEN*
UMEBOSHI: 2,500 YEN**
CHA-CHING

*ABOUT 155 USD **ABOUT 23 USD

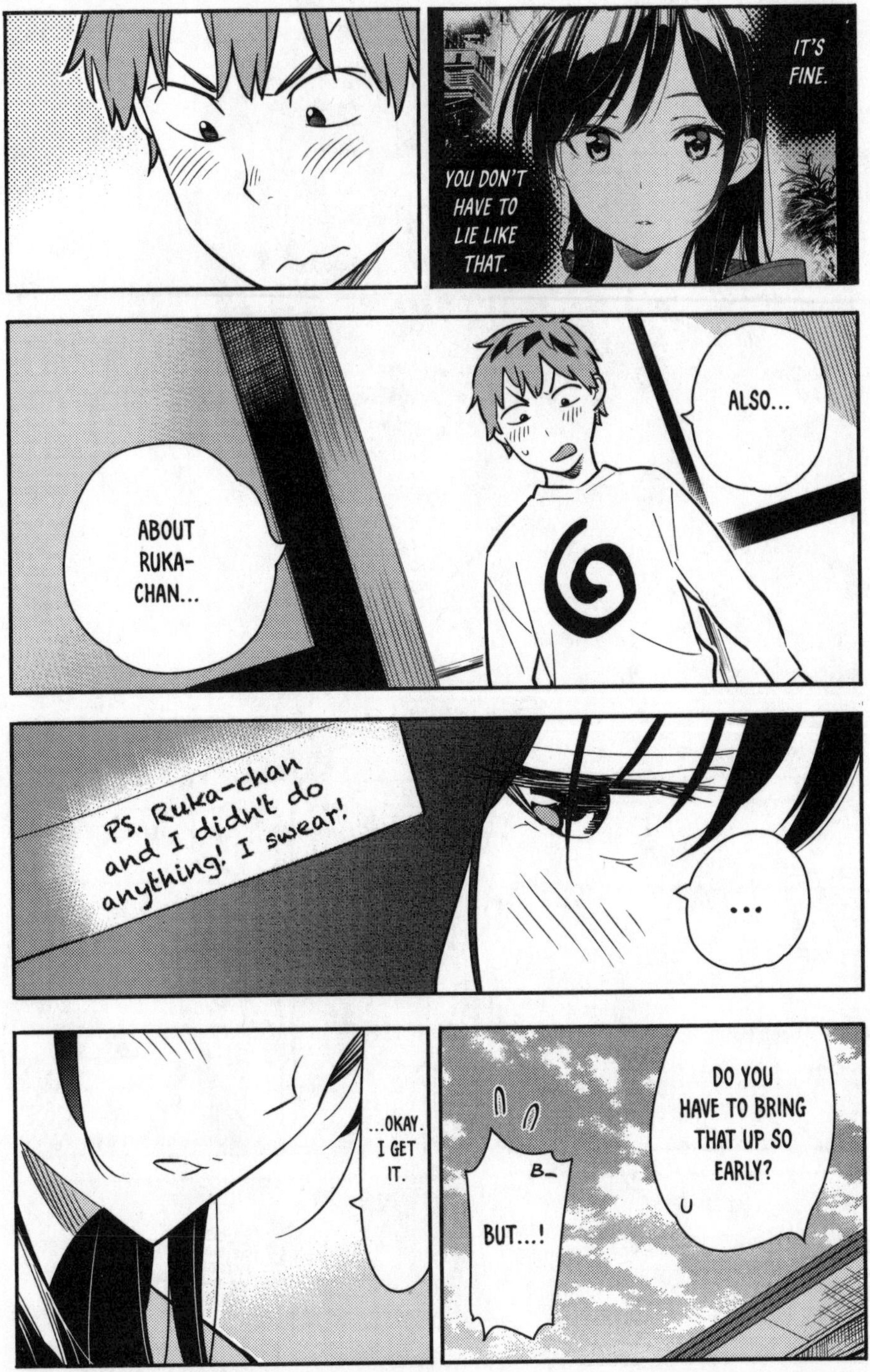
IT'S FINE.
YOU DON'T HAVE TO LIE LIKE THAT.
ALSO...
ABOUT RUKA-CHAN...
PS. Ruka-chan and I didn't do anything! I swear!
...
DO YOU HAVE TO BRING THAT UP SO EARLY?
B—
BUT...!
...OKAY. I GET IT.

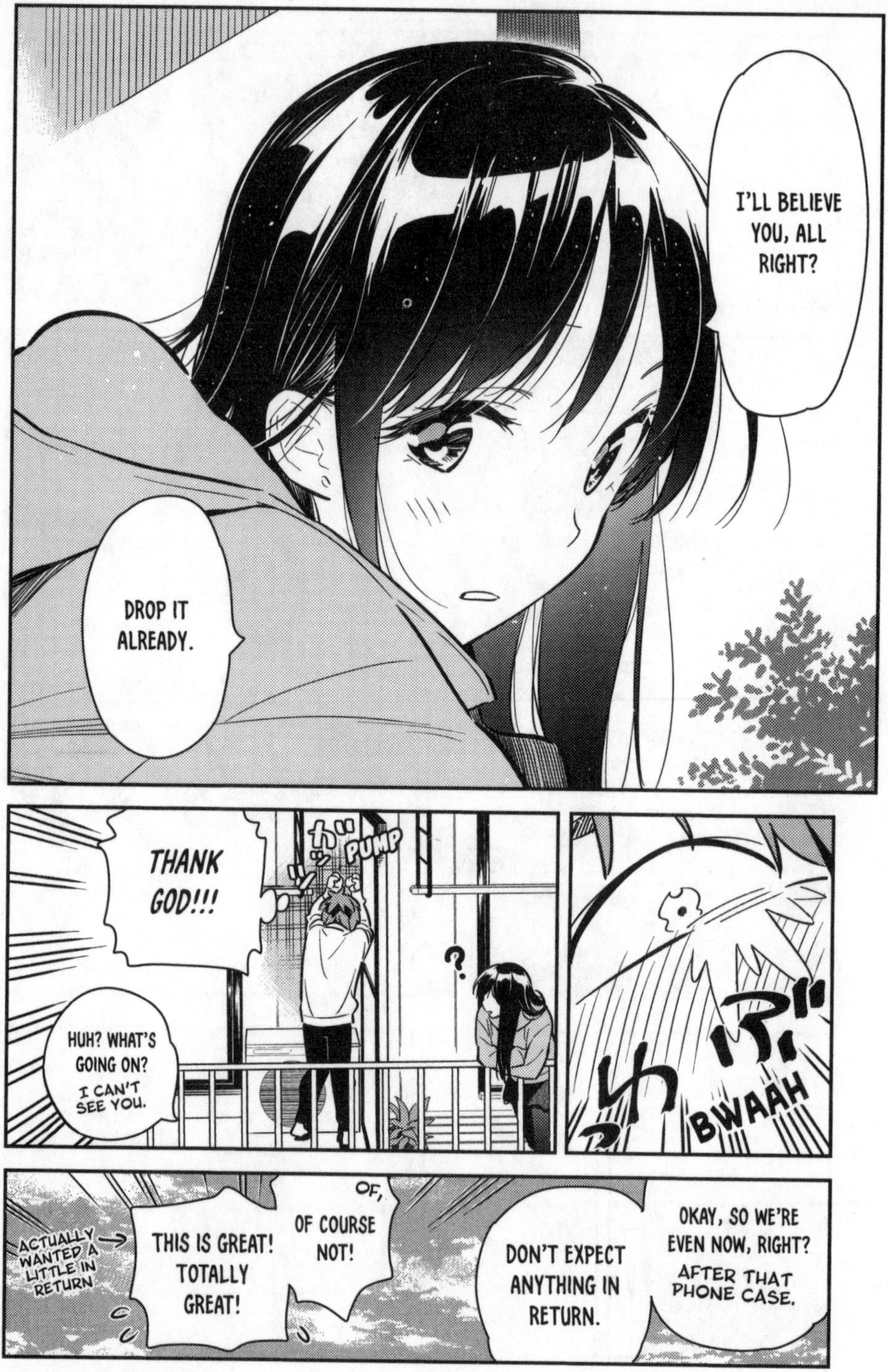
I'LL BELIEVE YOU, ALL RIGHT?
DROP IT ALREADY.
BWAAH
THANK GOD!!!
PUMP
?
HUH? WHAT'S GOING ON? I CAN'T SEE YOU.
OKAY, SO WE'RE EVEN NOW, RIGHT? AFTER THAT PHONE CASE.
DON'T EXPECT ANYTHING IN RETURN.
OF, OF COURSE NOT!
THIS IS GREAT! TOTALLY GREAT!
ACTUALLY WANTED A LITTLE IN RETURN

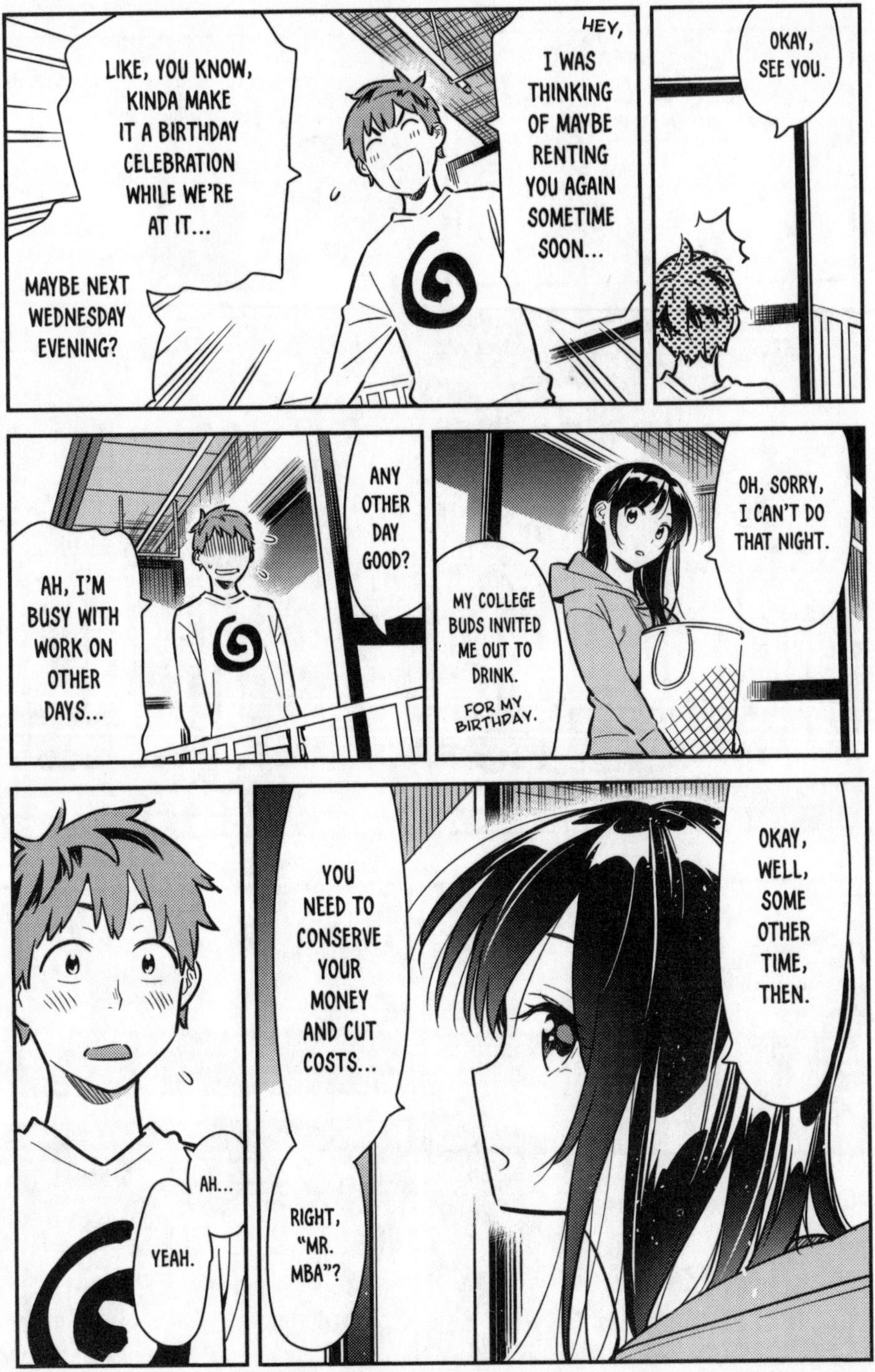
OKAY, SEE YOU.
HEY, I WAS THINKING OF MAYBE RENTING YOU AGAIN SOMETIME SOON...
LIKE, YOU KNOW, KINDA MAKE IT A BIRTHDAY CELEBRATION WHILE WE'RE AT IT...
MAYBE NEXT WEDNESDAY EVENING?
OH, SORRY, I CAN'T DO THAT NIGHT.
MY COLLEGE BUDS INVITED ME OUT TO DRINK.
FOR MY BIRTHDAY.
ANY OTHER DAY GOOD?
AH, I'M BUSY WITH WORK ON OTHER DAYS...
OKAY, WELL, SOME OTHER TIME, THEN.
YOU NEED TO CONSERVE YOUR MONEY AND CUT COSTS...
RIGHT, "MR. MBA"?
AH...
YEAH.

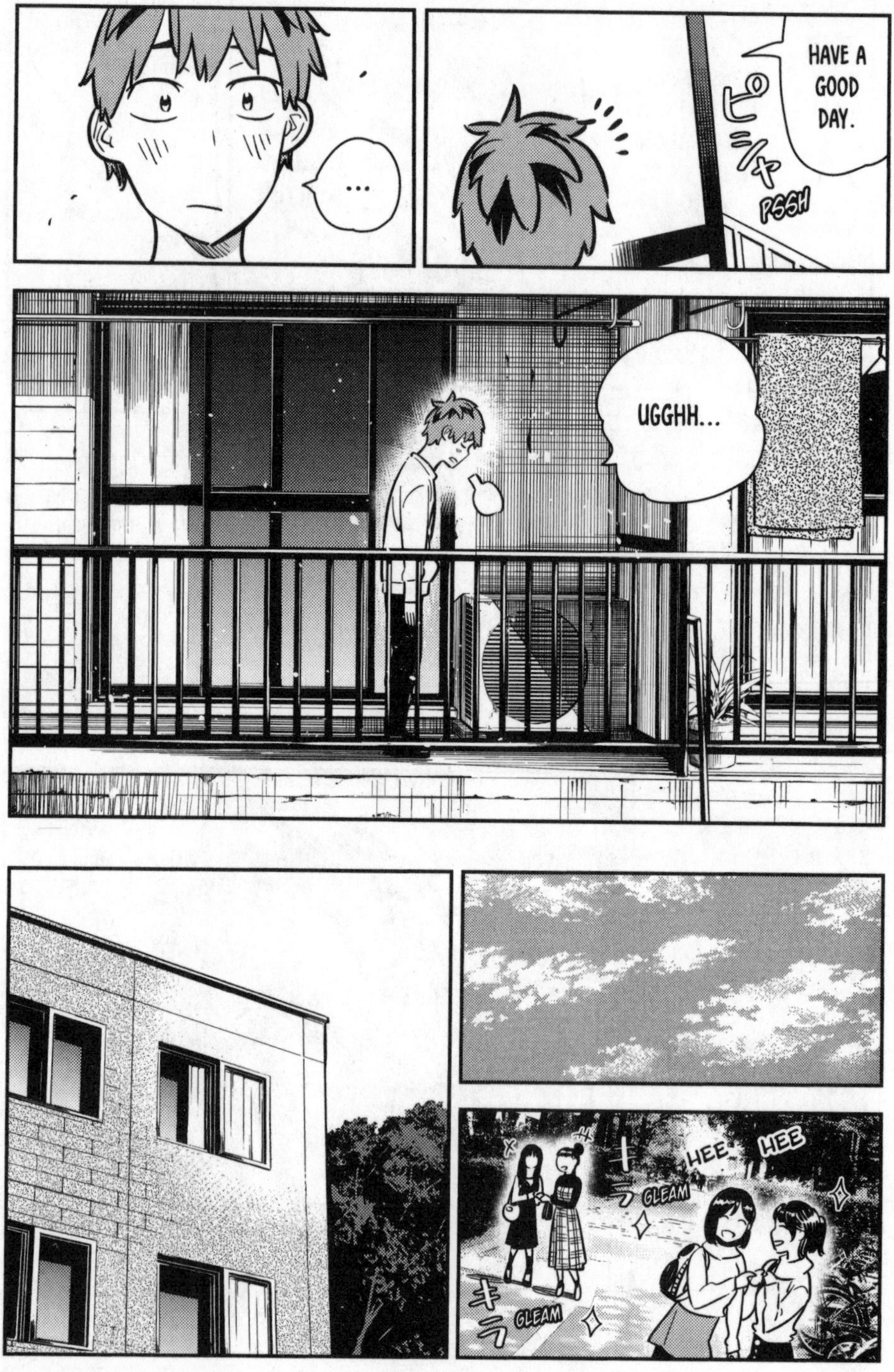
HAVE A GOOD DAY.
ピシャ
PSSH
...
UGGHH...
HEE HEE
キラ
GLEAM
キラ
GLEAM

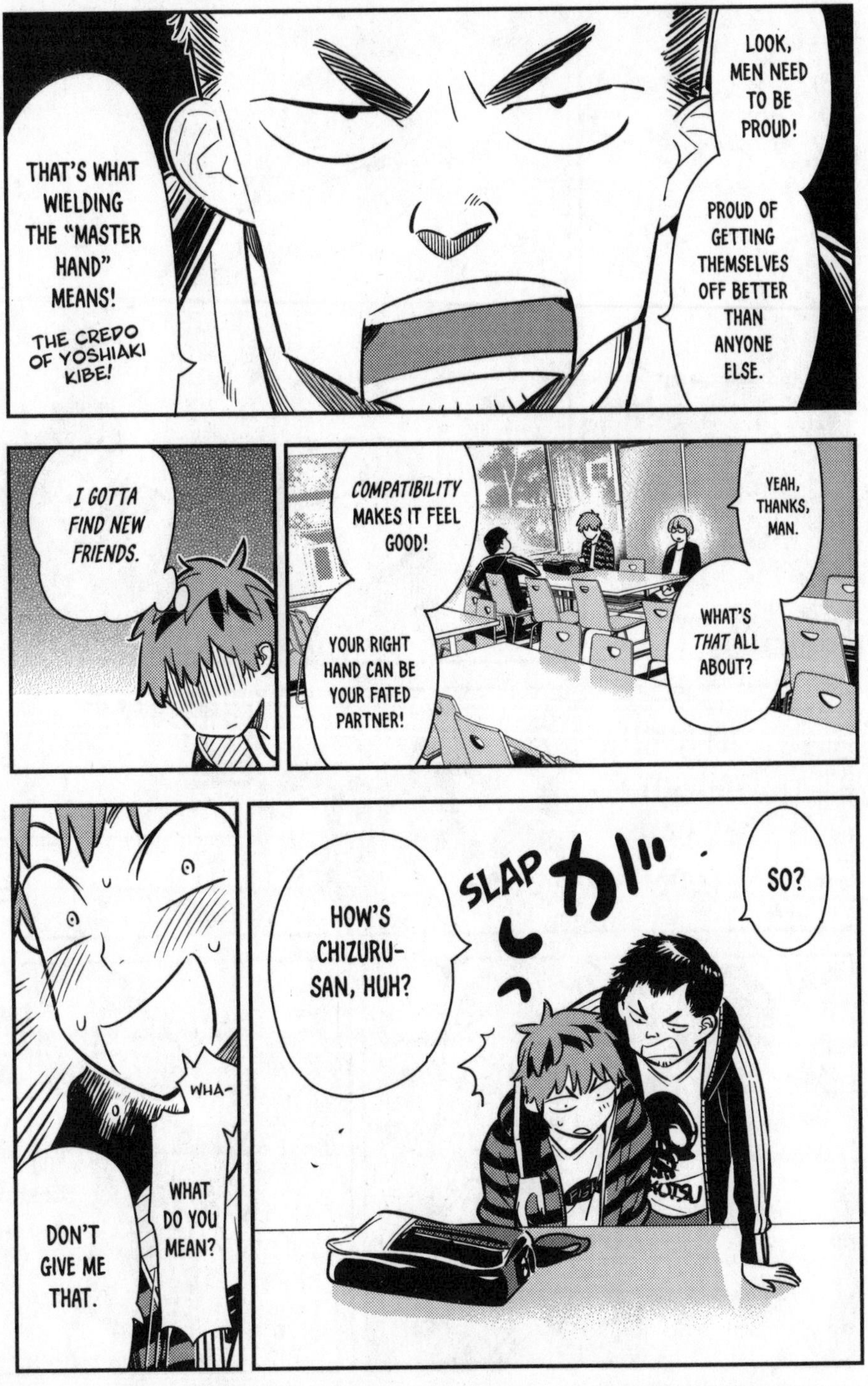
LOOK, MEN NEED TO BE PROUD!
PROUD OF GETTING THEMSELVES OFF BETTER THAN ANYONE ELSE.
THAT'S WHAT WIELDING THE "MASTER HAND" MEANS!
THE CREDO OF YOSHIAKI KIBE!
YEAH, THANKS, MAN.
COMPATIBILITY MAKES IT FEEL GOOD!
WHAT'S *THAT* ALL ABOUT?
YOUR RIGHT HAND CAN BE YOUR FATED PARTNER!
I GOTTA FIND NEW FRIENDS.
SO?
SLAP
HOW'S CHIZURU-SAN, HUH?
WHA-
WHAT DO YOU MEAN?
DON'T GIVE ME THAT.

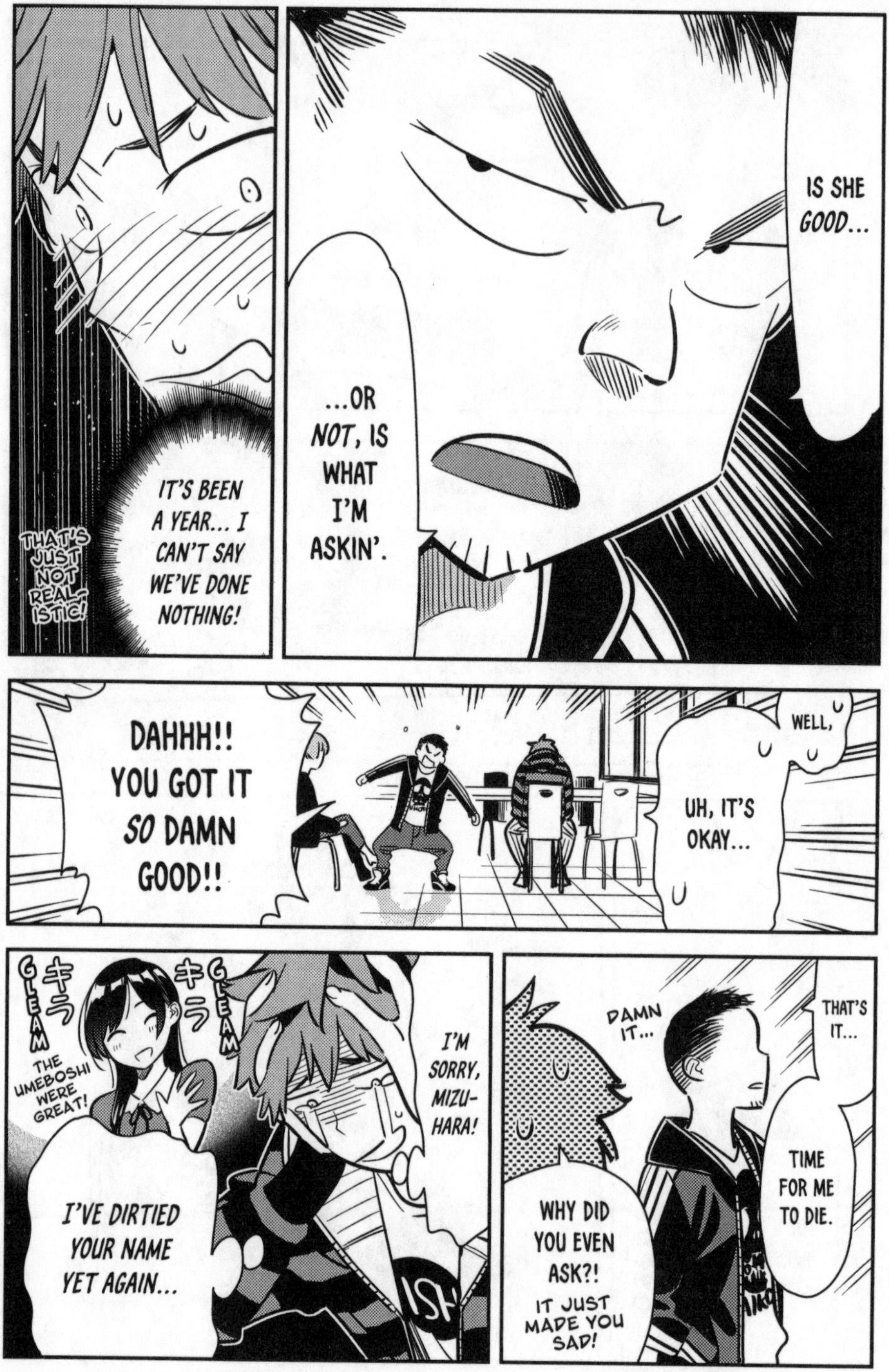
IS SHE GOOD...
...OR NOT, IS WHAT I'M ASKIN'.
IT'S BEEN A YEAR... I CAN'T SAY WE'VE DONE NOTHING!
THAT'S JUST NOT REAL-ISTIC!
WELL,
UH, IT'S OKAY...
DAHHH!! YOU GOT IT SO DAMN GOOD!!
THAT'S IT...
TIME FOR ME TO DIE.
DAMN IT...
WHY DID YOU EVEN ASK?!
IT JUST MADE YOU SAD!
I'M SORRY, MIZU-HARA!
キラ GLEAM
キラ GLEAM
THE UMEBOSHI WERE GREAT!
I'VE DIRTIED YOUR NAME YET AGAIN...

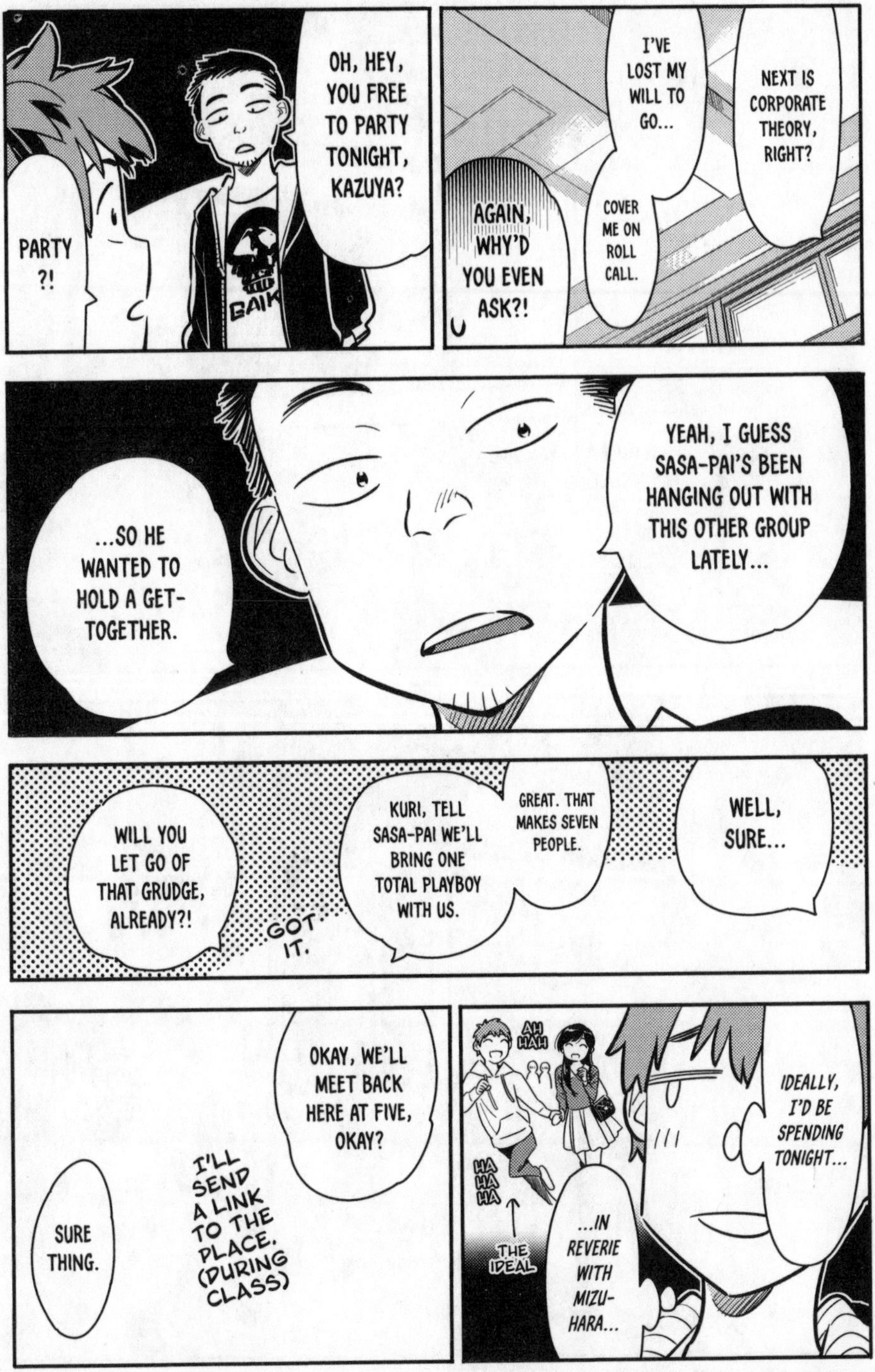
NEXT IS CORPORATE THEORY, RIGHT?
I'VE LOST MY WILL TO GO...
COVER ME ON ROLL CALL.
AGAIN, WHY'D YOU EVEN ASK?!
OH, HEY, YOU FREE TO PARTY TONIGHT, KAZUYA?
PARTY?!
YEAH, I GUESS SASA-PAI'S BEEN HANGING OUT WITH THIS OTHER GROUP LATELY...
...SO HE WANTED TO HOLD A GET-TOGETHER.
WELL, SURE...
GREAT. THAT MAKES SEVEN PEOPLE.
KURI, TELL SASA-PAI WE'LL BRING ONE TOTAL PLAYBOY WITH US.
GOT IT.
WILL YOU LET GO OF THAT GRUDGE, ALREADY?!
IDEALLY, I'D BE SPENDING TONIGHT...
AH HAH
HA HA HA
THE IDEAL
...IN REVERIE WITH MIZU-HARA...
OKAY, WE'LL MEET BACK HERE AT FIVE, OKAY?
I'LL SEND A LINK TO THE PLACE. (DURING CLASS)
SURE THING.

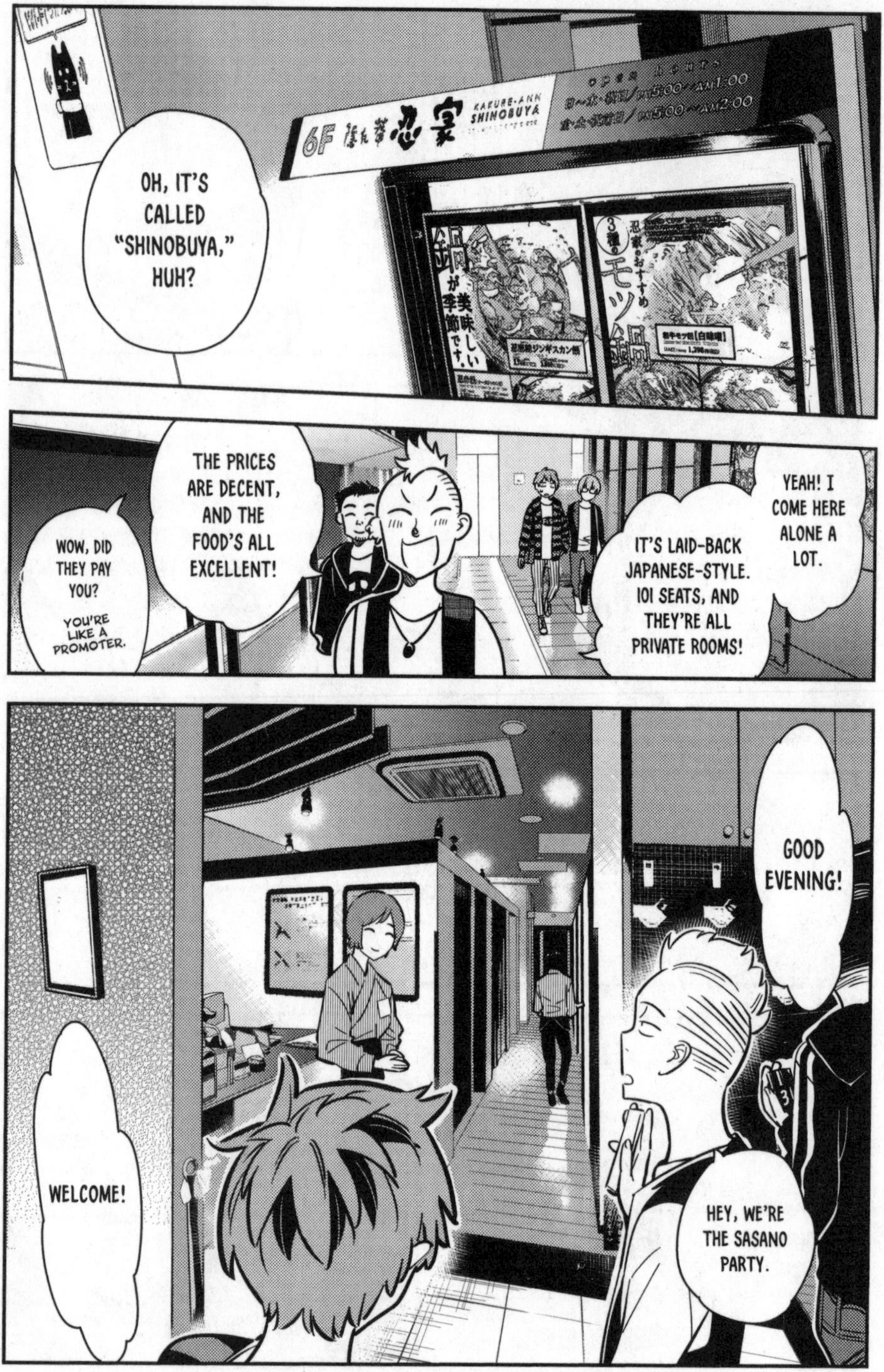
6F 隠れ庵 忍家
KAKURE-ANN SHINOBUYA
鍋が美味しい季節です。
3種の忍家おすすめモツ鍋
OH, IT'S CALLED "SHINOBUYA," HUH?
YEAH! I COME HERE ALONE A LOT.
IT'S LAID-BACK JAPANESE-STYLE. 101 SEATS, AND THEY'RE ALL PRIVATE ROOMS!
THE PRICES ARE DECENT, AND THE FOOD'S ALL EXCELLENT!
WOW, DID THEY PAY YOU?
YOU'RE LIKE A PROMOTER.
GOOD EVENING!
HEY, WE'RE THE SASANO PARTY.
WELCOME!

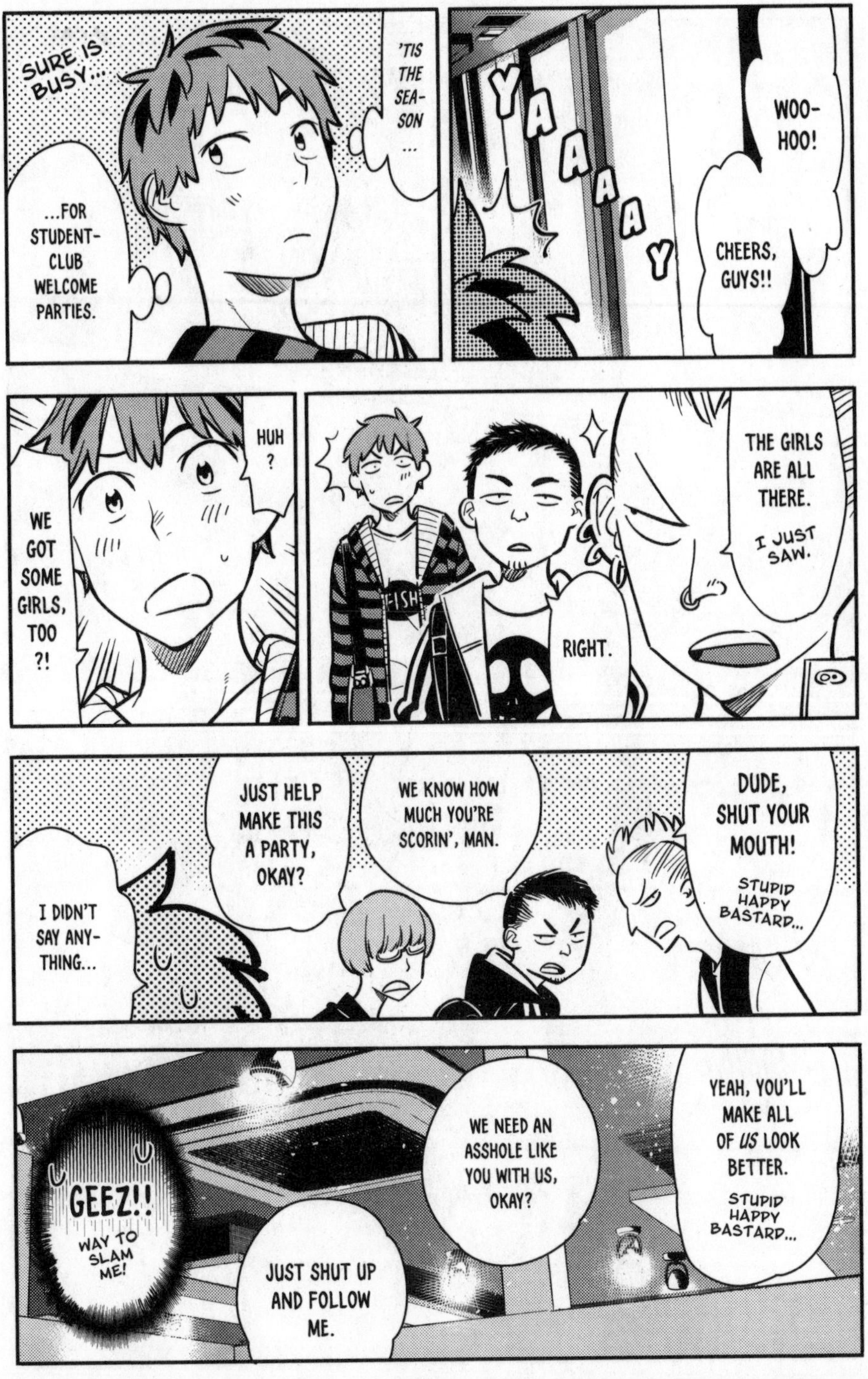
WOO-HOO!
CHEERS, GUYS!!
YAAAAAY
'TIS THE SEASON...
SURE IS BUSY...
...FOR STUDENT-CLUB WELCOME PARTIES.
THE GIRLS ARE ALL THERE.
I JUST SAW.
RIGHT.
HUH?
WE GOT SOME GIRLS, TOO?!
DUDE, SHUT YOUR MOUTH!
STUPID HAPPY BASTARD...
WE KNOW HOW MUCH YOU'RE SCORIN', MAN.
JUST HELP MAKE THIS A PARTY, OKAY?
I DIDN'T SAY ANYTHING...
YEAH, YOU'LL MAKE ALL OF US LOOK BETTER.
STUPID HAPPY BASTARD...
WE NEED AN ASSHOLE LIKE YOU WITH US, OKAY?
JUST SHUT UP AND FOLLOW ME.
GEEZ!!
WAY TO SLAM ME!

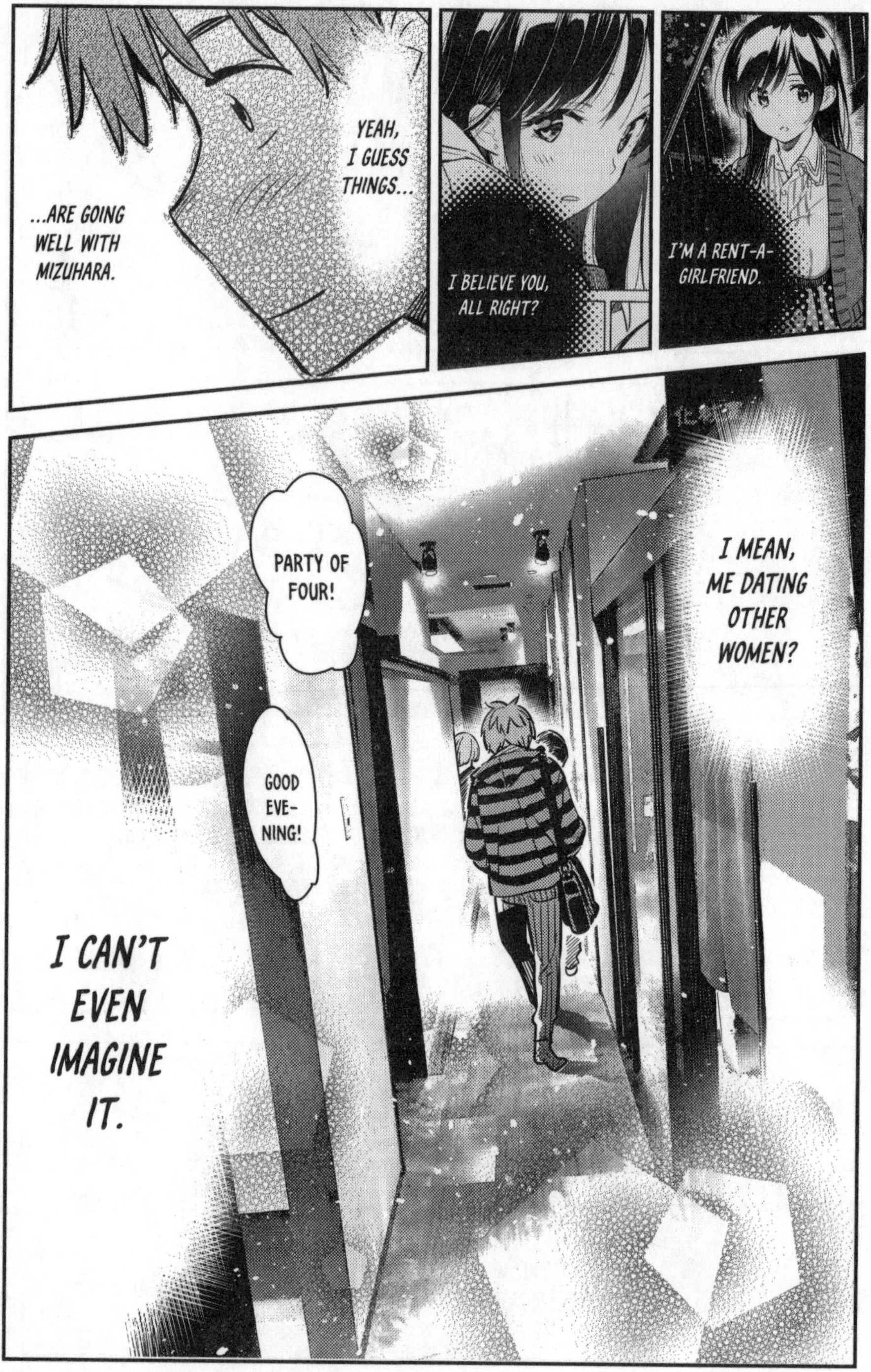
I'M A RENT-A-GIRLFRIEND.
I BELIEVE YOU, ALL RIGHT?
YEAH, I GUESS THINGS...
...ARE GOING WELL WITH MIZUHARA.
I MEAN, ME DATING OTHER WOMEN?
PARTY OF FOUR!
GOOD EVE-NING!
I CAN'T EVEN IMAGINE IT.

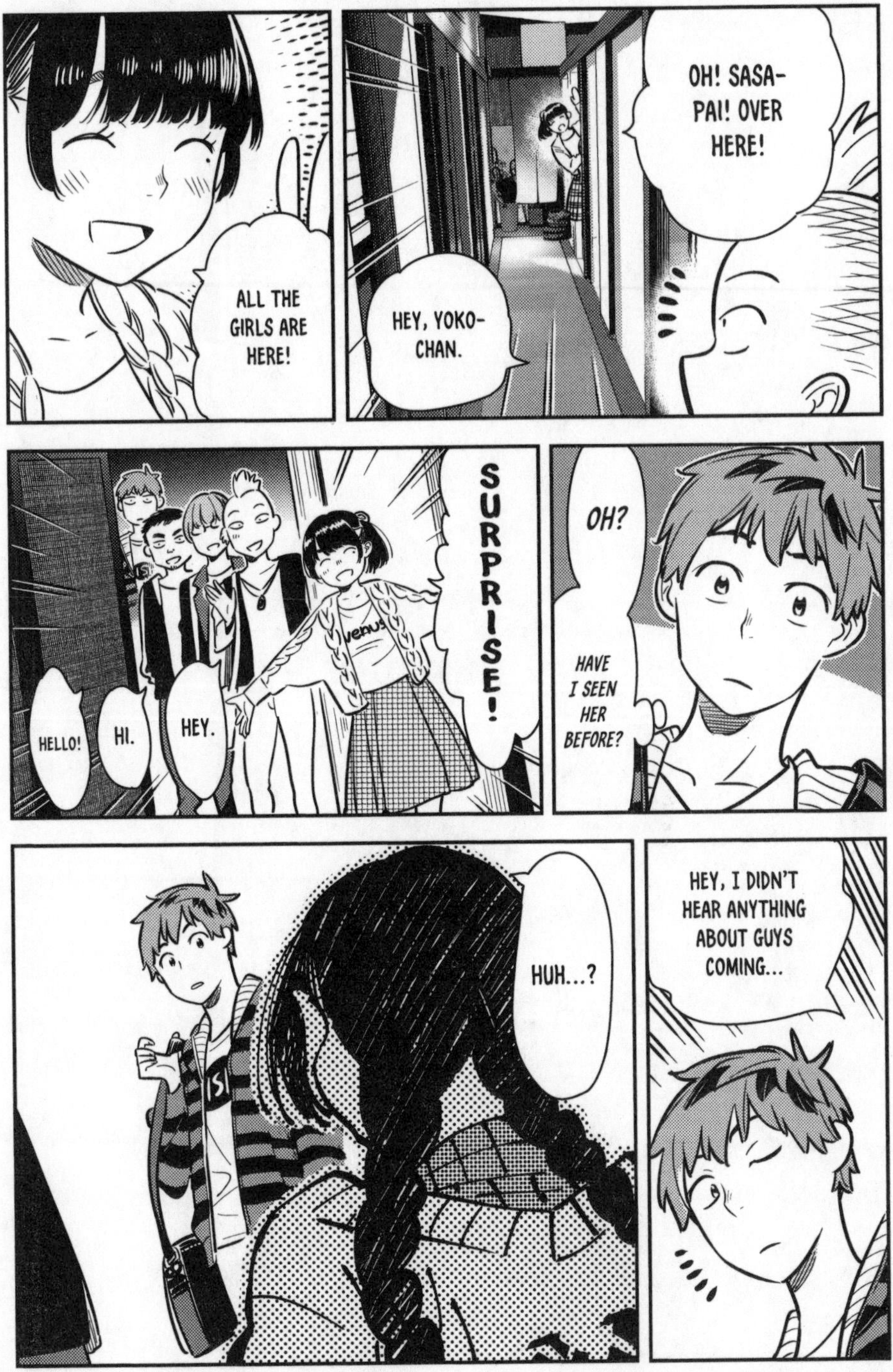
OH! SASA-PAI! OVER HERE!
HEY, YOKO-CHAN.
ALL THE GIRLS ARE HERE!
OH?
HAVE I SEEN HER BEFORE?
SURPRISE!
HEY.
HI.
HELLO!
HEY, I DIDN'T HEAR ANYTHING ABOUT GUYS COMING...
HUH...?

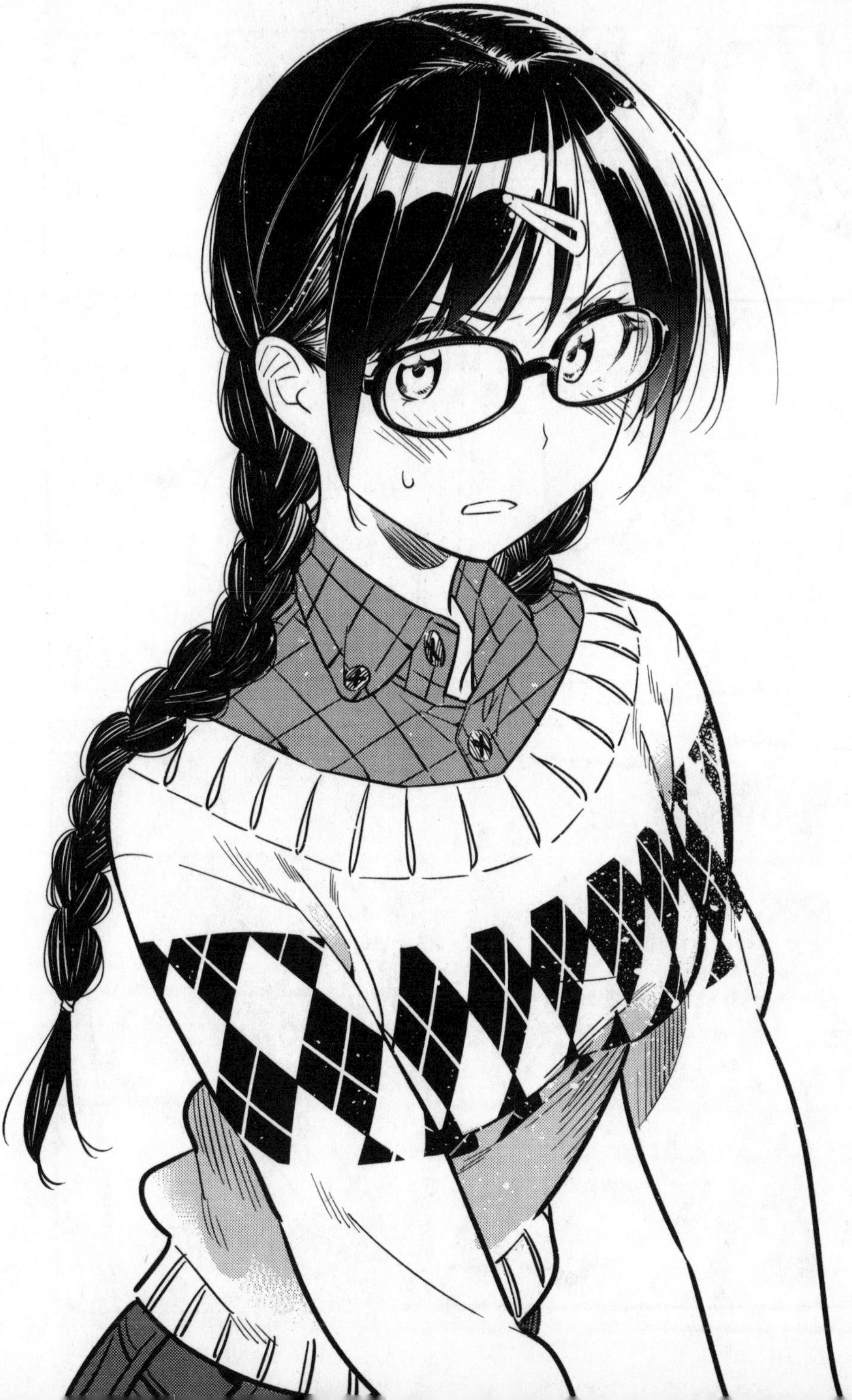

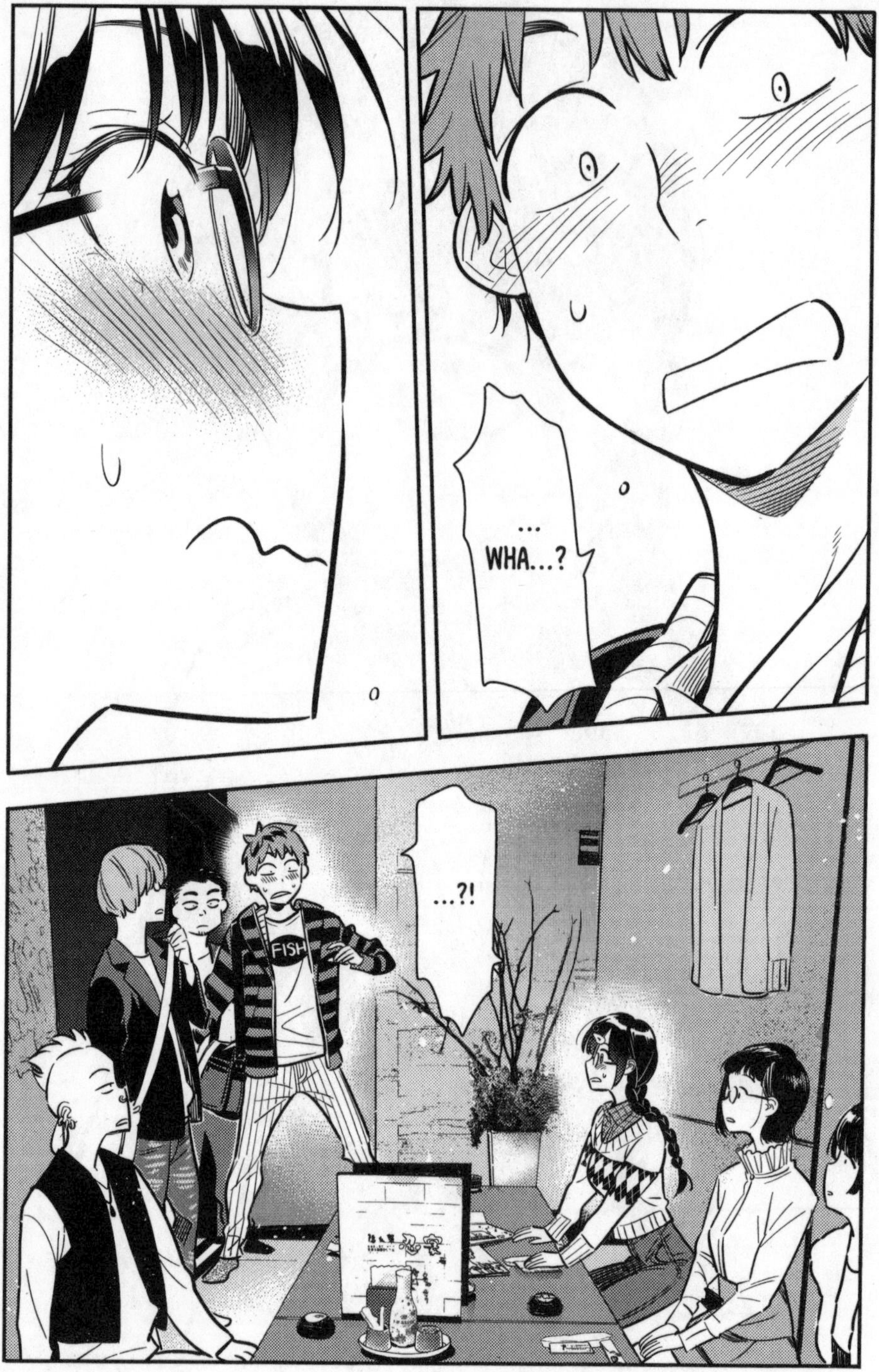
...
WHA...?
FISH
...?!

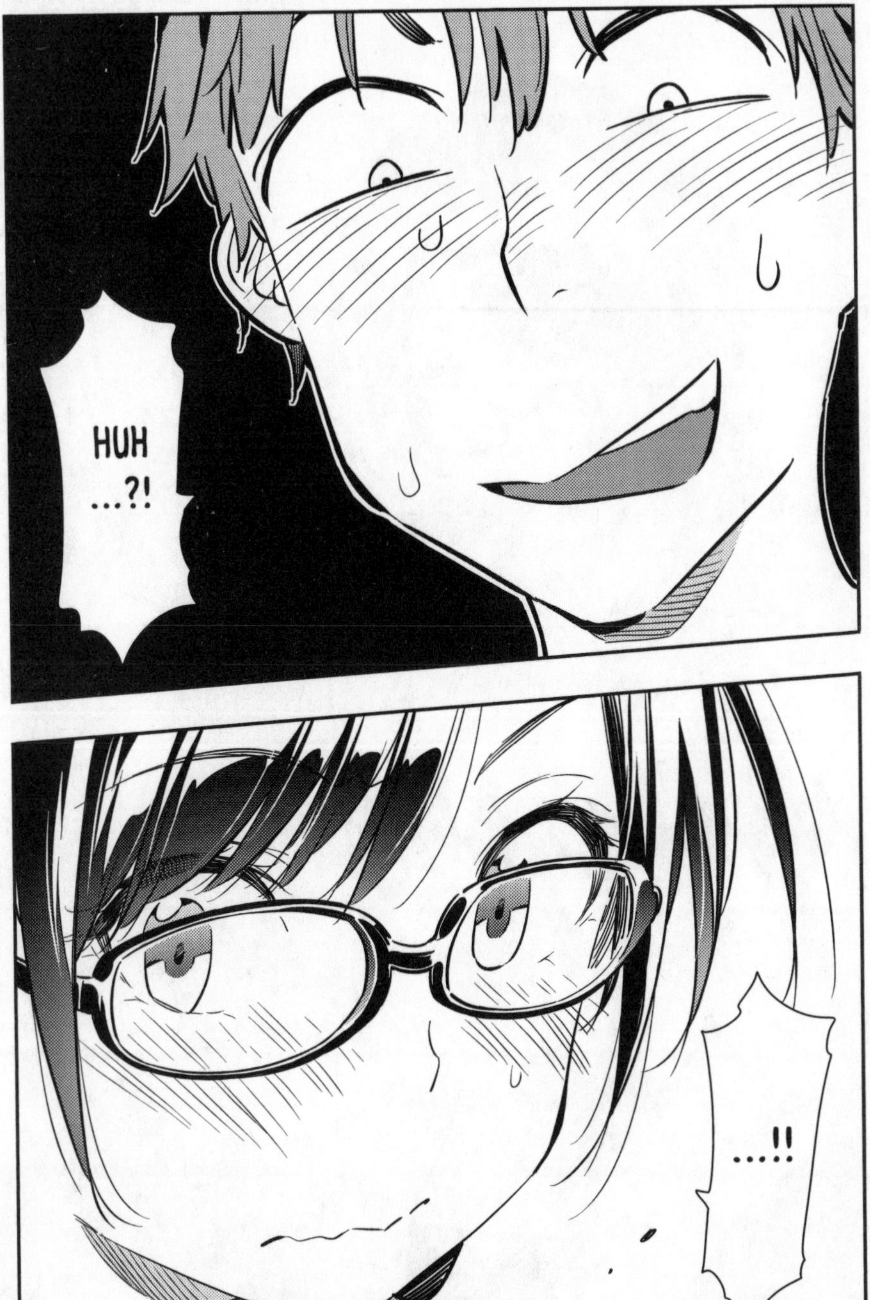
HUH ...?!
...!!

RATING 71 ALCOHOL AND MY GIRLFRIEND 2

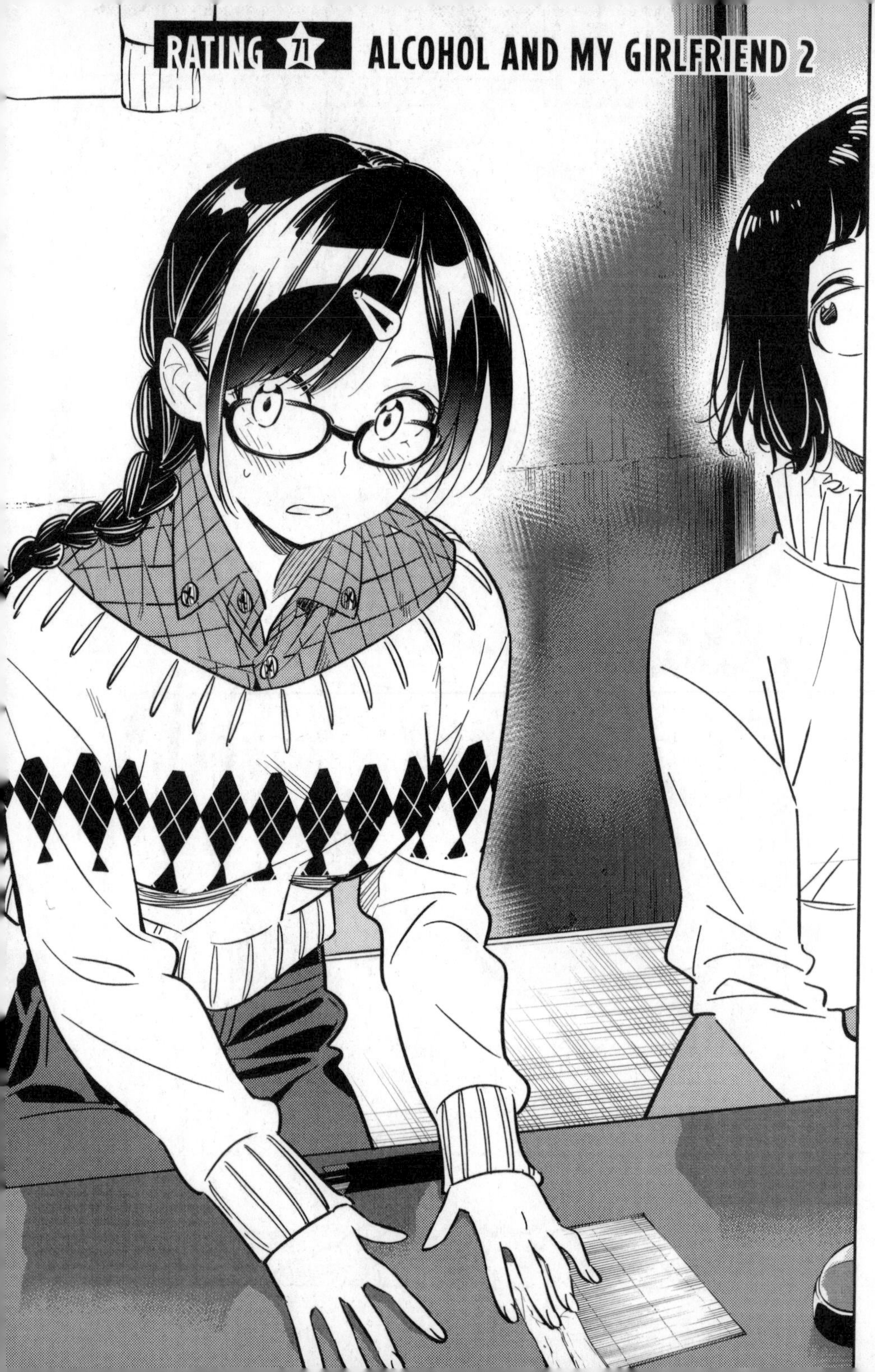

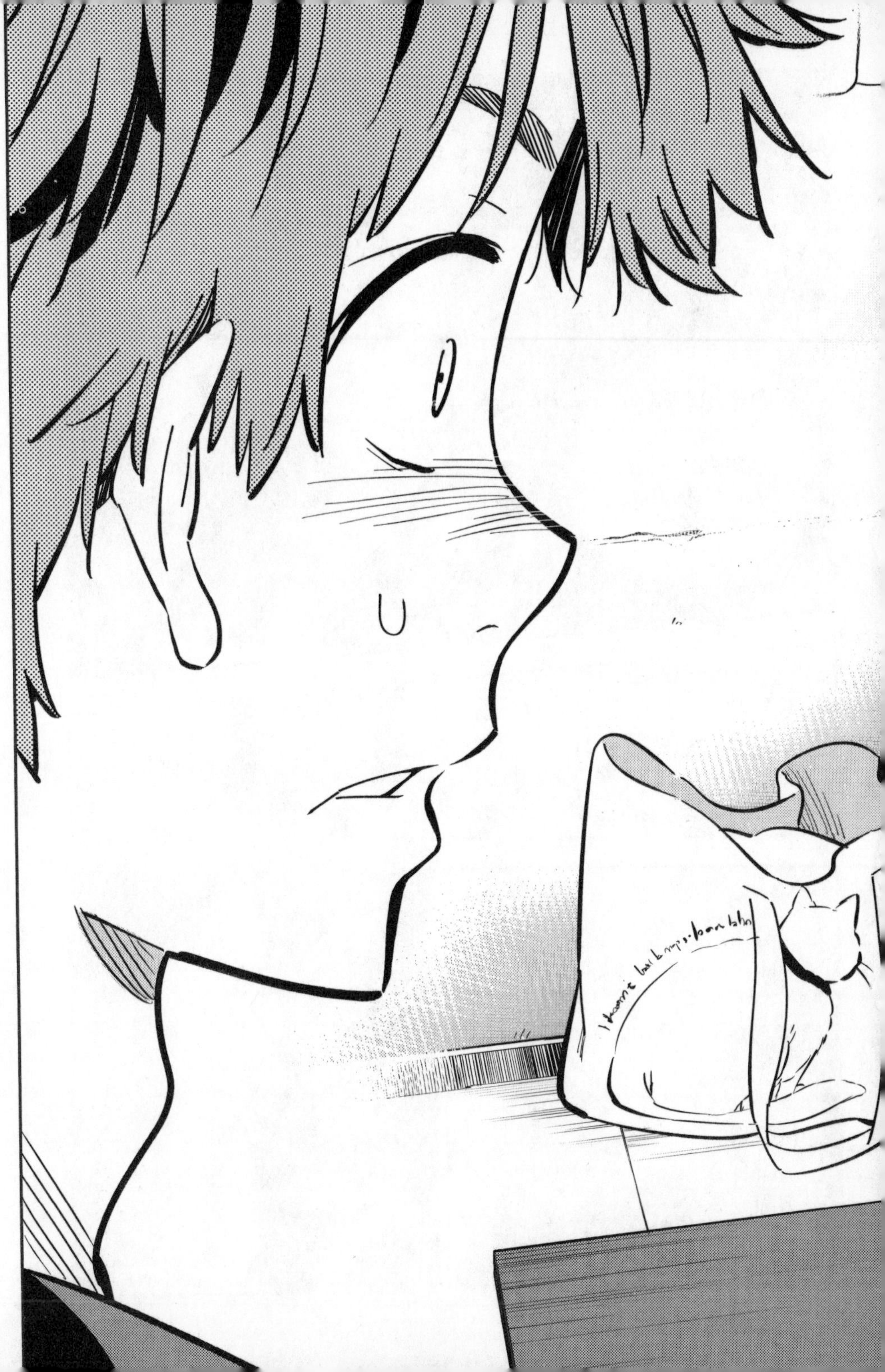

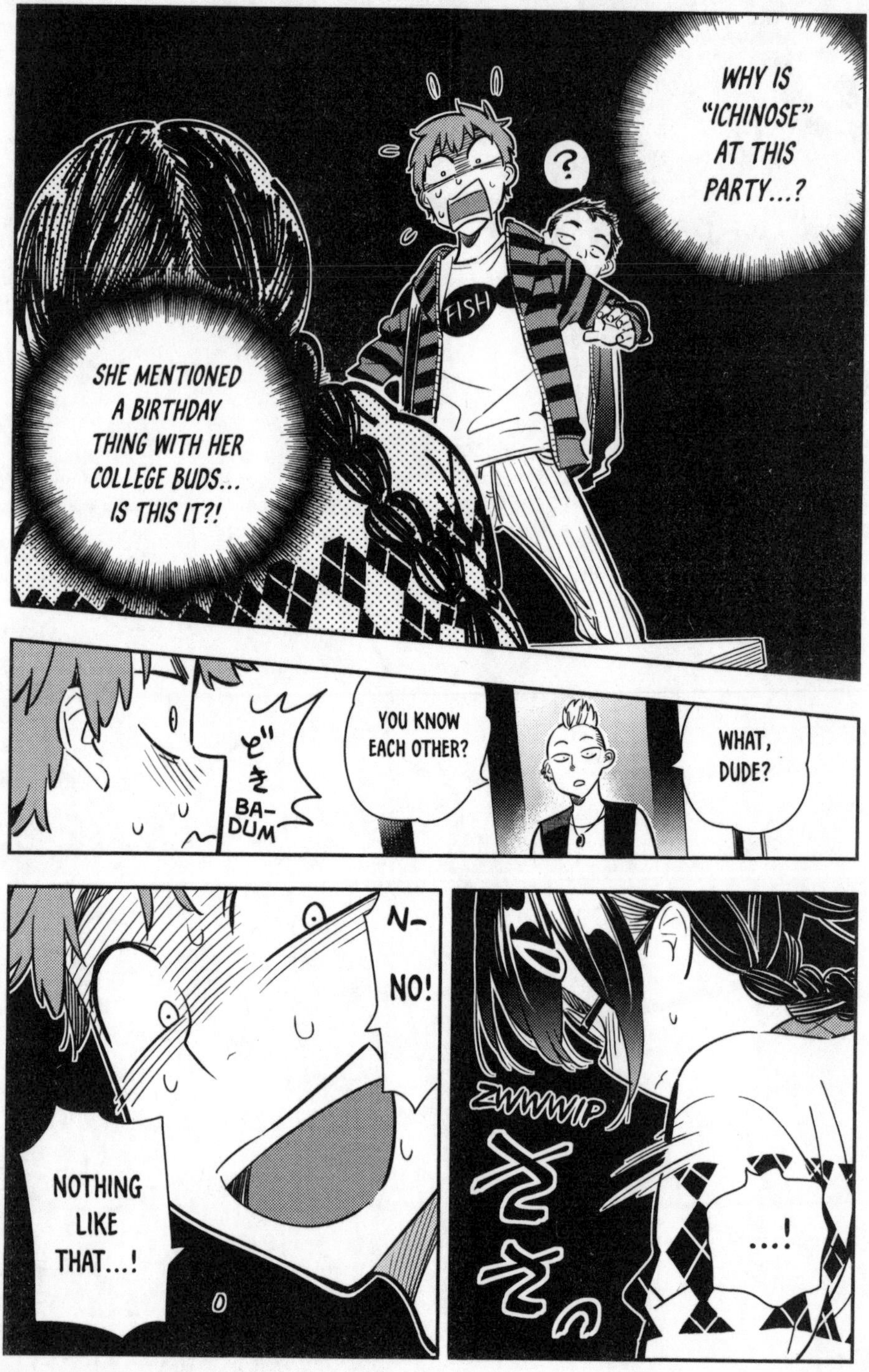

WHY IS "ICHINOSE" AT THIS PARTY...?
SHE MENTIONED A BIRTHDAY THING WITH HER COLLEGE BUDS... IS THIS IT?!
WHAT, DUDE?
YOU KNOW EACH OTHER?
どき
BA-DUM
ZWWWIP
そそっ
...!
N-
NO!
NOTHING LIKE THAT...!

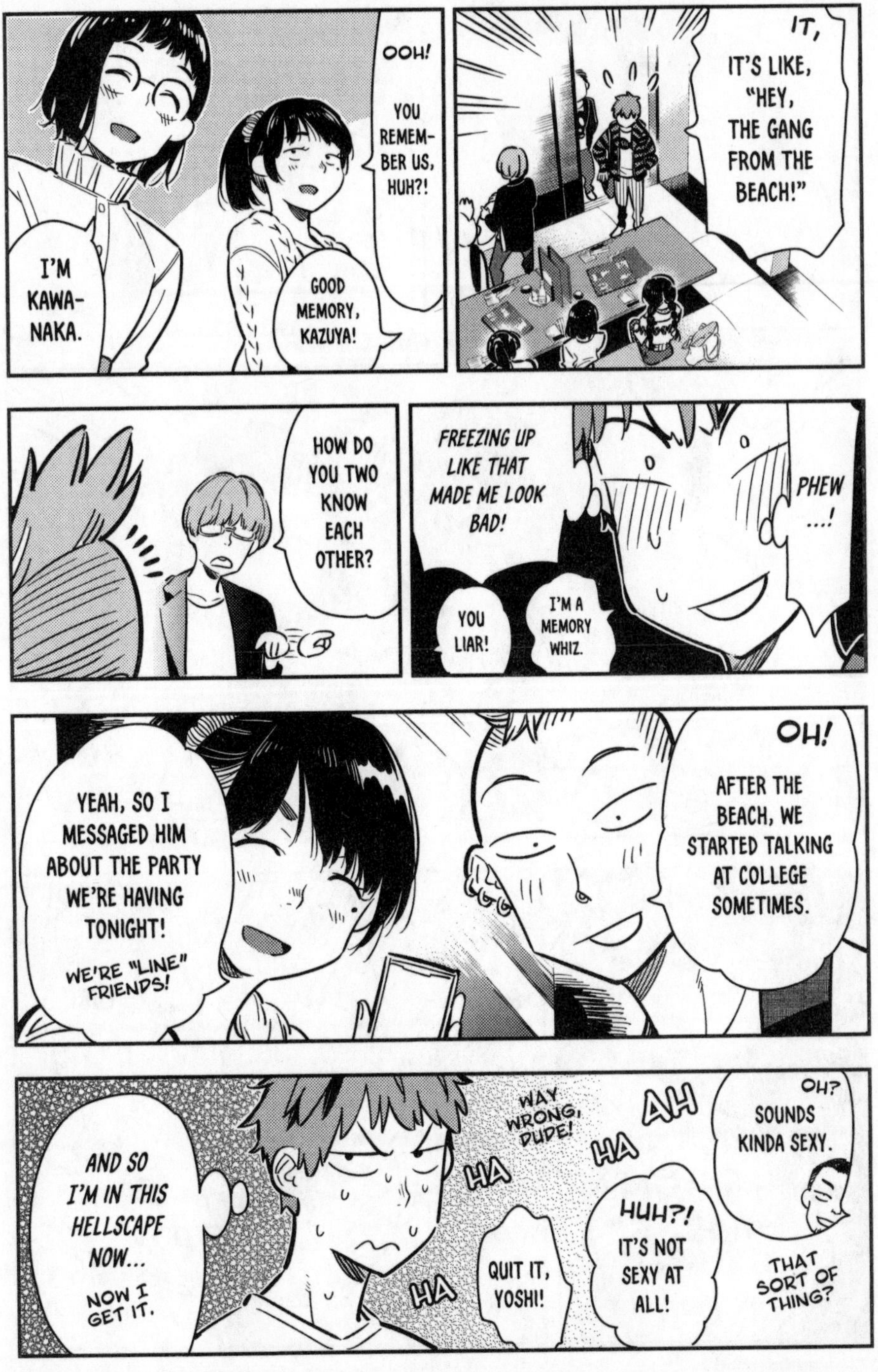
IT,
IT'S LIKE, "HEY, THE GANG FROM THE BEACH!"
OOH!
YOU REMEMBER US, HUH?!
GOOD MEMORY, KAZUYA!
I'M KAWANAKA.
PHEW ...!
FREEZING UP LIKE THAT MADE ME LOOK BAD!
I'M A MEMORY WHIZ.
YOU LIAR!
HOW DO YOU TWO KNOW EACH OTHER?
OH!
AFTER THE BEACH, WE STARTED TALKING AT COLLEGE SOMETIMES.
YEAH, SO I MESSAGED HIM ABOUT THE PARTY WE'RE HAVING TONIGHT!
WE'RE "LINE" FRIENDS!
OH?
SOUNDS KINDA SEXY.
THAT SORT OF THING?
AH
HA
HA
HA
HA
WAY WRONG, DUDE!
HUH?!
IT'S NOT SEXY AT ALL!
QUIT IT, YOSHI!
AND SO I'M IN THIS HELLSCAPE NOW...
NOW I GET IT.

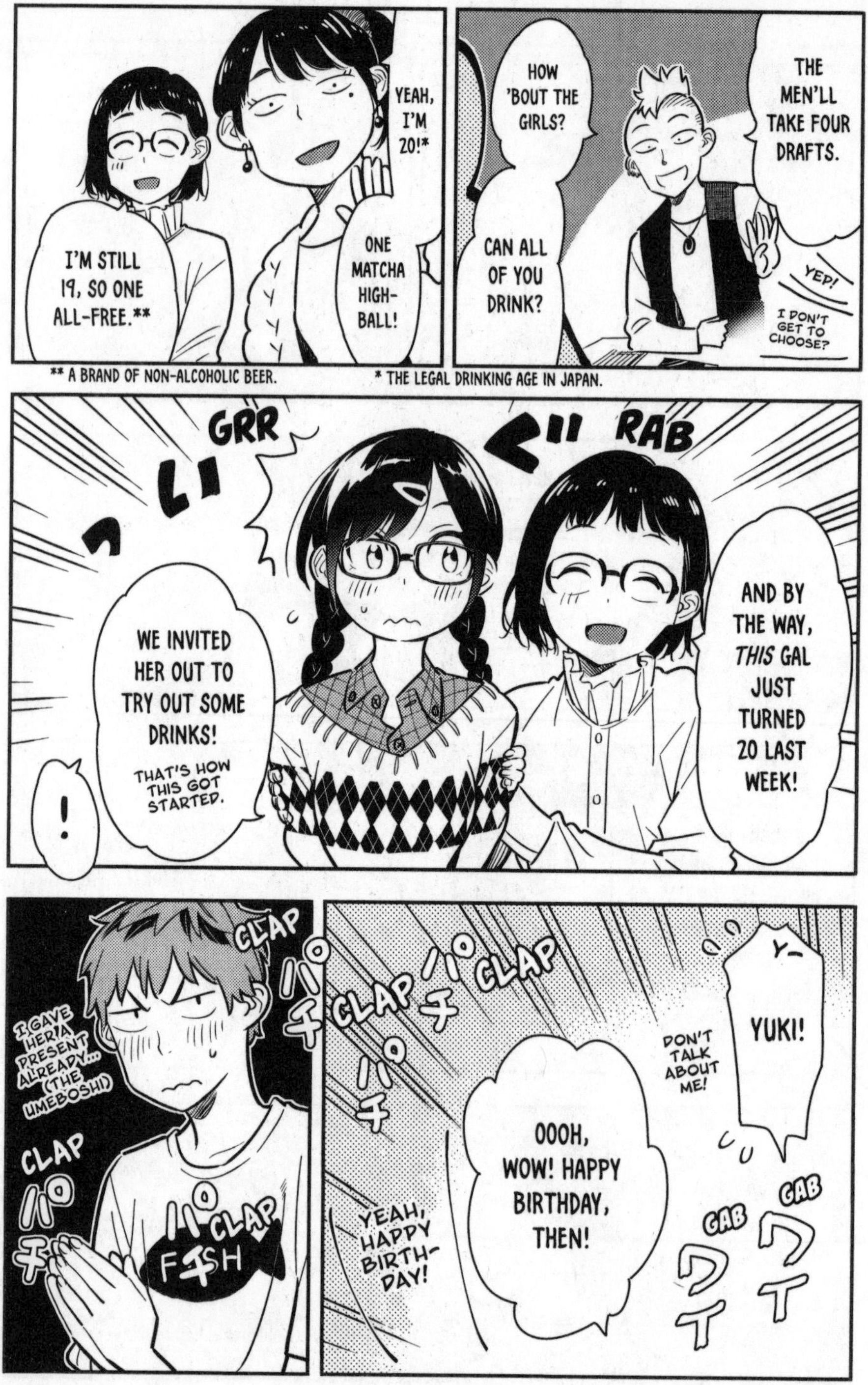
THE MEN'LL TAKE FOUR DRAFTS.
YEP!
I DON'T GET TO CHOOSE?
HOW 'BOUT THE GIRLS?
CAN ALL OF YOU DRINK?
YEAH, I'M 20!*
ONE MATCHA HIGH-BALL!
I'M STILL 19, SO ONE ALL-FREE.**
AND BY THE WAY, *THIS* GAL JUST TURNED 20 LAST WEEK!
RAB
GRR
WE INVITED HER OUT TO TRY OUT SOME DRINKS!
THAT'S HOW THIS GOT STARTED.
!
Y—
YUKI!
DON'T TALK ABOUT ME!
GAB
GAB
OOOH, WOW! HAPPY BIRTHDAY, THEN!
YEAH, HAPPY BIRTH-DAY!
CLAP
CLAP
CLAP
I GAVE HER A PRESENT ALREADY... (THE UMEBOSHI)
CLAP
CLAP
FISH

* THE LEGAL DRINKING AGE IN JAPAN.

** A BRAND OF NON-ALCOHOLIC BEER.

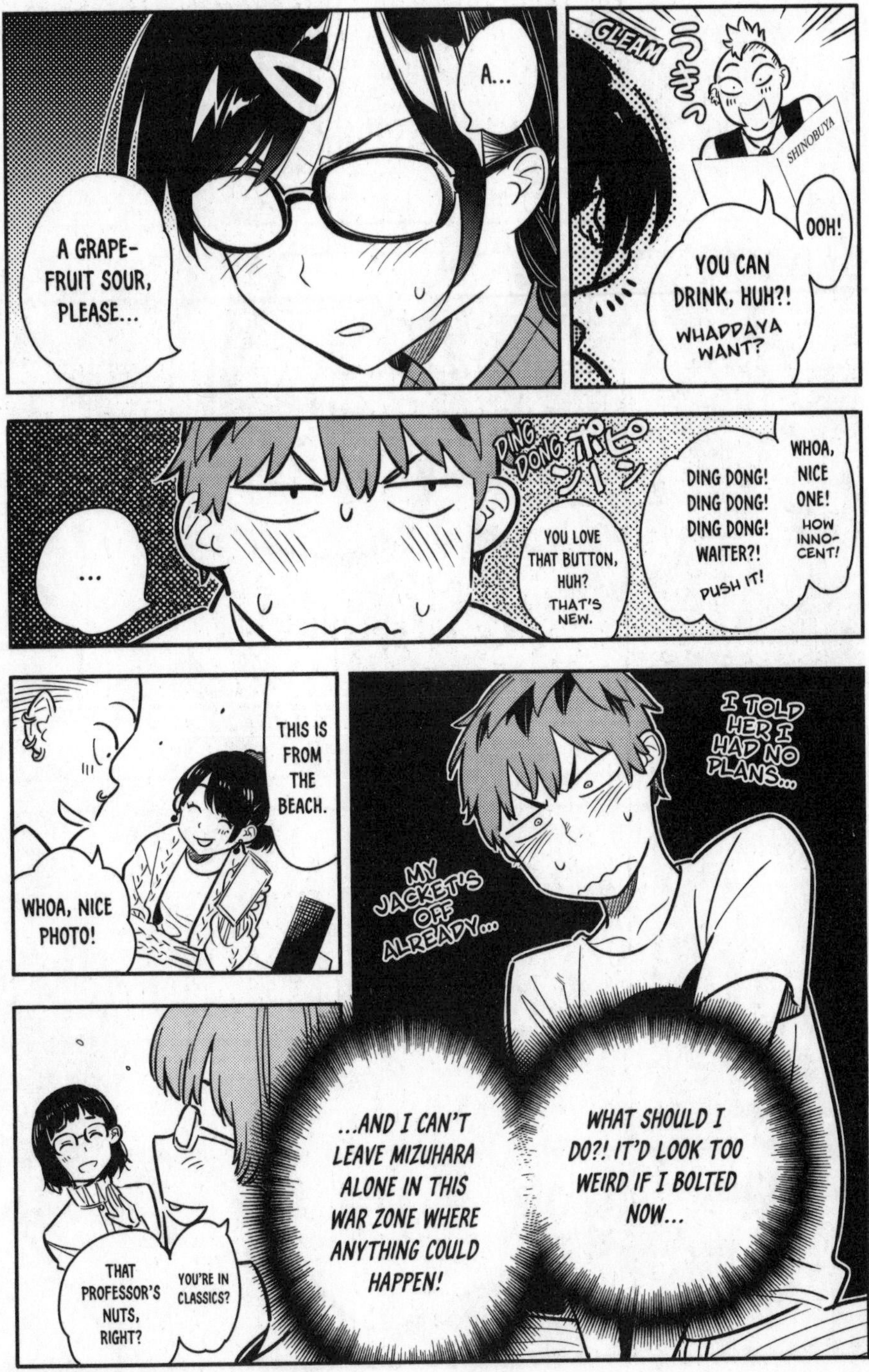
GLEAM
うきっ
SHINOBUYA
OOH!
YOU CAN DRINK, HUH?!
WHADDAYA WANT?
A...
A GRAPE-FRUIT SOUR, PLEASE...
WHOA, NICE ONE!
HOW INNO-CENT!
DING DONG! DING DONG! DING DONG! WAITER?!
PUSH IT!
DING DONG
ポピーン
YOU LOVE THAT BUTTON, HUH?
THAT'S NEW.
...
I TOLD HER I HAD NO PLANS...
MY JACKET'S OFF ALREADY...
WHAT SHOULD I DO?! IT'D LOOK TOO WEIRD IF I BOLTED NOW...
...AND I CAN'T LEAVE MIZUHARA ALONE IN THIS WAR ZONE WHERE ANYTHING COULD HAPPEN!
THIS IS FROM THE BEACH.
WHOA, NICE PHOTO!
YOU'RE IN CLASSICS?
THAT PROFESSOR'S NUTS, RIGHT?

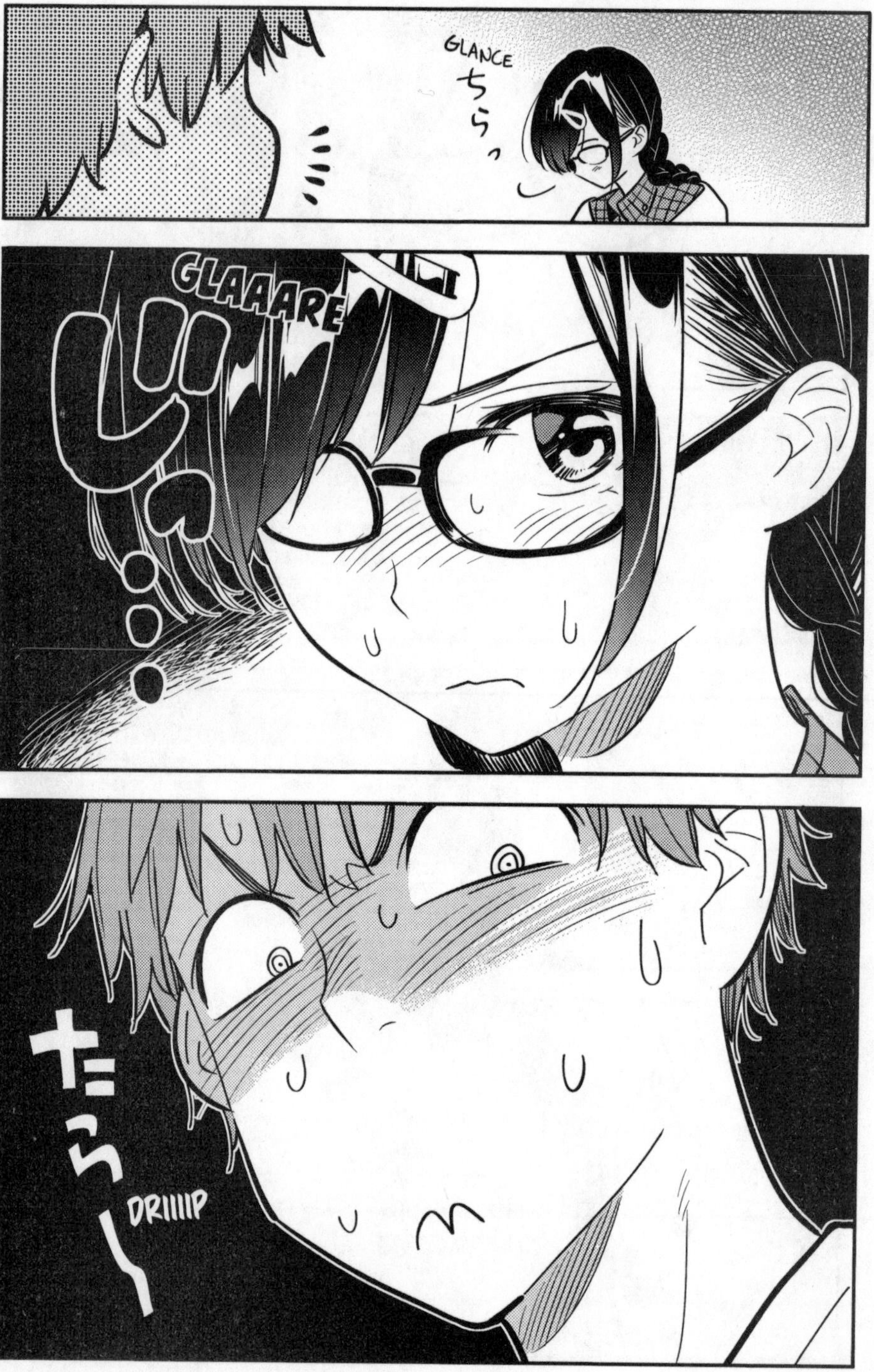
GLANCE
ちらっ
GLAAARE
じーっ…
DRIIIIP
たら～

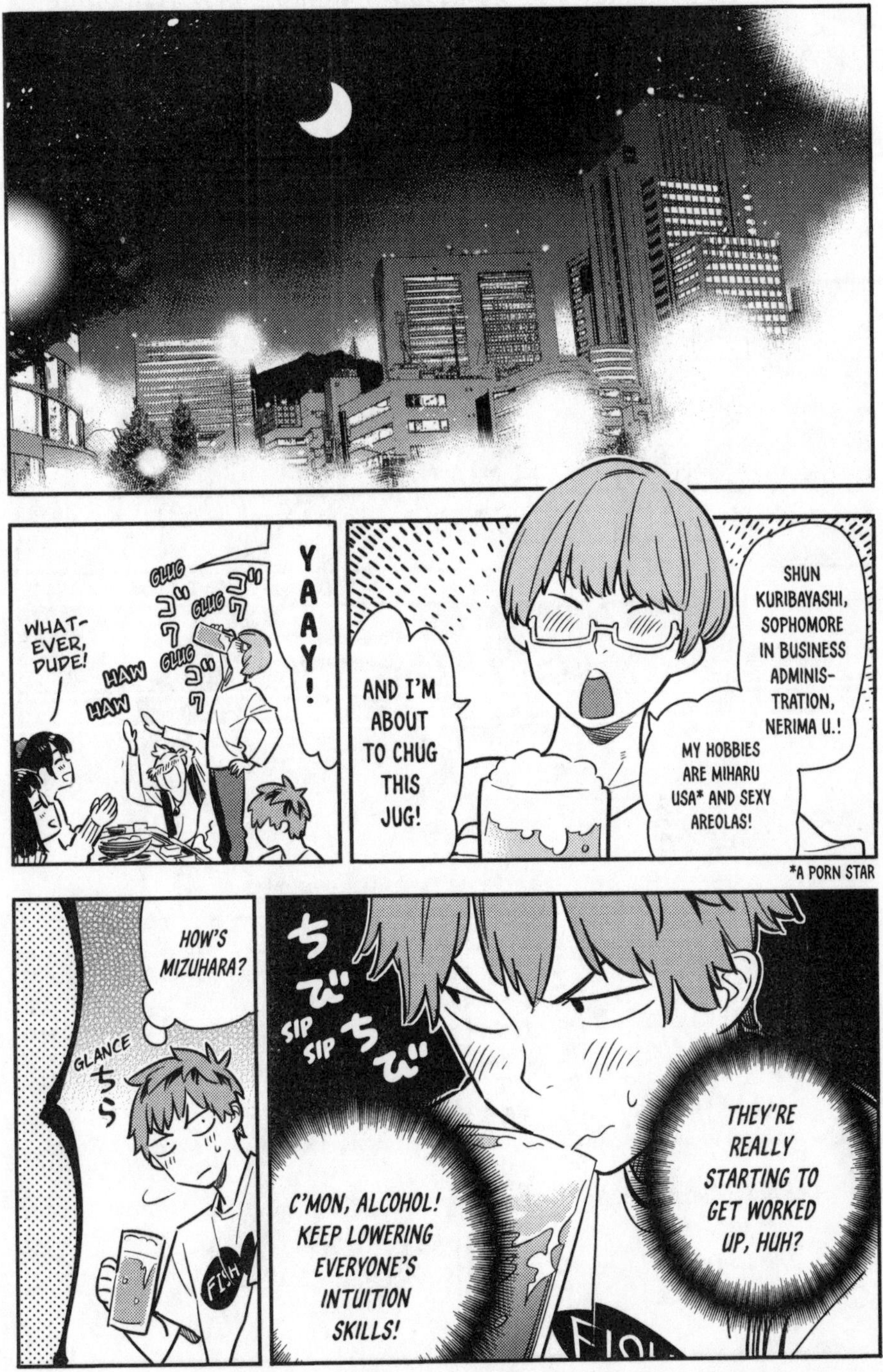
SHUN KURIBAYASHI, SOPHOMORE IN BUSINESS ADMINIS-TRATION, NERIMA U.!
MY HOBBIES ARE MIHARU USA* AND SEXY AREOLAS!
AND I'M ABOUT TO CHUG THIS JUG!
YAAAY!
GLUG ゴク
GLUG ゴク
GLUG ゴク
HAW HAW
WHAT-EVER, DUDE!
*A PORN STAR
ちび SIP SIP ちび
THEY'RE REALLY STARTING TO GET WORKED UP, HUH?
C'MON, ALCOHOL! KEEP LOWERING EVERYONE'S INTUITION SKILLS!
FISH
HOW'S MIZUHARA?
GLANCE ちら
FISH

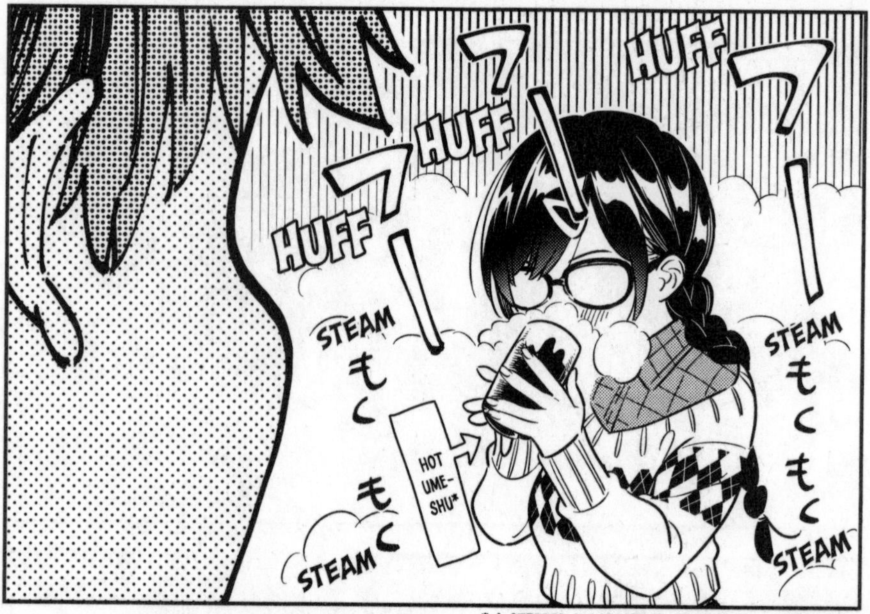
HUFF
HUFF
HUFF
HUFF
フー
フー
STEAM
もくもく
STEAM
STEAM
もく
STEAM
もく
HOT UME-SHU*

* A STEEPED PLUM LIQUOR, 10-15% ABV.

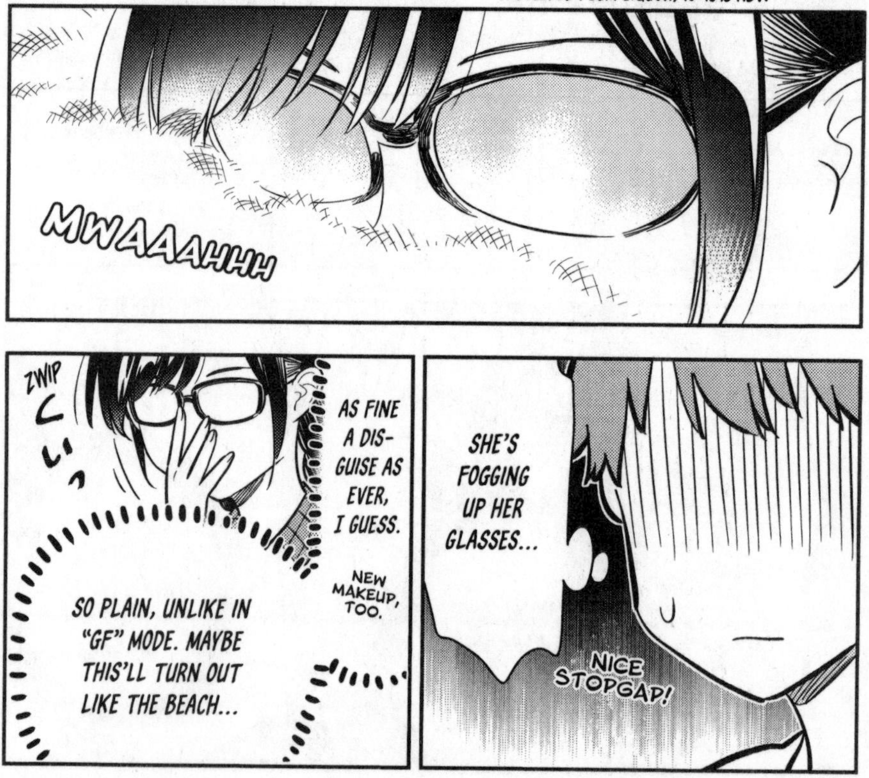
MWAAAHHH
SHE'S FOGGING UP HER GLASSES...
NICE STOPGAP!
ZWIP
くいっ
AS FINE A DIS-GUISE AS EVER, I GUESS.
NEW MAKEUP, TOO.
SO PLAIN, UNLIKE IN "GF" MODE. MAYBE THIS'LL TURN OUT LIKE THE BEACH...

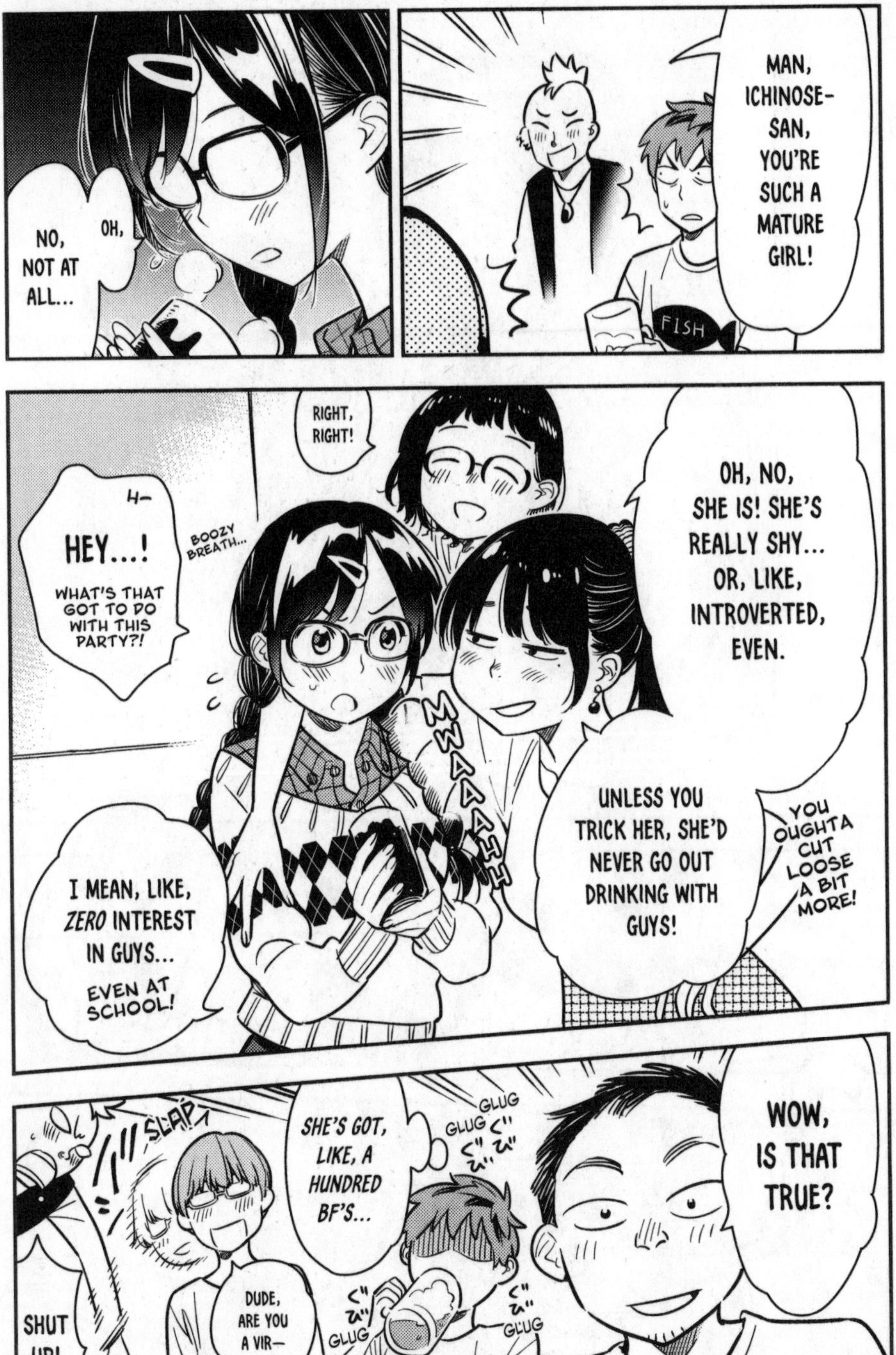
MAN, ICHINOSE-SAN, YOU'RE SUCH A MATURE GIRL!
FISH
OH,
NO, NOT AT ALL...
OH, NO, SHE IS! SHE'S REALLY SHY... OR, LIKE, INTROVERTED, EVEN.
RIGHT, RIGHT!
H— HEY...! WHAT'S THAT GOT TO DO WITH THIS PARTY?!
BOOZY BREATH...
MWAAAAHH
YOU OUGHTA CUT LOOSE A BIT MORE!
UNLESS YOU TRICK HER, SHE'D NEVER GO OUT DRINKING WITH GUYS!
I MEAN, LIKE, *ZERO* INTEREST IN GUYS... EVEN AT SCHOOL!
WOW, IS THAT TRUE?
GLUG GLUG
SHE'S GOT, LIKE, A HUNDRED BF'S...
GLUG GLUG
DUDE, ARE YOU A VIR—
SLAP
SHUT UP!

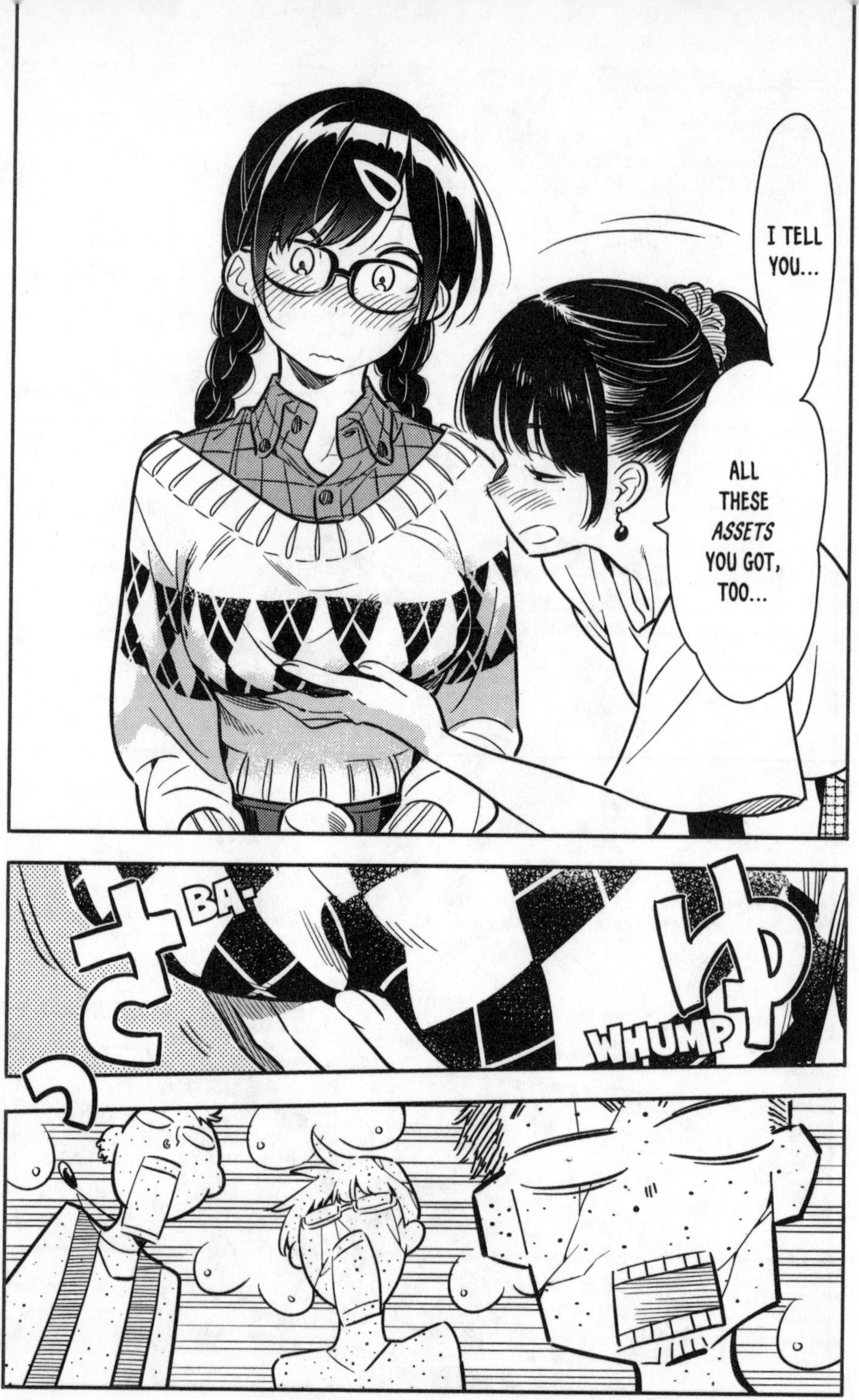
I TELL YOU...
ALL THESE *ASSETS* YOU GOT, TOO...
ゆ
BA-
さ
WHUMP
っ

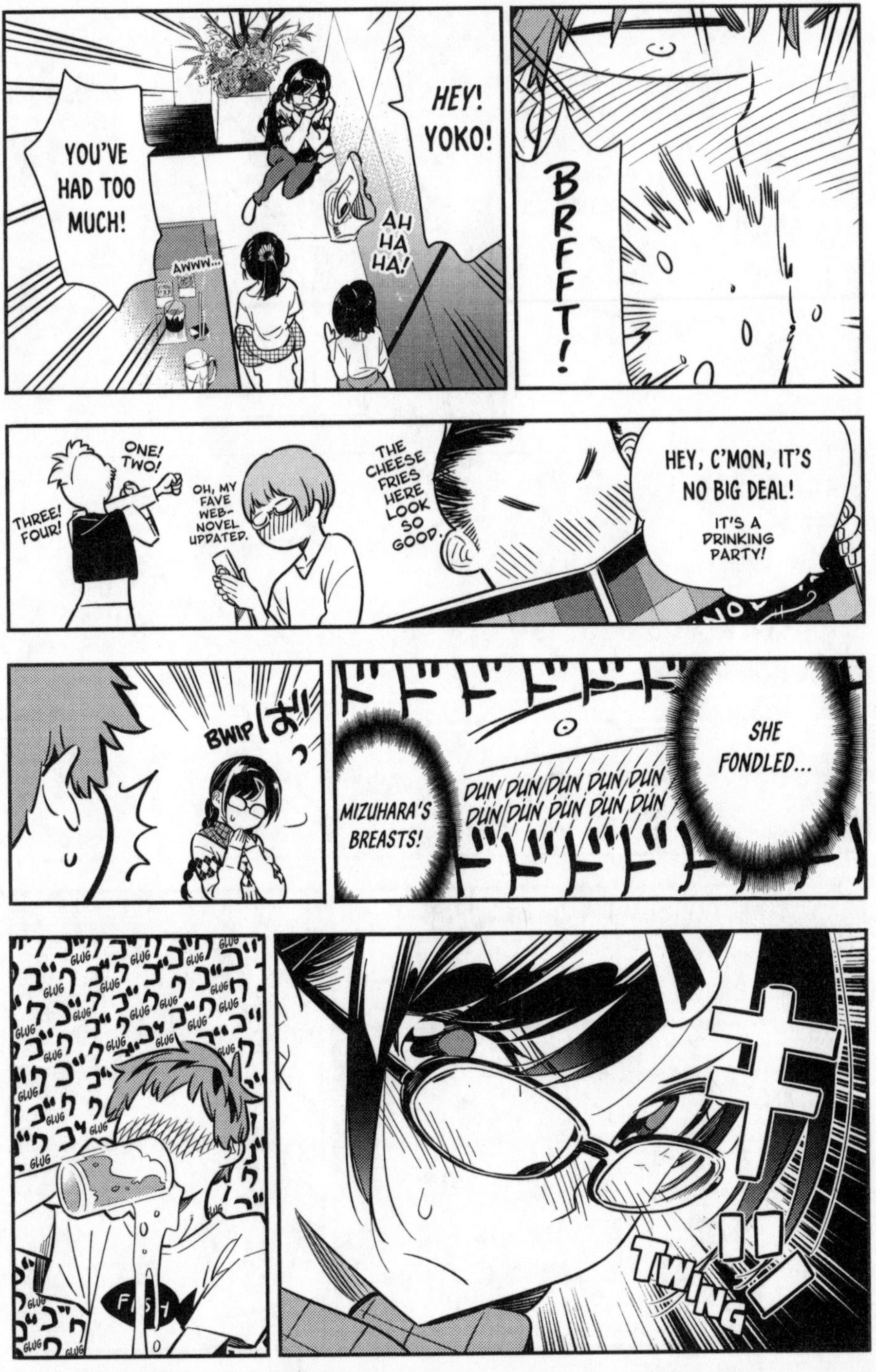
BRFFT!
HEY! YOKO!
AH HA HA!
AWWW...
YOU'VE HAD TOO MUCH!
HEY, C'MON, IT'S NO BIG DEAL!
IT'S A DRINKING PARTY!
THE CHEESE FRIES HERE LOOK SO GOOD.
OH, MY FAVE WEB-NOVEL UPDATED.
ONE! TWO!
THREE! FOUR!
SHE FONDLED...
DUN DUN DUN DUN DUN DUN DUN DUN DUN DUN
MIZUHARA'S BREASTS!
BWIP
TWING
GLUG GLUG GLUG
FISH

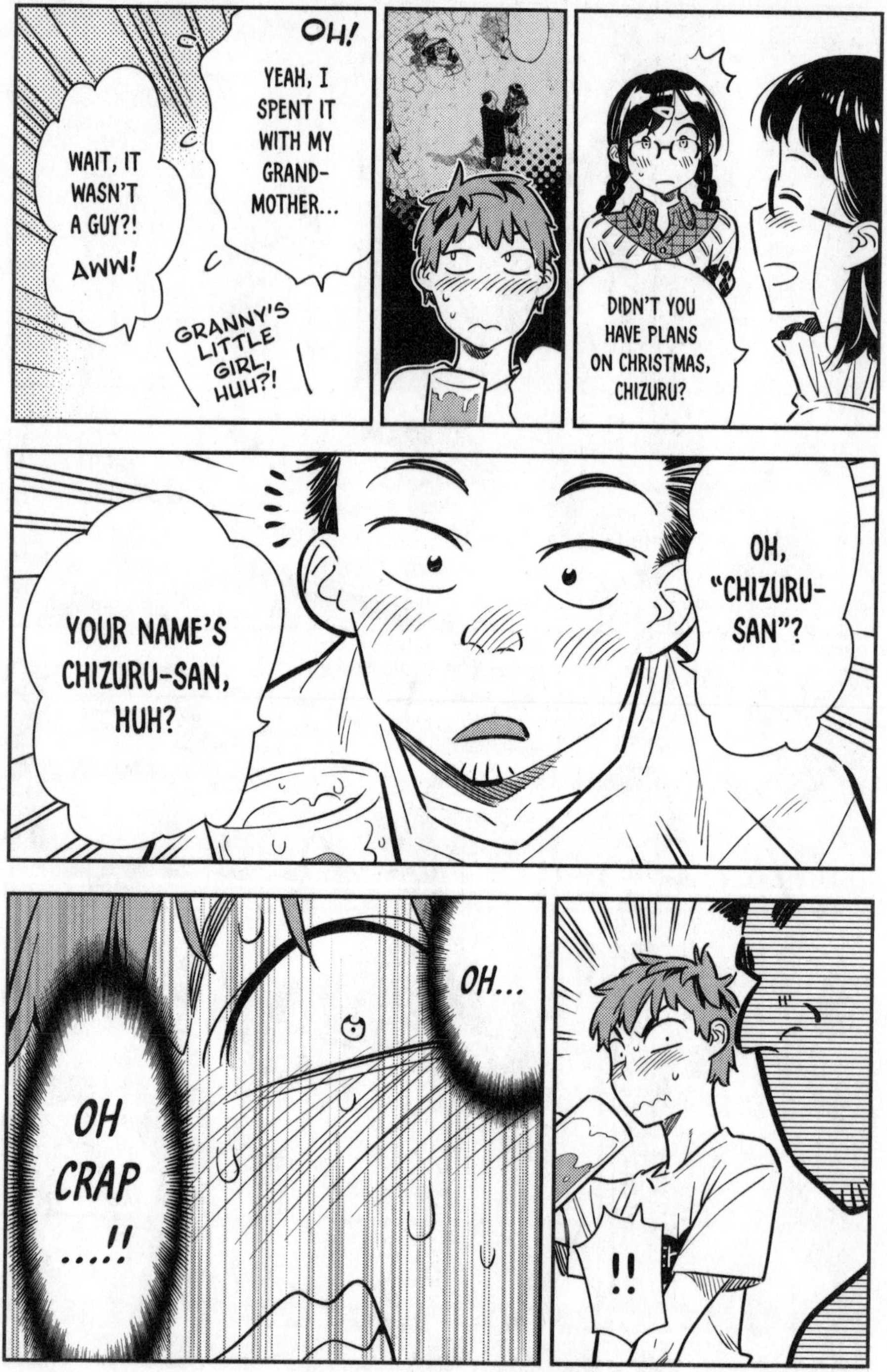
DIDN'T YOU HAVE PLANS ON CHRISTMAS, CHIZURU?
OH!
YEAH, I SPENT IT WITH MY GRAND-MOTHER...
WAIT, IT WASN'T A GUY?! AWW!
GRANNY'S LITTLE GIRL, HUH?!
OH, "CHIZURU-SAN"?
YOUR NAME'S CHIZURU-SAN, HUH?
!!
OH...
OH CRAP ...!!

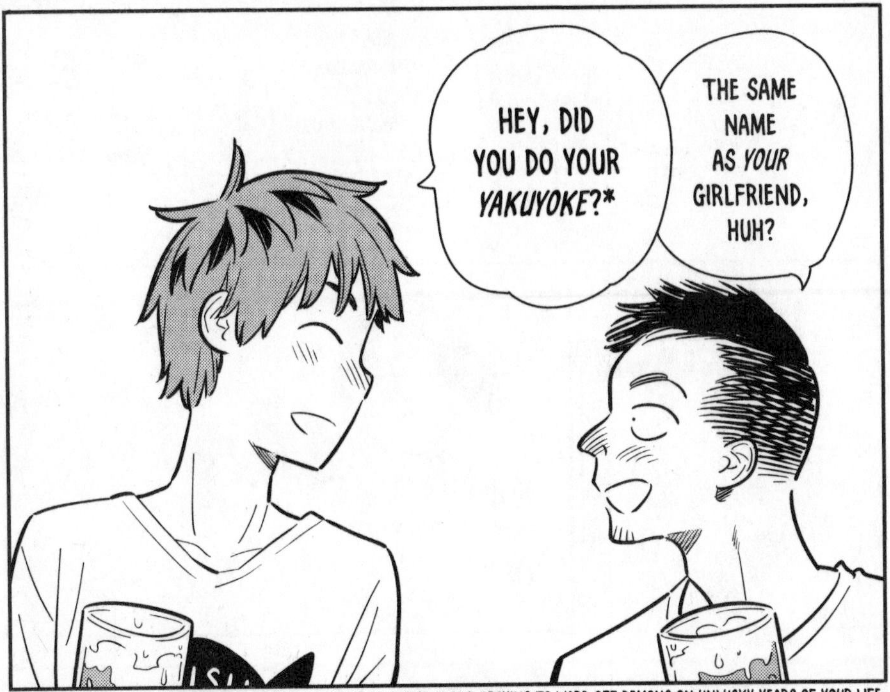
THE SAME NAME AS *YOUR* GIRLFRIEND, HUH?
HEY, DID YOU DO YOUR *YAKUYOKE*?*

* IN JAPANESE TRADITION, GOING TO A SHRINE AND PRAYING TO WARD OFF DEMONS ON UNLUCKY YEARS OF YOUR LIFE.

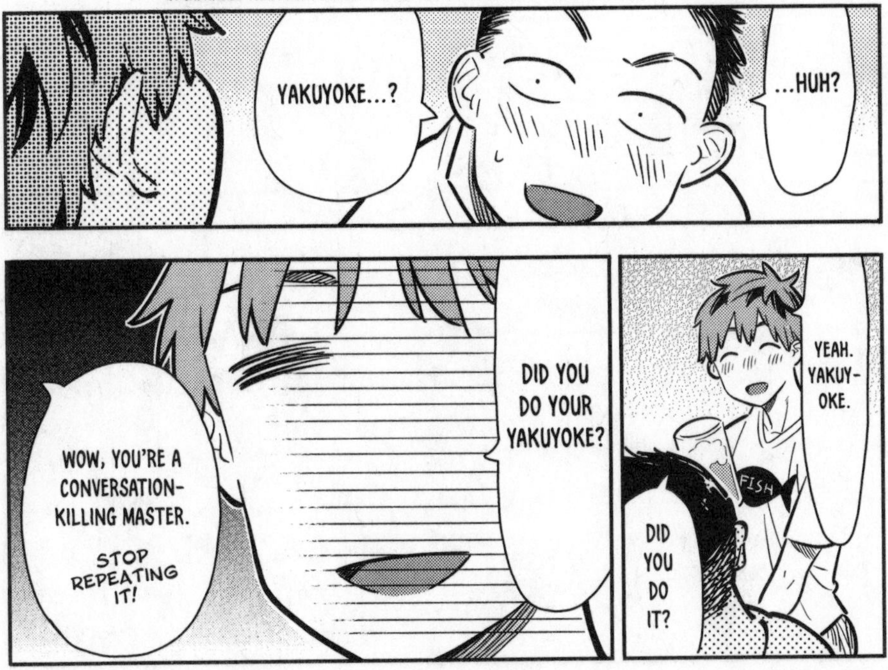
...HUH?
YAKUYOKE...?
YEAH. YAKUY-OKE.
FISH
DID YOU DO IT?
DID YOU DO YOUR YAKUYOKE?
WOW, YOU'RE A CONVERSATION-KILLING MASTER.
STOP REPEATING IT!

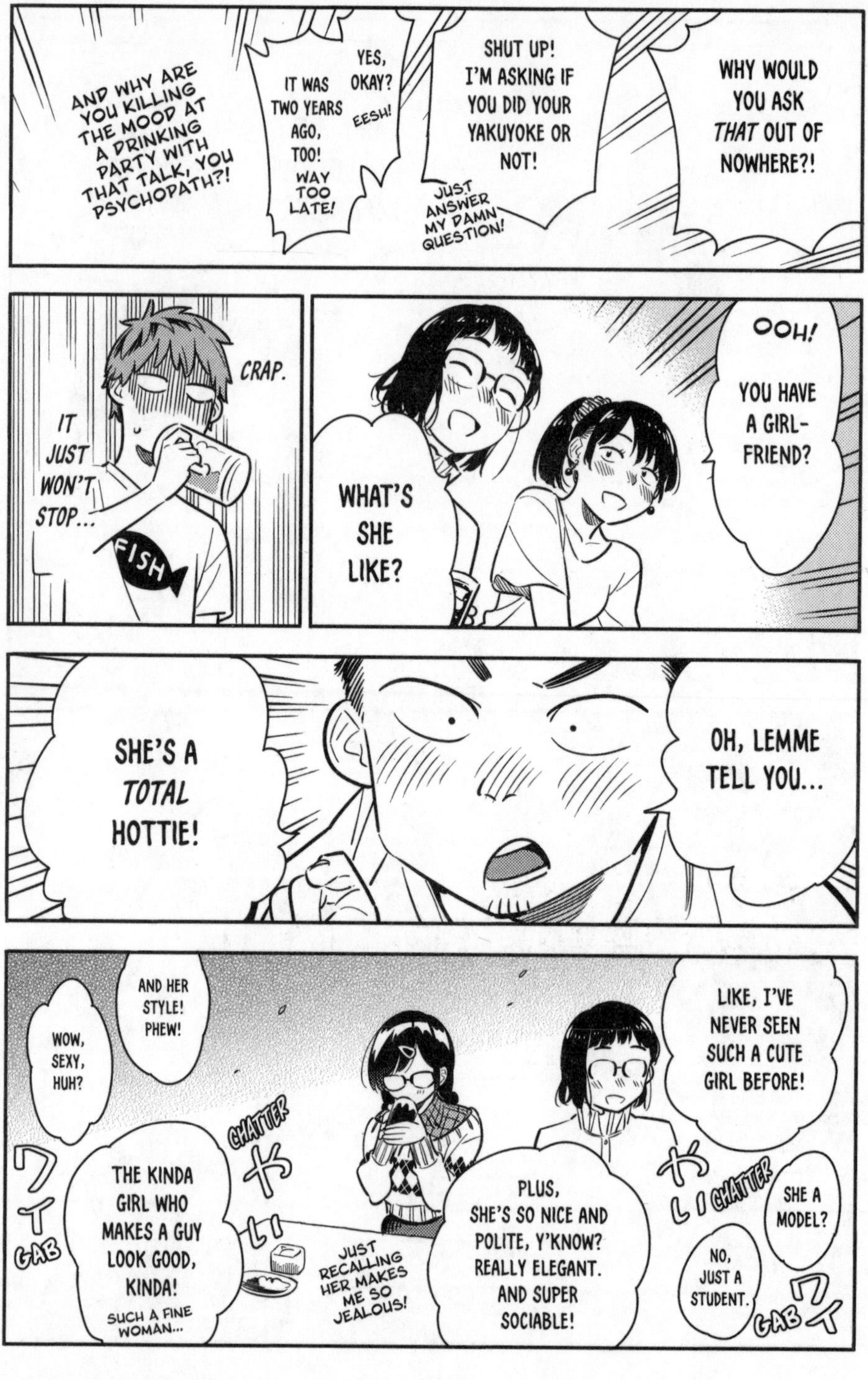
WHY WOULD YOU ASK *THAT* OUT OF NOWHERE?!
SHUT UP! I'M ASKING IF YOU DID YOUR YAKUYOKE OR NOT!
JUST ANSWER MY DAMN QUESTION!
YES, OKAY?
EESH!
IT WAS TWO YEARS AGO, TOO!
WAY TOO LATE!
AND WHY ARE YOU KILLING THE MOOD AT A DRINKING PARTY WITH THAT TALK, YOU PSYCHOPATH?!
OOH!
YOU HAVE A GIRL-FRIEND?
WHAT'S SHE LIKE?
CRAP.
IT JUST WON'T STOP...
FISH
OH, LEMME TELL YOU...
SHE'S A *TOTAL* HOTTIE!
LIKE, I'VE NEVER SEEN SUCH A CUTE GIRL BEFORE!
SHE A MODEL?
NO, JUST A STUDENT.
ワイ
GAB
やい
CHATTER
PLUS, SHE'S SO NICE AND POLITE, Y'KNOW? REALLY ELEGANT. AND SUPER SOCIABLE!
JUST RECALLING HER MAKES ME SO JEALOUS!
やい
CHATTER
THE KINDA GIRL WHO MAKES A GUY LOOK GOOD, KINDA!
SUCH A FINE WOMAN...
AND HER STYLE! PHEW!
WOW, SEXY, HUH?
ワイ
GAB

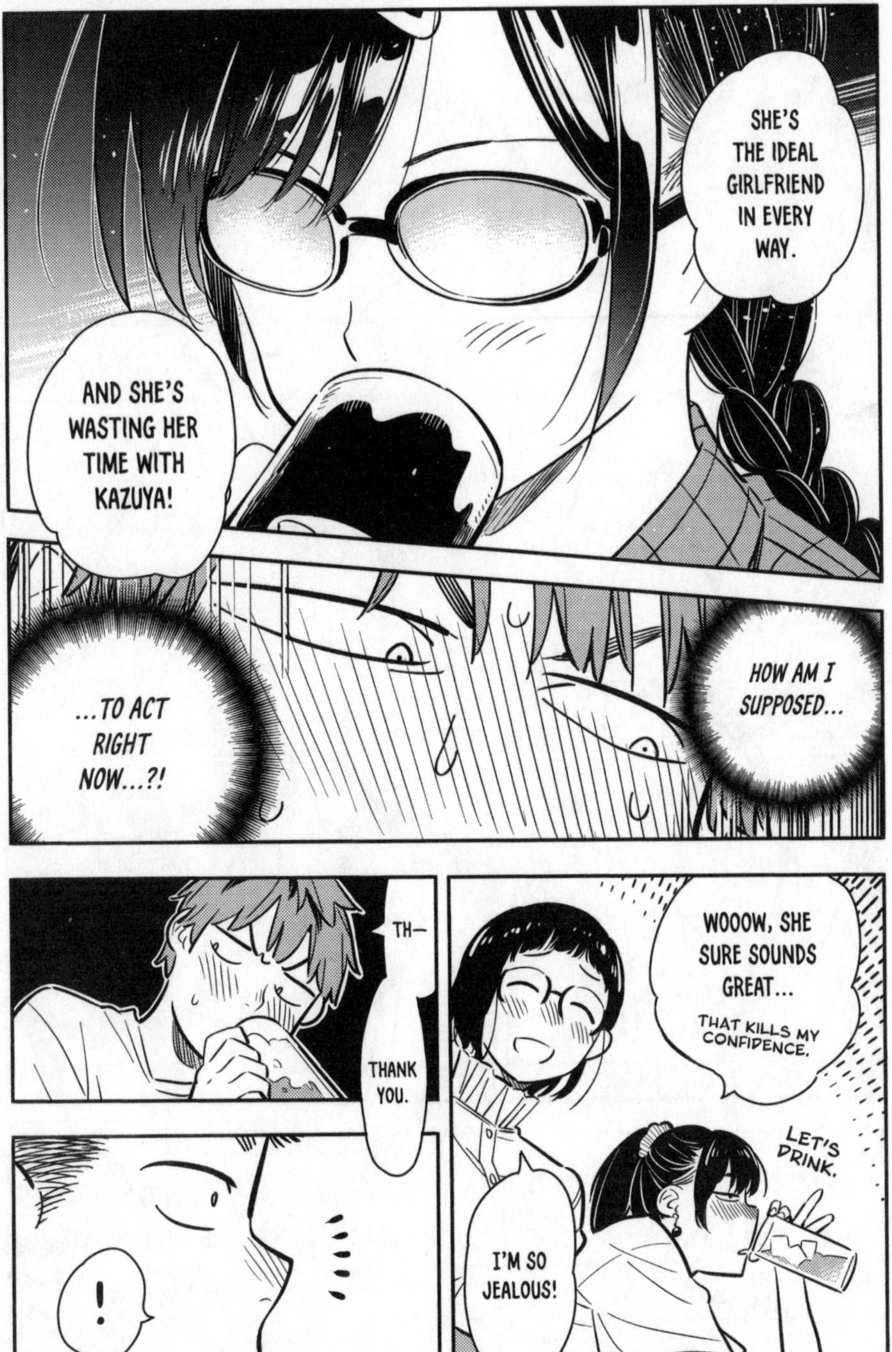
SHE'S THE IDEAL GIRLFRIEND IN EVERY WAY.
AND SHE'S WASTING HER TIME WITH KAZUYA!
HOW AM I SUPPOSED...
...TO ACT RIGHT NOW...?!
WOOOW, SHE SURE SOUNDS GREAT...
THAT KILLS MY CONFIDENCE.
LET'S DRINK.
I'M SO JEALOUS!
TH—
THANK YOU.
!

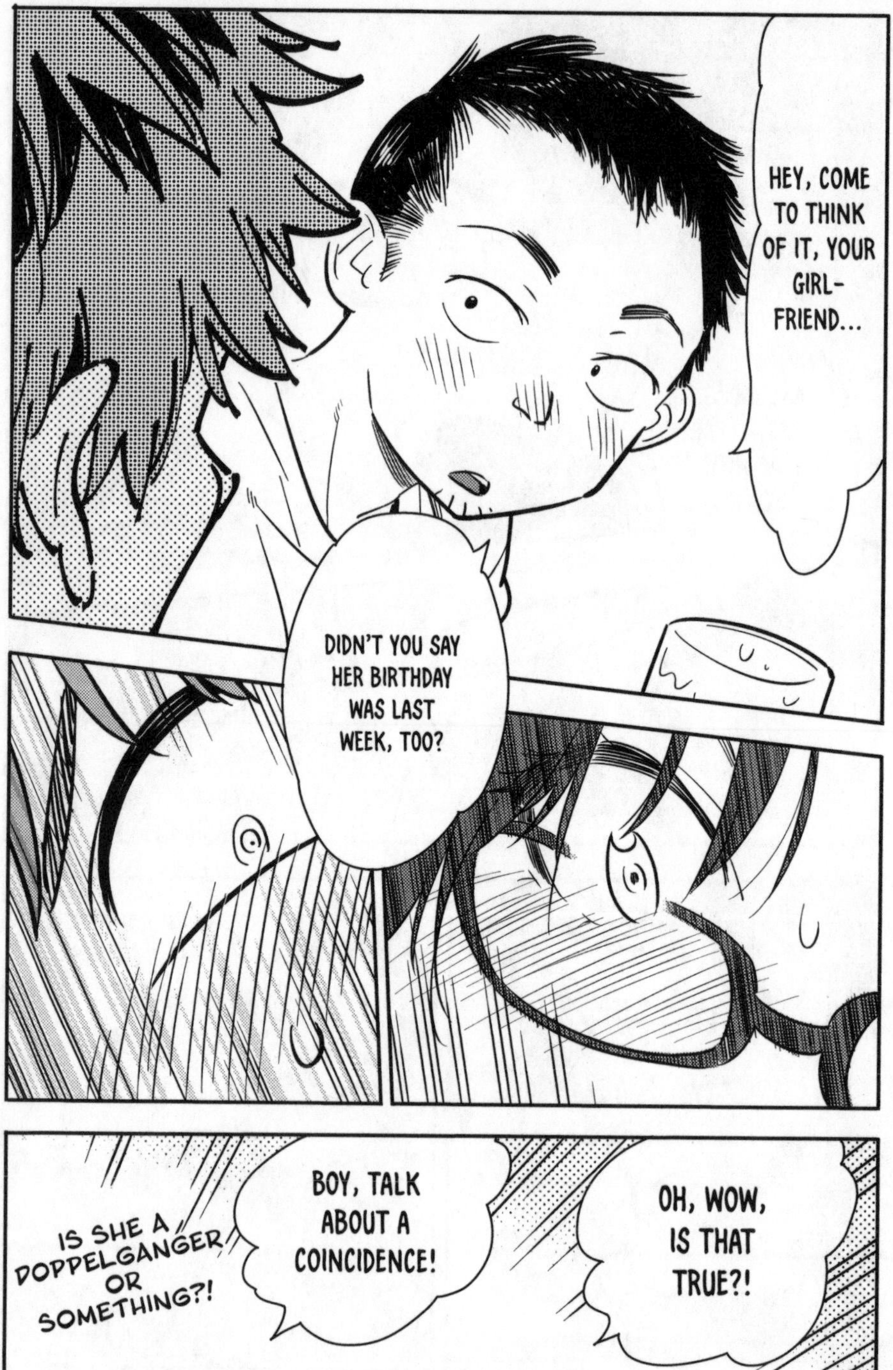
HEY, COME TO THINK OF IT, YOUR GIRL-FRIEND...
DIDN'T YOU SAY HER BIRTHDAY WAS LAST WEEK, TOO?
OH, WOW, IS THAT TRUE?!
BOY, TALK ABOUT A COINCIDENCE!
IS SHE A DOPPELGANGER OR SOMETHING?!

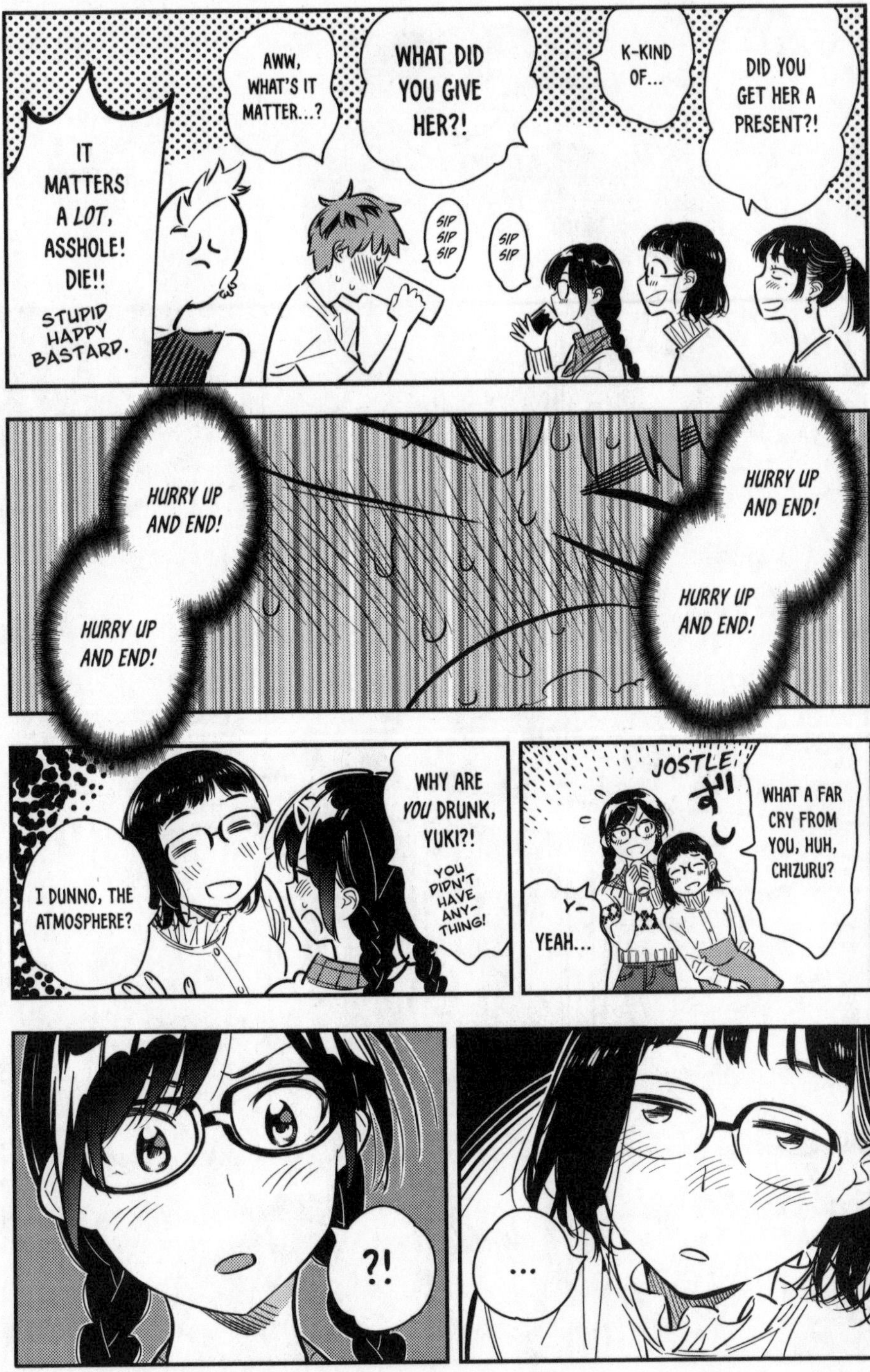
DID YOU GET HER A PRESENT?!
K-KIND OF...
WHAT DID YOU GIVE HER?!
AWW, WHAT'S IT MATTER...?
SIP SIP
SIP SIP SIP
IT MATTERS A LOT, ASSHOLE! DIE!!
STUPID HAPPY BASTARD.
HURRY UP AND END!
HURRY UP AND END!
HURRY UP AND END!
HURRY UP AND END!
WHAT A FAR CRY FROM YOU, HUH, CHIZURU?
JOSTLE
ずし
Y-
YEAH...
WHY ARE YOU DRUNK, YUKI?!
YOU DIDN'T HAVE ANYTHING!
I DUNNO, THE ATMOSPHERE?
...
?!

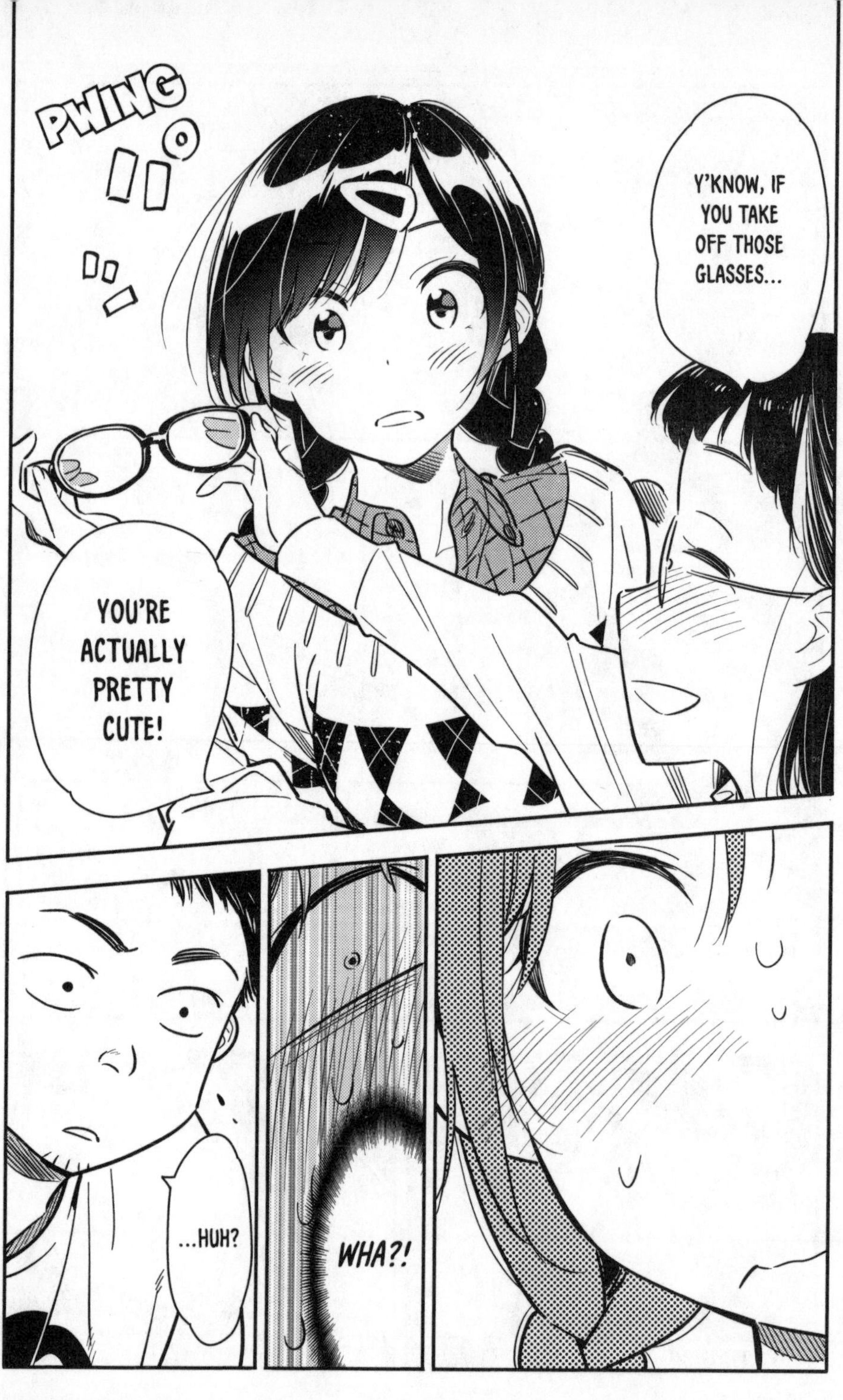
PWING
Y'KNOW, IF YOU TAKE OFF THOSE GLASSES...
YOU'RE ACTUALLY PRETTY CUTE!
WHA?!
...HUH?

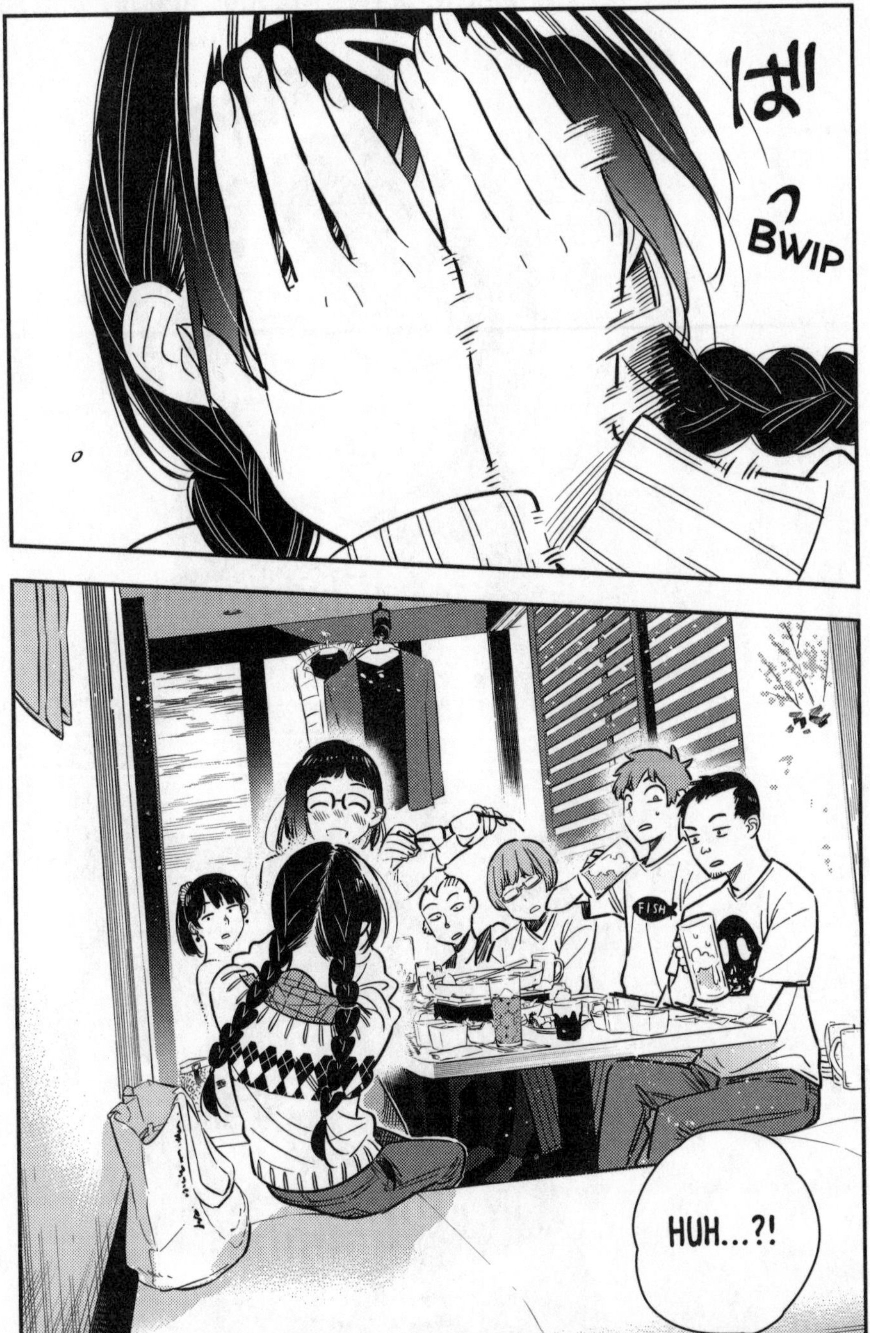

ぱっ
BWIP
HUH...?!
FISH

RATING 72 ALCOHOL AND MY GIRLFRIEND 3

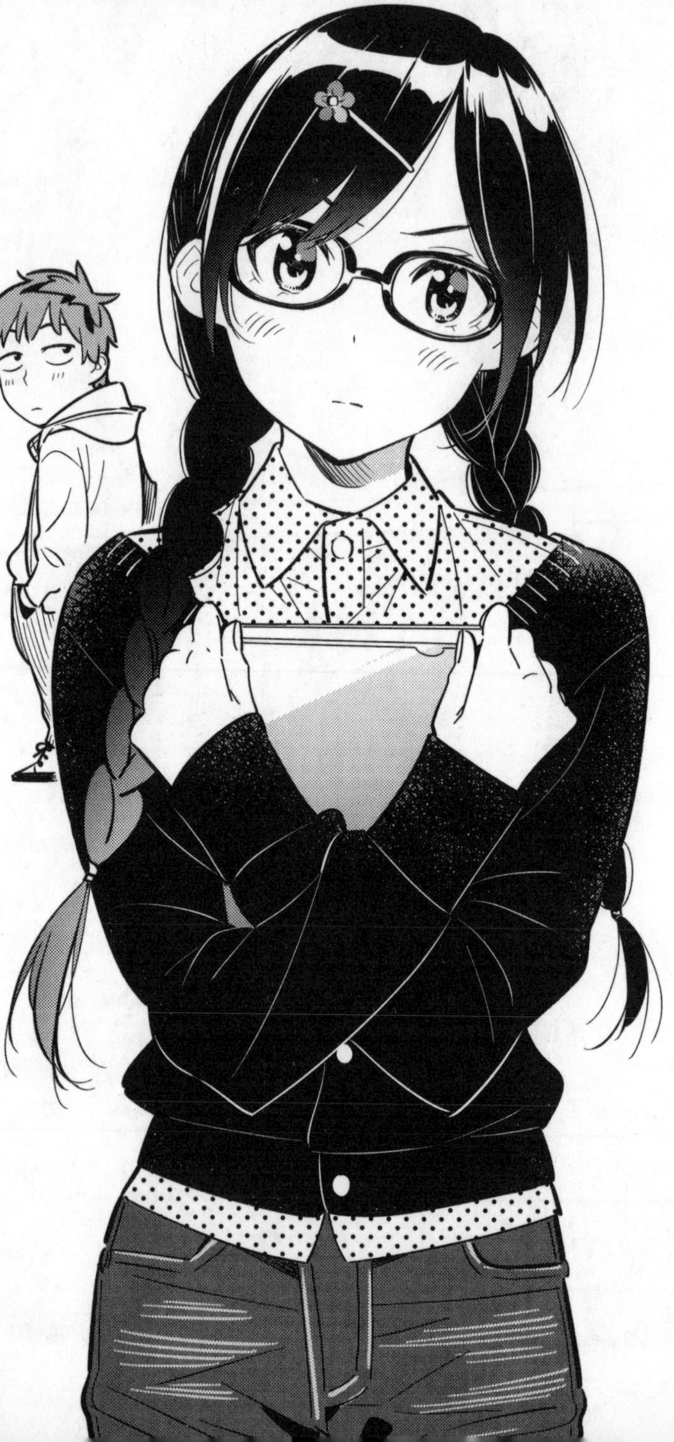

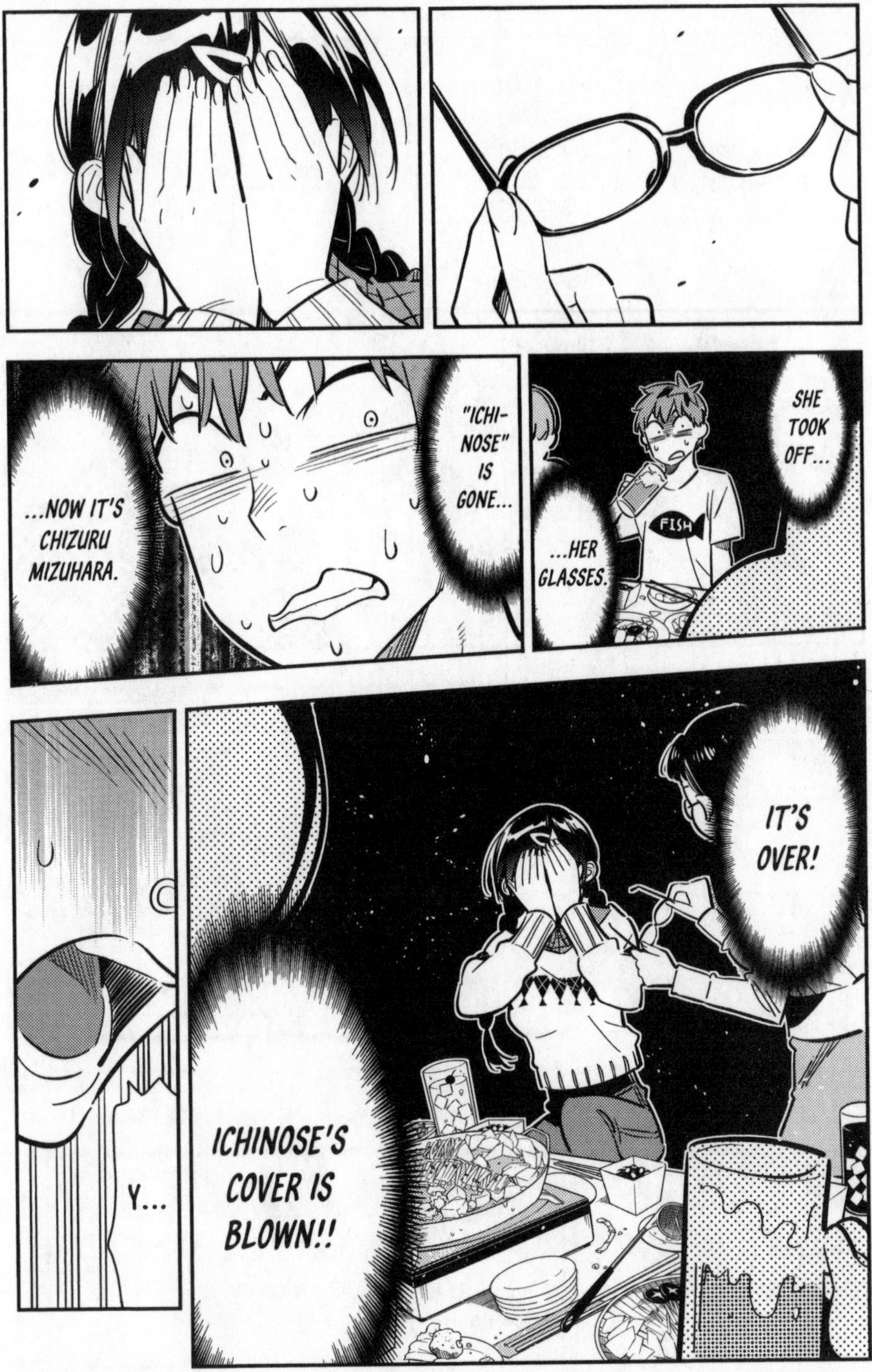
SHE TOOK OFF...
...HER GLASSES.
"ICHI-NOSE" IS GONE...
...NOW IT'S CHIZURU MIZUHARA.
IT'S OVER!
ICHINOSE'S COVER IS BLOWN!!
Y...

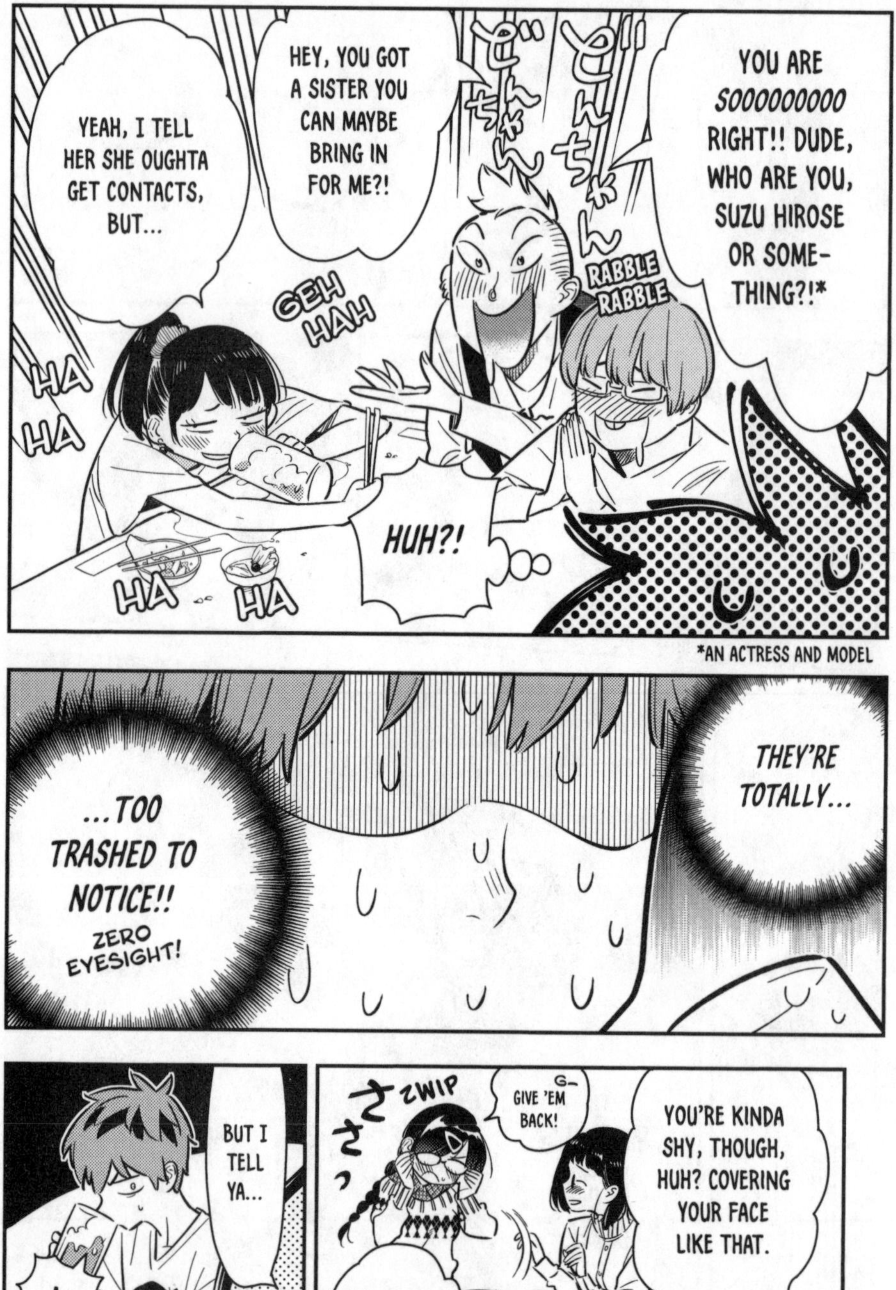
YOU ARE SOOOOOOOOO RIGHT!! DUDE, WHO ARE YOU, SUZU HIROSE OR SOMETHING?!*
どんちゃん
どんちゃん
HEY, YOU GOT A SISTER YOU CAN MAYBE BRING IN FOR ME?!
RABBLE RABBLE
YEAH, I TELL HER SHE OUGHTA GET CONTACTS, BUT...
GEH HAH
HUH?!
HA HA
HA
HA
THEY'RE TOTALLY...
...TOO TRASHED TO NOTICE!!
ZERO EYESIGHT!
YOU'RE KINDA SHY, THOUGH, HUH? COVERING YOUR FACE LIKE THAT.
G- GIVE 'EM BACK!
ZWIP
ささっ
HEY, IT WAS A COMPLIMENT!
BUT I TELL YA...
!
FISH

*AN ACTRESS AND MODEL

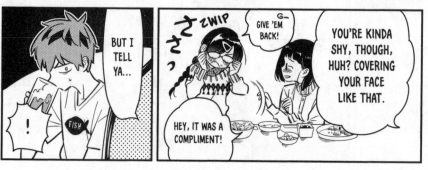

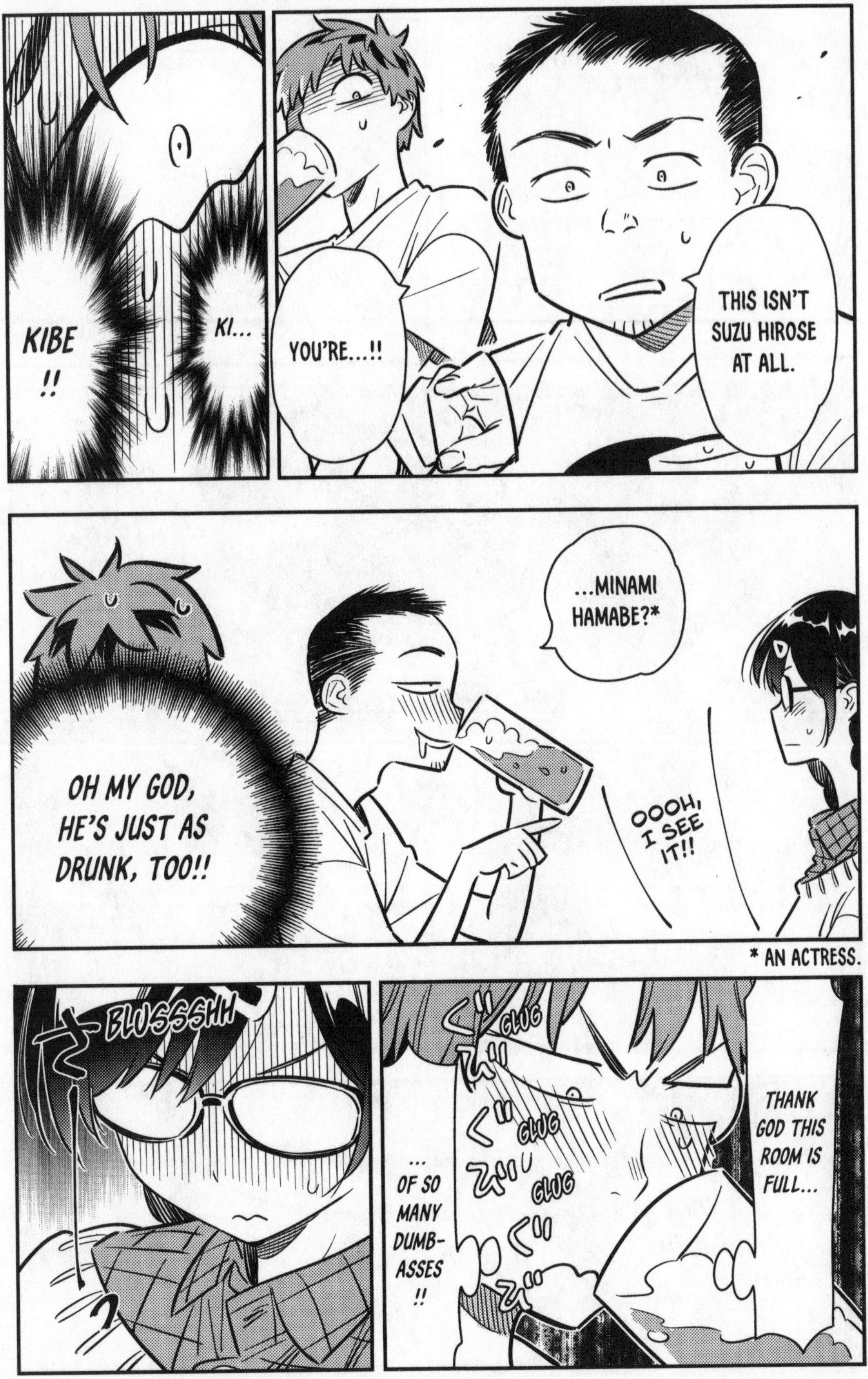
THIS ISN'T SUZU HIROSE AT ALL.
YOU'RE...!!
KI...
KIBE !!
...MINAMI HAMABE?*
OOOH, I SEE IT!!
OH MY GOD, HE'S JUST AS DRUNK, TOO!!
* AN ACTRESS.
THANK GOD THIS ROOM IS FULL...
GLUG
GLUG
GLUG
... OF SO MANY DUMB-ASSES !!
BLUSSSHH

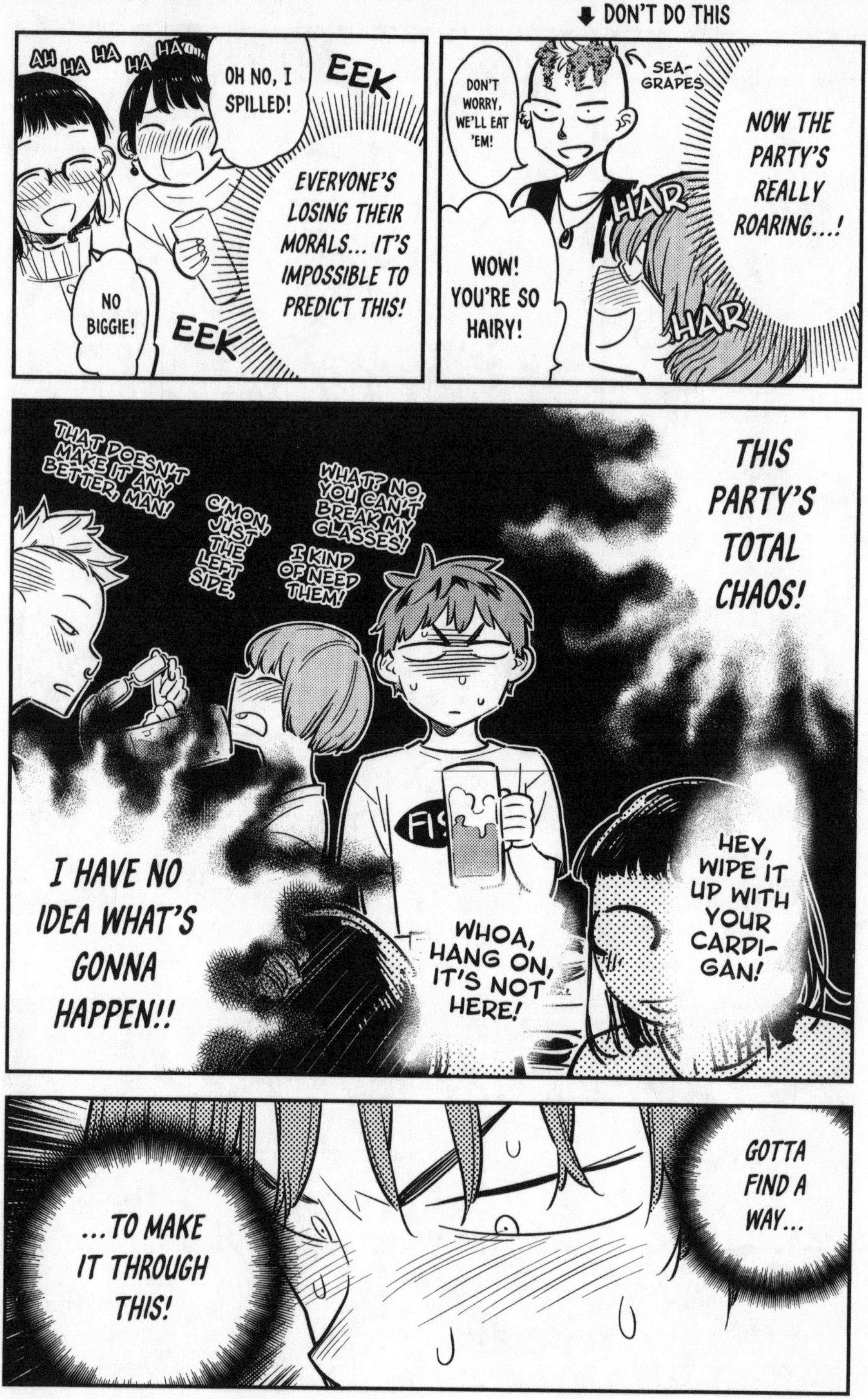
DON'T DO THIS
NOW THE PARTY'S REALLY ROARING...!
SEA-GRAPES
DON'T WORRY, WE'LL EAT 'EM!
HAR
WOW! YOU'RE SO HAIRY!
HAR
EEK
OH NO, I SPILLED!
AH HA HA HA HA
EVERYONE'S LOSING THEIR MORALS... IT'S IMPOSSIBLE TO PREDICT THIS!
EEK
NO BIGGIE!
THIS PARTY'S TOTAL CHAOS!
WHAT? NO, YOU CAN'T BREAK MY GLASSES!
I KIND OF NEED THEM!
C'MON, JUST THE LEFT SIDE.
THAT DOESN'T MAKE IT ANY BETTER, MAN!
HEY, WIPE IT UP WITH YOUR CARDIGAN!
WHOA, HANG ON, IT'S NOT HERE!
I HAVE NO IDEA WHAT'S GONNA HAPPEN!!
GOTTA FIND A WAY...
...TO MAKE IT THROUGH THIS!

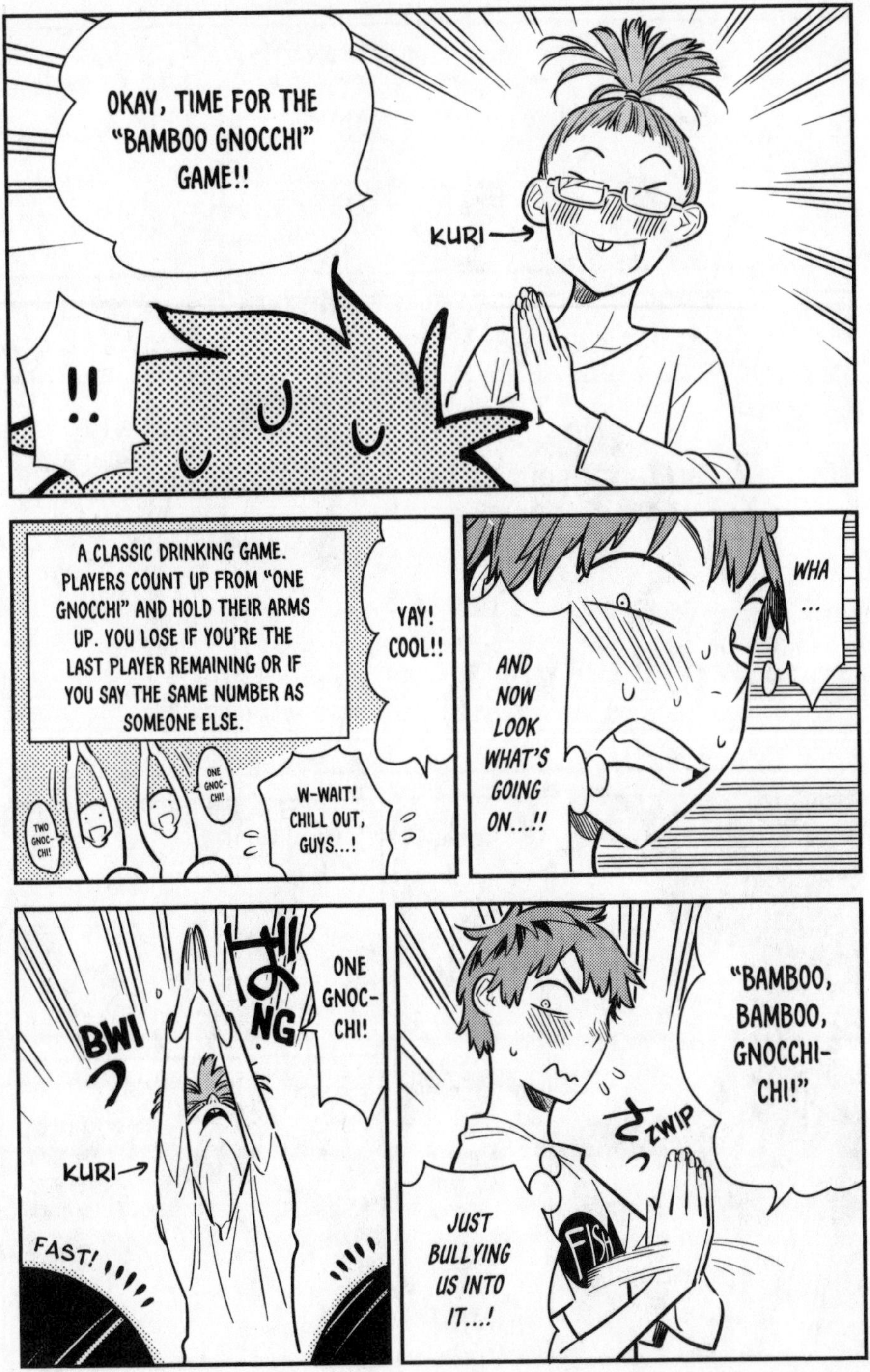
OKAY, TIME FOR THE "BAMBOO GNOCCHI" GAME!!
KURI →
!!
WHA...
AND NOW LOOK WHAT'S GOING ON...!!
YAY! COOL!!
A CLASSIC DRINKING GAME. PLAYERS COUNT UP FROM "ONE GNOCCHI" AND HOLD THEIR ARMS UP. YOU LOSE IF YOU'RE THE LAST PLAYER REMAINING OR IF YOU SAY THE SAME NUMBER AS SOMEONE ELSE.
ONE GNOC-CHI!
W-WAIT! CHILL OUT, GUYS...!
TWO GNOC-CHI!
"BAMBOO, BAMBOO, GNOCCHI-CHI!"
ZWIP
JUST BULLYING US INTO IT...!
FISH
ONE GNOC-CHI!
BWI
NG
KURI →
FAST!

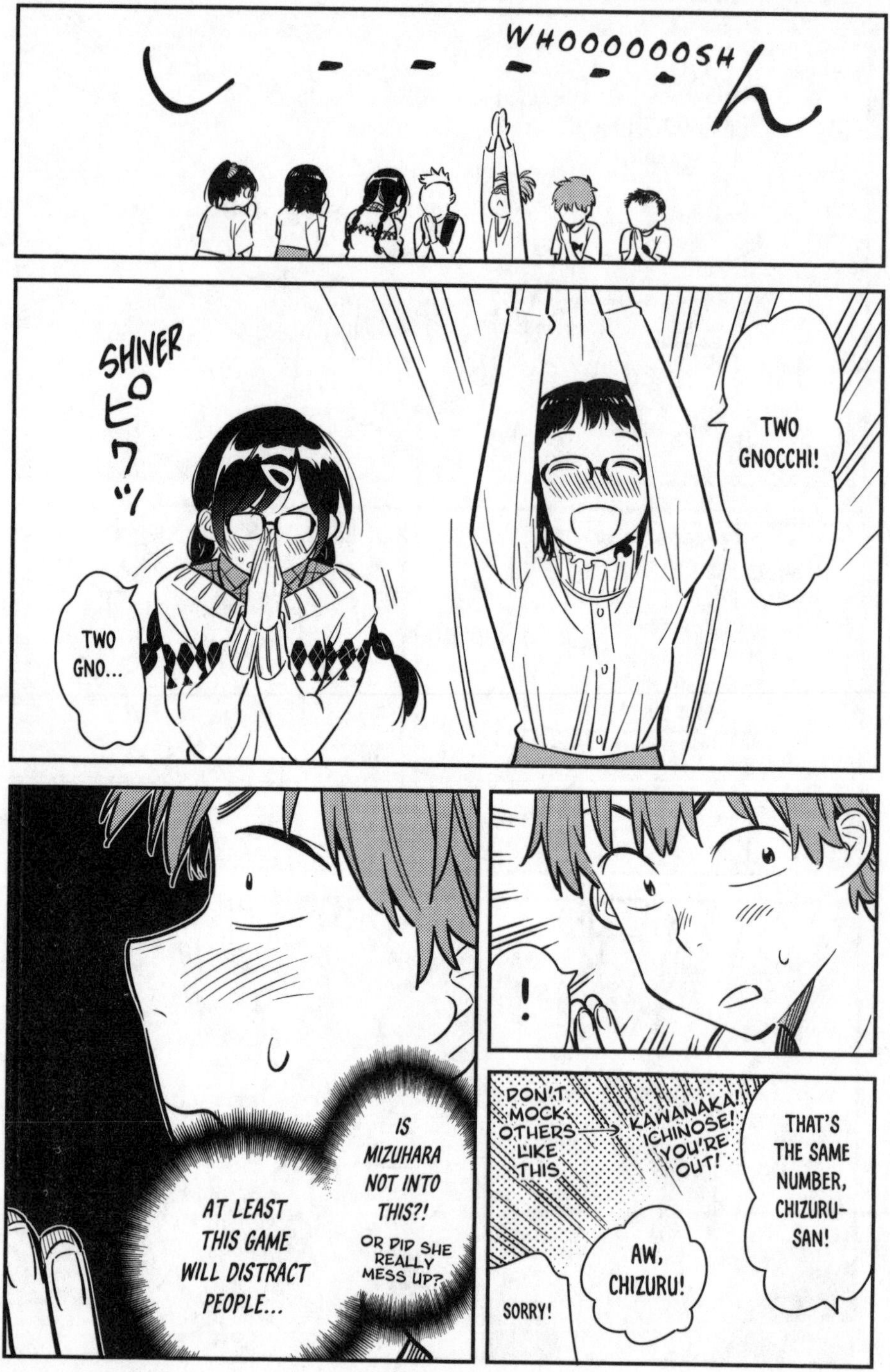
WHOOOOOOSH
TWO GNOCCHI!
SHIVER
ピクッ
TWO GNO...
!
THAT'S THE SAME NUMBER, CHIZURU-SAN!
KAWANAKA! ICHINOSE! YOU'RE OUT!
DON'T MOCK OTHERS LIKE THIS
AW, CHIZURU!
SORRY!
IS MIZUHARA NOT INTO THIS?!
OR DID SHE REALLY MESS UP?
AT LEAST THIS GAME WILL DISTRACT PEOPLE...

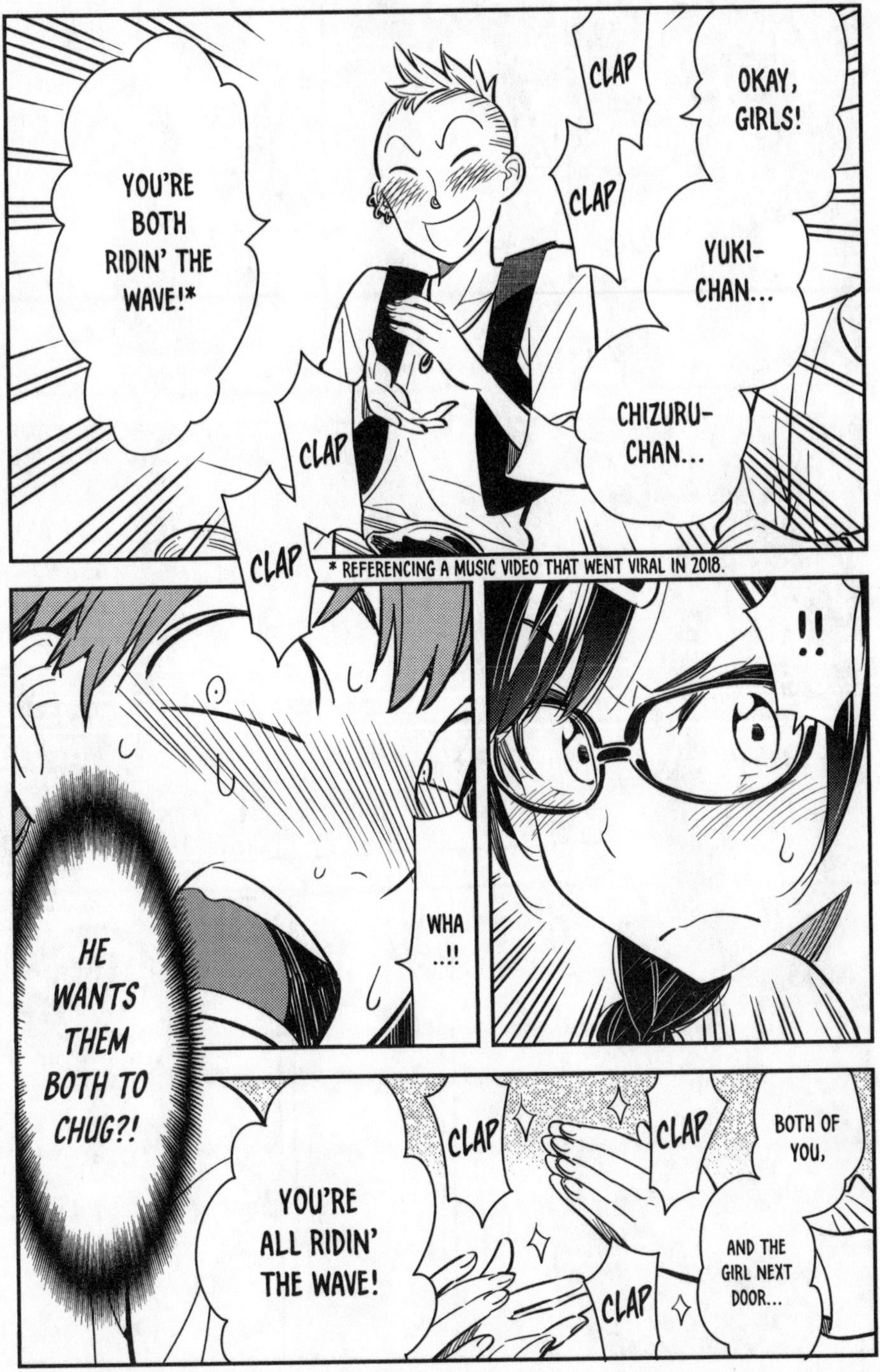
OKAY, GIRLS!
CLAP
CLAP
YUKI-CHAN...
CHIZURU-CHAN...
CLAP
CLAP
YOU'RE BOTH RIDIN' THE WAVE!*
* REFERENCING A MUSIC VIDEO THAT WENT VIRAL IN 2018.
!!
WHA...!!
HE WANTS THEM BOTH TO CHUG?!
BOTH OF YOU,
CLAP
AND THE GIRL NEXT DOOR...
CLAP
CLAP
YOU'RE ALL RIDIN' THE WAVE!

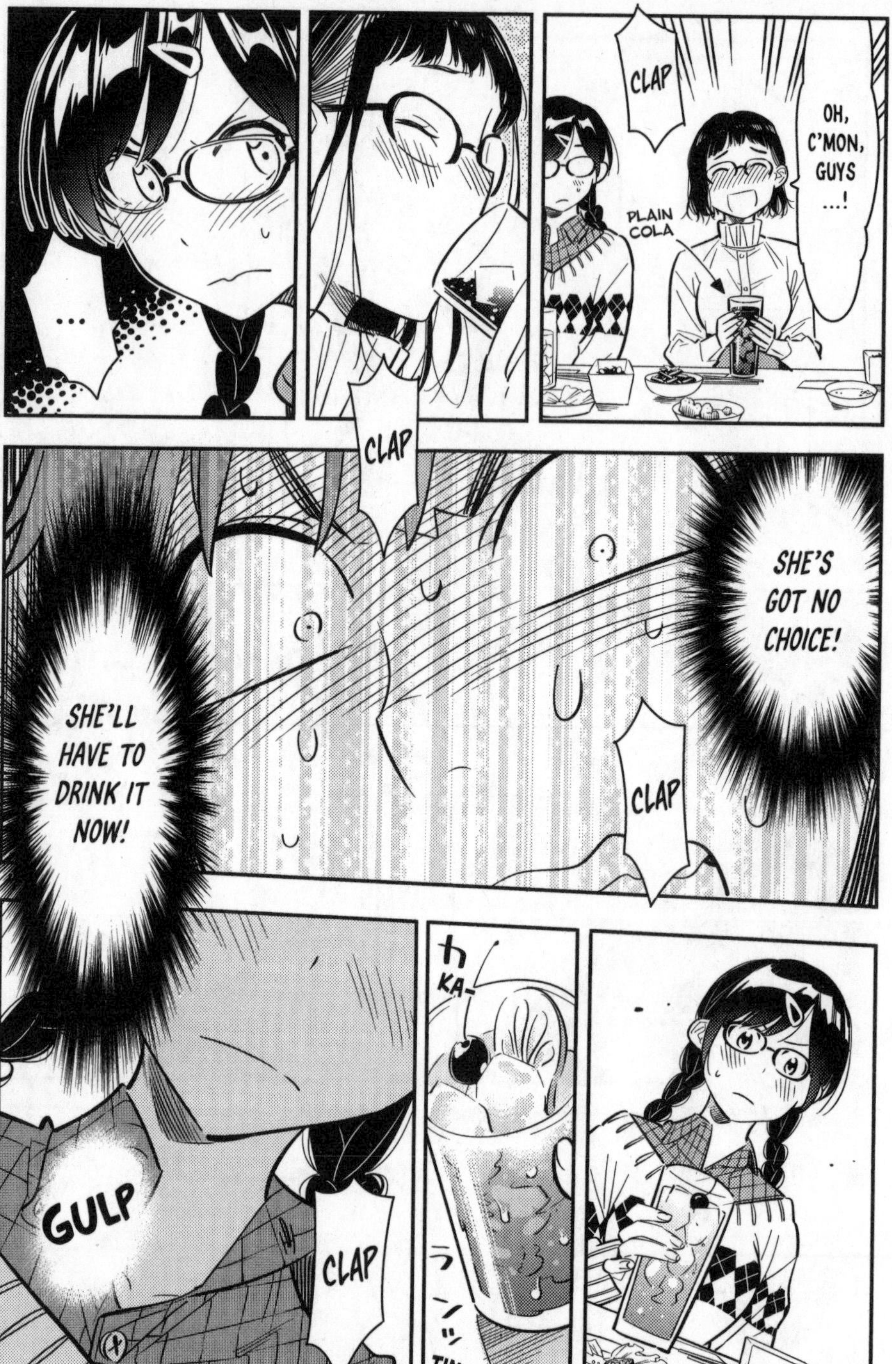
CLAP
OH, C'MON, GUYS ...!
PLAIN COLA
CLAP
...
SHE'S GOT NO CHOICE!
CLAP
SHE'LL HAVE TO DRINK IT NOW!
カ
KA-
ラーンッ
TINK
GULP
CLAP

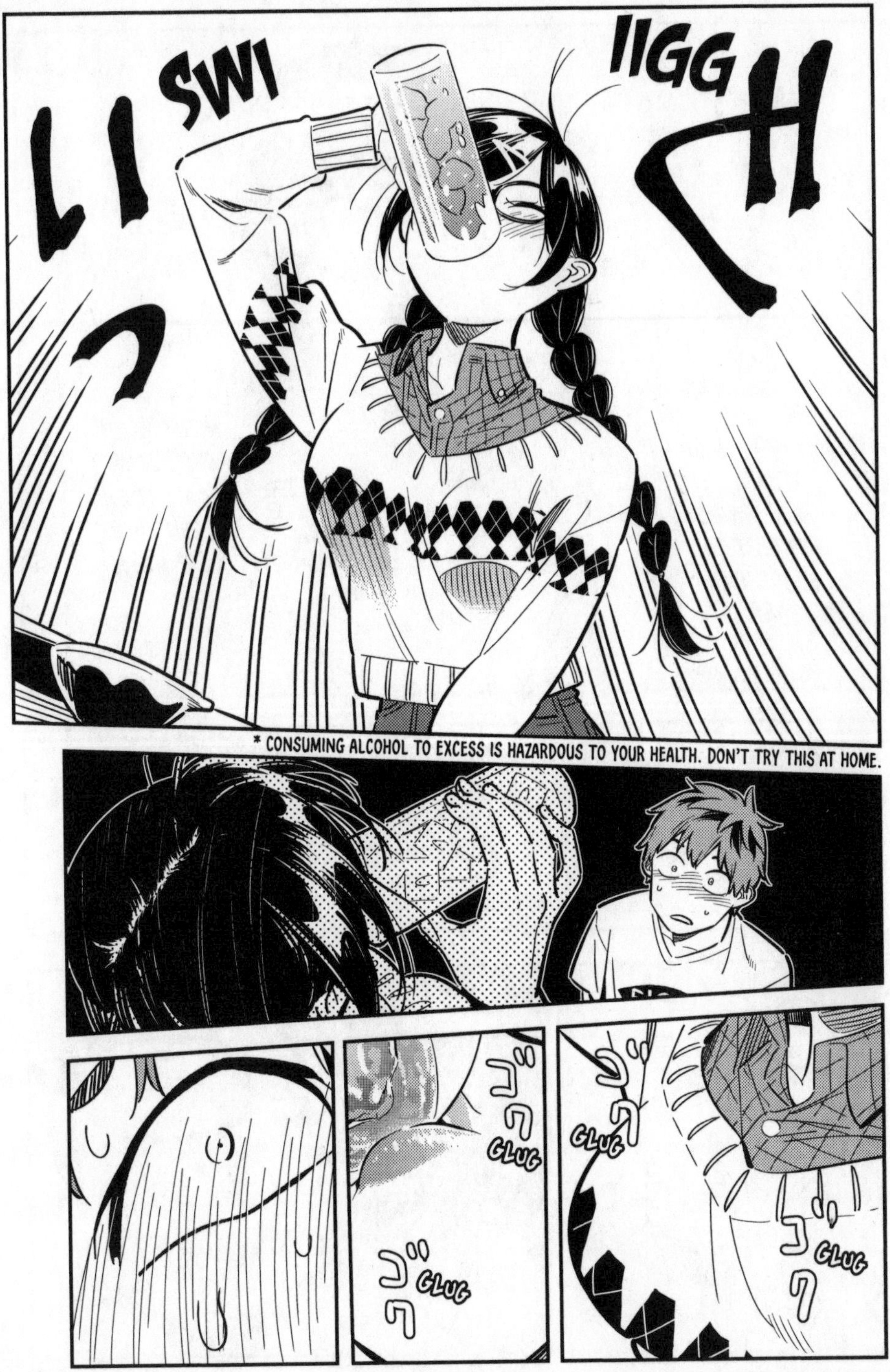
SWI
IIGG H
ゴク
GLUG
ゴク
GLUG
ゴク
GLUG
ゴク
GLUG
* CONSUMING ALCOHOL TO EXCESS IS HAZARDOUS TO YOUR HEALTH. DON'T TRY THIS AT HOME.

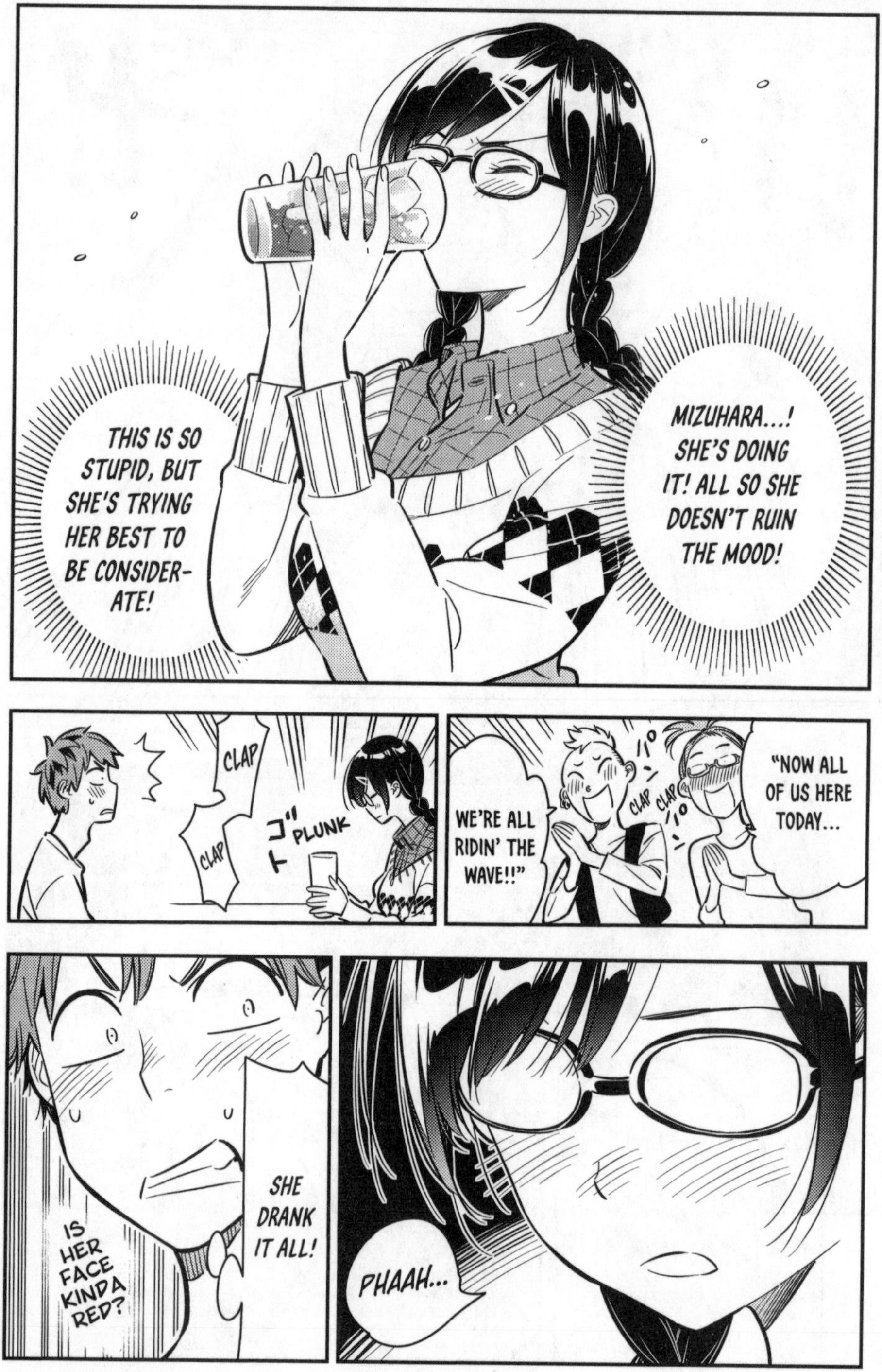
MIZUHARA...! SHE'S DOING IT! ALL SO SHE DOESN'T RUIN THE MOOD!
THIS IS SO STUPID, BUT SHE'S TRYING HER BEST TO BE CONSIDER-ATE!
"NOW ALL OF US HERE TODAY...
CLAP
CLAP
WE'RE ALL RIDIN' THE WAVE!!"
PLUNK
CLAP
CLAP
PHAAH...
SHE DRANK IT ALL!
IS HER FACE KINDA RED?

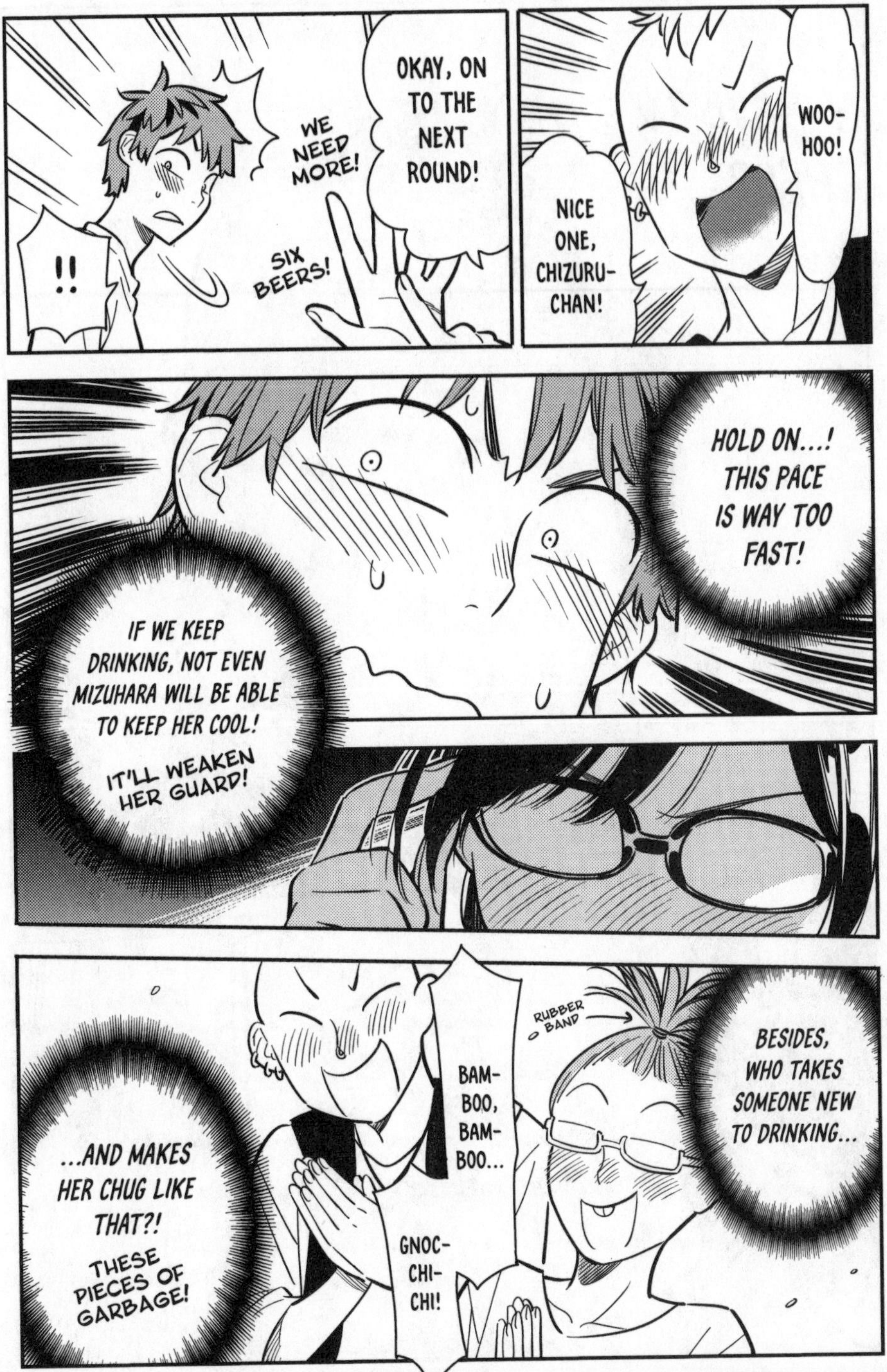
WOO-HOO!
NICE ONE, CHIZURU-CHAN!
OKAY, ON TO THE NEXT ROUND!
WE NEED MORE!
SIX BEERS!
!!
HOLD ON...! THIS PACE IS WAY TOO FAST!
IF WE KEEP DRINKING, NOT EVEN MIZUHARA WILL BE ABLE TO KEEP HER COOL!
IT'LL WEAKEN HER GUARD!
BESIDES, WHO TAKES SOMEONE NEW TO DRINKING...
RUBBER BAND
BAM-BOO, BAM-BOO...
GNOC-CHI-CHI!
...AND MAKES HER CHUG LIKE THAT?!
THESE PIECES OF GARBAGE!

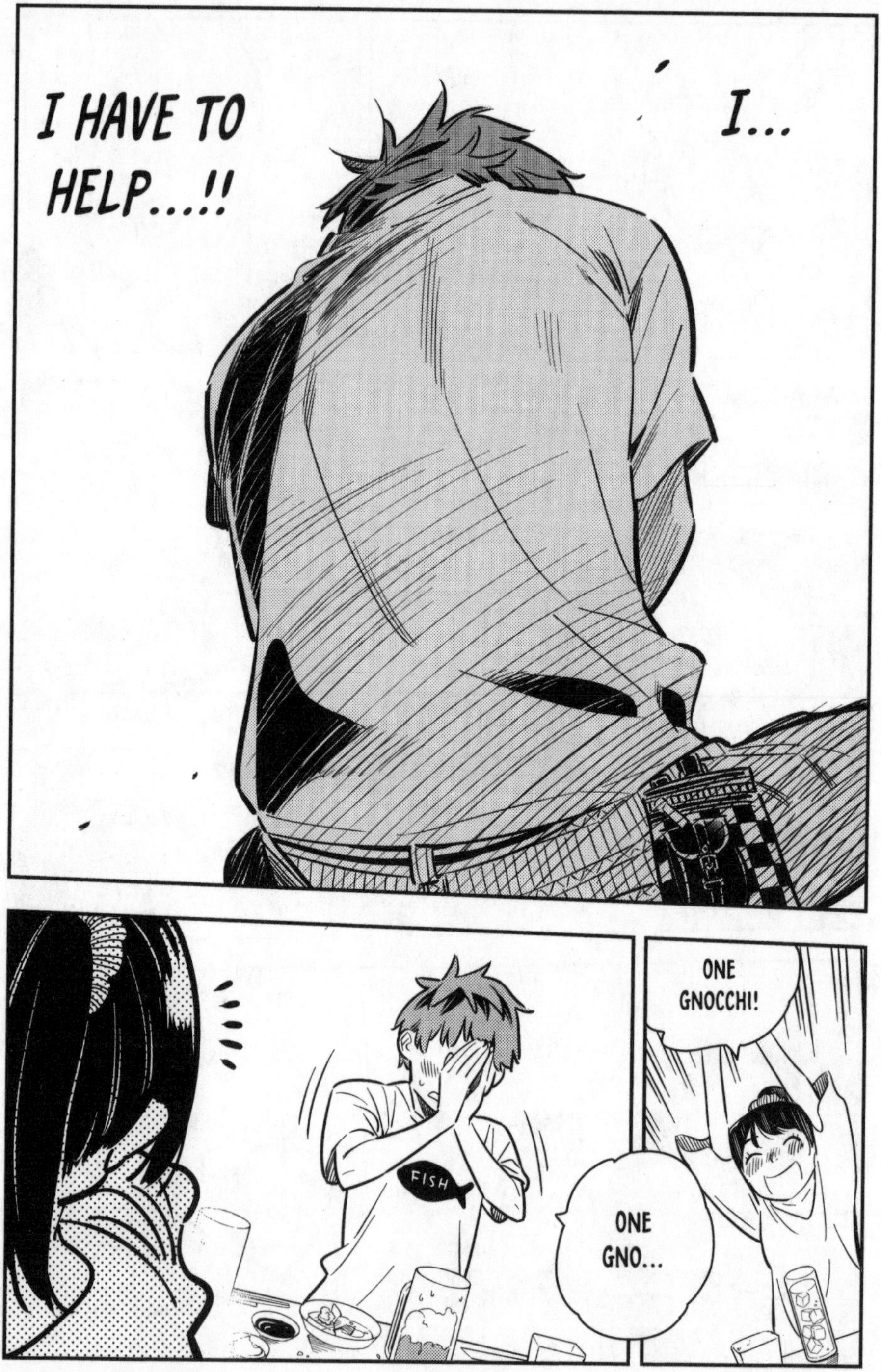
I...
I HAVE TO HELP...!!
ONE GNOCCHI!
ONE GNO...
FISH

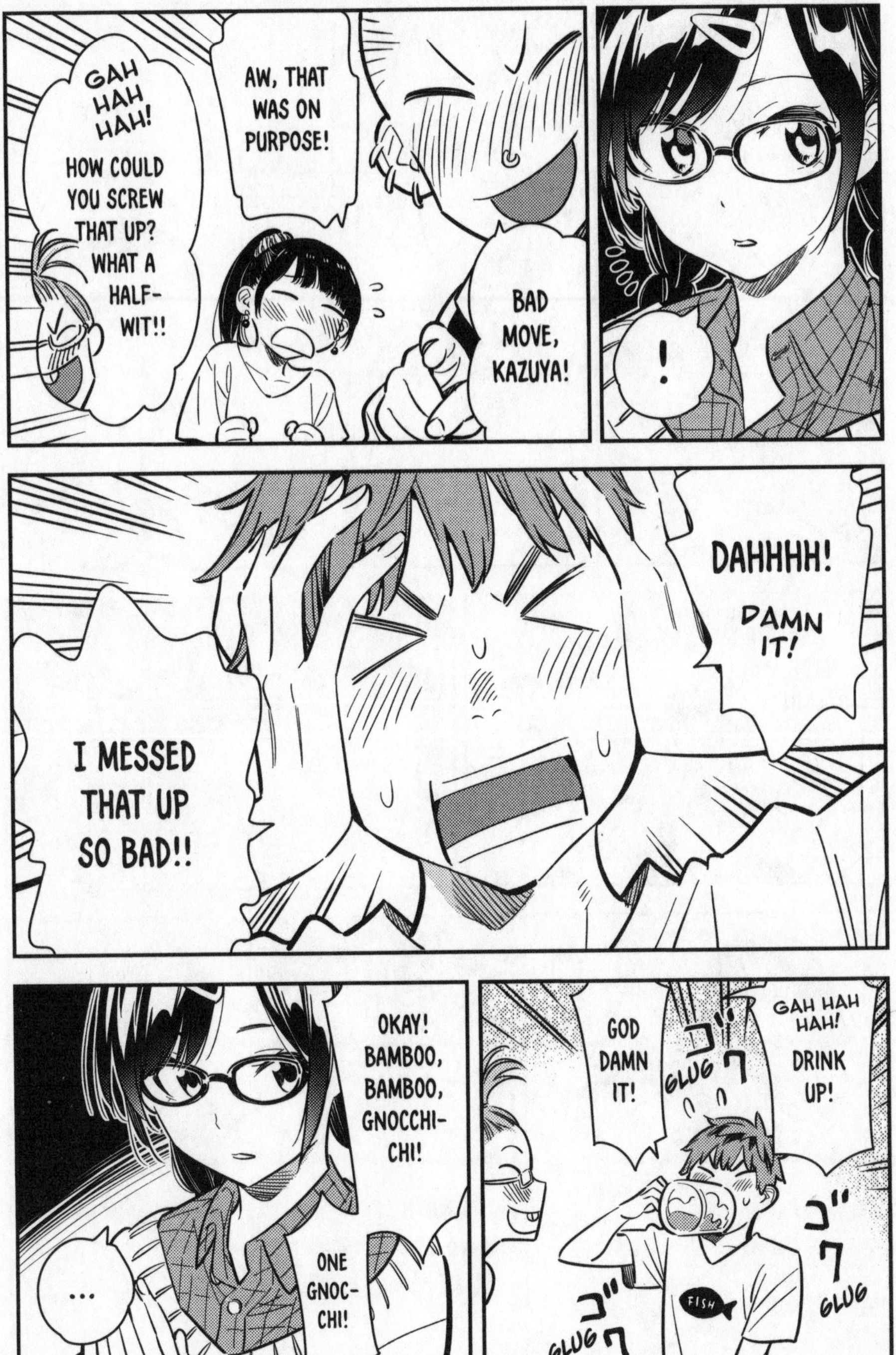
!
BAD MOVE, KAZUYA!
AW, THAT WAS ON PURPOSE!
GAH HAH HAH! HOW COULD YOU SCREW THAT UP? WHAT A HALF-WIT!!
DAHHHH! DAMN IT!
I MESSED THAT UP SO BAD!!
GAH HAH HAH! DRINK UP!
ゴク GLUG
GOD DAMN IT!
ゴク GLUG
ゴク GLUG
OKAY! BAMBOO, BAMBOO, GNOCCHI-CHI!
ONE GNOC-CHI!
...

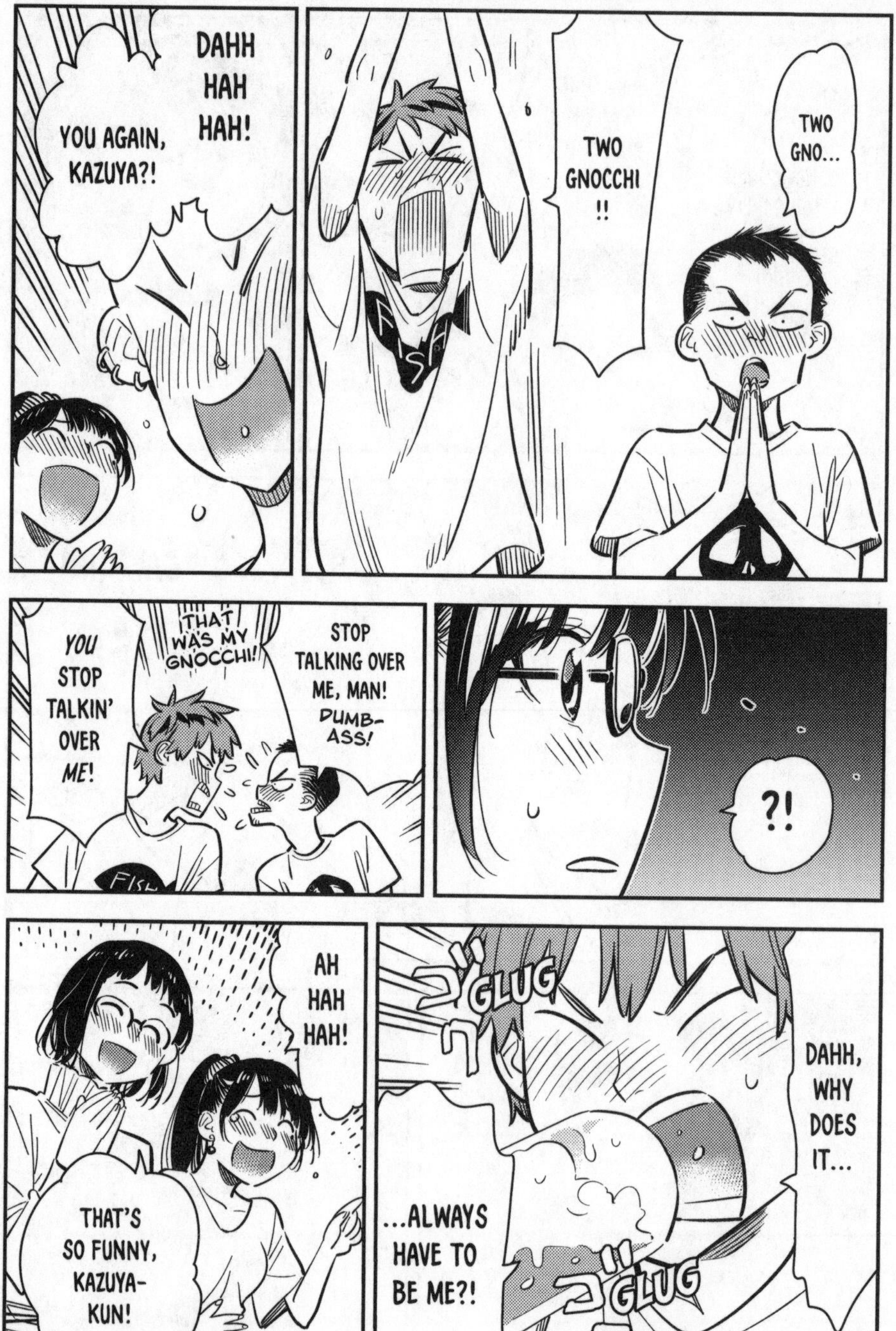
TWO GNO...
TWO GNOCCHI !!
DAHH HAH HAH!
YOU AGAIN, KAZUYA?!
?!
STOP TALKING OVER ME, MAN! DUMB-ASS!
THAT WAS MY GNOCCHI!
YOU STOP TALKIN' OVER ME!
GLUG
DAHH, WHY DOES IT...
...ALWAYS HAVE TO BE ME?!
GLUG
AH HAH HAH!
THAT'S SO FUNNY, KAZUYA-KUN!

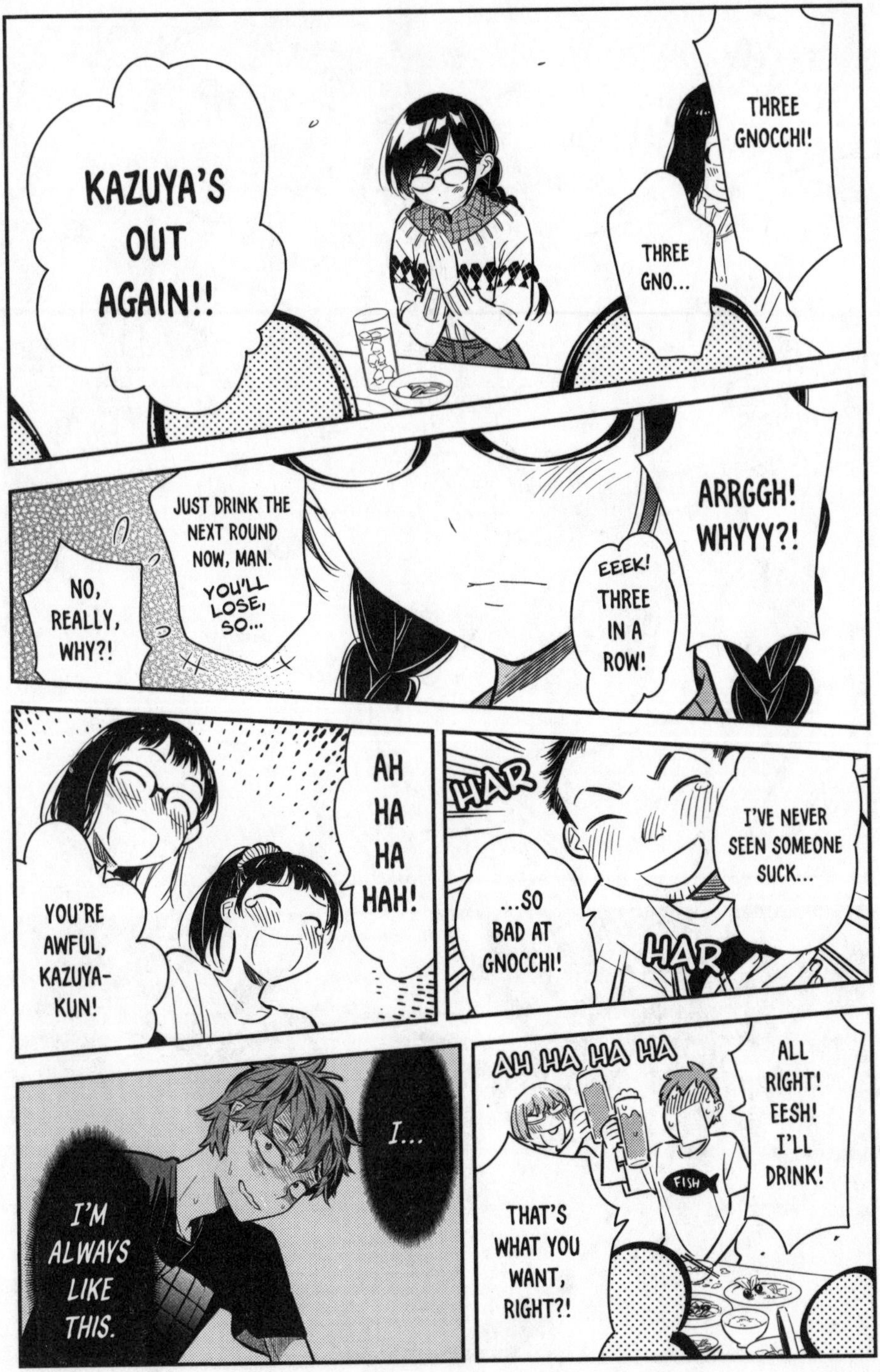
THREE GNOCCHI!
THREE GNO...
KAZUYA'S OUT AGAIN!!
ARRGGH! WHYYY?!
EEEK! THREE IN A ROW!
JUST DRINK THE NEXT ROUND NOW, MAN.
YOU'LL LOSE, SO...
NO, REALLY, WHY?!
I'VE NEVER SEEN SOMEONE SUCK...
HAR
HAR
...SO BAD AT GNOCCHI!
AH HA HA HAH!
YOU'RE AWFUL, KAZUYA-KUN!
ALL RIGHT! EESH! I'LL DRINK!
AH HA HA HA
FISH
THAT'S WHAT YOU WANT, RIGHT?!
I...
I'M ALWAYS LIKE THIS.

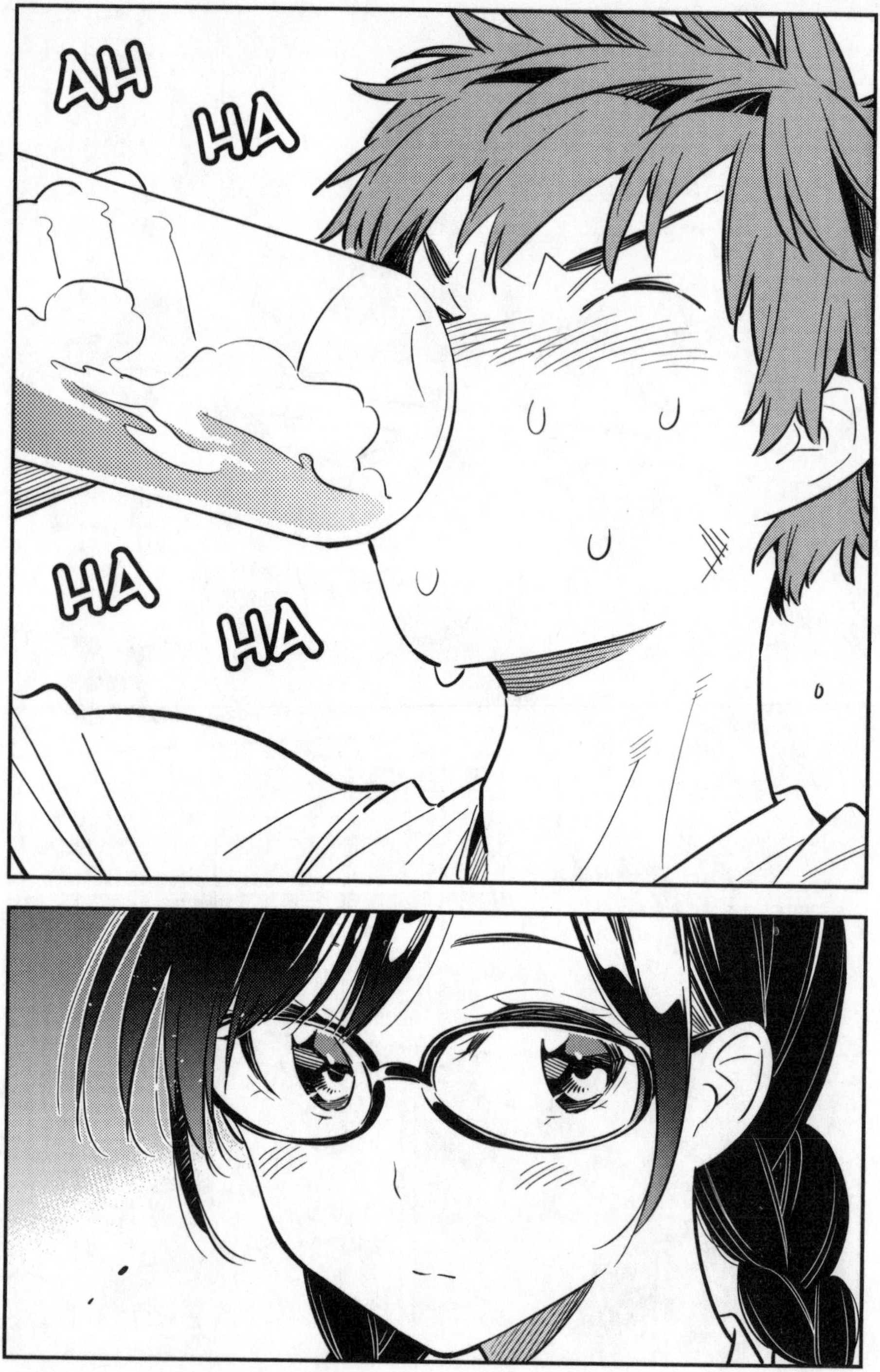
AH
HA
HA
HA

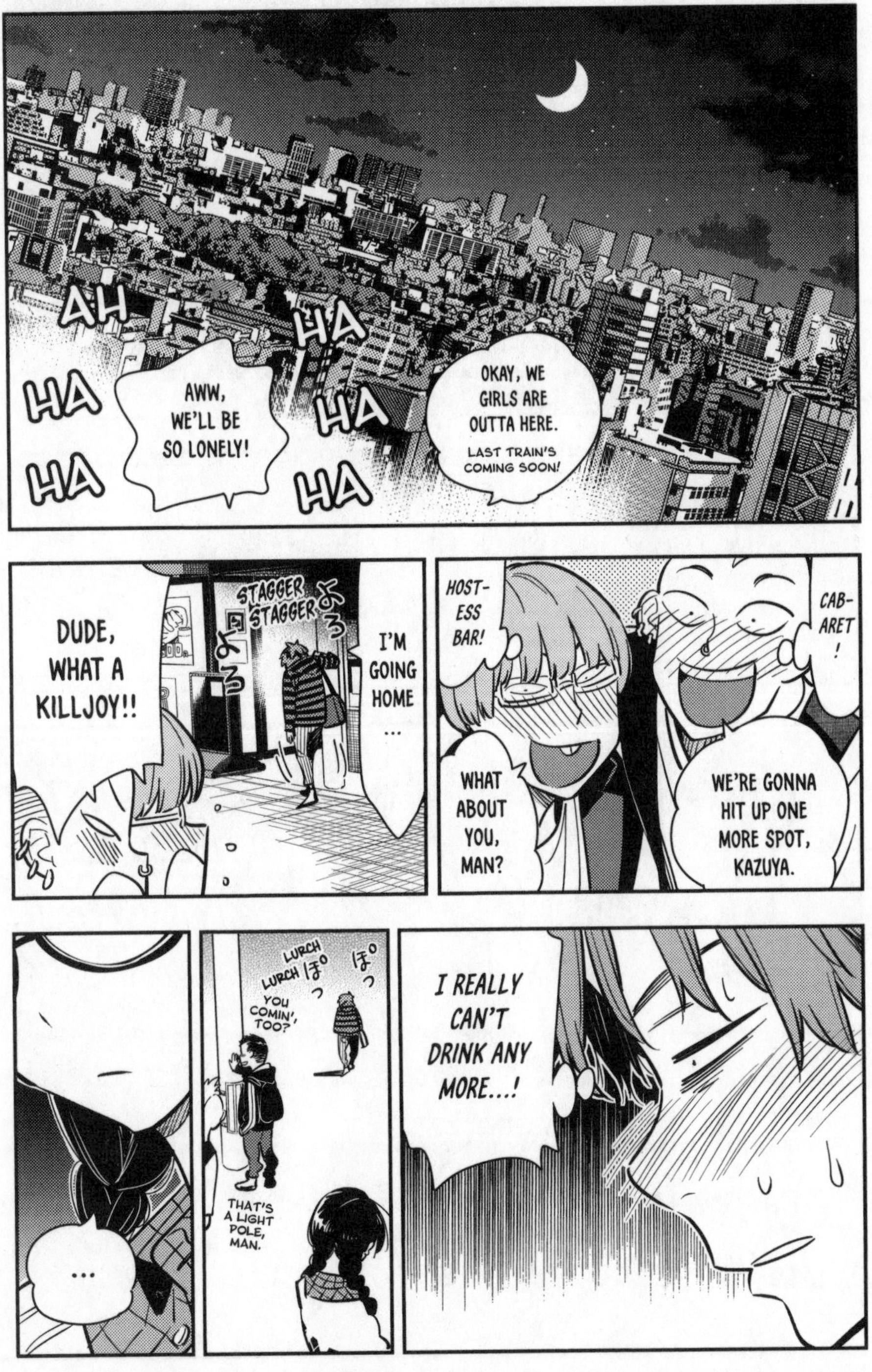
OKAY, WE GIRLS ARE OUTTA HERE.
LAST TRAIN'S COMING SOON!
HA
HA
HA
AWW, WE'LL BE SO LONELY!
AH
HA
HA
CAB-ARET!
WE'RE GONNA HIT UP ONE MORE SPOT, KAZUYA.
HOST-ESS BAR!
WHAT ABOUT YOU, MAN?
I'M GOING HOME...
STAGGER STAGGER
よろよろ
DUDE, WHAT A KILLJOY!!
I REALLY CAN'T DRINK ANY MORE...!
ぽっぽっ
LURCH LURCH
YOU COMIN', TOO?
THAT'S A LIGHT POLE, MAN.
...

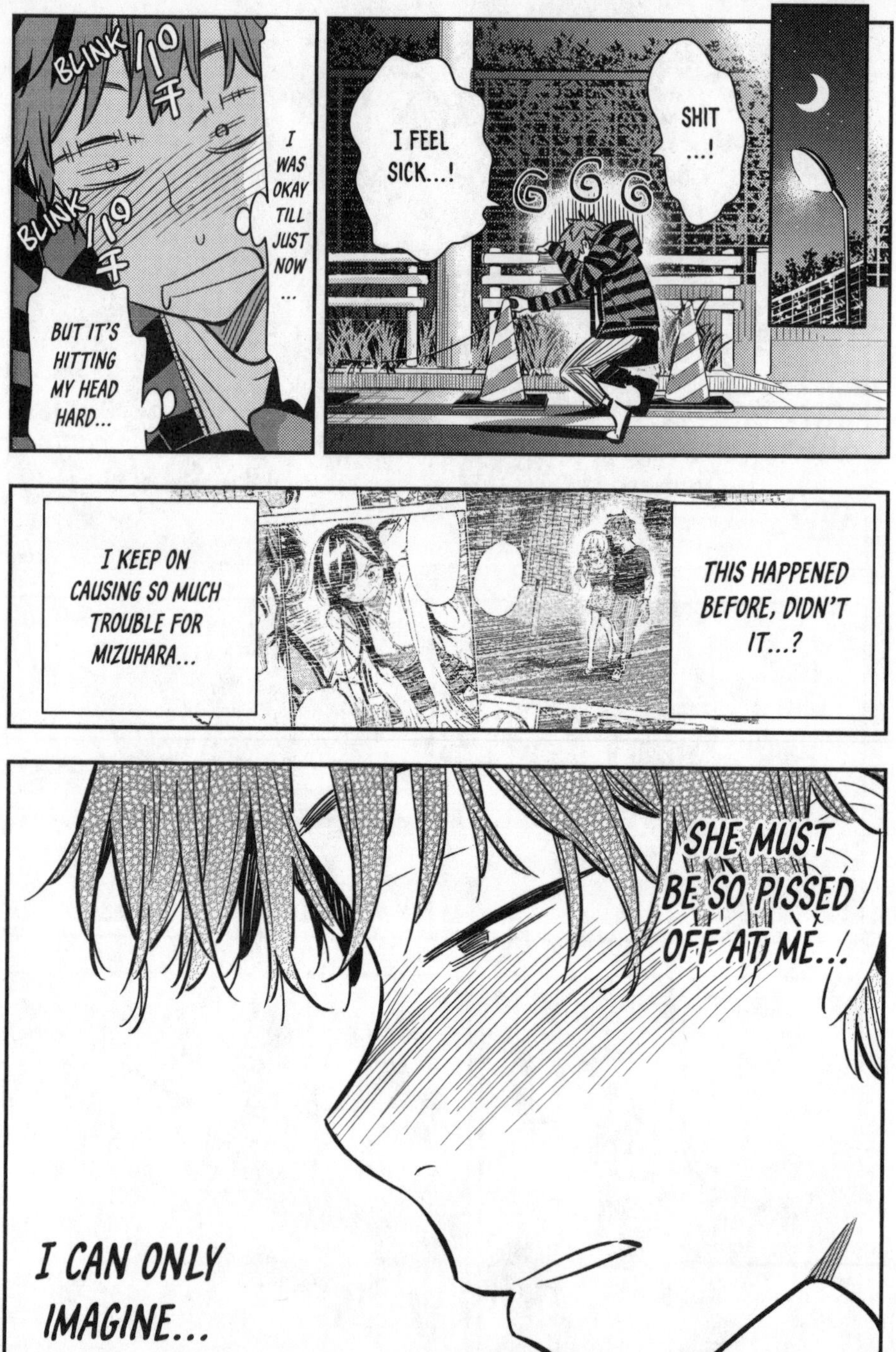
SHIT ...!
GGG
I FEEL SICK...!
I WAS OKAY TILL JUST NOW ...
BLINK
BLINK
BUT IT'S HITTING MY HEAD HARD...
THIS HAPPENED BEFORE, DIDN'T IT...?
I KEEP ON CAUSING SO MUCH TROUBLE FOR MIZUHARA...
SHE MUST BE SO PISSED OFF AT ME...
I CAN ONLY IMAGINE...

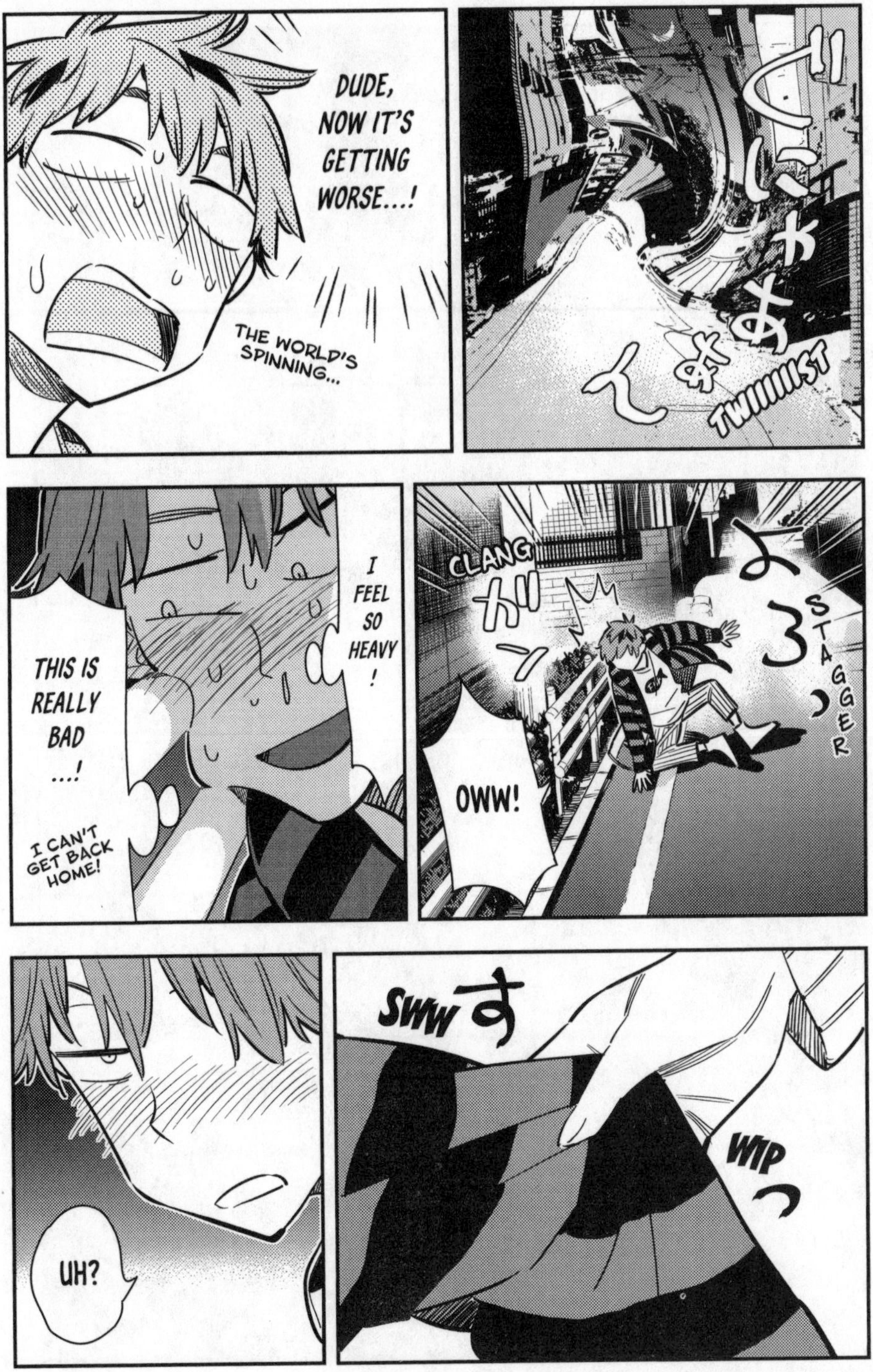
TWIIIIIIST
DUDE, NOW IT'S GETTING WORSE...!
THE WORLD'S SPINNING...
CLANG
STAGGER
OWW!
I FEEL SO HEAVY!
THIS IS REALLY BAD...!
I CAN'T GET BACK HOME!
SWW
WIP
UH?

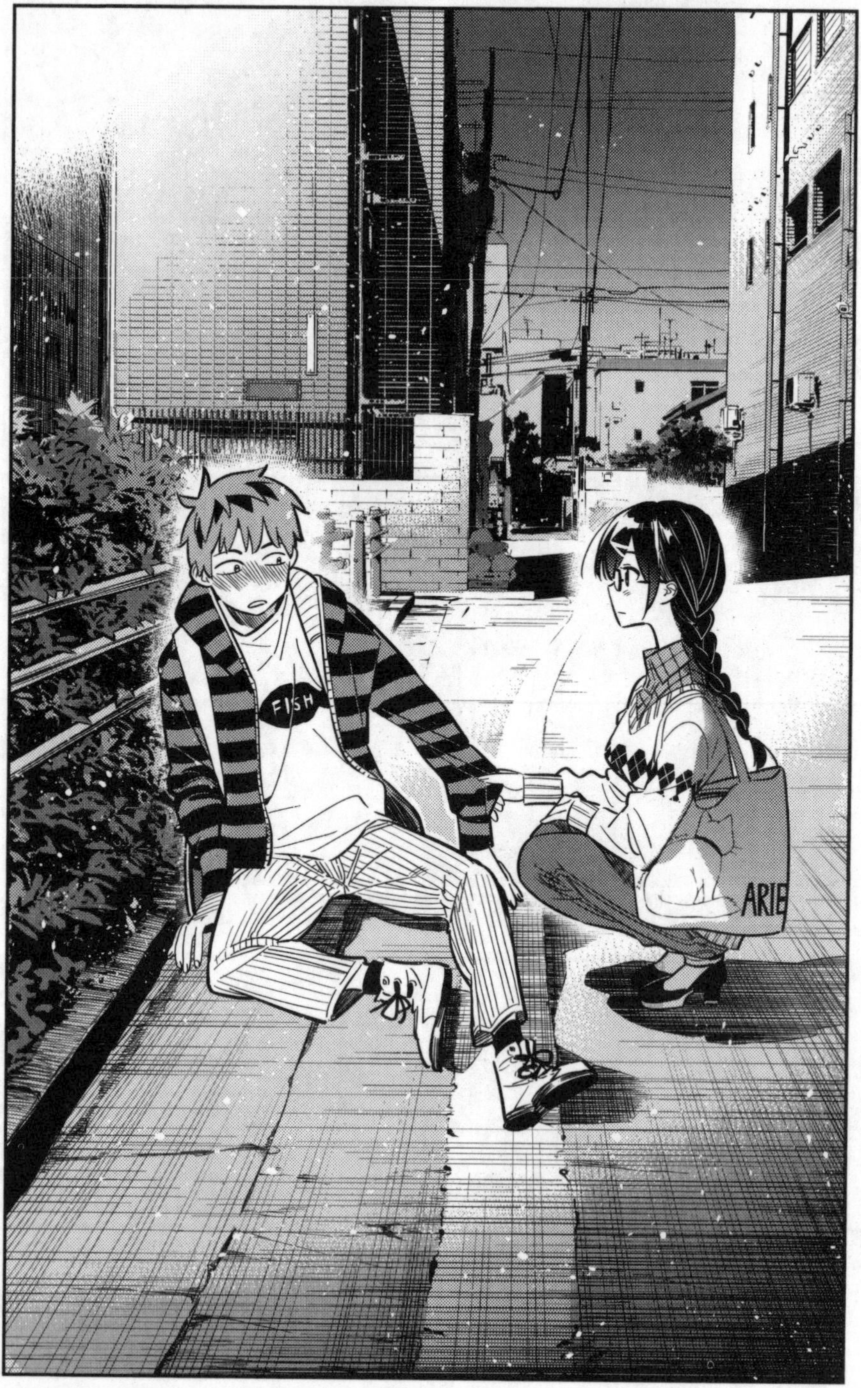
FISH
ARIE

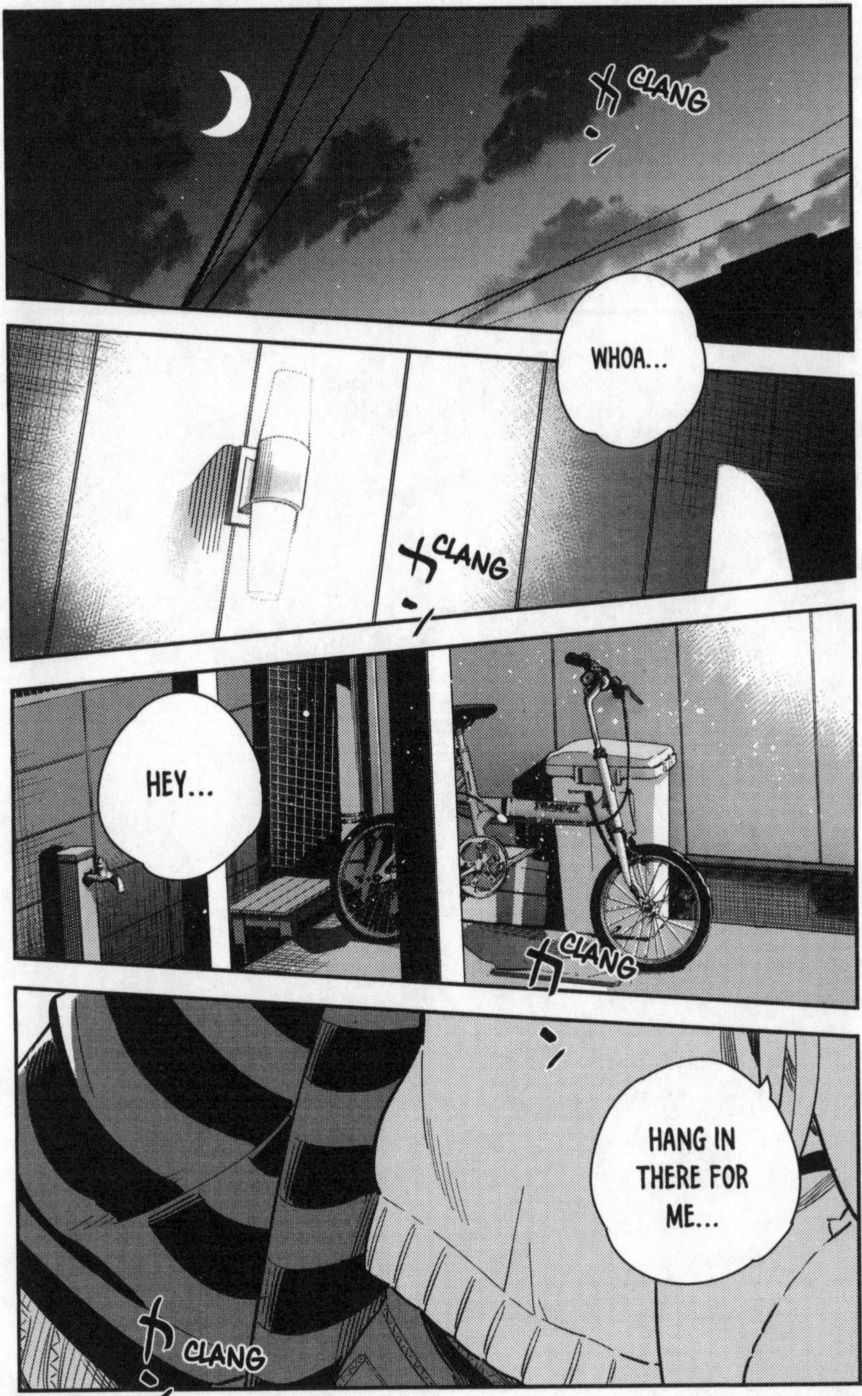
CLANG
WHOA...
CLANG
CLANG
HEY...
HANG IN THERE FOR ME...
CLANG

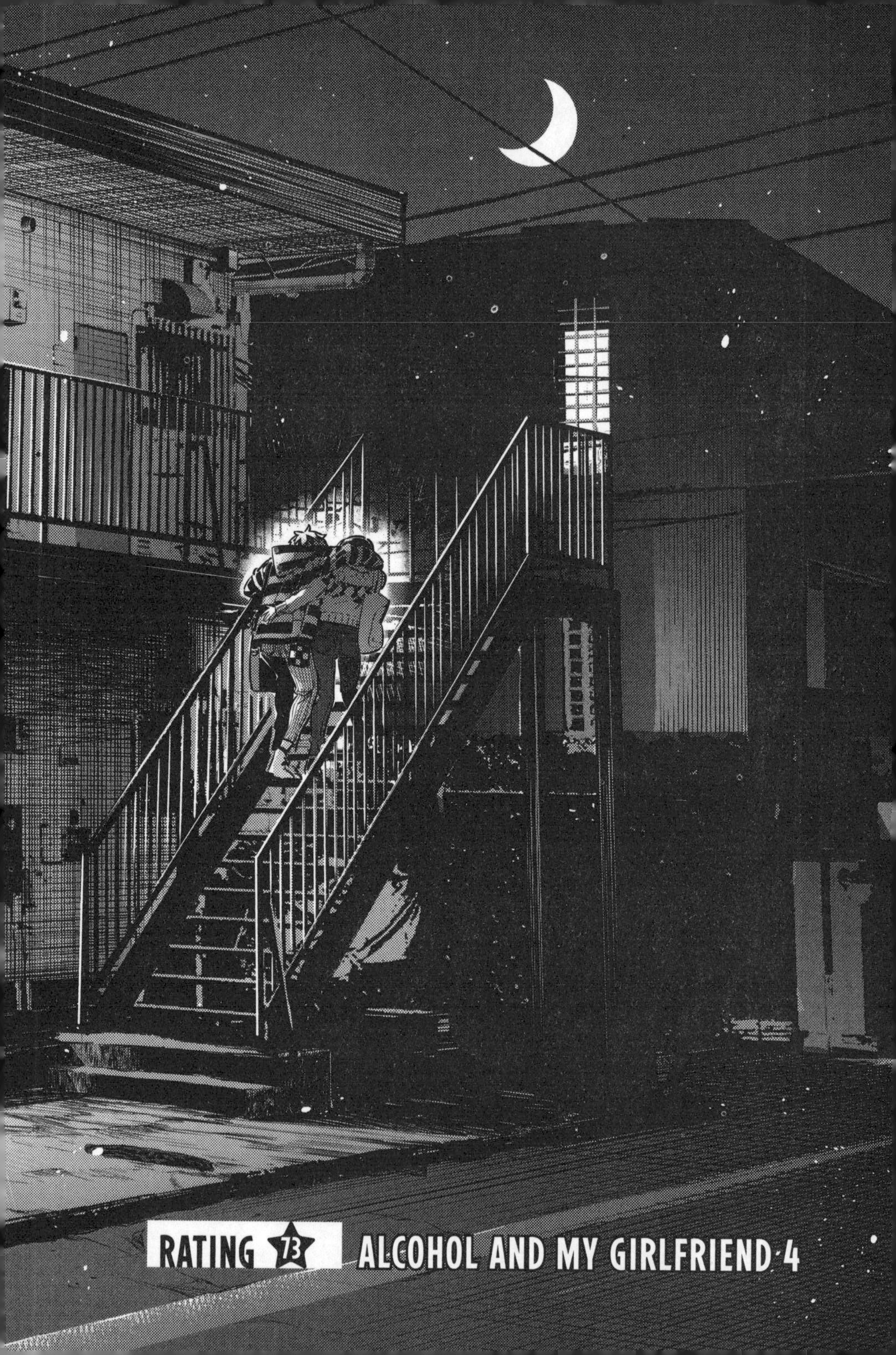
RATING 73 ALCOHOL AND MY GIRLFRIEND 4

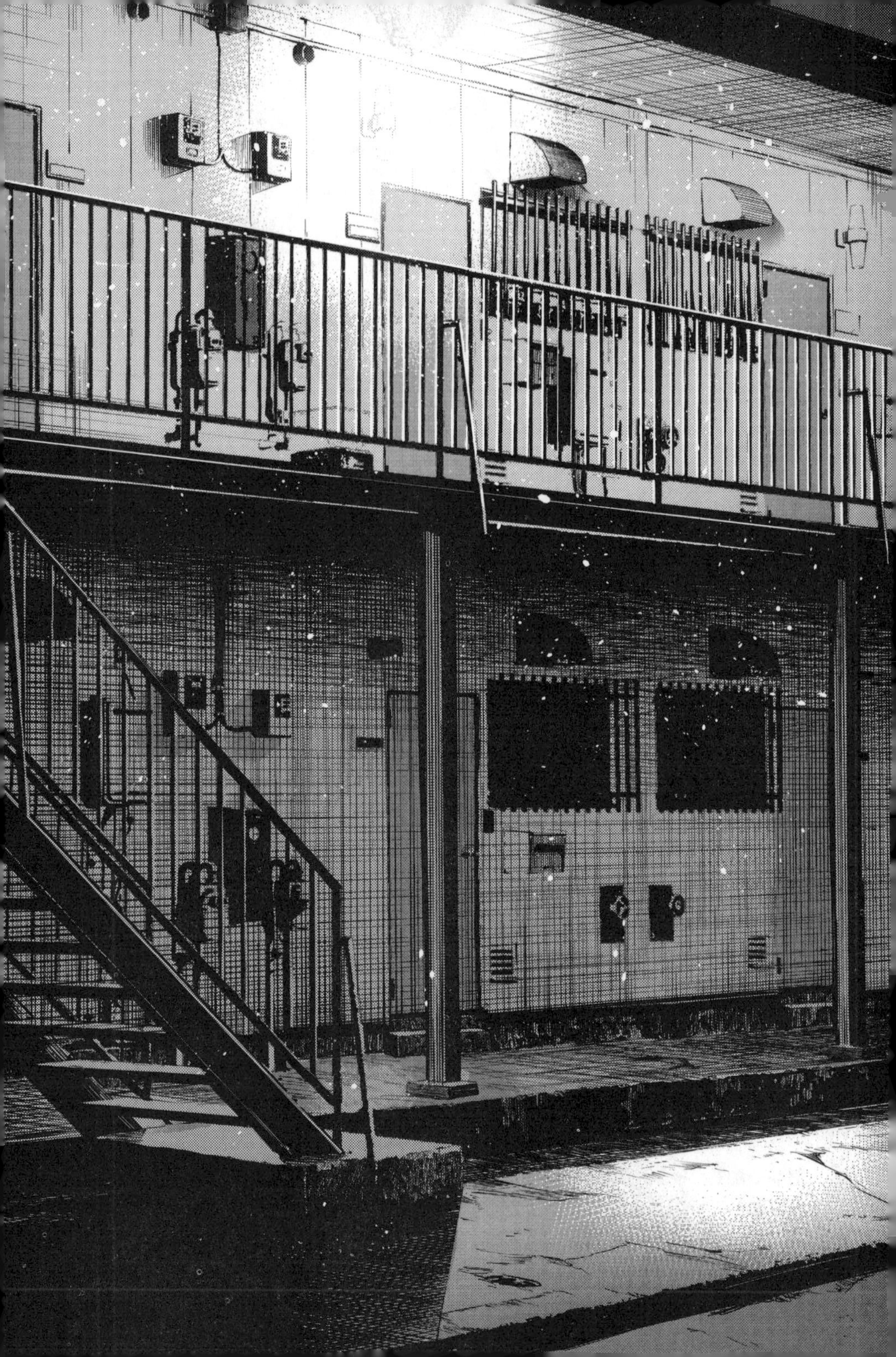

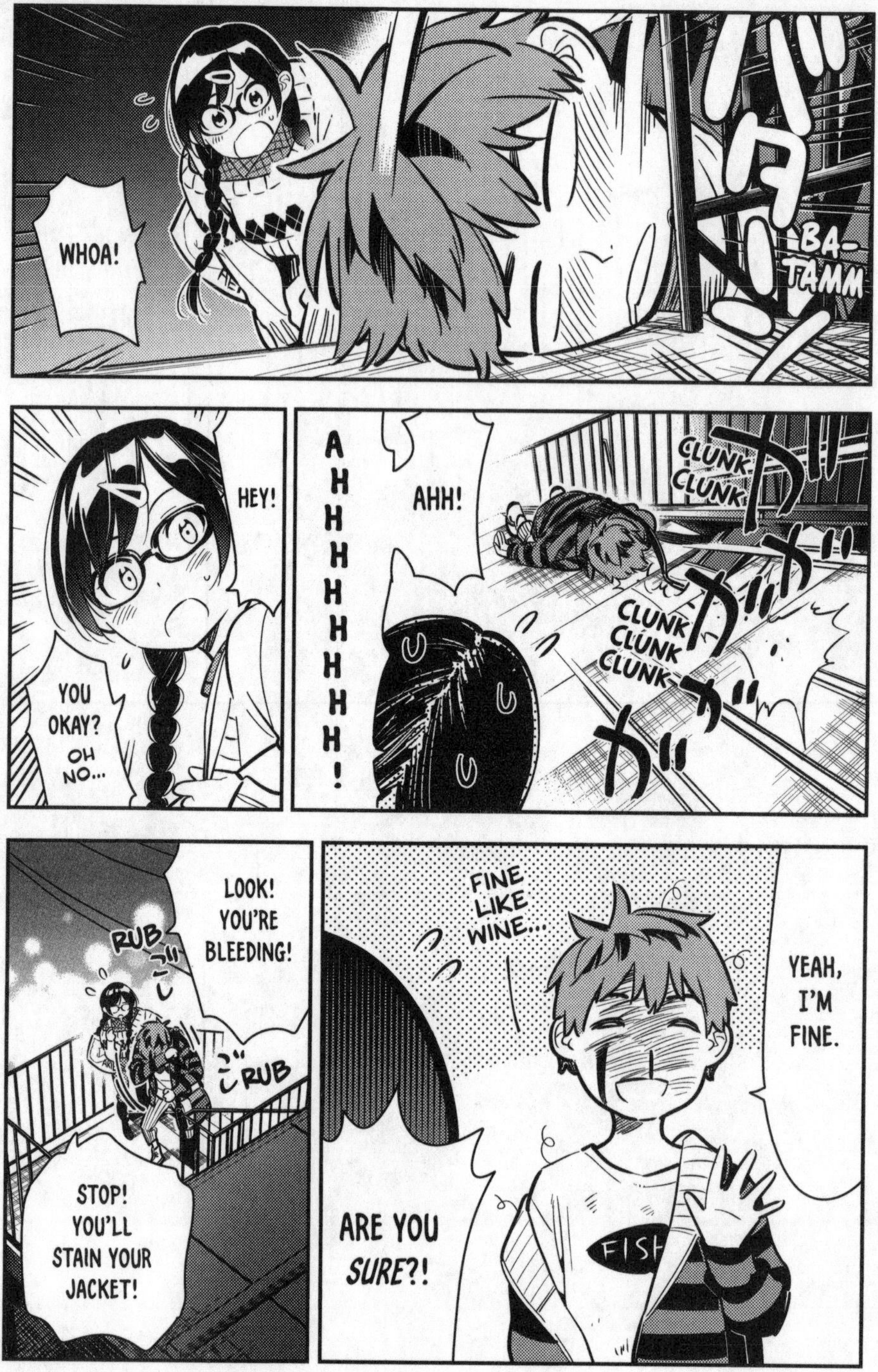
BA-
TAMM
WHOA!
AHH!
AHHHHHHHH!
CLUNK
CLUNK
CLUNK
CLUNK
CLUNK
HEY!
YOU OKAY?
OH NO...
YEAH, I'M FINE.
FINE LIKE WINE...
ARE YOU SURE?!
LOOK! YOU'RE BLEEDING!
RUB
RUB
STOP! YOU'LL STAIN YOUR JACKET!

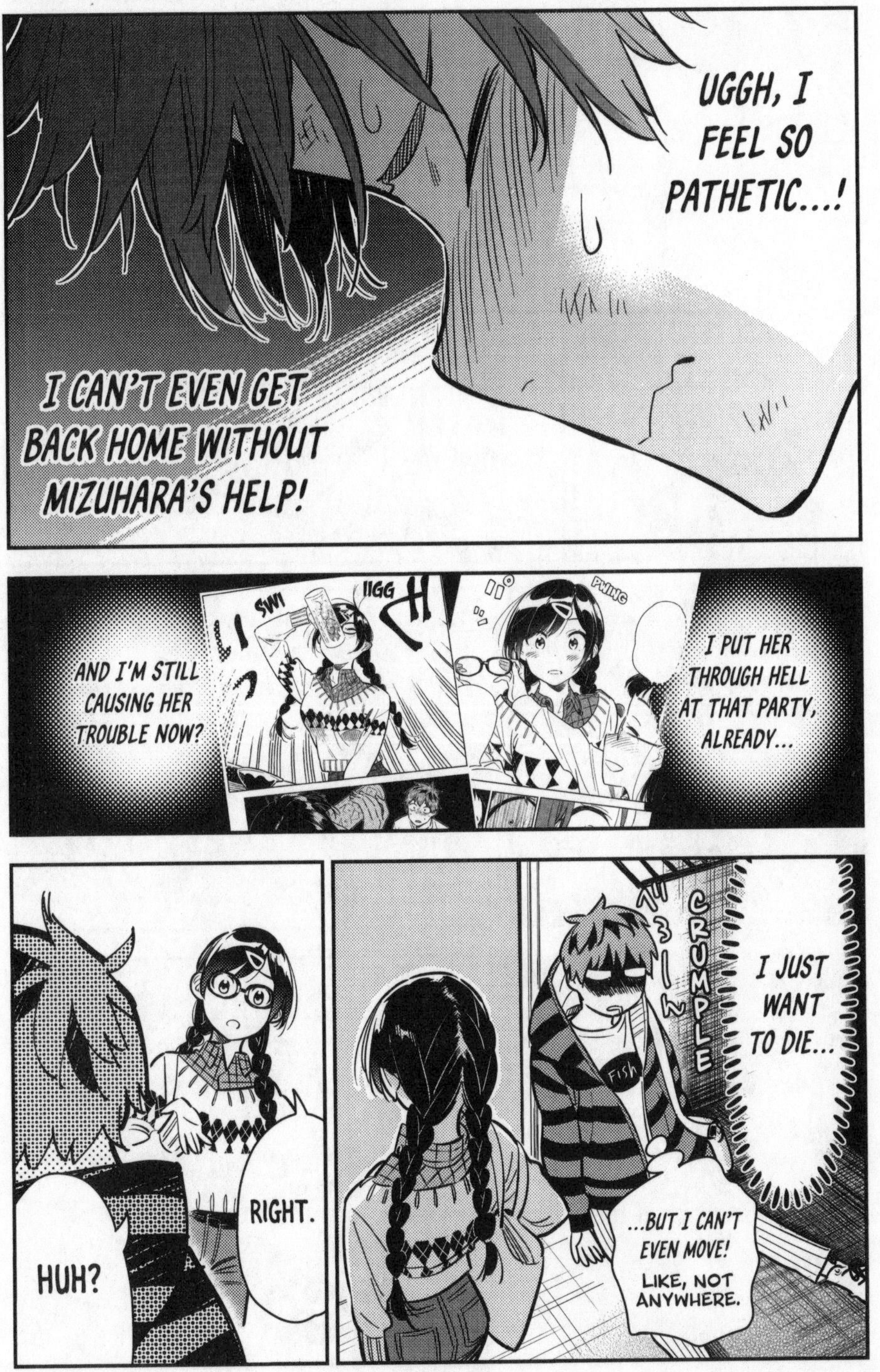
UGGH, I FEEL SO PATHETIC...!
I CAN'T EVEN GET BACK HOME WITHOUT MIZUHARA'S HELP!
I PUT HER THROUGH HELL AT THAT PARTY, ALREADY...
PWING
SWI
IIGG
AND I'M STILL CAUSING HER TROUBLE NOW?
I JUST WANT TO DIE...
CRUMPLE
...BUT I CAN'T EVEN MOVE! LIKE, NOT ANYWHERE.
RIGHT.
HUH?

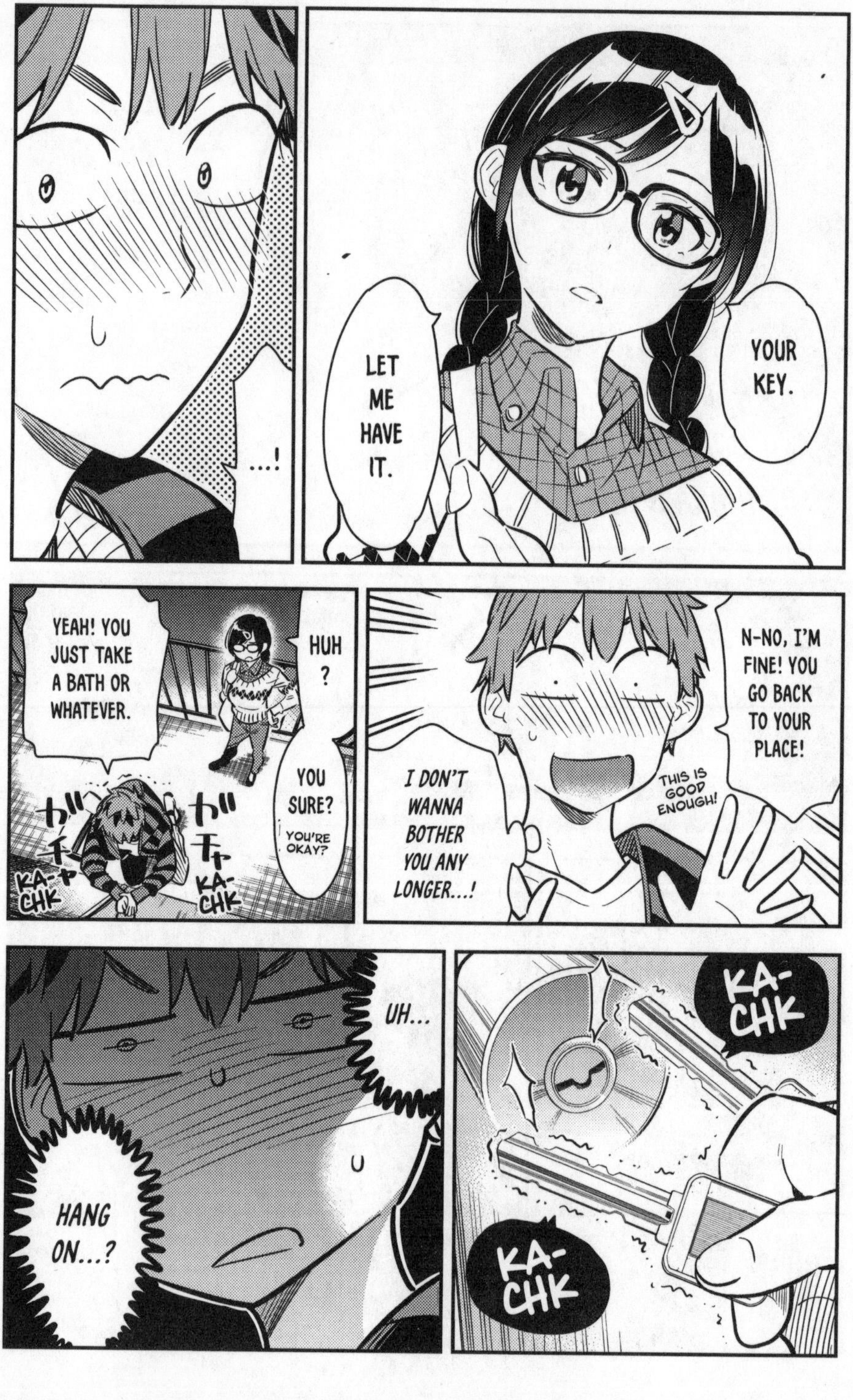
YOUR KEY.
LET ME HAVE IT.
...!
N-NO, I'M FINE! YOU GO BACK TO YOUR PLACE!
THIS IS GOOD ENOUGH!
I DON'T WANNA BOTHER YOU ANY LONGER...!
HUH?
YOU SURE?
YOU'RE OKAY?
YEAH! YOU JUST TAKE A BATH OR WHATEVER.
ガチャ
KA-CHK
ガチャ
KA-CHK
KA-CHK
KA-CHK
UH...
HANG ON...?

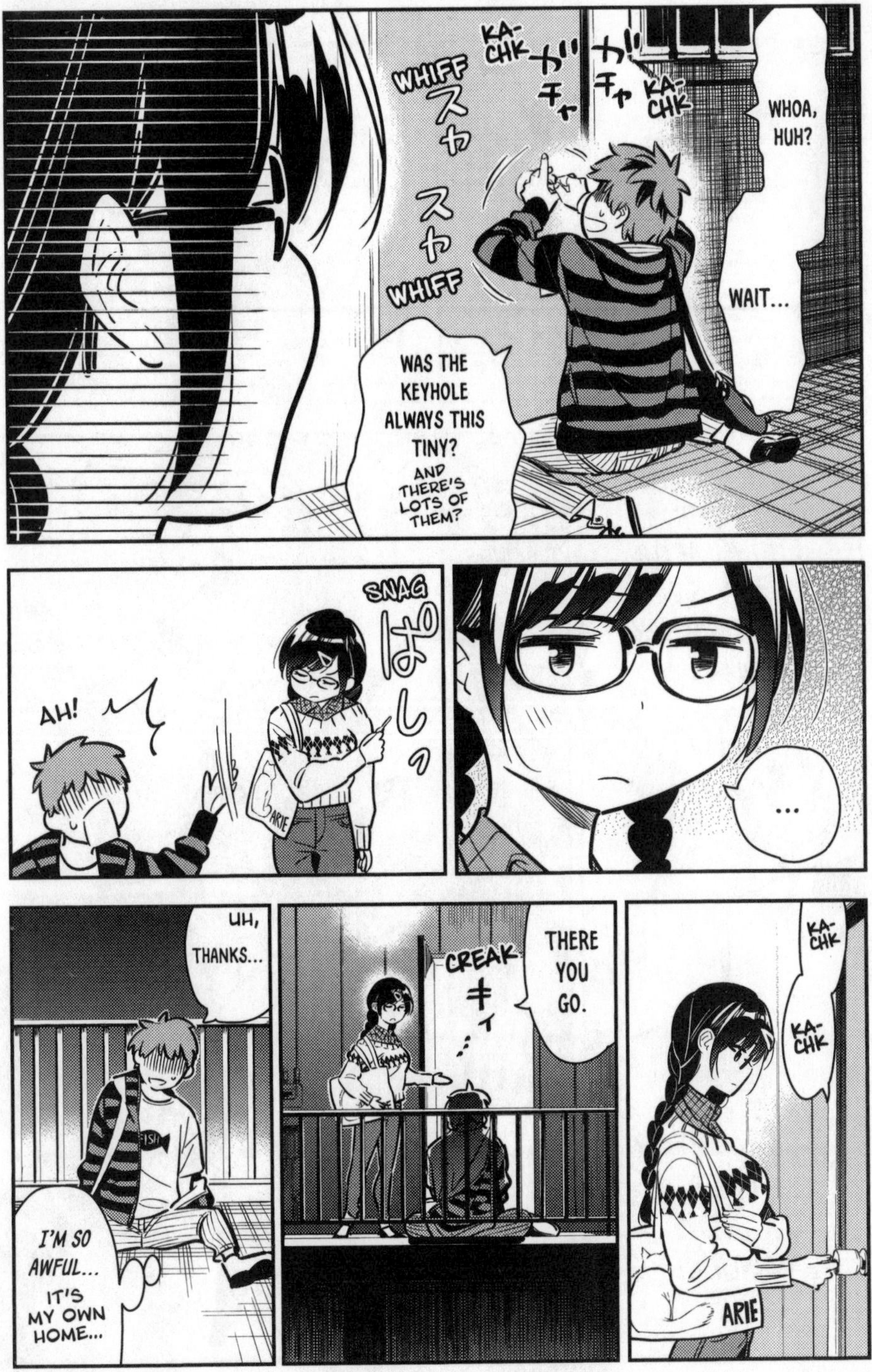
KA-CHK ガチャ
KA-CHK ガチャ
WHOA, HUH?
WAIT...
WHIFF スヵ
スヵ WHIFF
WAS THE KEYHOLE ALWAYS THIS TINY?
AND THERE'S LOTS OF THEM?
...
SNAG ぱしっ
AH!
KA-CHK
KA-CHK
THERE YOU GO.
CREAK キィ
UH, THANKS...
I'M SO AWFUL... IT'S MY OWN HOME...

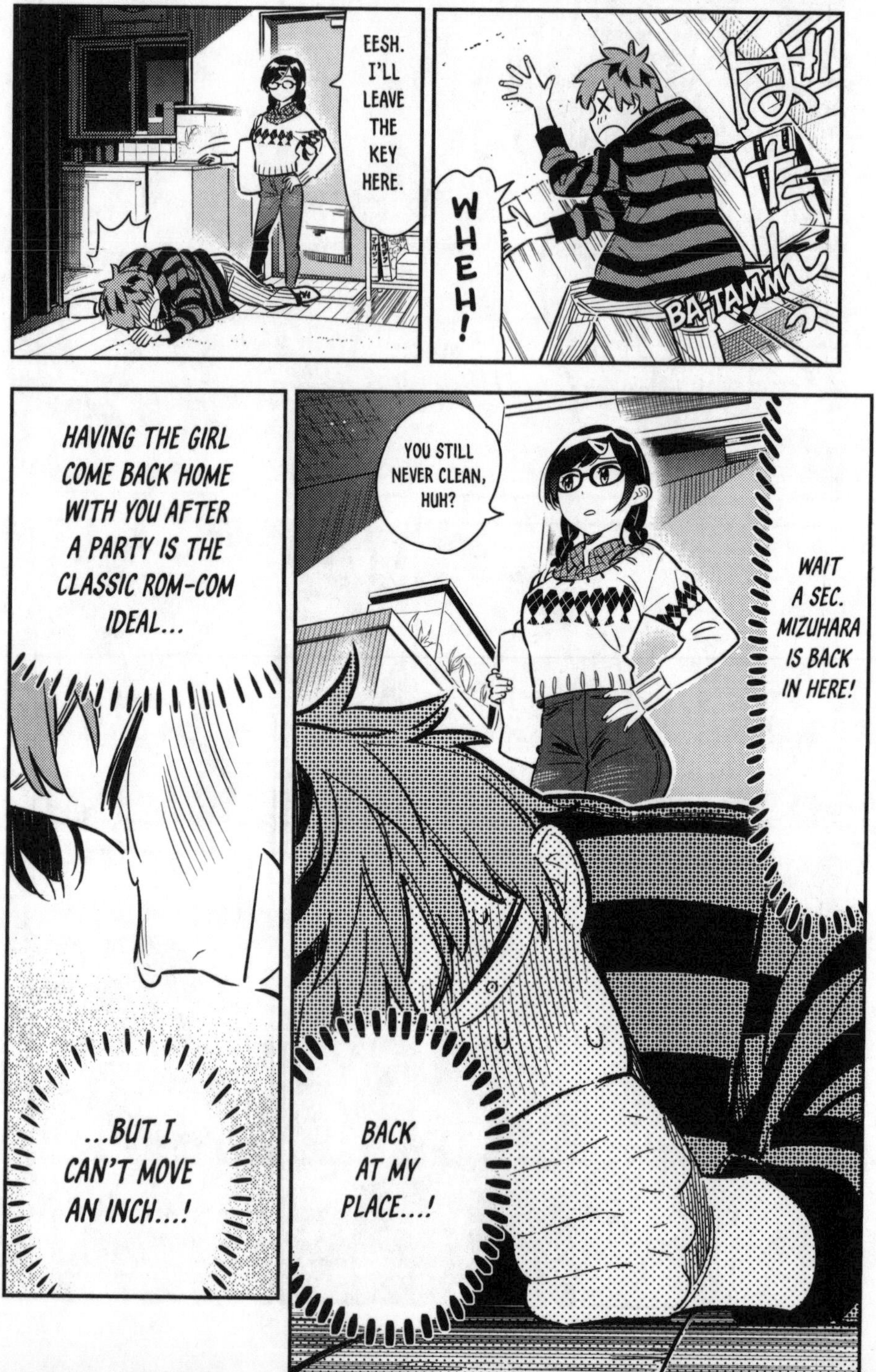
WHEH!
BA-TAMM
EESH. I'LL LEAVE THE KEY HERE.
WAIT A SEC. MIZUHARA IS BACK IN HERE!
YOU STILL NEVER CLEAN, HUH?
BACK AT MY PLACE...!
HAVING THE GIRL COME BACK HOME WITH YOU AFTER A PARTY IS THE CLASSIC ROM-COM IDEAL...
...BUT I CAN'T MOVE AN INCH...!

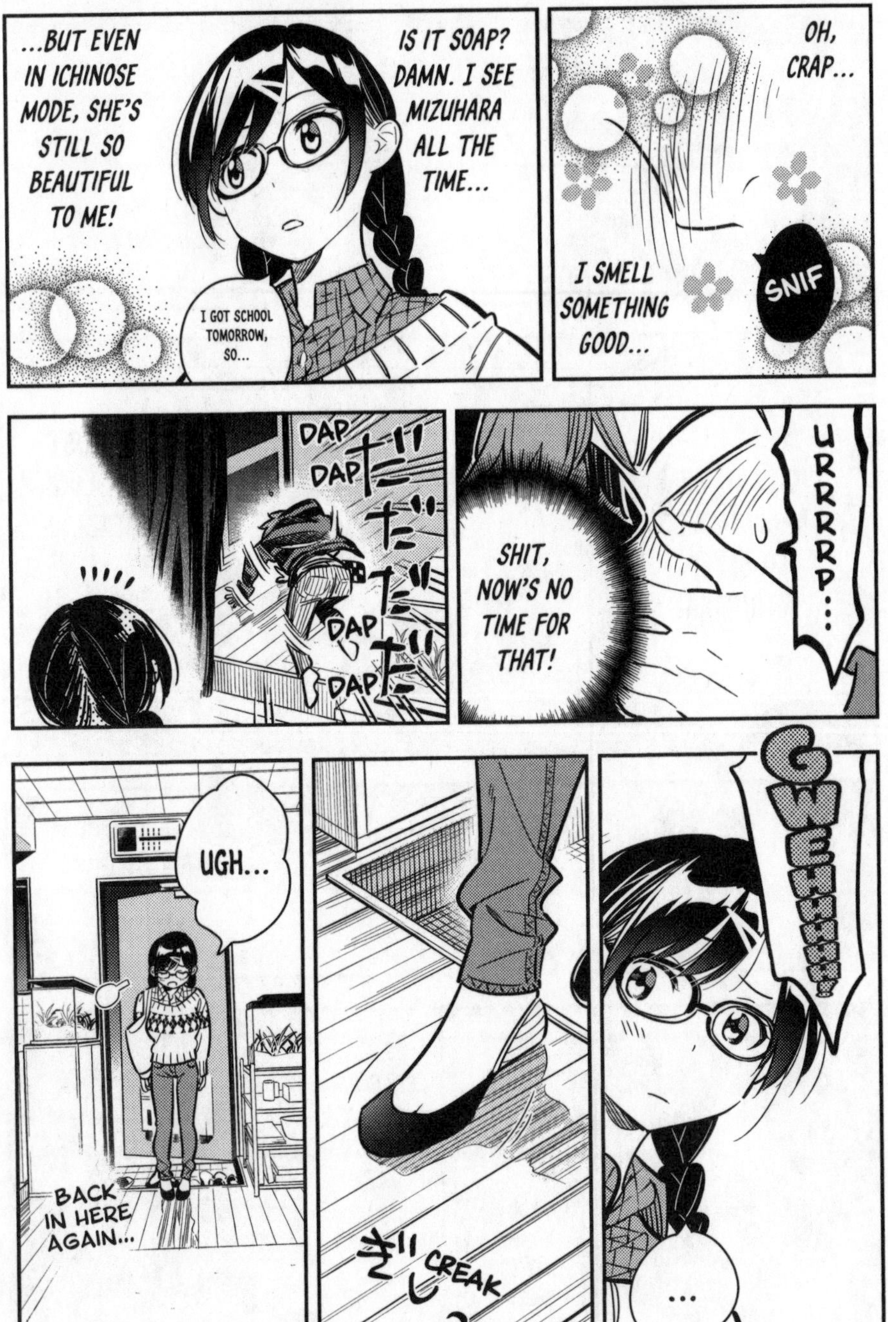
OH, CRAP...
I SMELL SOMETHING GOOD...
SNIF
IS IT SOAP? DAMN. I SEE MIZUHARA ALL THE TIME...
...BUT EVEN IN ICHINOSE MODE, SHE'S STILL SO BEAUTIFUL TO ME!
I GOT SCHOOL TOMORROW, SO...
URRRRP...
SHIT, NOW'S NO TIME FOR THAT!
DAP
DAP
DAP
DAP
...
CREAK
UGH...
BACK IN HERE AGAIN...

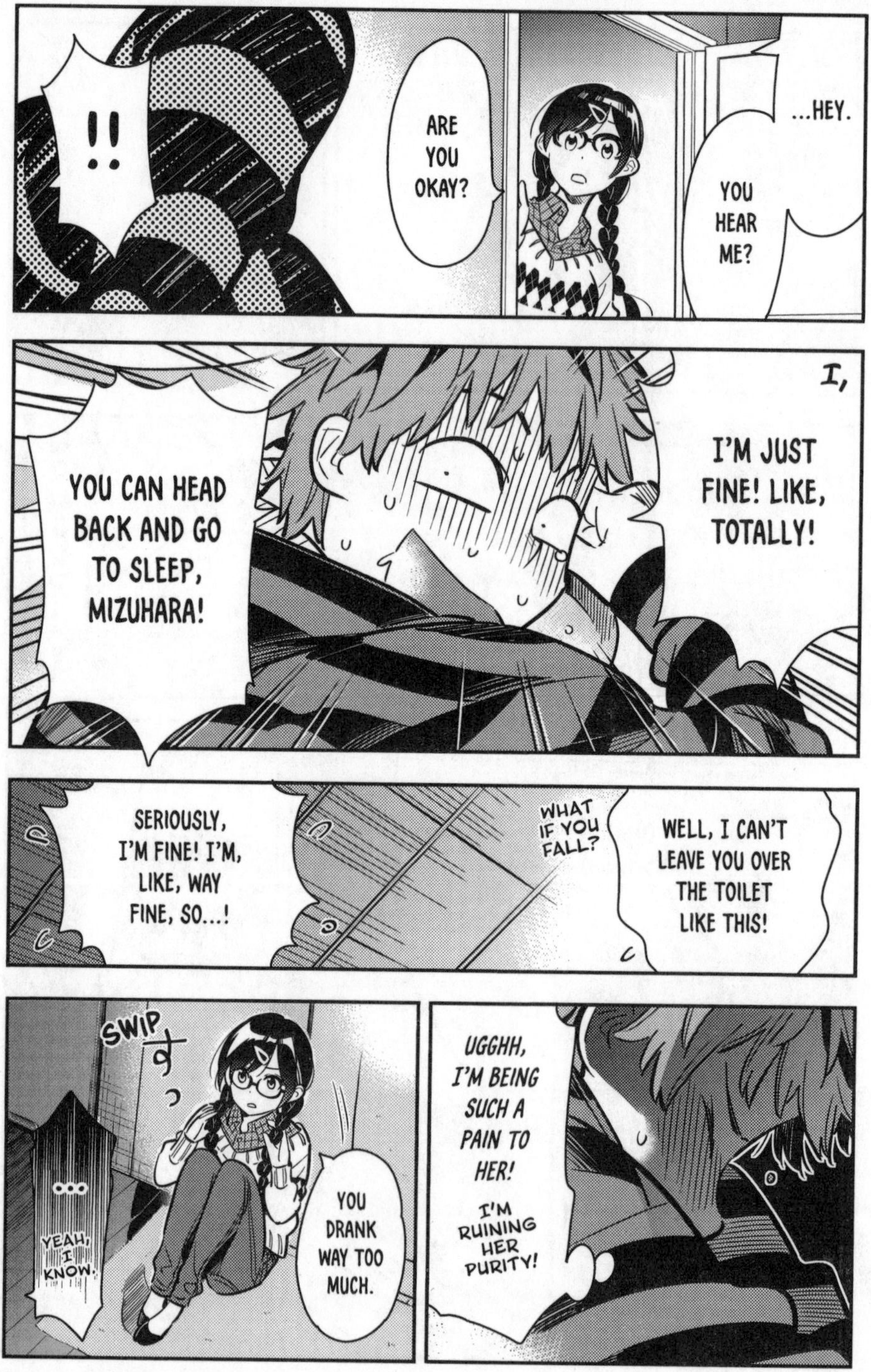
...HEY.
YOU HEAR ME?
ARE YOU OKAY?
!!
I,
I'M JUST FINE! LIKE, TOTALLY!
YOU CAN HEAD BACK AND GO TO SLEEP, MIZUHARA!
WELL, I CAN'T LEAVE YOU OVER THE TOILET LIKE THIS!
WHAT IF YOU FALL?
SERIOUSLY, I'M FINE! I'M, LIKE, WAY FINE, SO...!
UGGHH, I'M BEING SUCH A PAIN TO HER!
I'M RUINING HER PURITY!
SWIP
YOU DRANK WAY TOO MUCH.
...
YEAH, I KNOW.

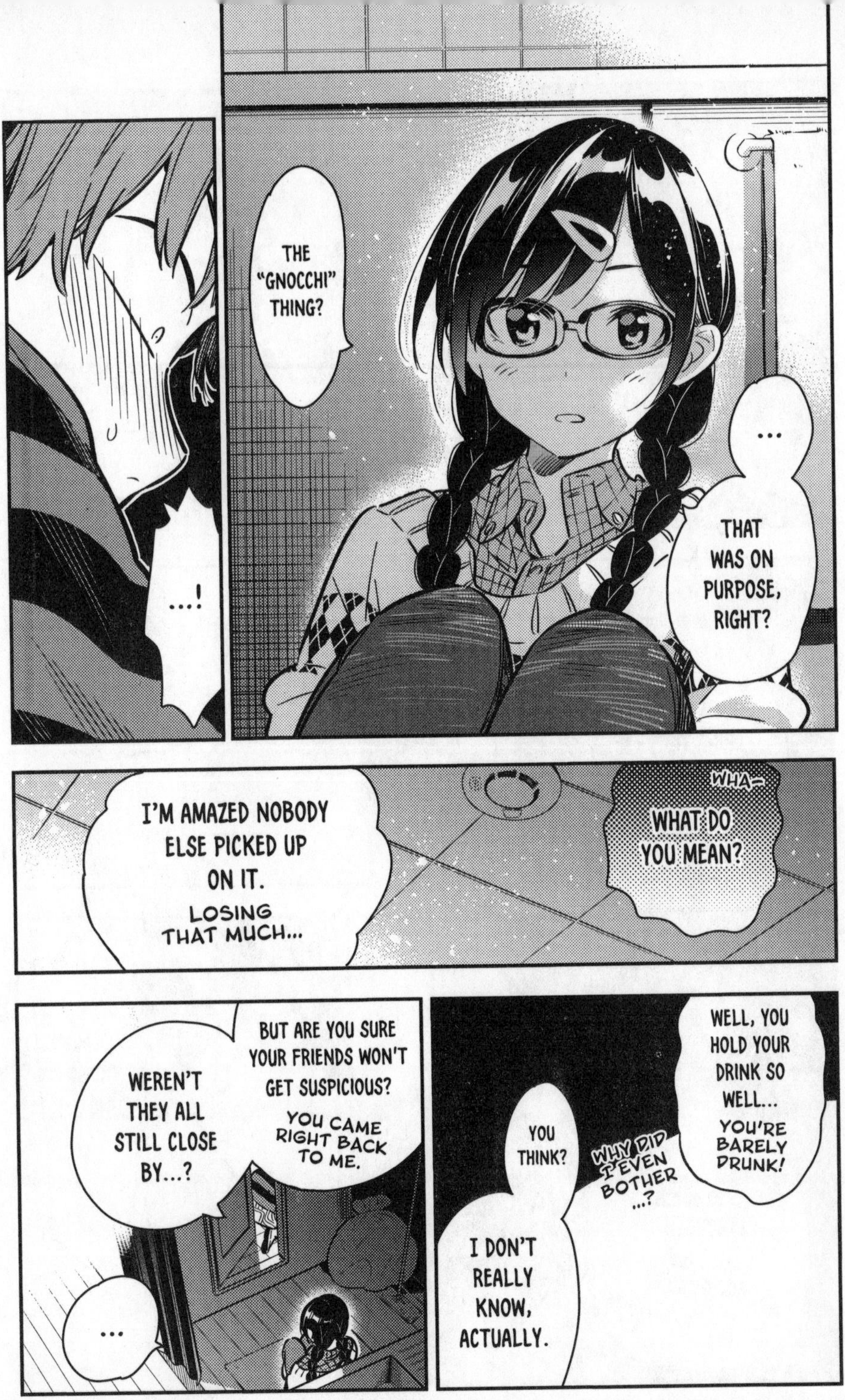
THE "GNOCCHI" THING?
...
THAT WAS ON PURPOSE, RIGHT?
...!
WHA-
WHAT DO YOU MEAN?
I'M AMAZED NOBODY ELSE PICKED UP ON IT.
LOSING THAT MUCH...
WELL, YOU HOLD YOUR DRINK SO WELL...
YOU'RE BARELY DRUNK!
WHY DID I EVEN BOTHER ...?
YOU THINK?
I DON'T REALLY KNOW, ACTUALLY.
BUT ARE YOU SURE YOUR FRIENDS WON'T GET SUSPICIOUS?
YOU CAME RIGHT BACK TO ME.
WEREN'T THEY ALL STILL CLOSE BY...?
...

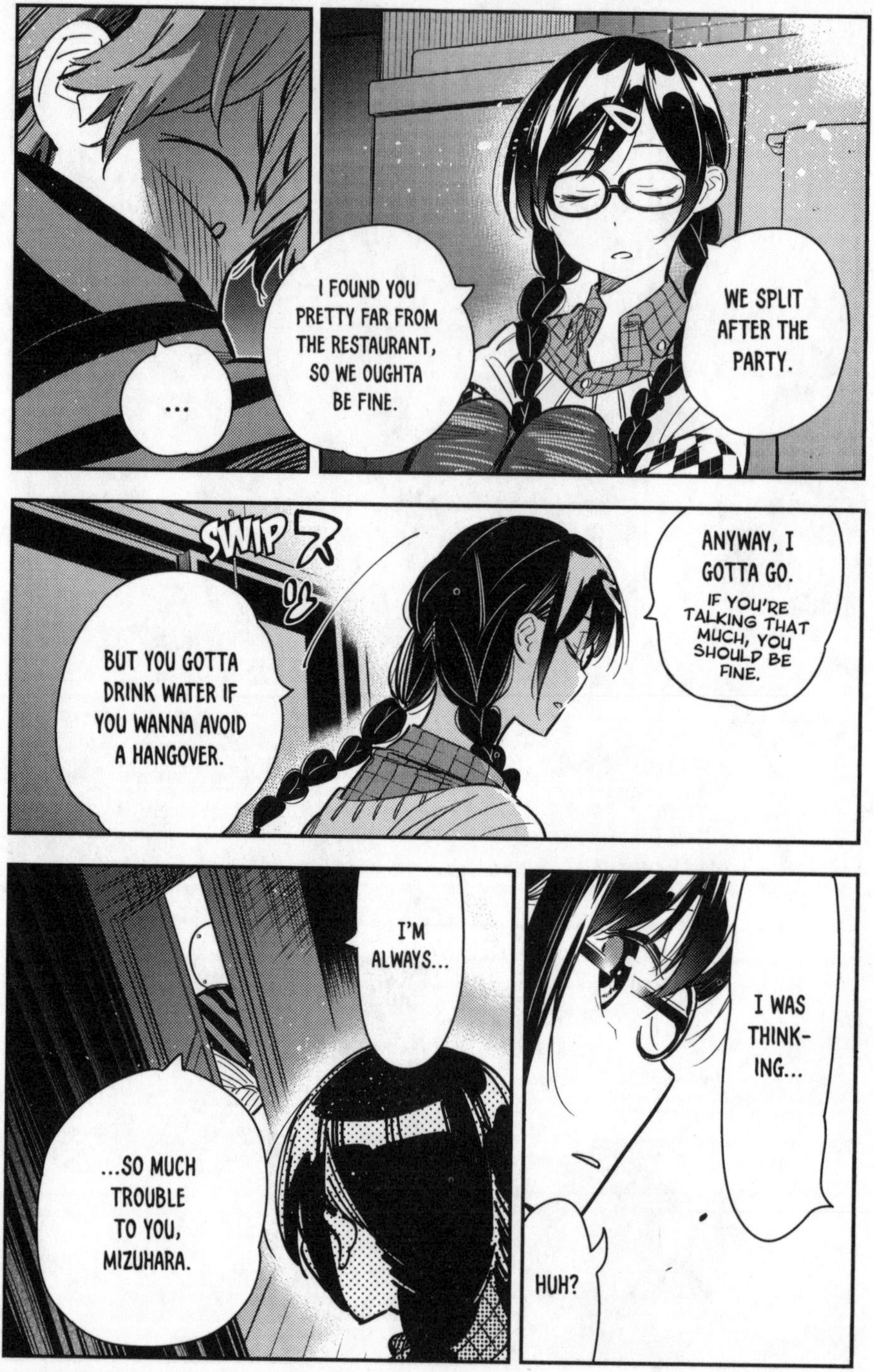
WE SPLIT AFTER THE PARTY.
I FOUND YOU PRETTY FAR FROM THE RESTAURANT, SO WE OUGHTA BE FINE.
...
ANYWAY, I GOTTA GO.
IF YOU'RE TALKING THAT MUCH, YOU SHOULD BE FINE.
SWIP
BUT YOU GOTTA DRINK WATER IF YOU WANNA AVOID A HANGOVER.
I WAS THINKING...
HUH?
I'M ALWAYS...
...SO MUCH TROUBLE TO YOU, MIZUHARA.

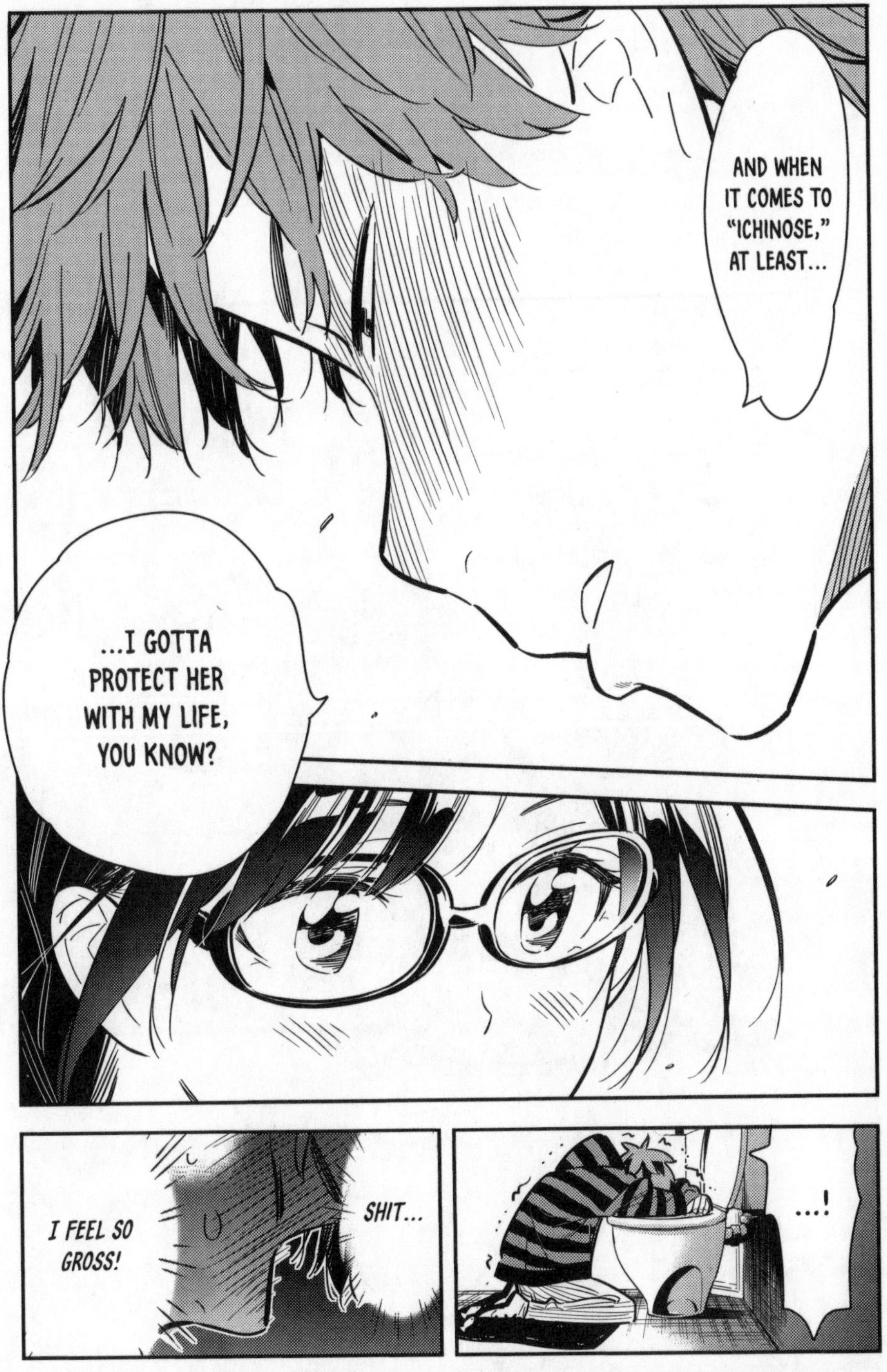
AND WHEN IT COMES TO "ICHINOSE," AT LEAST...
...I GOTTA PROTECT HER WITH MY LIFE, YOU KNOW?
...!
SHIT...
I FEEL SO GROSS!

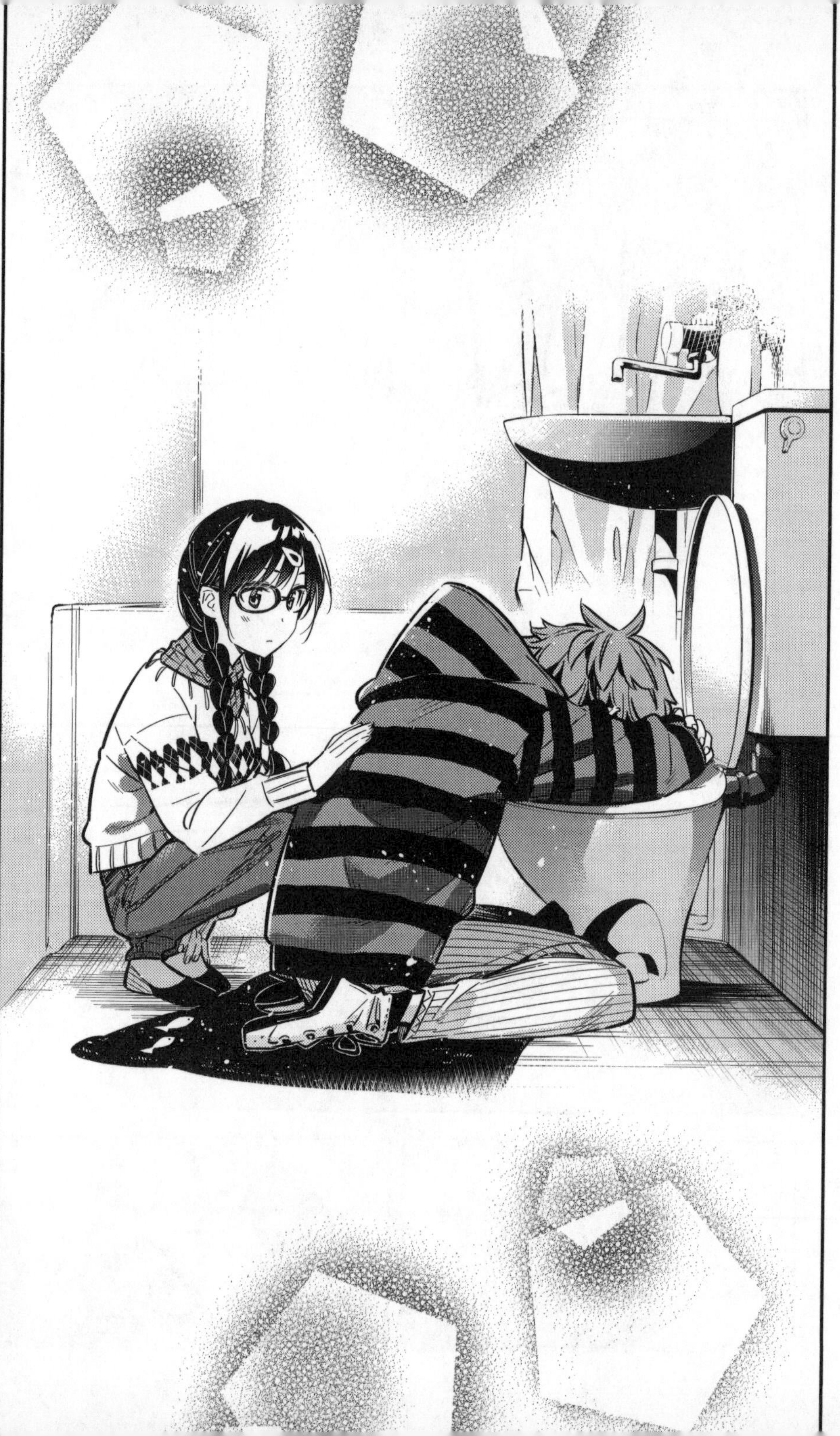

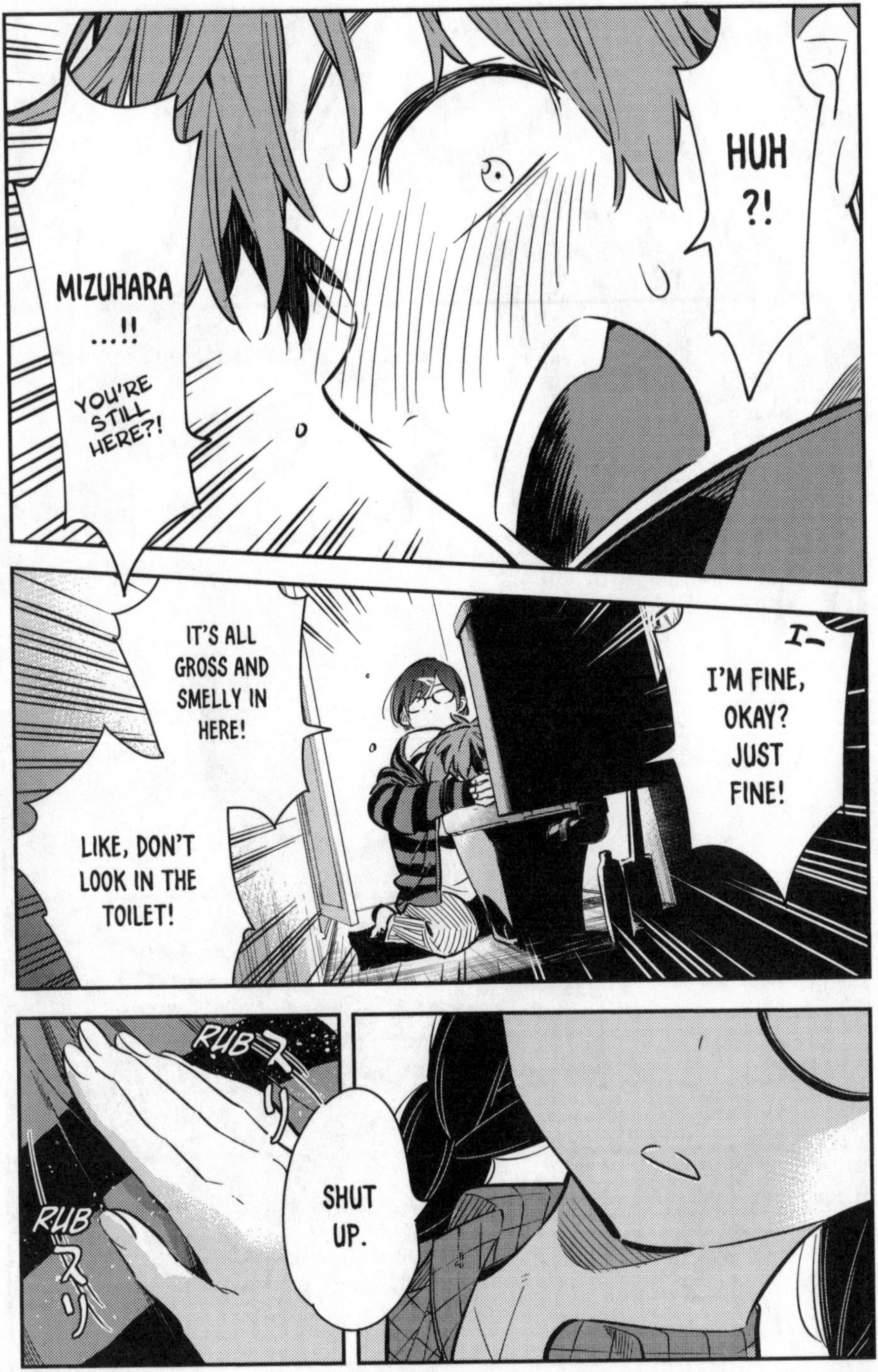
HUH ?!
MIZUHARA ...!!
YOU'RE STILL HERE?!
I—
I'M FINE, OKAY? JUST FINE!
IT'S ALL GROSS AND SMELLY IN HERE!
LIKE, DON'T LOOK IN THE TOILET!
SHUT UP.
RUB
RUB

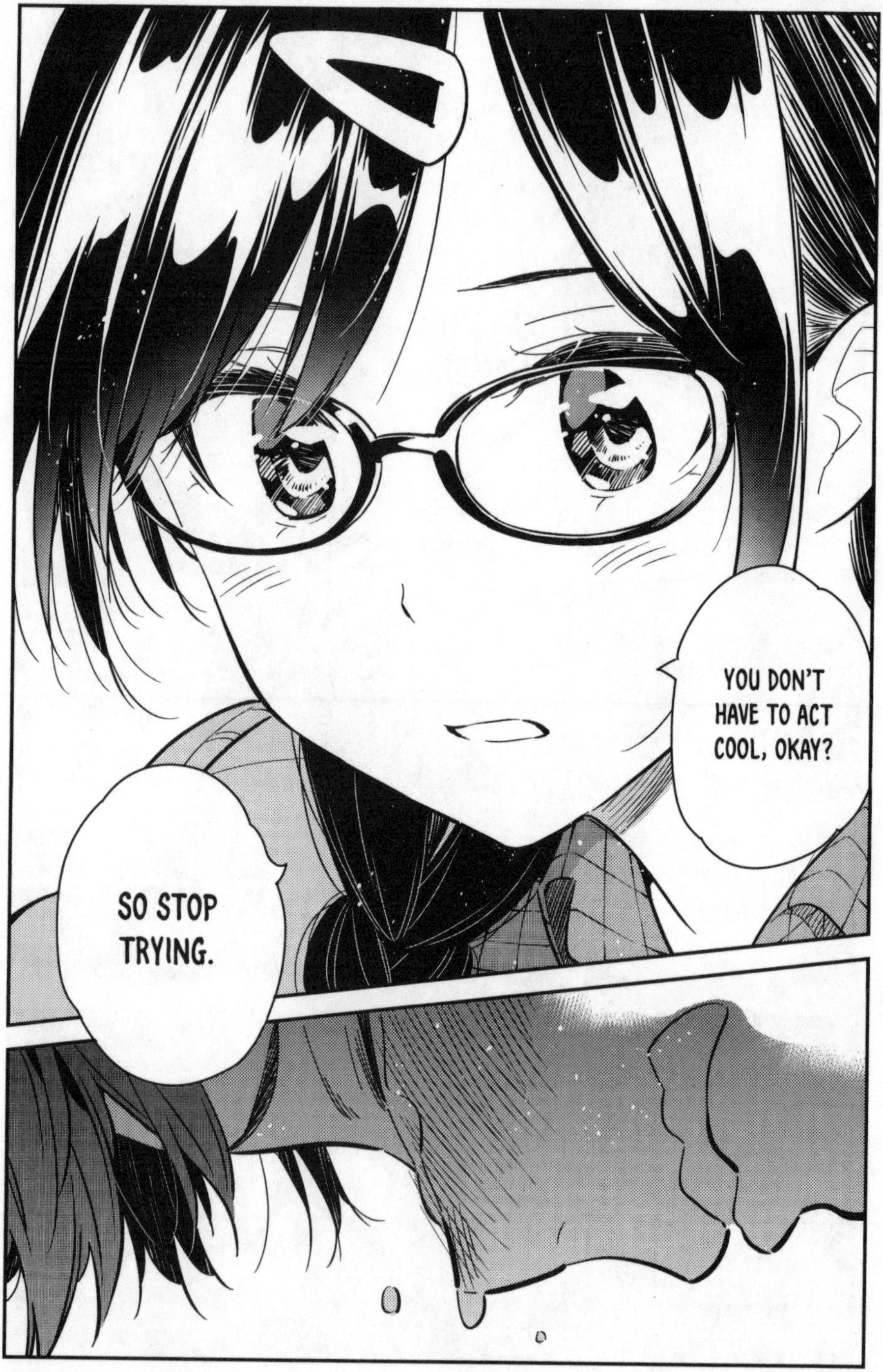
YOU DON'T HAVE TO ACT COOL, OKAY?
SO STOP TRYING.

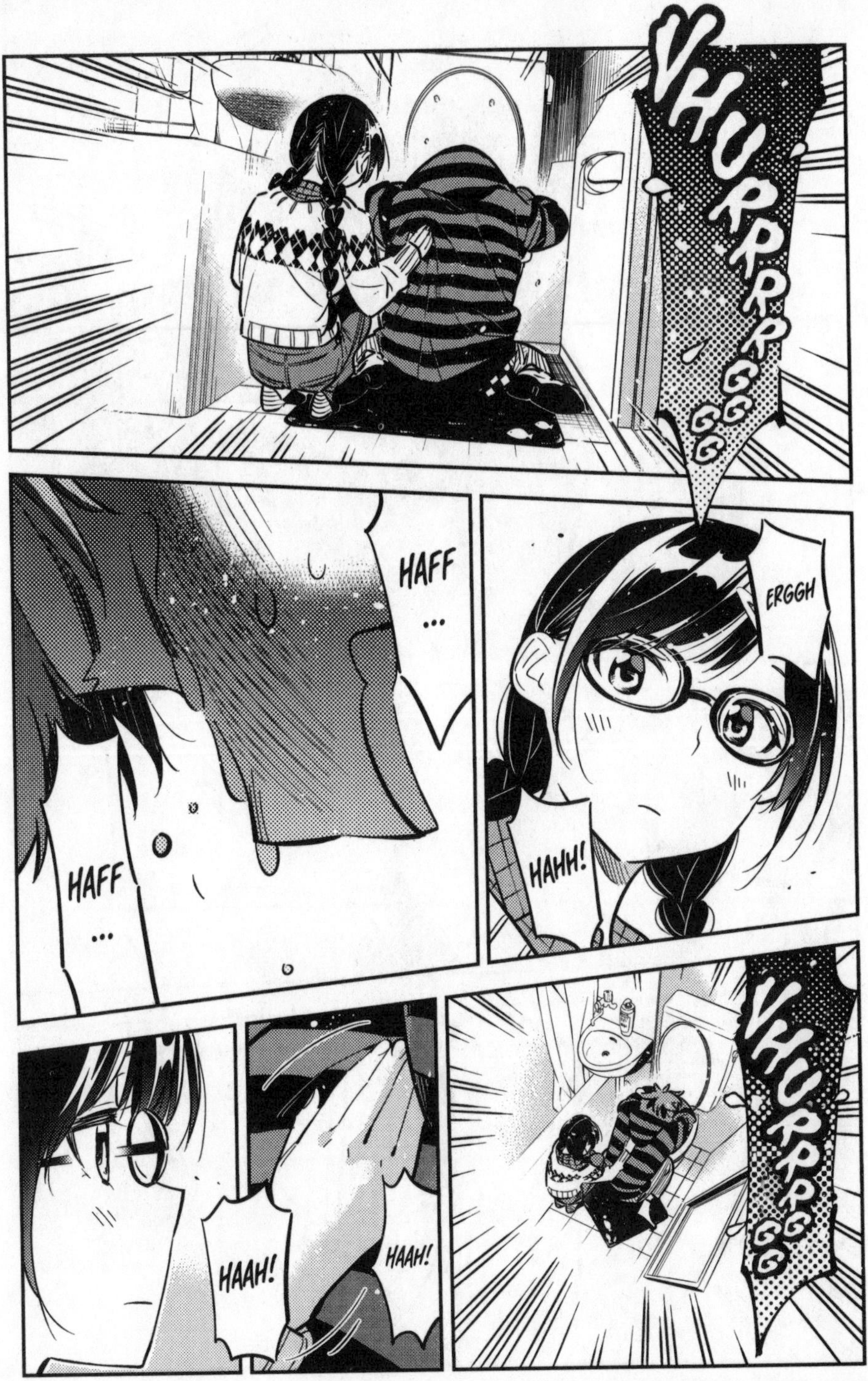
VHURRRRGGGG
ERGGH
HAHH!
HAFF...
HAFF...
VHURRRGG
HAAH!
HAAH!

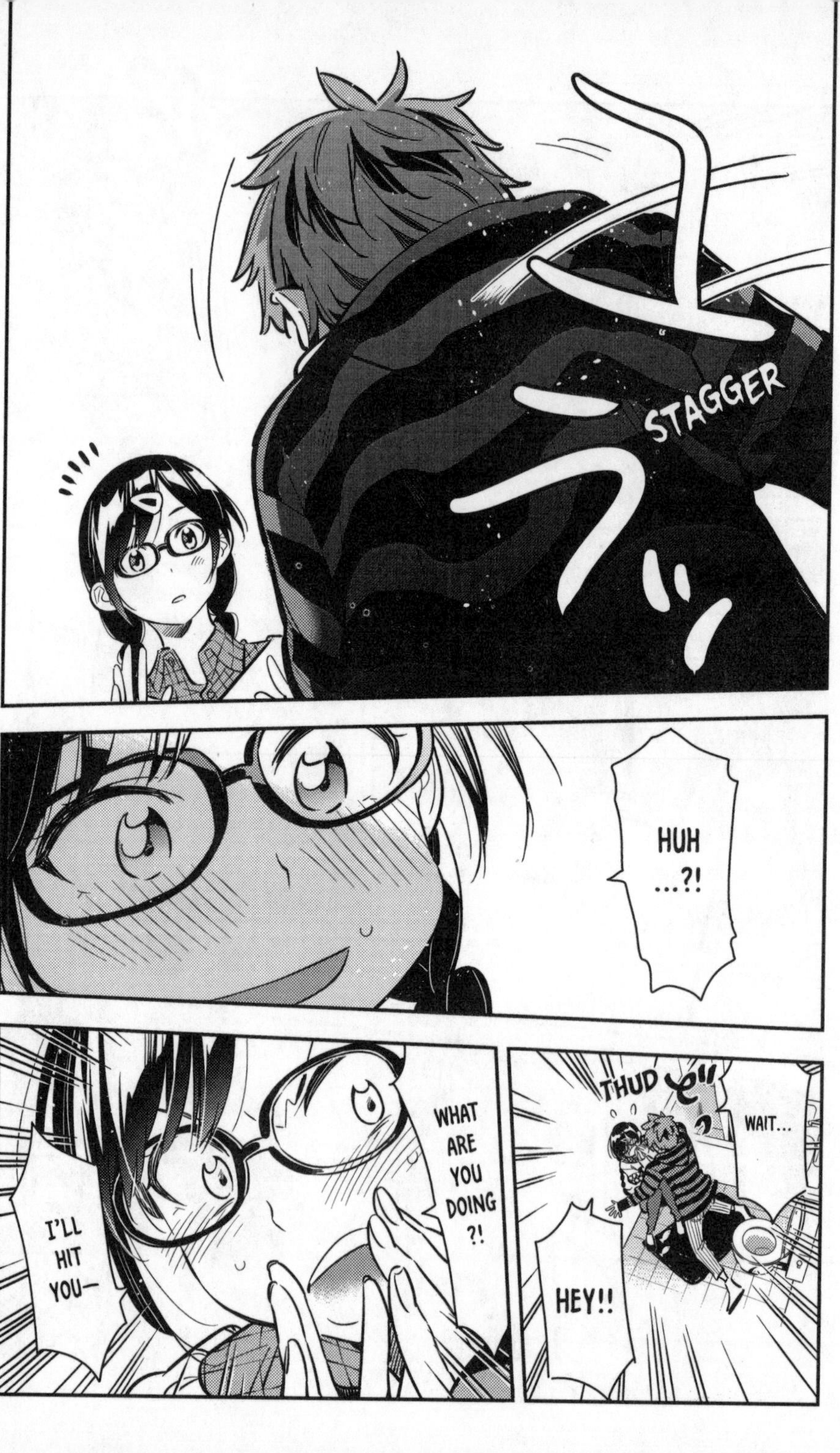
STAGGER
HUH ...?!
THUD
WAIT...
HEY!!
WHAT ARE YOU DOING ?!
I'LL HIT YOU—

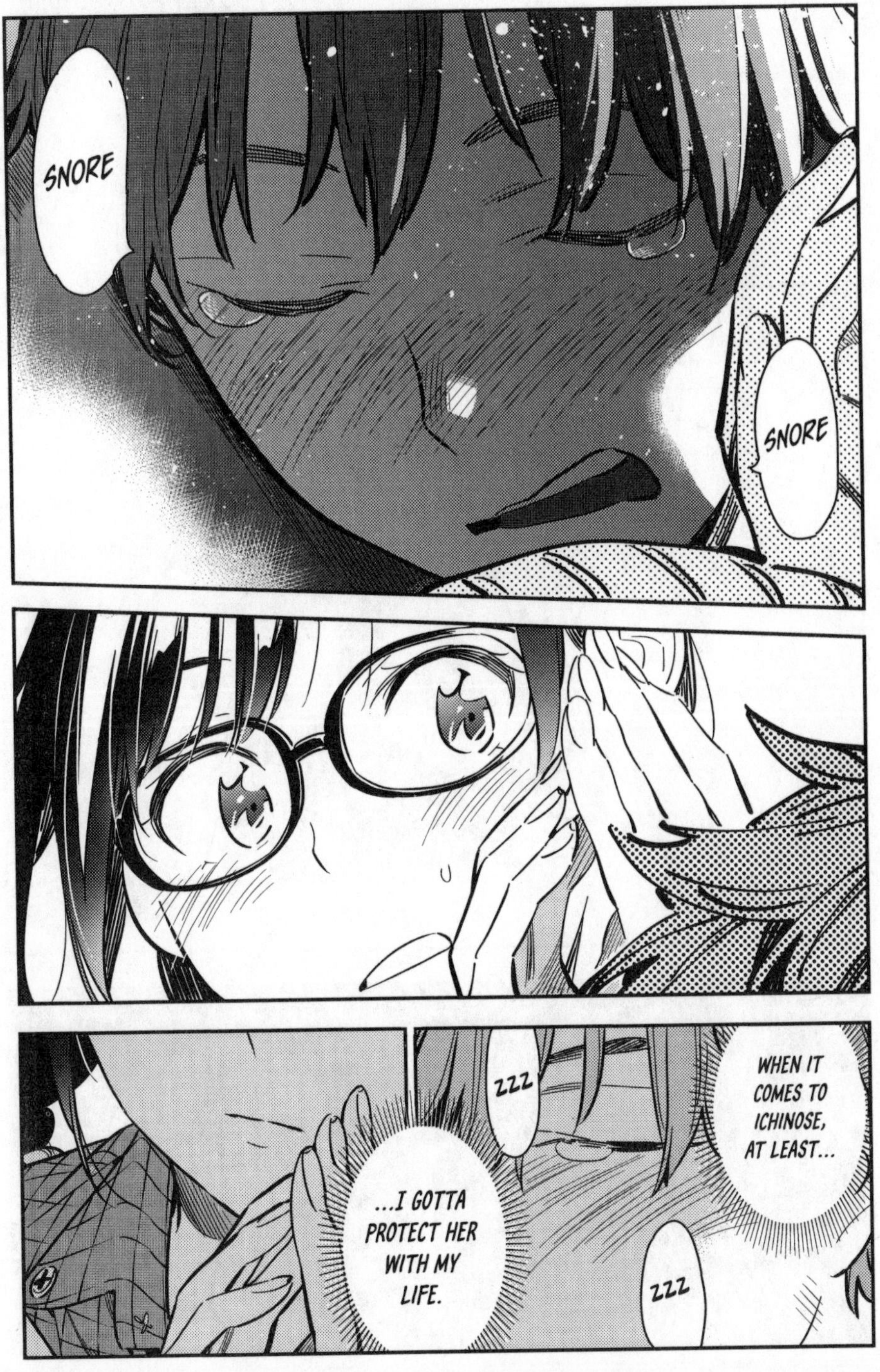
SNORE
SNORE
WHEN IT COMES TO ICHINOSE, AT LEAST...
ZZZ
...I GOTTA PROTECT HER WITH MY LIFE.
ZZZ

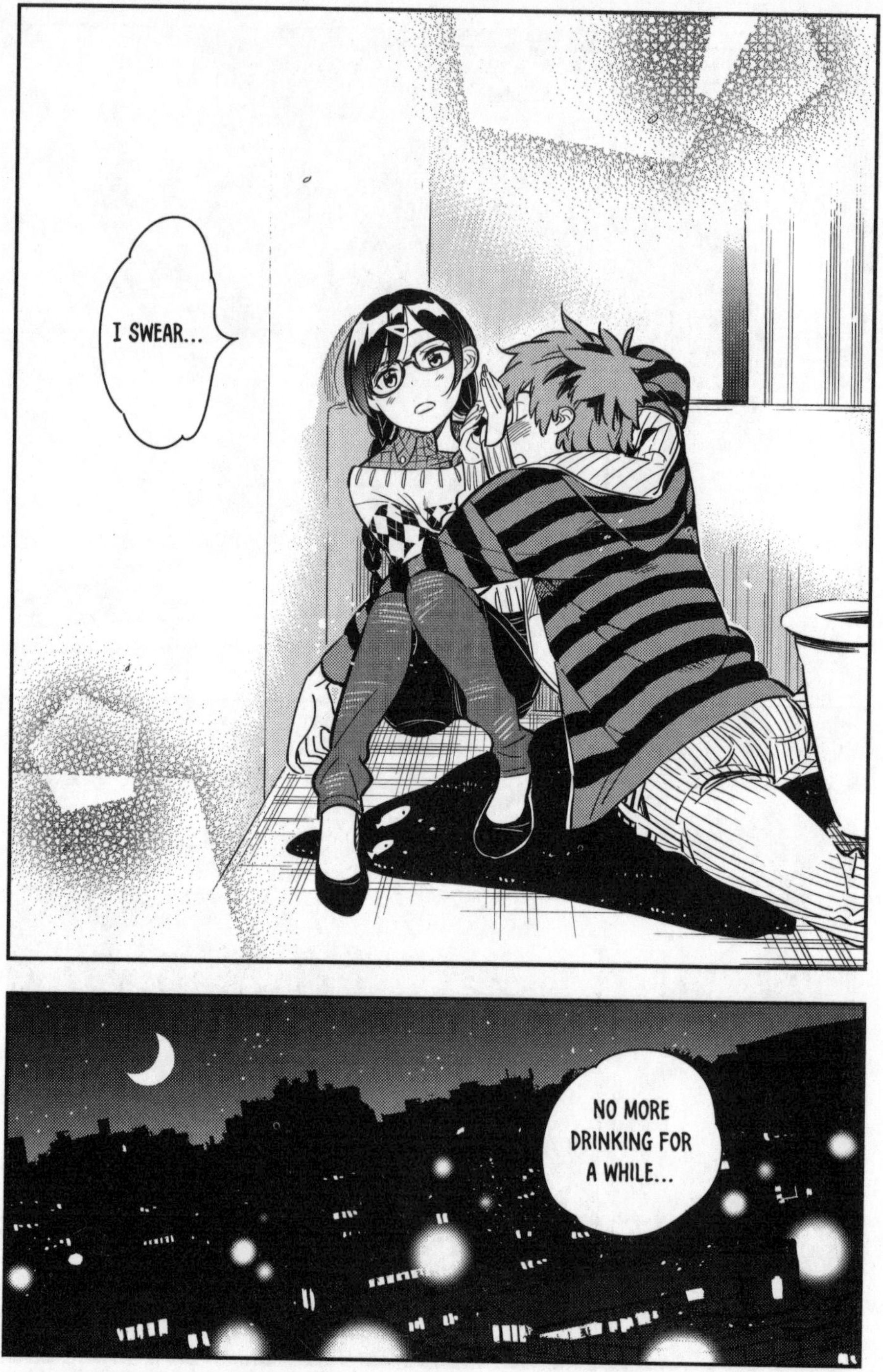
I SWEAR...
NO MORE DRINKING FOR A WHILE...

RATING 74 THE HANGOVER AND MY GIRLFRIEND

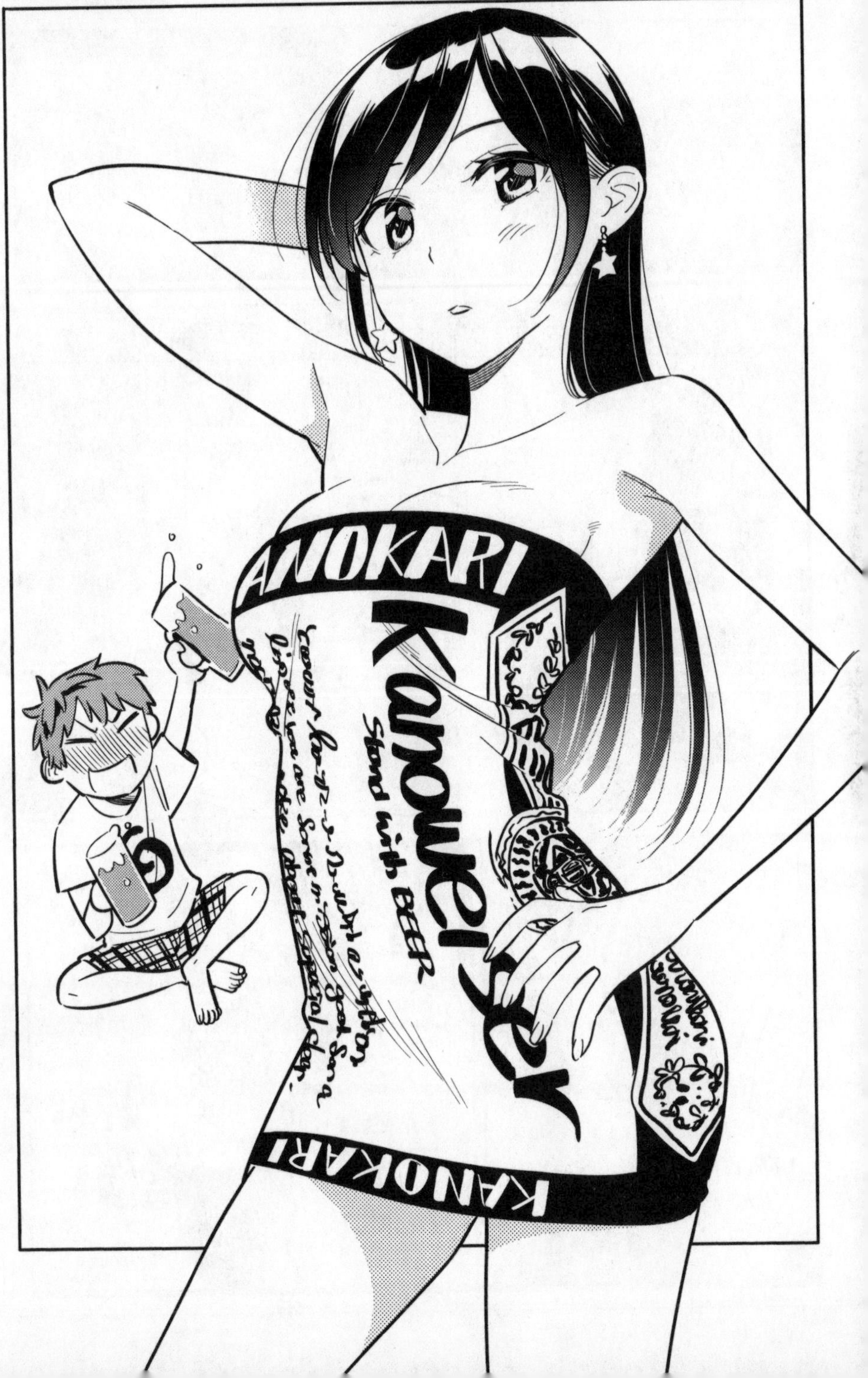
KANOKARI
Stand with BEER
KANOKARI

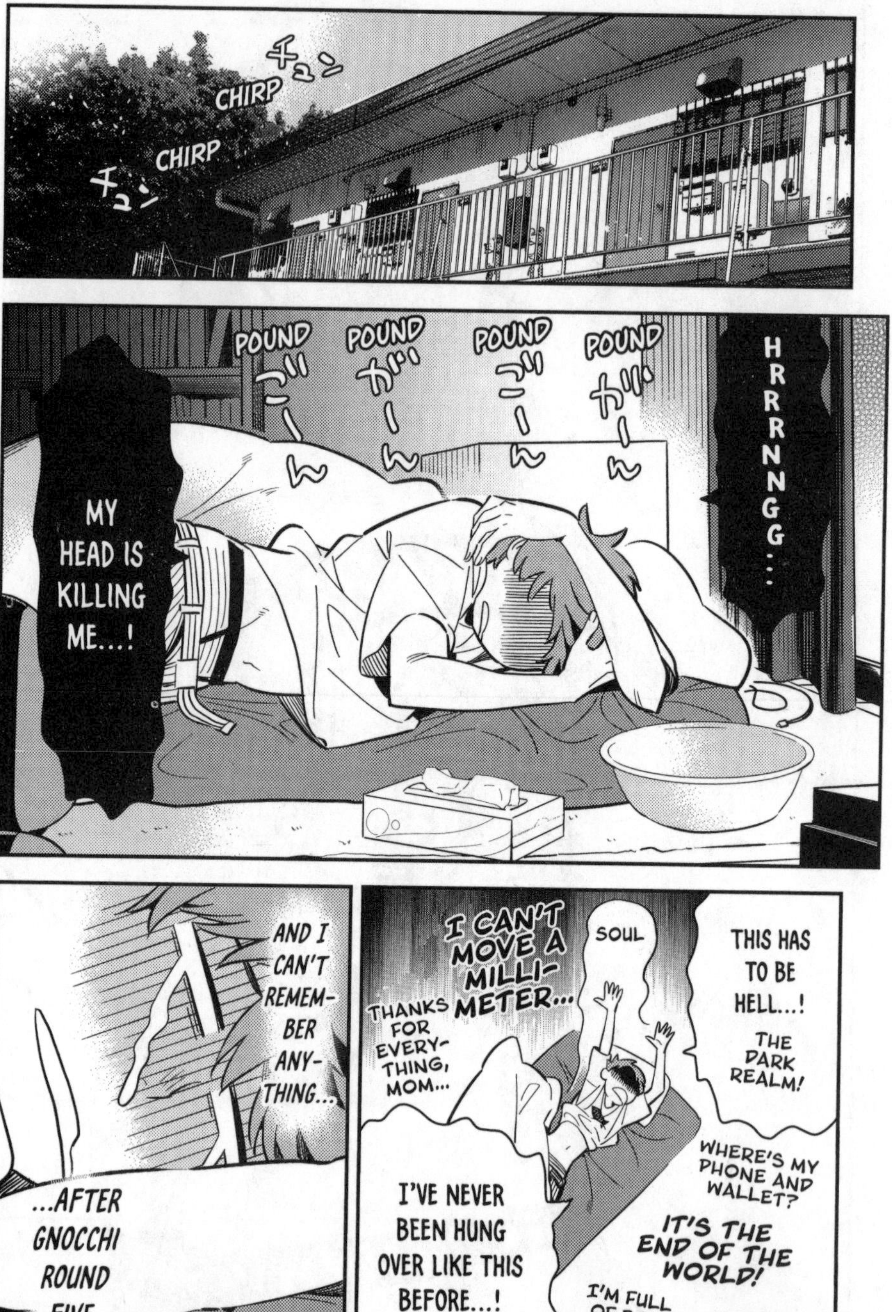
チュン
CHIRP
CHIRP
チュン
HRRRNNGG...
POUND がーん
POUND ごーん
POUND がーん
POUND ごーん
MY HEAD IS KILLING ME...!
THIS HAS TO BE HELL...!
THE DARK REALM!
SOUL
I CAN'T MOVE A MILLI-METER...
THANKS FOR EVERY-THING, MOM...
WHERE'S MY PHONE AND WALLET?
IT'S THE END OF THE WORLD!
I'VE NEVER BEEN HUNG OVER LIKE THIS BEFORE...!
I'M FULL OF BAD ENERGY
SMILE PRECURE REFERENCE
AND I CAN'T REMEM-BER ANY-THING...
...AFTER GNOCCHI ROUND FIVE.

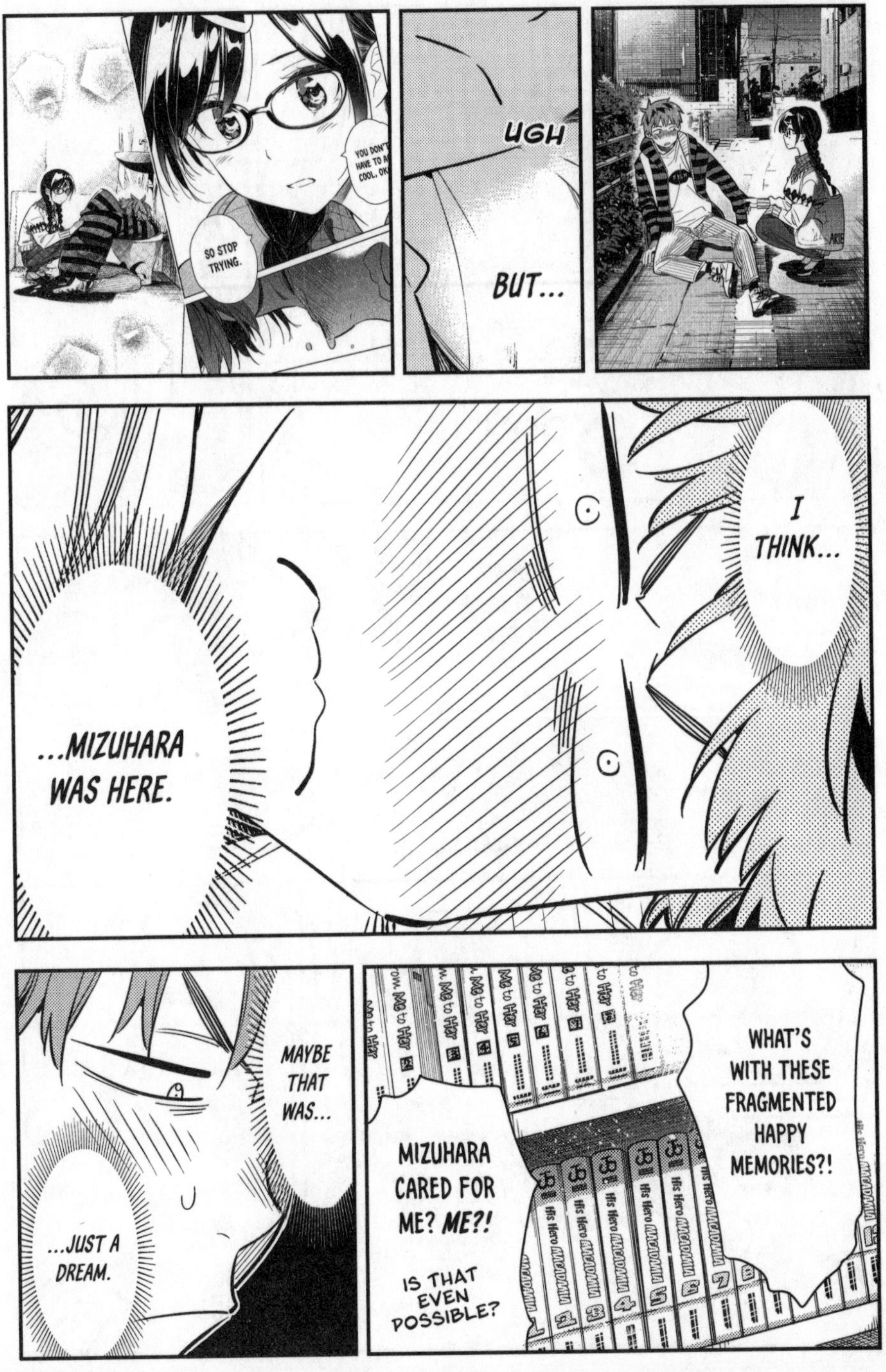
UGH
BUT...
YOU DON'T HAVE TO A COOL, OK
SO STOP TRYING.
I THINK...
...MIZUHARA WAS HERE.
WHAT'S WITH THESE FRAGMENTED HAPPY MEMORIES?!
MIZUHARA CARED FOR ME? *ME?!*
IS THAT EVEN POSSIBLE?
MAYBE THAT WAS...
...JUST A DREAM.

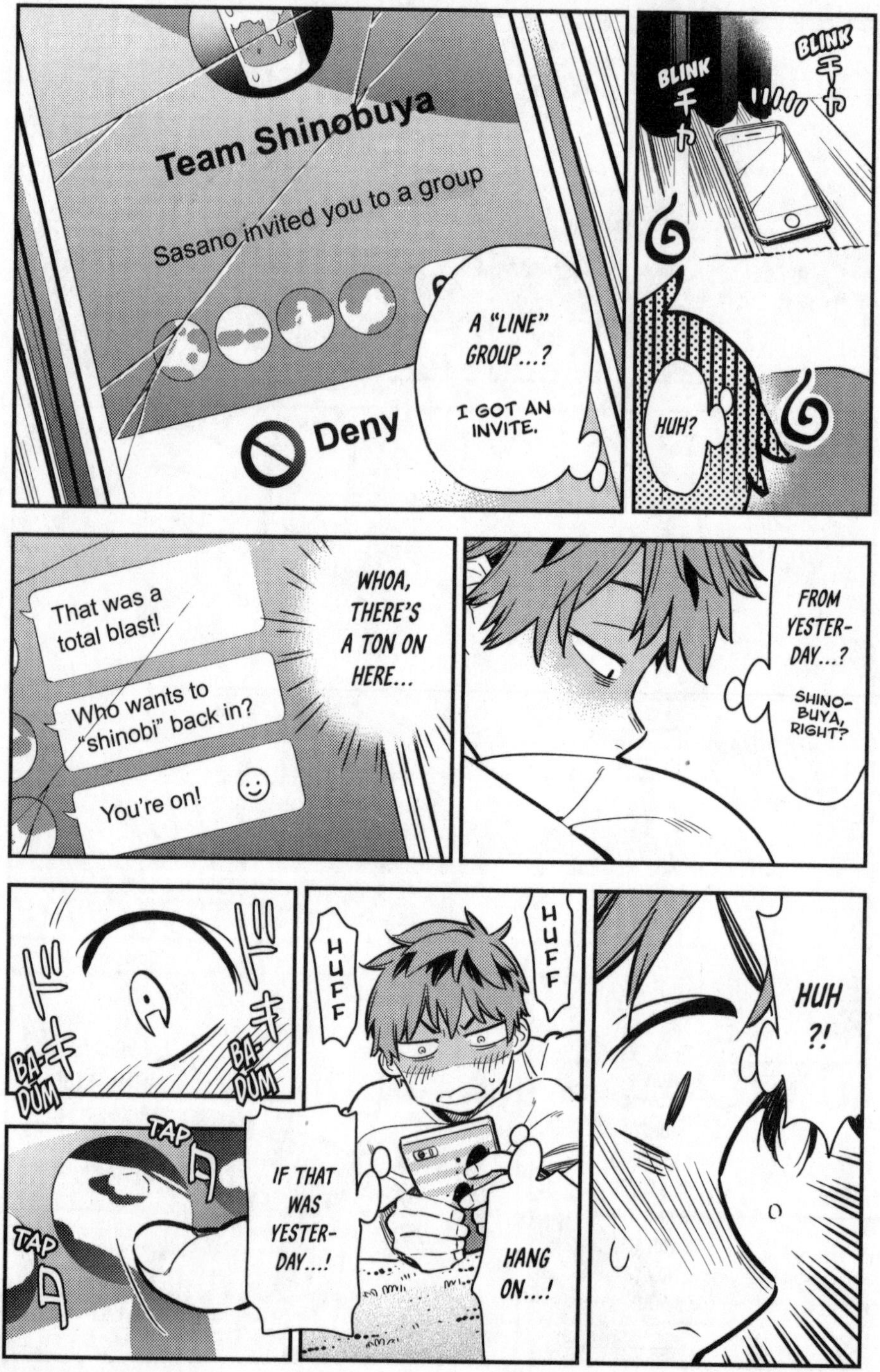
BLINK
BLINK
HUH?
Team Shinobuya
Sasano invited you to a group
Deny
A "LINE" GROUP...?
I GOT AN INVITE.
FROM YESTER-DAY...?
SHINOBUYA, RIGHT?
WHOA, THERE'S A TON ON HERE...
That was a total blast!
Who wants to "shinobi" back in?
You're on!
HUH ?!
HUFF
HUFF
IF THAT WAS YESTER-DAY...!
HANG ON...!
BA-DUM
BA-DUM
TAP
TAP

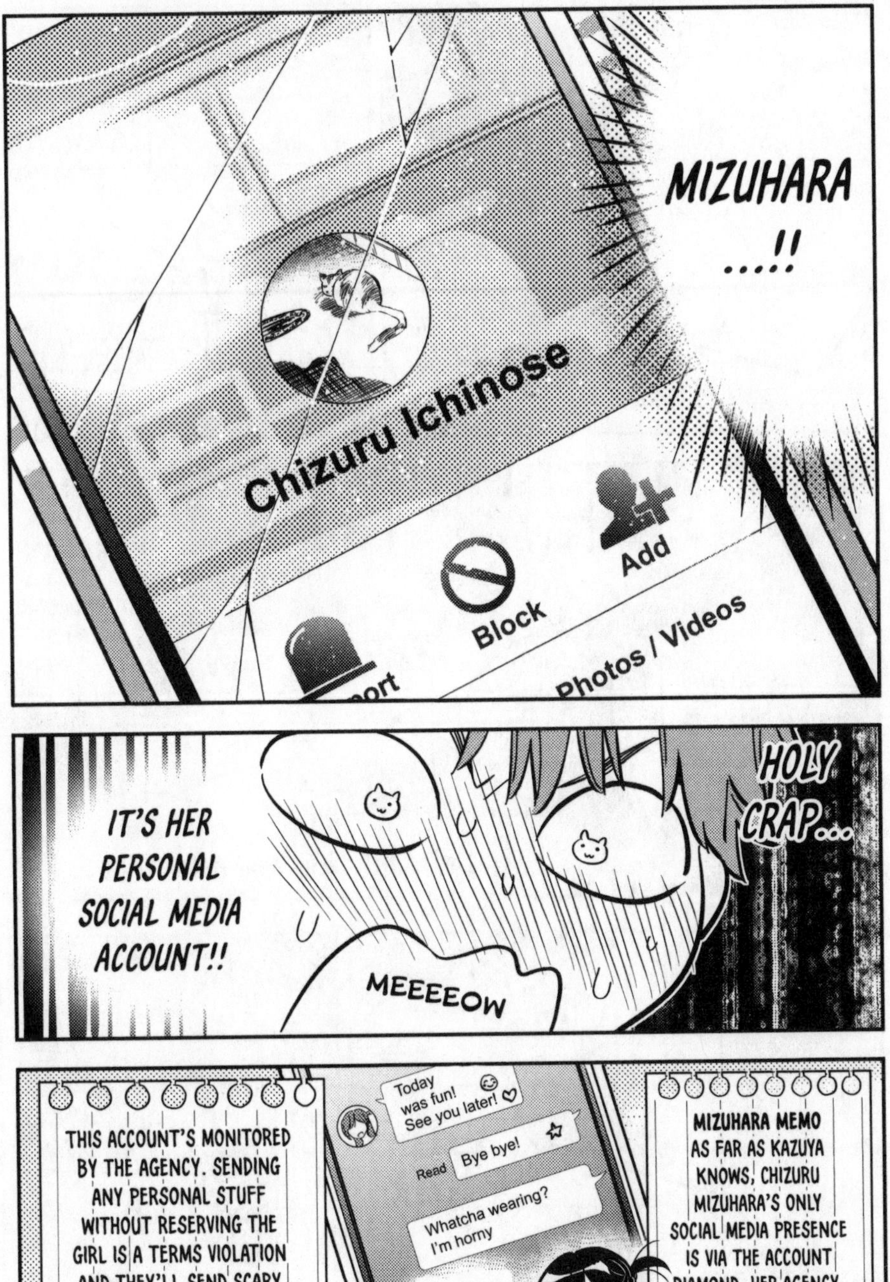
MIZUHARA ...!!
Chizuru Ichinose
Add
Block
Photos / Videos
HOLY CRAP...
MEEEEOW
IT'S HER PERSONAL SOCIAL MEDIA ACCOUNT!!
MIZUHARA MEMO
AS FAR AS KAZUYA KNOWS, CHIZURU MIZUHARA'S ONLY SOCIAL MEDIA PRESENCE IS VIA THE ACCOUNT DIAMOND, HER AGENCY, SET UP FOR HER.
Today was fun! See you later!
Read
Bye bye!
Whatcha wearing? I'm horny
YOU ALL BE CAREFUL, TOO!
THIS ACCOUNT'S MONITORED BY THE AGENCY. SENDING ANY PERSONAL STUFF WITHOUT RESERVING THE GIRL IS A TERMS VIOLATION AND THEY'LL SEND SCARY DUDES AFTER YOU!

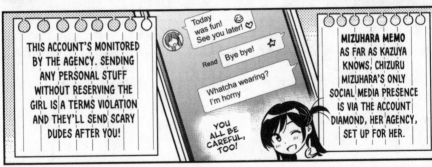

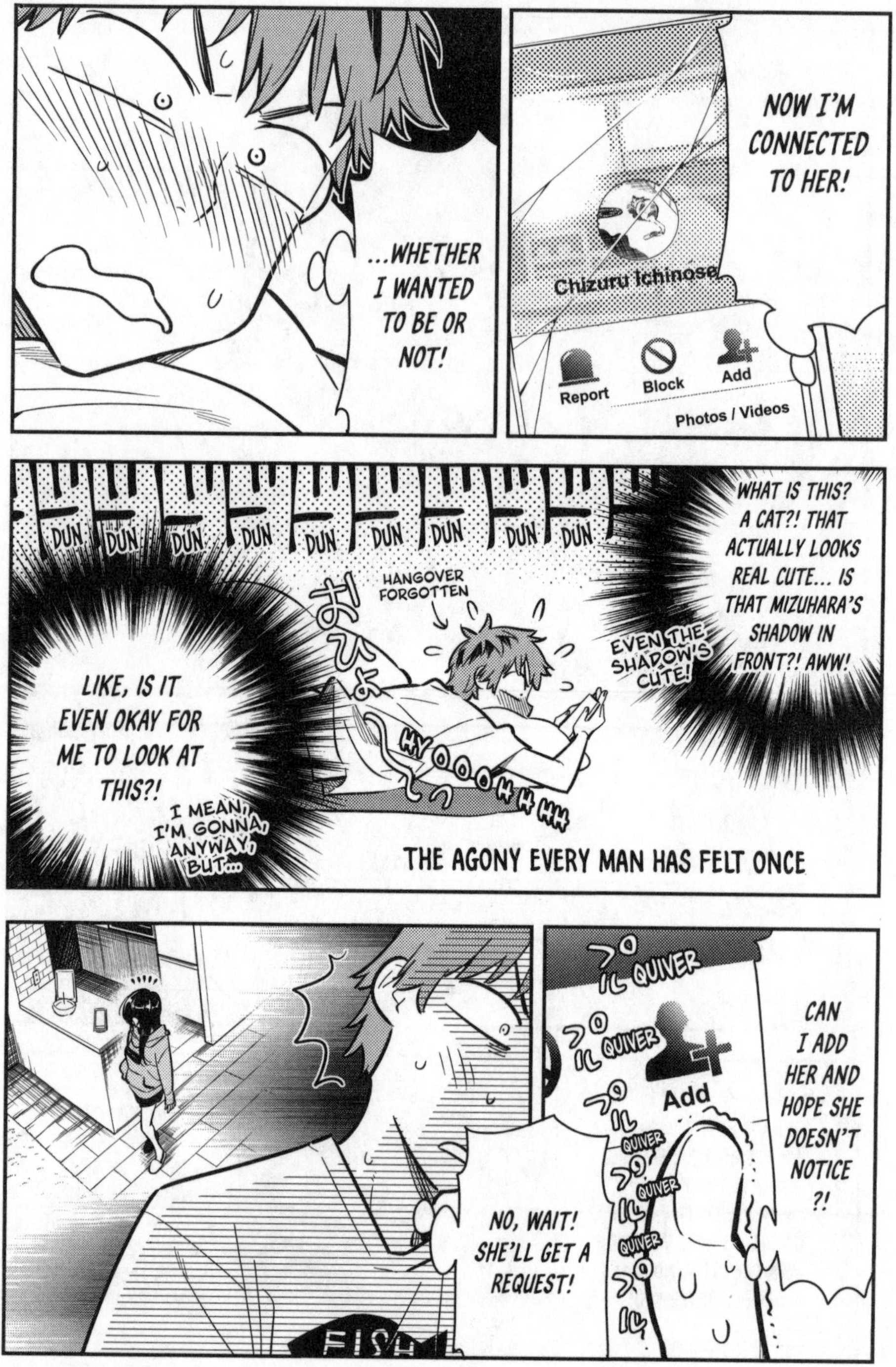
NOW I'M CONNECTED TO HER!
Chizuru Ichinose
Report
Block
Add
Photos / Videos
...WHETHER I WANTED TO BE OR NOT!
DUN DUN DUN DUN DUN DUN DUN DUN DUN
WHAT IS THIS? A CAT?! THAT ACTUALLY LOOKS REAL CUTE... IS THAT MIZUHARA'S SHADOW IN FRONT?! AWW!
EVEN THE SHADOW'S CUTE!
HANGOVER FORGOTTEN
HYOOOOHHHHH
LIKE, IS IT EVEN OKAY FOR ME TO LOOK AT THIS?!
I MEAN, I'M GONNA, ANYWAY, BUT...
THE AGONY EVERY MAN HAS FELT ONCE
QUIVER
QUIVER
Add
QUIVER
QUIVER
QUIVER
CAN I ADD HER AND HOPE SHE DOESN'T NOTICE ?!
NO, WAIT! SHE'LL GET A REQUEST!

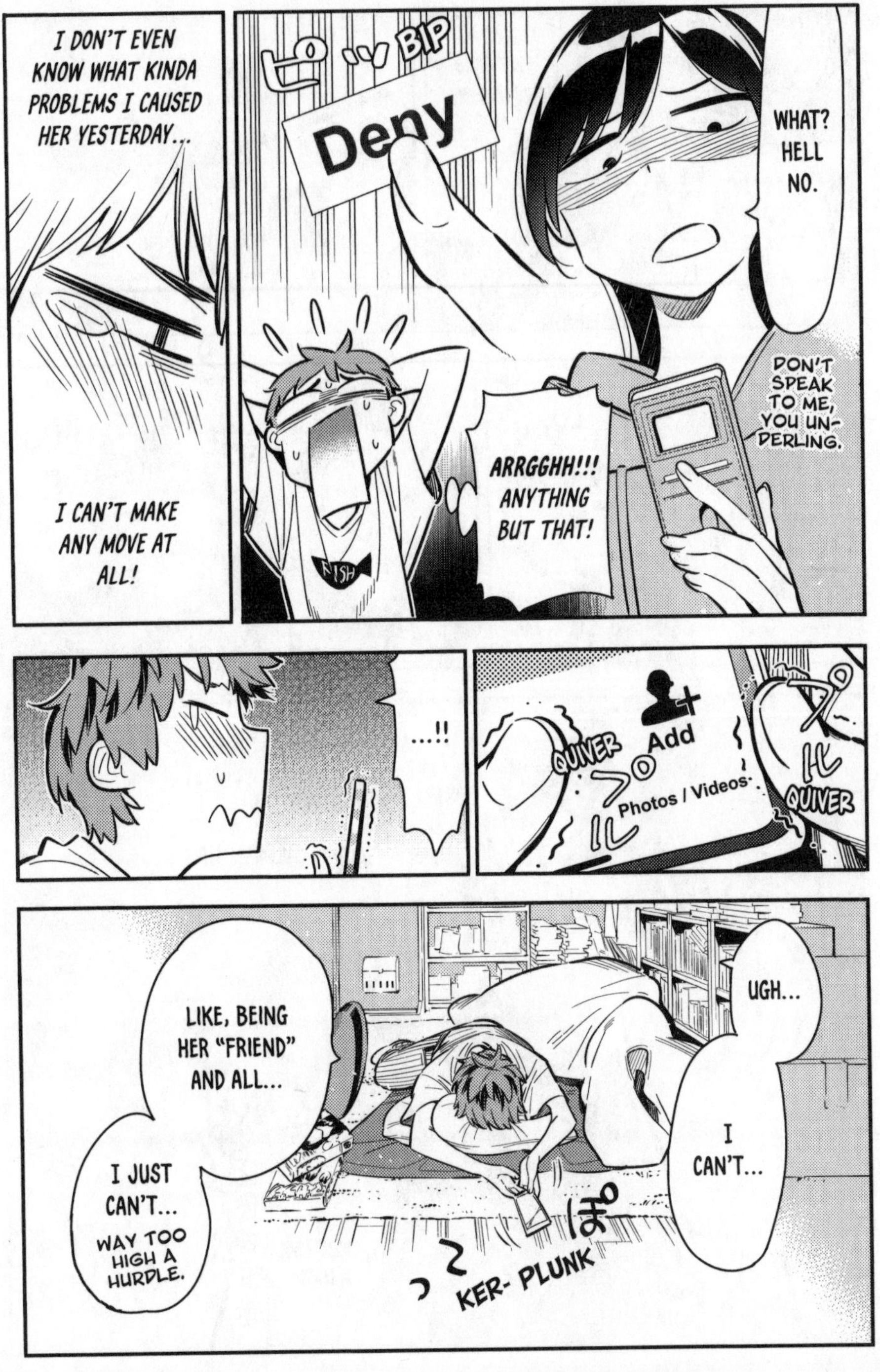
BIP
Deny
WHAT? HELL NO.
DON'T SPEAK TO ME, YOU UN-DERLING.
ARRGGHH!!! ANYTHING BUT THAT!
I DON'T EVEN KNOW WHAT KINDA PROBLEMS I CAUSED HER YESTERDAY...
I CAN'T MAKE ANY MOVE AT ALL!
Add
Photos / Videos
QUIVER
QUIVER
...!!
UGH...
I CAN'T...
LIKE, BEING HER "FRIEND" AND ALL...
I JUST CAN'T...
WAY TOO HIGH A HURDLE.
KER- PLUNK

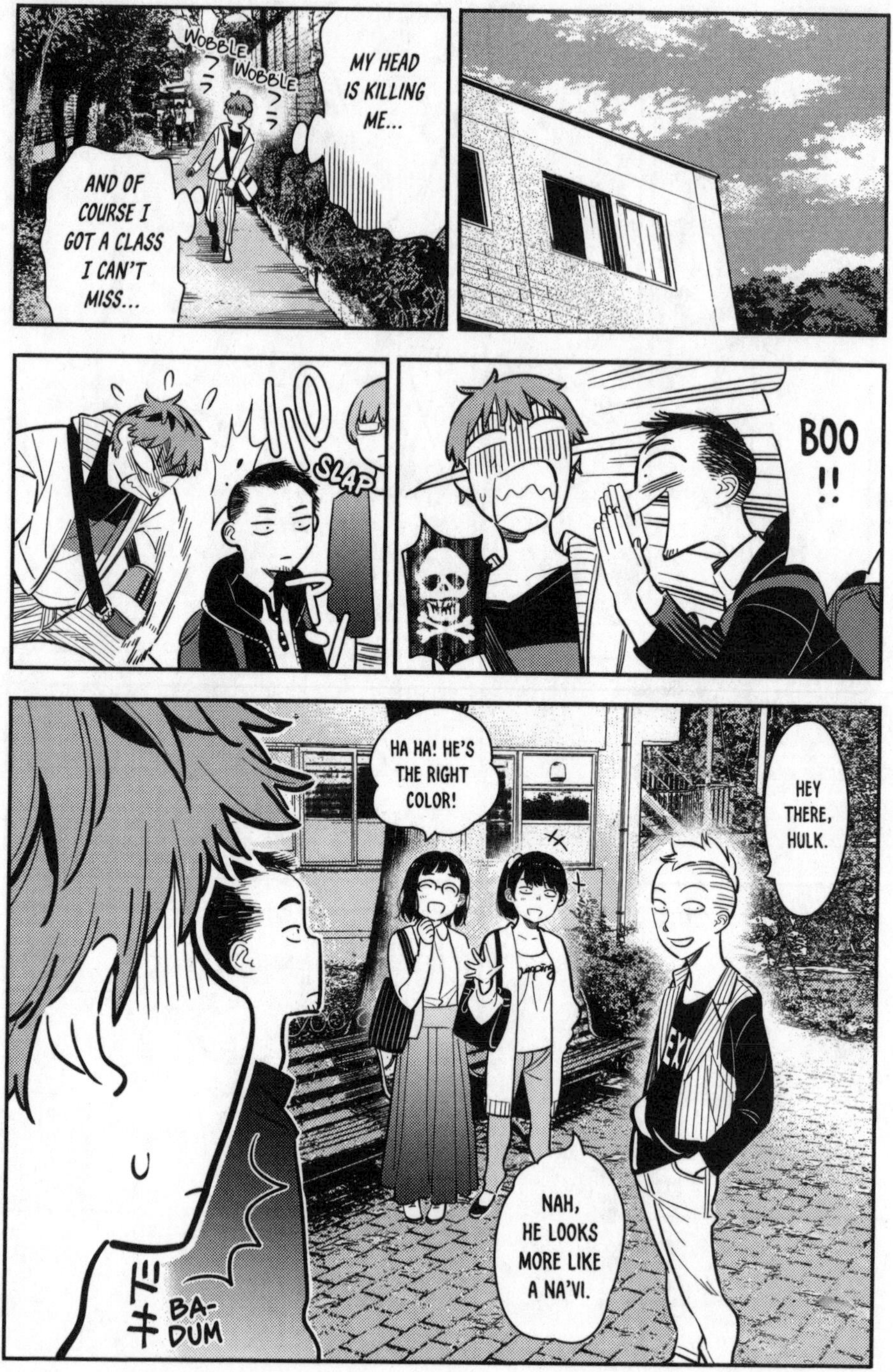
WOBBLE
フラ
WOBBLE
フラ
MY HEAD IS KILLING ME...
AND OF COURSE I GOT A CLASS I CAN'T MISS...
BOO !!
SLAP
HEY THERE, HULK.
HA HA! HE'S THE RIGHT COLOR!
NAH, HE LOOKS MORE LIKE A NA'VI.
ドキ
BA-DUM

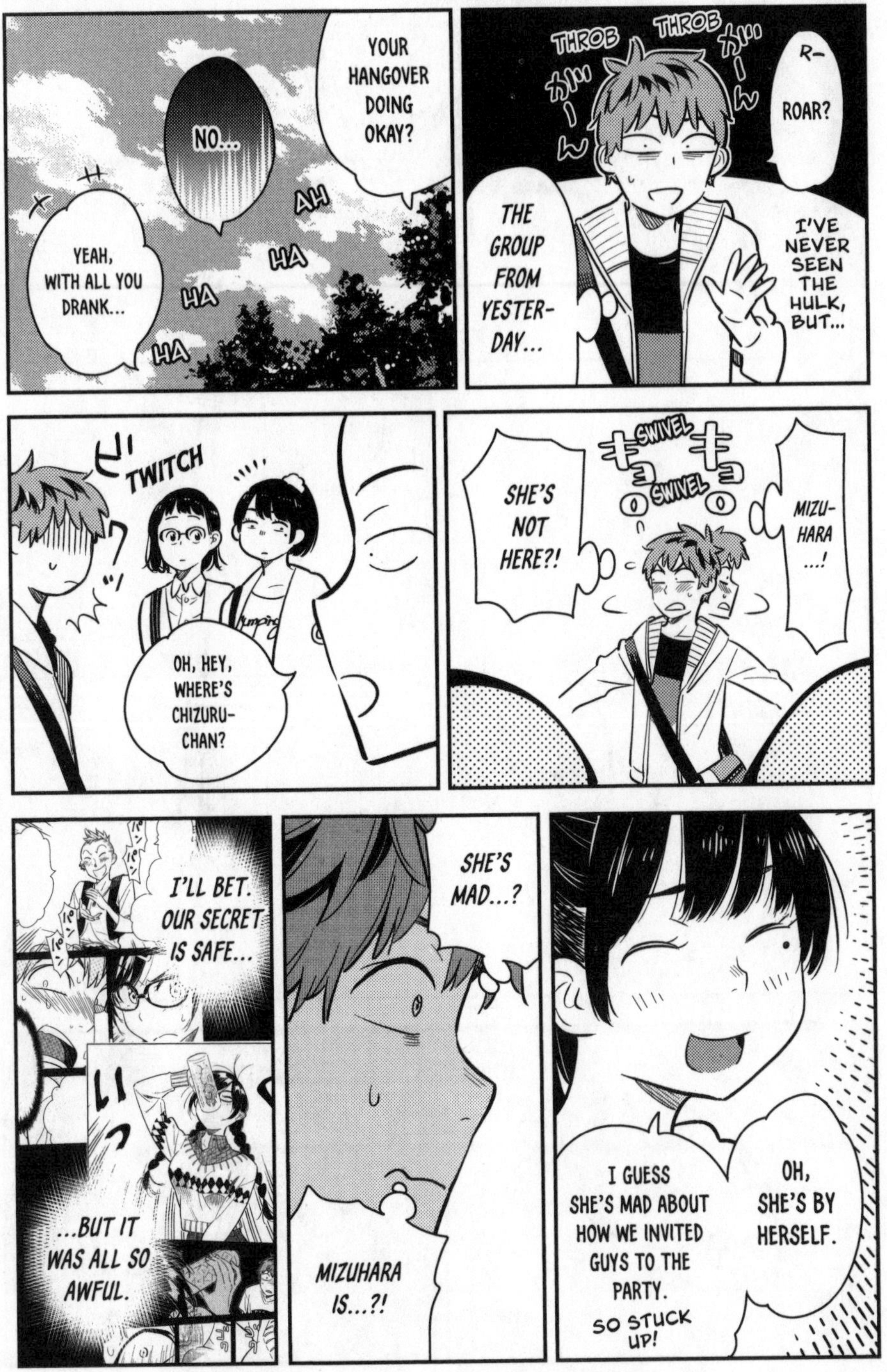
THROB THROB
R–
ROAR?
I'VE NEVER SEEN THE HULK, BUT...
THE GROUP FROM YESTER-DAY...
YOUR HANGOVER DOING OKAY?
NO...
AH HA HA HA
YEAH, WITH ALL YOU DRANK...
SWIVEL SWIVEL
MIZU-HARA ...!
SHE'S NOT HERE?!
TWITCH
OH, HEY, WHERE'S CHIZURU-CHAN?
OH, SHE'S BY HERSELF.
I GUESS SHE'S MAD ABOUT HOW WE INVITED GUYS TO THE PARTY.
SO STUCK UP!
SHE'S MAD...?
MIZUHARA IS...?!
I'LL BET. OUR SECRET IS SAFE...
...BUT IT WAS ALL SO AWFUL.

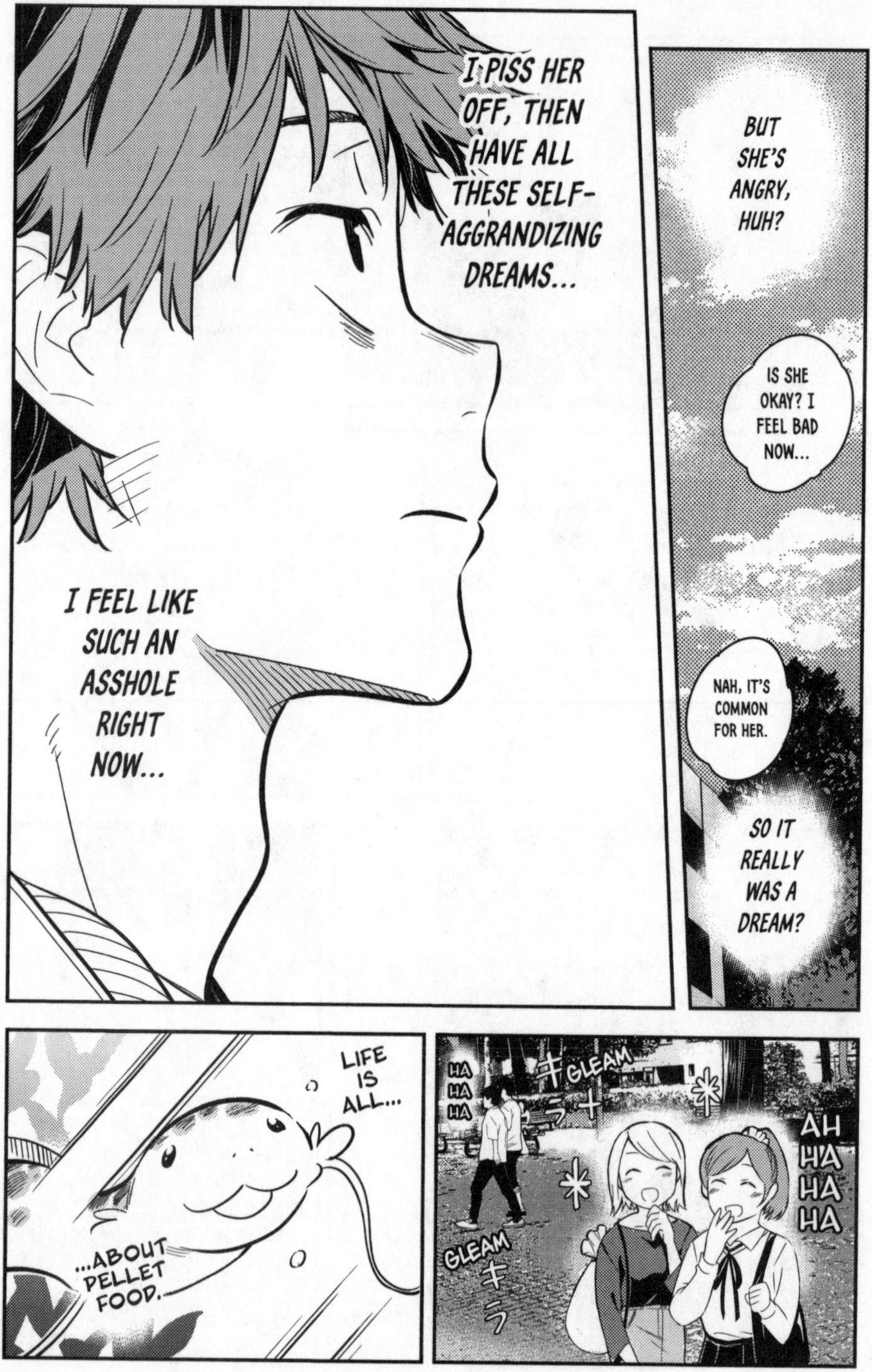
BUT SHE'S ANGRY, HUH?
IS SHE OKAY? I FEEL BAD NOW...
NAH, IT'S COMMON FOR HER.
SO IT REALLY WAS A DREAM?
I PISS HER OFF, THEN HAVE ALL THESE SELF-AGGRANDIZING DREAMS...
I FEEL LIKE SUCH AN ASSHOLE RIGHT NOW...
AH HA HA HA HA
GLEAM
HA HA HA
GLEAM
LIFE IS ALL...
...ABOUT PELLET FOOD.

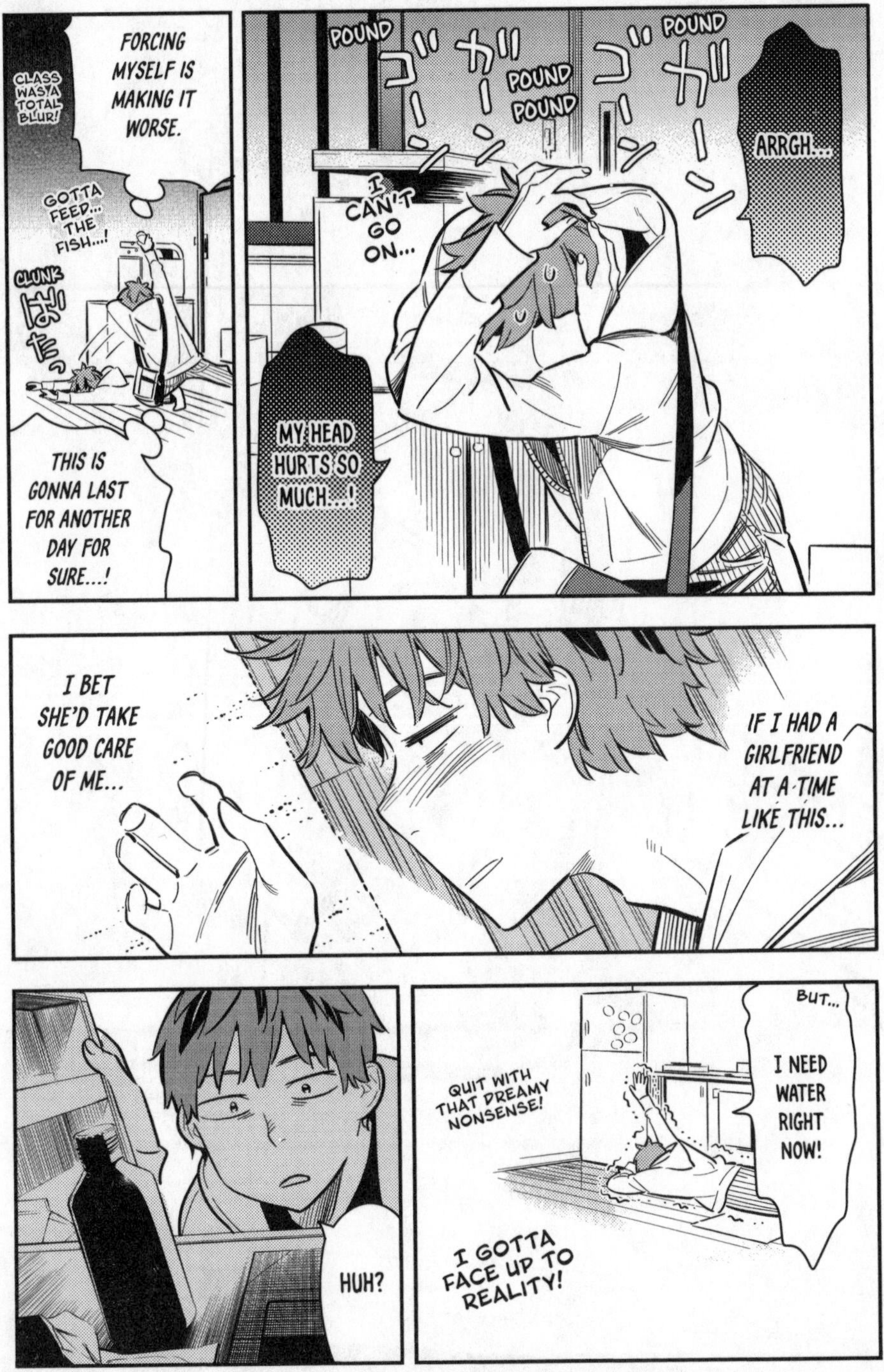

POUND
ゴガーン
POUND POUND
POUND
ゴガーン
ARRGH...
I CAN'T GO ON...
MY HEAD HURTS SO MUCH...!
FORCING MYSELF IS MAKING IT WORSE.
CLASS WAS A TOTAL BLUR!
GOTTA FEED... THE FISH...!
CLUNK
ばたっ
THIS IS GONNA LAST FOR ANOTHER DAY FOR SURE...!
IF I HAD A GIRLFRIEND AT A TIME LIKE THIS...
I BET SHE'D TAKE GOOD CARE OF ME...
BUT...
I NEED WATER RIGHT NOW!
QUIT WITH THAT DREAMY NONSENSE!
I GOTTA FACE UP TO REALITY!
HUH?

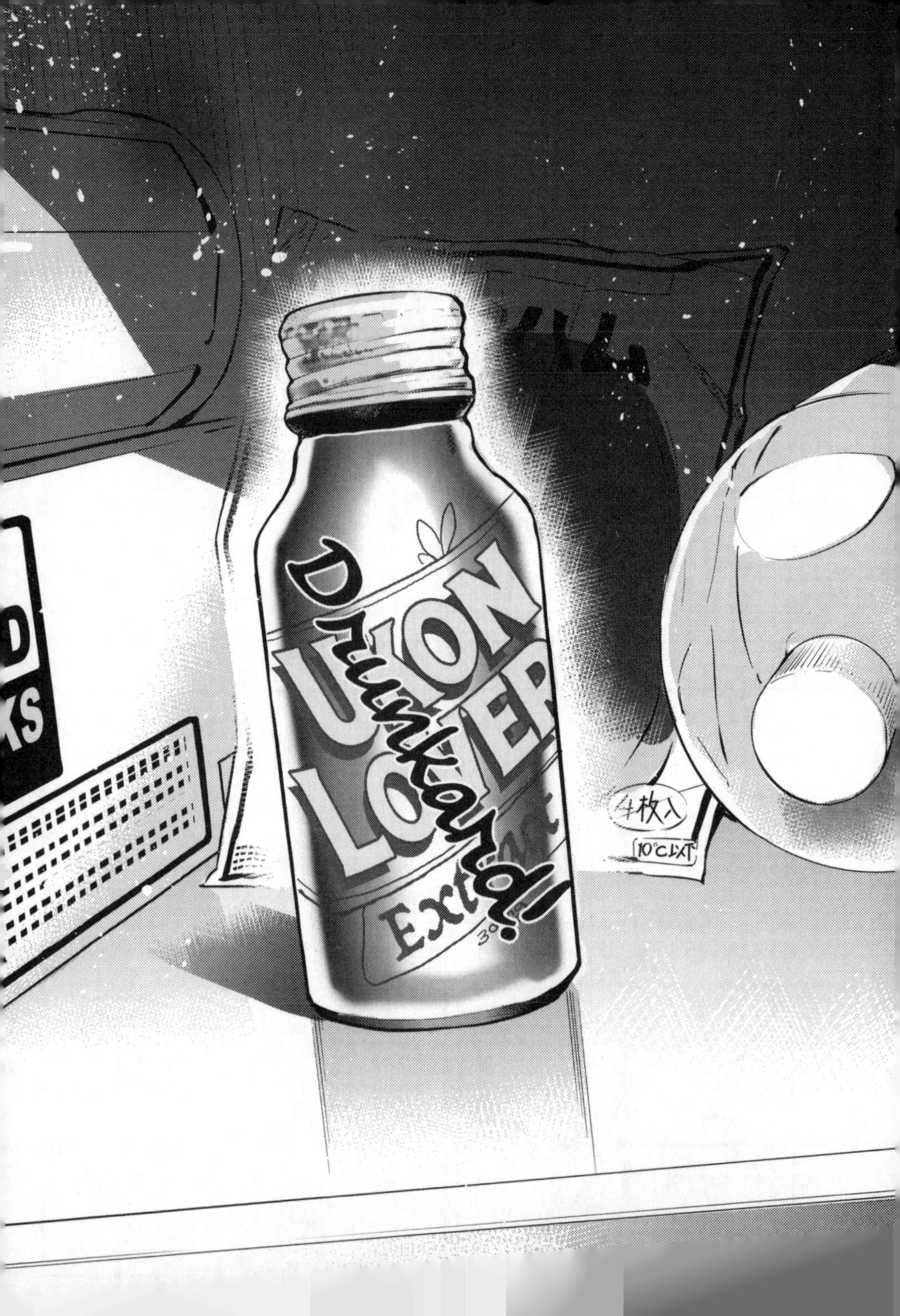

Drunkard!
4枚入
10℃以下

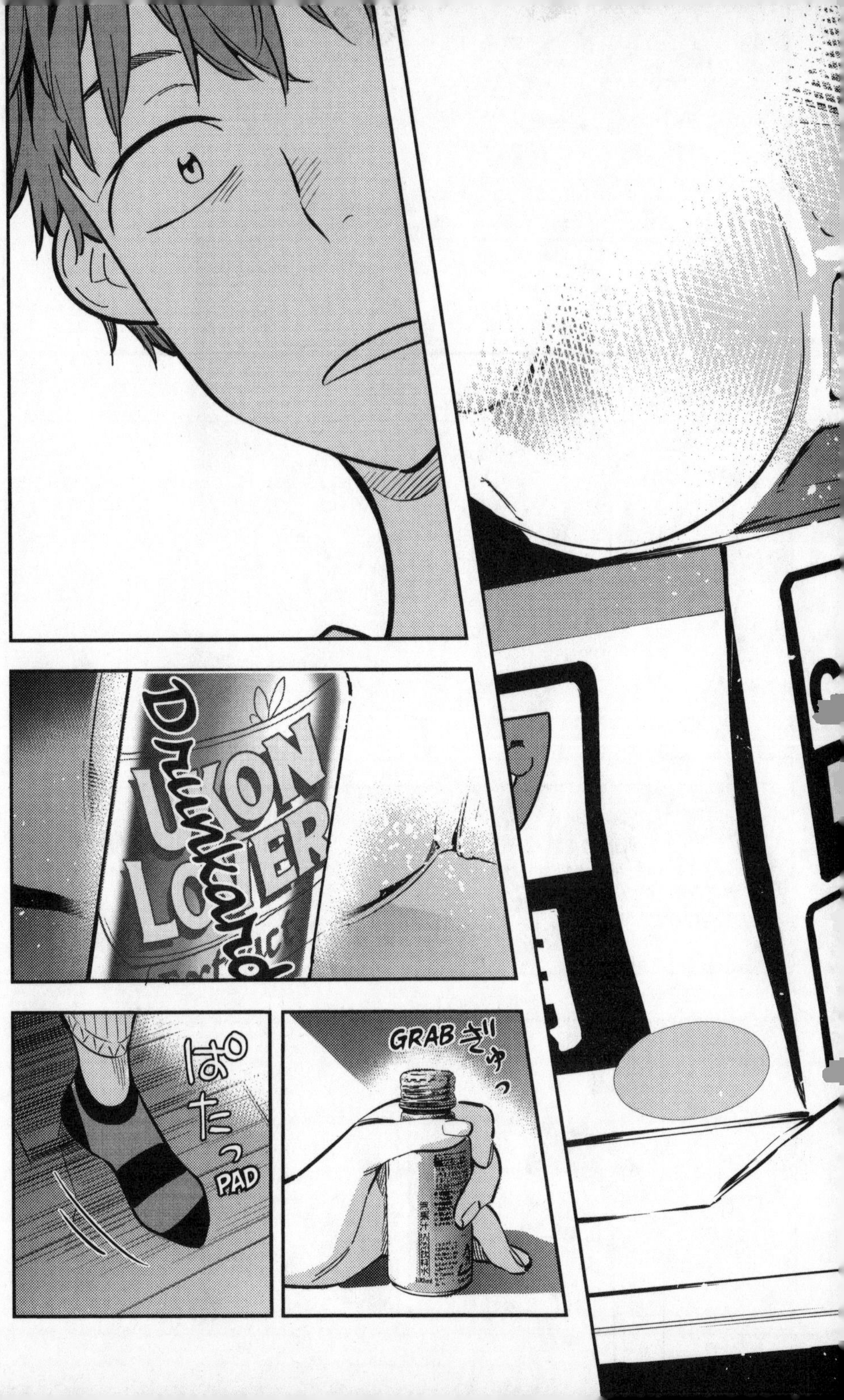
GRAB ぎゅっ
ぱたっ
PAD

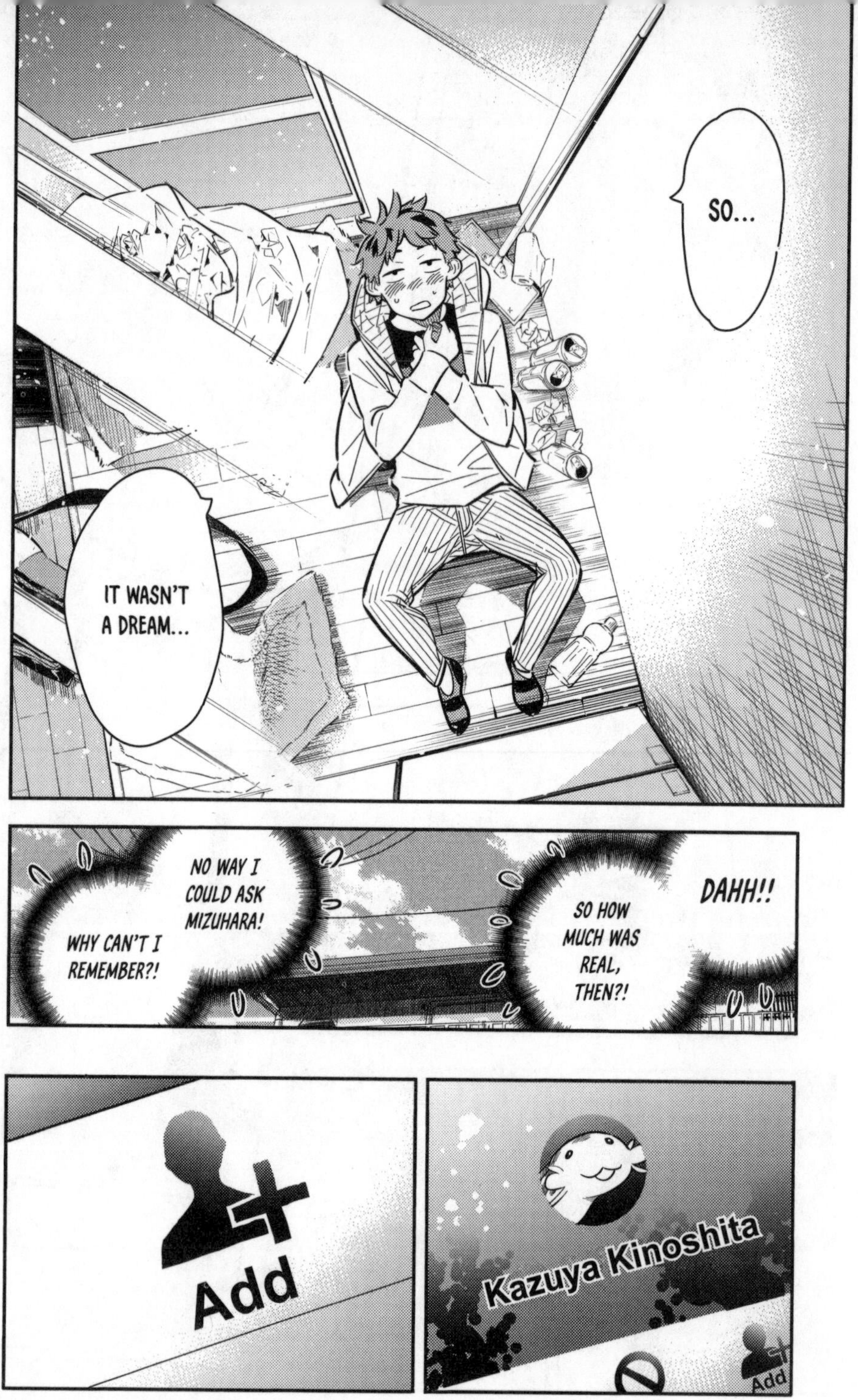
SO...
IT WASN'T A DREAM...
DAHH!!
SO HOW MUCH WAS REAL, THEN?!
NO WAY I COULD ASK MIZUHARA!
WHY CAN'T I REMEMBER?!
Kazuya Kinoshita
Add
Add

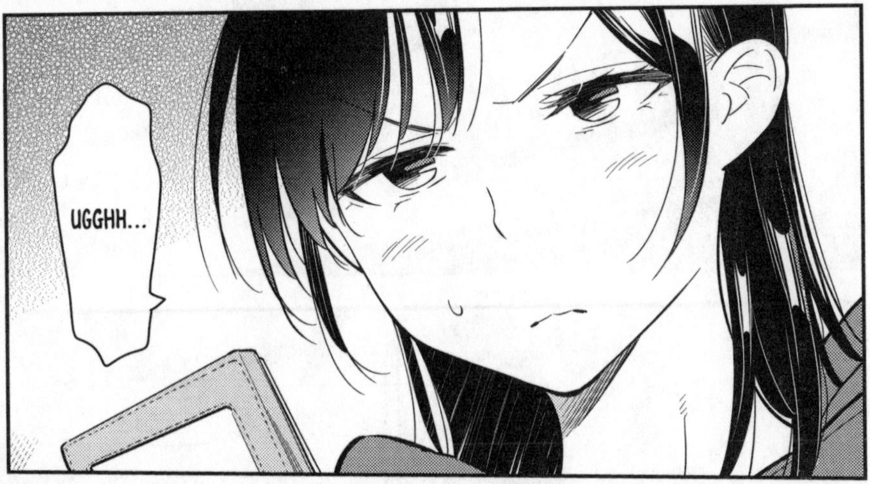
UGGHH...

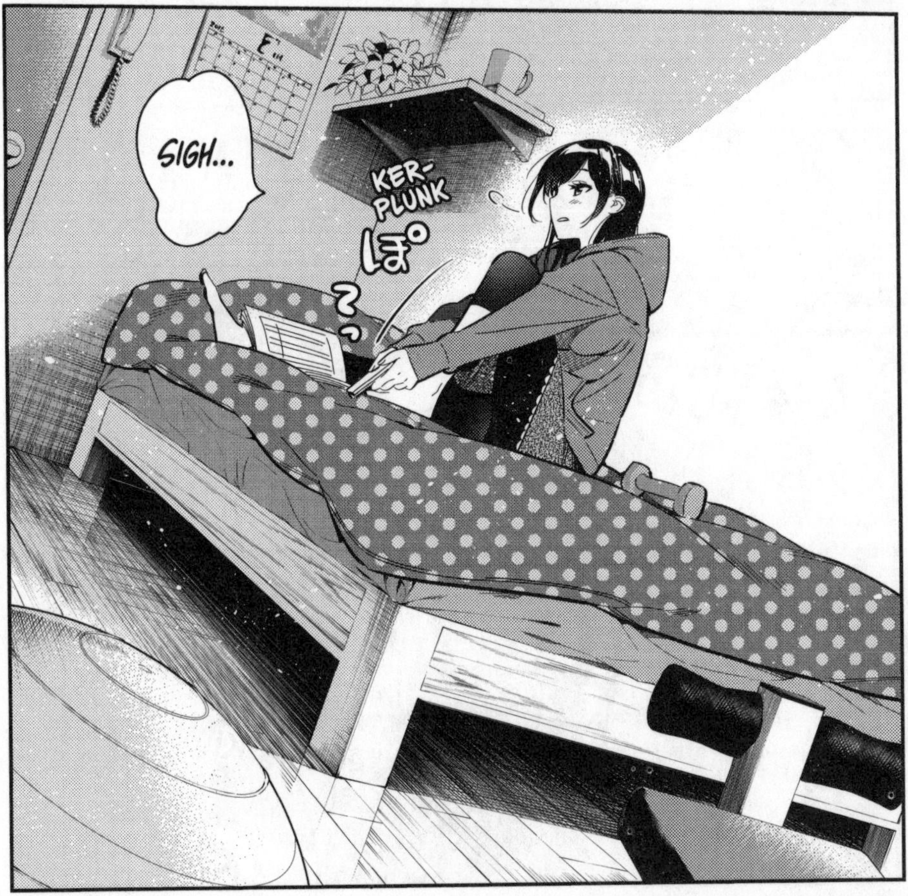
KER-
PLUNK
ぽっ
SIGH...

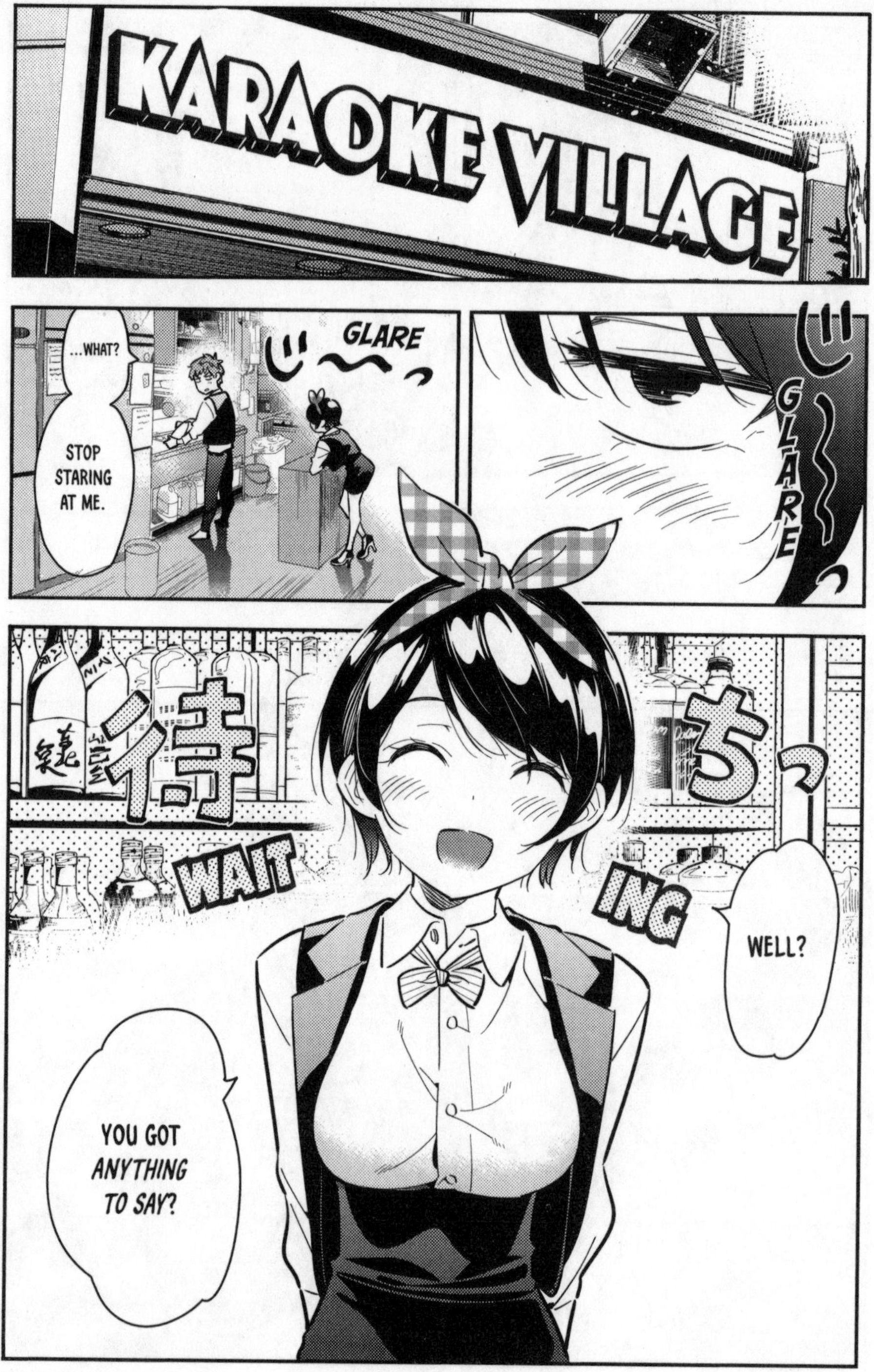
KARAOKE VILLAGE
じ〜っ
GLARE
じ〜っ
GLARE
...WHAT?
STOP STARING AT ME.
待ちっ
WAIT
ING
WELL?
YOU GOT *ANYTHING* TO SAY?

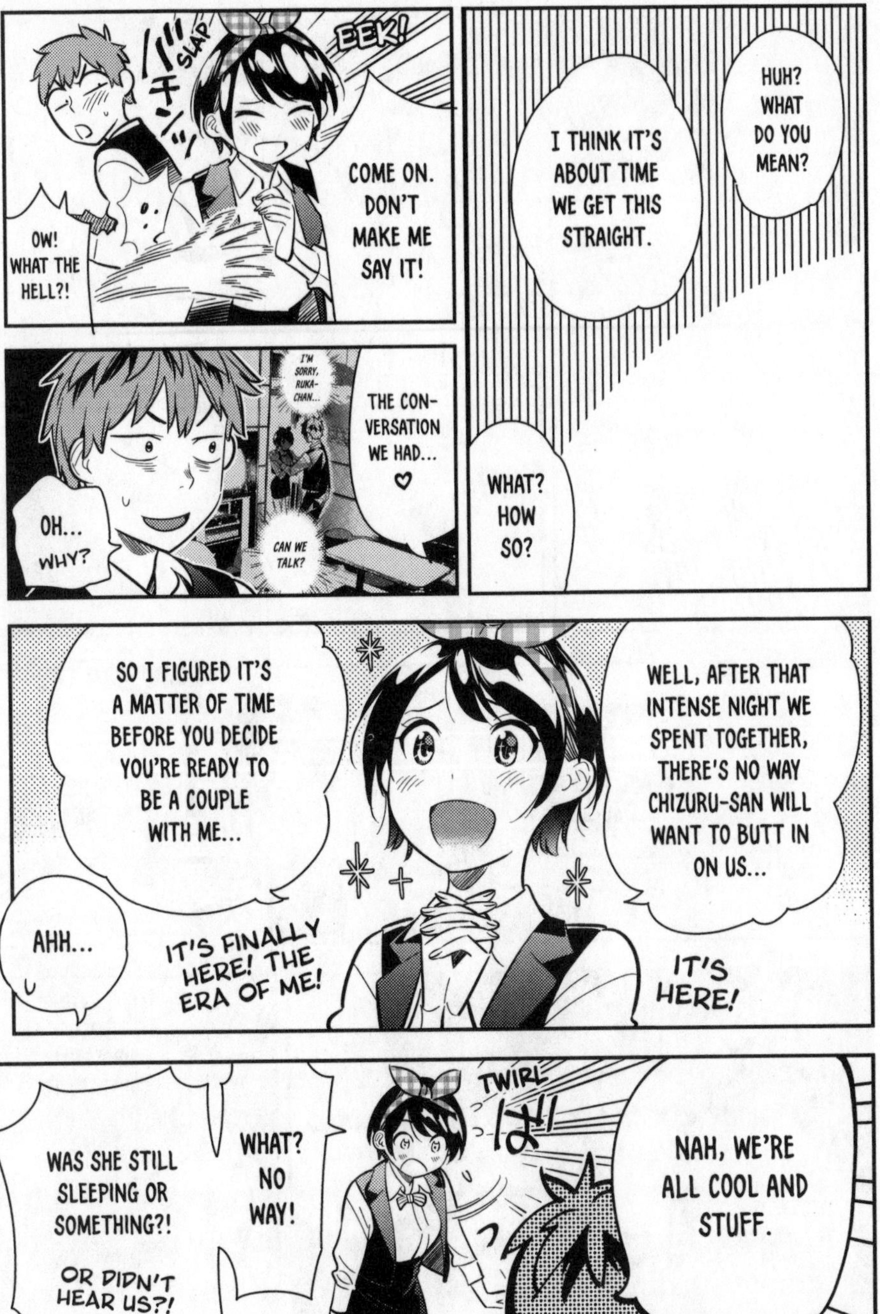
HUH? WHAT DO YOU MEAN?
I THINK IT'S ABOUT TIME WE GET THIS STRAIGHT.
WHAT? HOW SO?
EEK!
SLAP
COME ON. DON'T MAKE ME SAY IT!
OW! WHAT THE HELL?!
THE CON-VERSATION WE HAD... ♡
I'M SORRY, RUKA-CHAN...
CAN WE TALK?
OH... WHY?
WELL, AFTER THAT INTENSE NIGHT WE SPENT TOGETHER, THERE'S NO WAY CHIZURU-SAN WILL WANT TO BUTT IN ON US...
IT'S HERE!
SO I FIGURED IT'S A MATTER OF TIME BEFORE YOU DECIDE YOU'RE READY TO BE A COUPLE WITH ME...
IT'S FINALLY HERE! THE ERA OF ME!
AHH...
NAH, WE'RE ALL COOL AND STUFF.
TWIRL
WHAT? NO WAY!
WAS SHE STILL SLEEPING OR SOMETHING?!
OR DIDN'T HEAR US?!

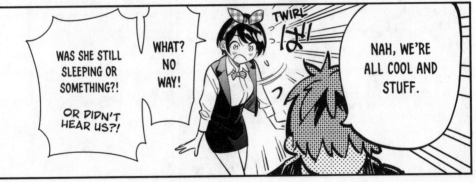

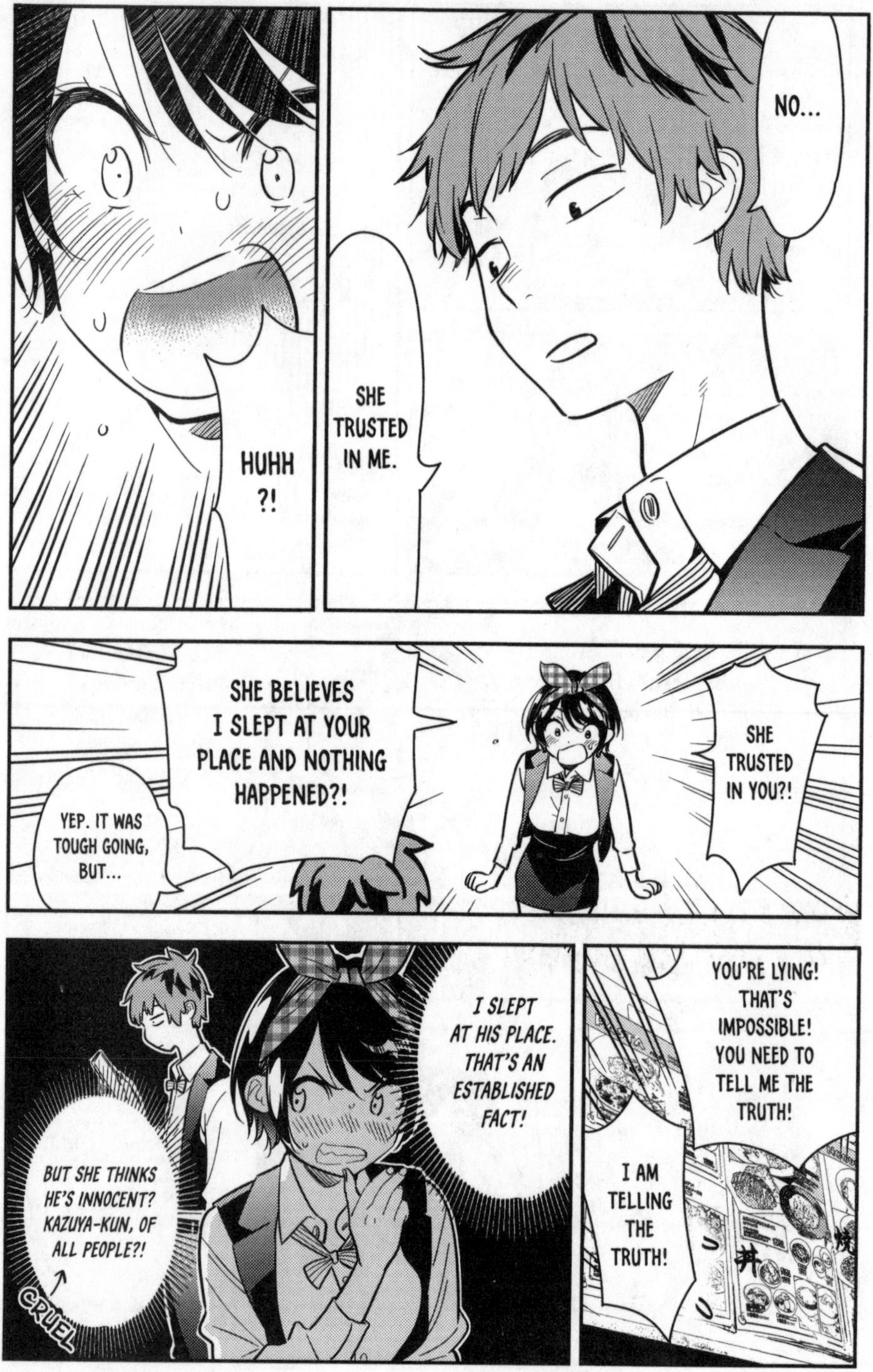
NO...
SHE TRUSTED IN ME.
HUHH ?!
SHE TRUSTED IN YOU?!
SHE BELIEVES I SLEPT AT YOUR PLACE AND NOTHING HAPPENED?!
YEP. IT WAS TOUGH GOING, BUT...
YOU'RE LYING! THAT'S IMPOSSIBLE! YOU NEED TO TELL ME THE TRUTH!
I AM TELLING THE TRUTH!
I SLEPT AT HIS PLACE. THAT'S AN ESTABLISHED FACT!
BUT SHE THINKS HE'S INNOCENT? KAZUYA-KUN, OF ALL PEOPLE?!
CRUEL

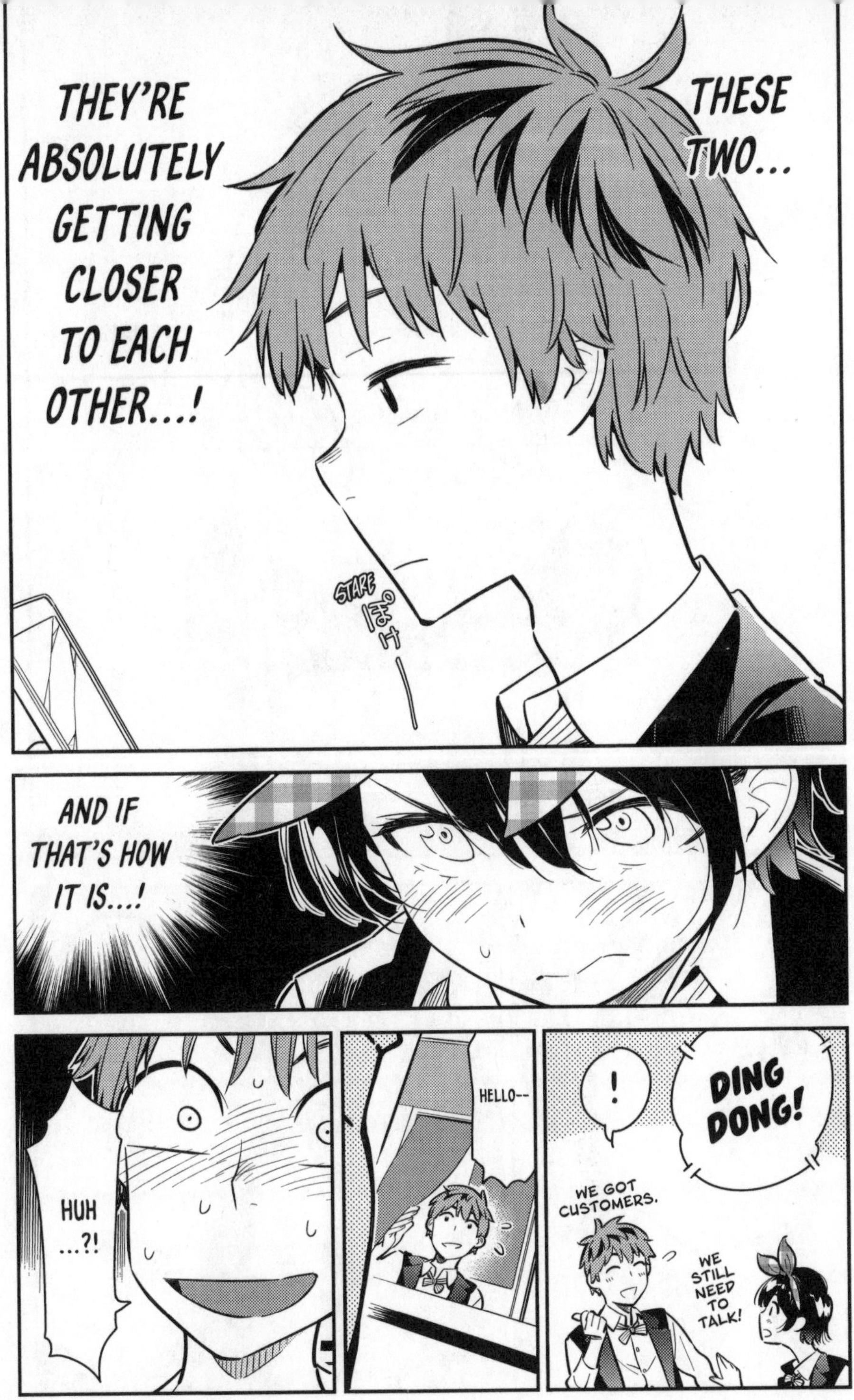
THESE TWO...
THEY'RE ABSOLUTELY GETTING CLOSER TO EACH OTHER...!
STARE
ぽけー
AND IF THAT'S HOW IT IS...!
DING DONG!
!
WE GOT CUSTOMERS.
WE STILL NEED TO TALK!
HELLO--
HUH ...?!

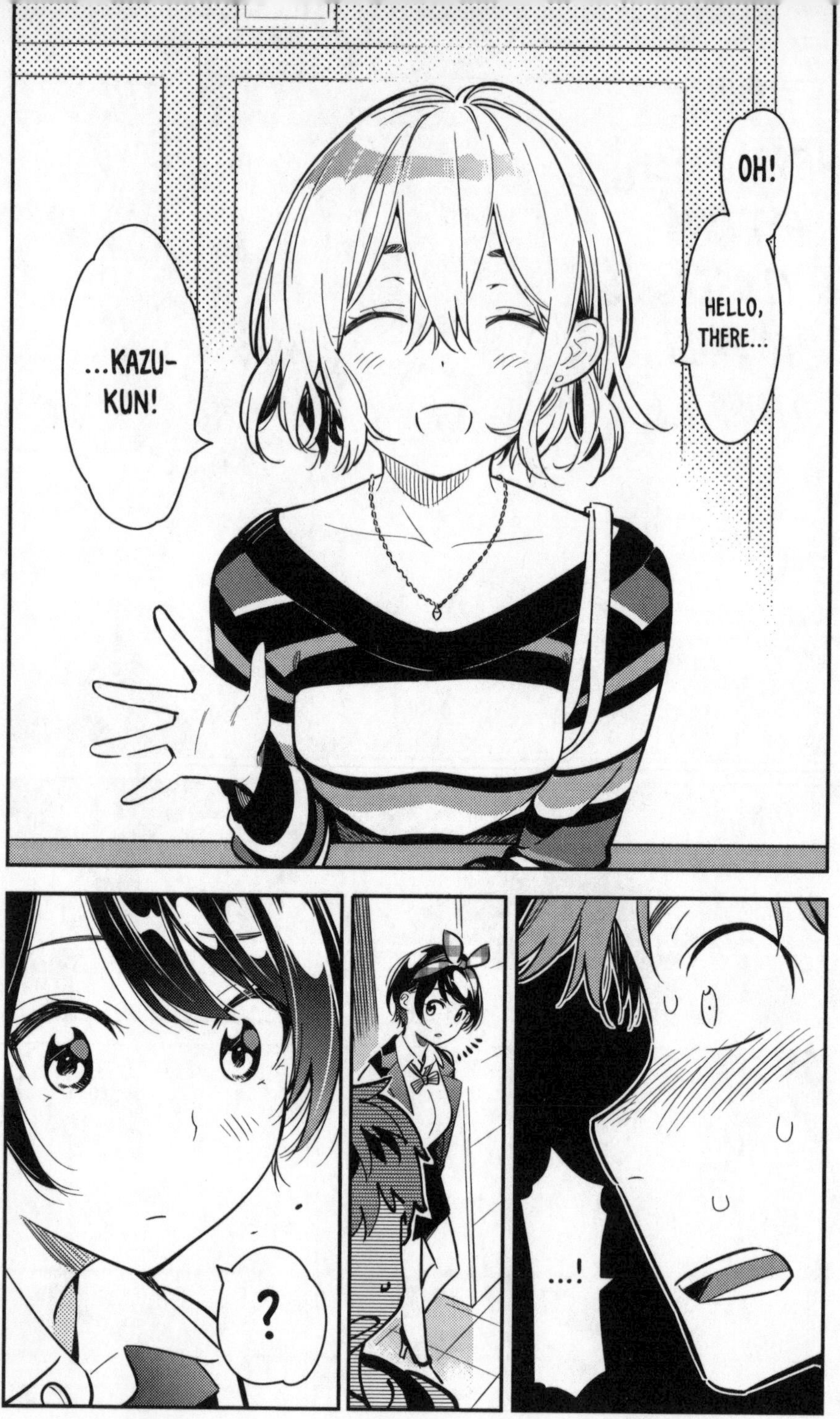
OH!
HELLO, THERE...
...KAZU-KUN!
...!
?

Check-in

HELLO...

KARAOKE VILLAGE

...KAZU-KUN!

?

RATING 75 MY EX-GIRLFRIEND AND MY "GIRLFRIEND" 1

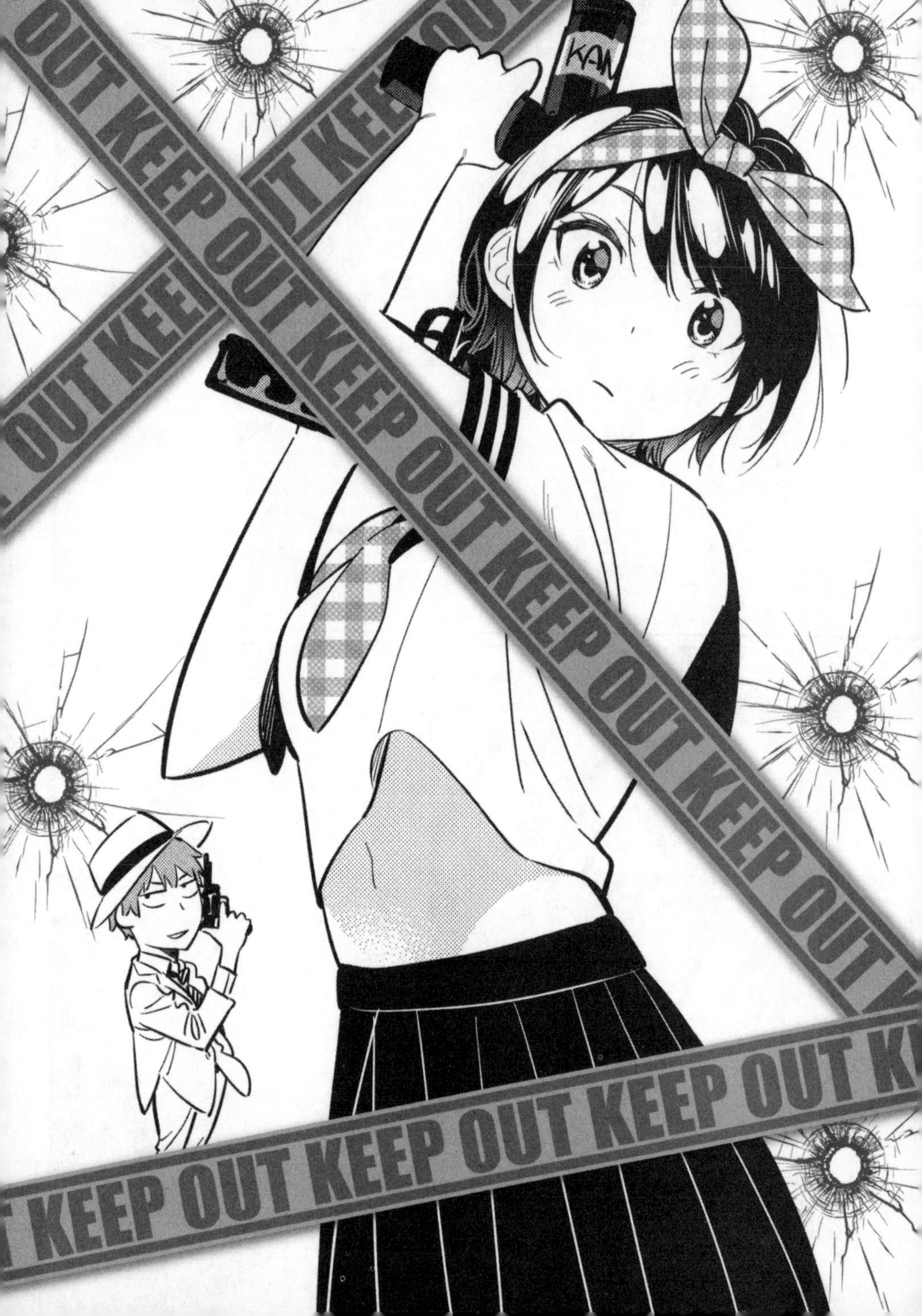
KEEP OUT KEEP OUT
KEEP OUT KEEP OUT
KEEP OUT KEEP OUT

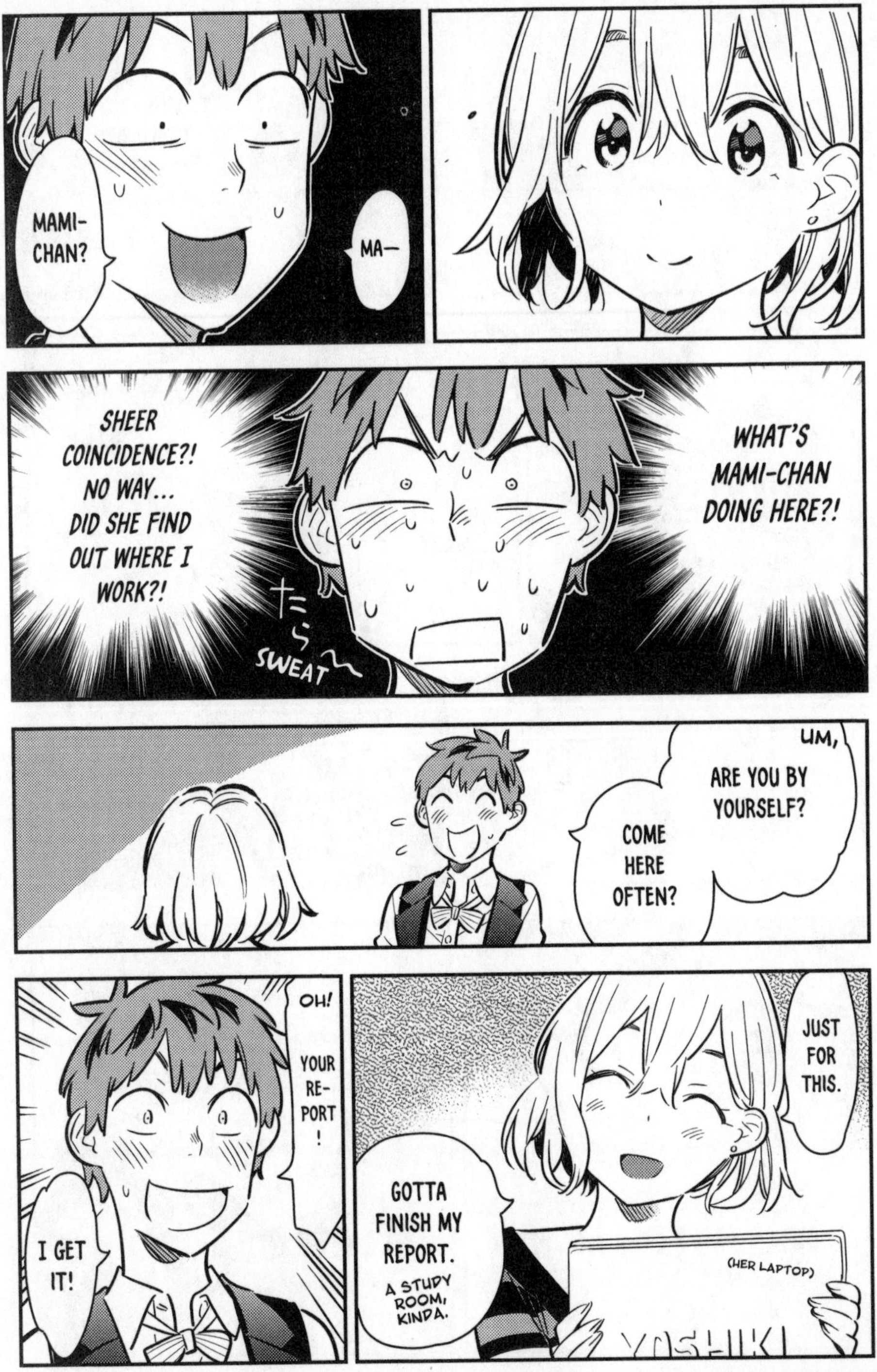
MA—
MAMI-CHAN?
WHAT'S MAMI-CHAN DOING HERE?!
SHEER COINCIDENCE?! NO WAY... DID SHE FIND OUT WHERE I WORK?!
たら
SWEAT
UM, ARE YOU BY YOURSELF?
COME HERE OFTEN?
JUST FOR THIS.
GOTTA FINISH MY REPORT.
A STUDY ROOM, KINDA.
(HER LAPTOP)
OH! YOUR REPORT!
I GET IT!

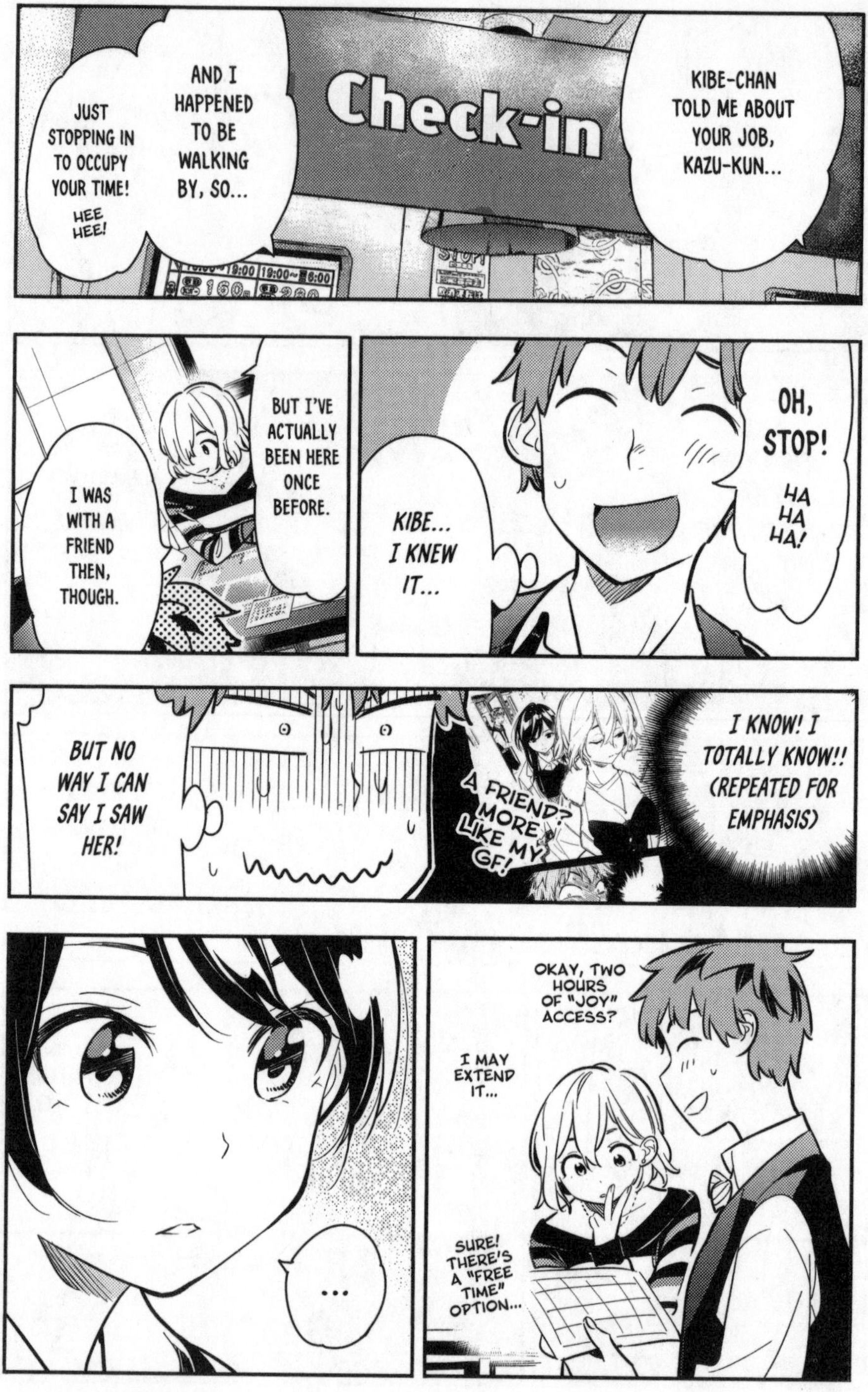
Check-in
KIBE-CHAN TOLD ME ABOUT YOUR JOB, KAZU-KUN...
AND I HAPPENED TO BE WALKING BY, SO...
JUST STOPPING IN TO OCCUPY YOUR TIME!
HEE HEE!
OH, STOP!
HA HA HA!
KIBE... I KNEW IT...
BUT I'VE ACTUALLY BEEN HERE ONCE BEFORE.
I WAS WITH A FRIEND THEN, THOUGH.
I KNOW! I TOTALLY KNOW!! (REPEATED FOR EMPHASIS)
A FRIEND? MORE LIKE MY GF!
BUT NO WAY I CAN SAY I SAW HER!
OKAY, TWO HOURS OF "JOY" ACCESS?
I MAY EXTEND IT...
SURE! THERE'S A "FREE TIME" OPTION...
...

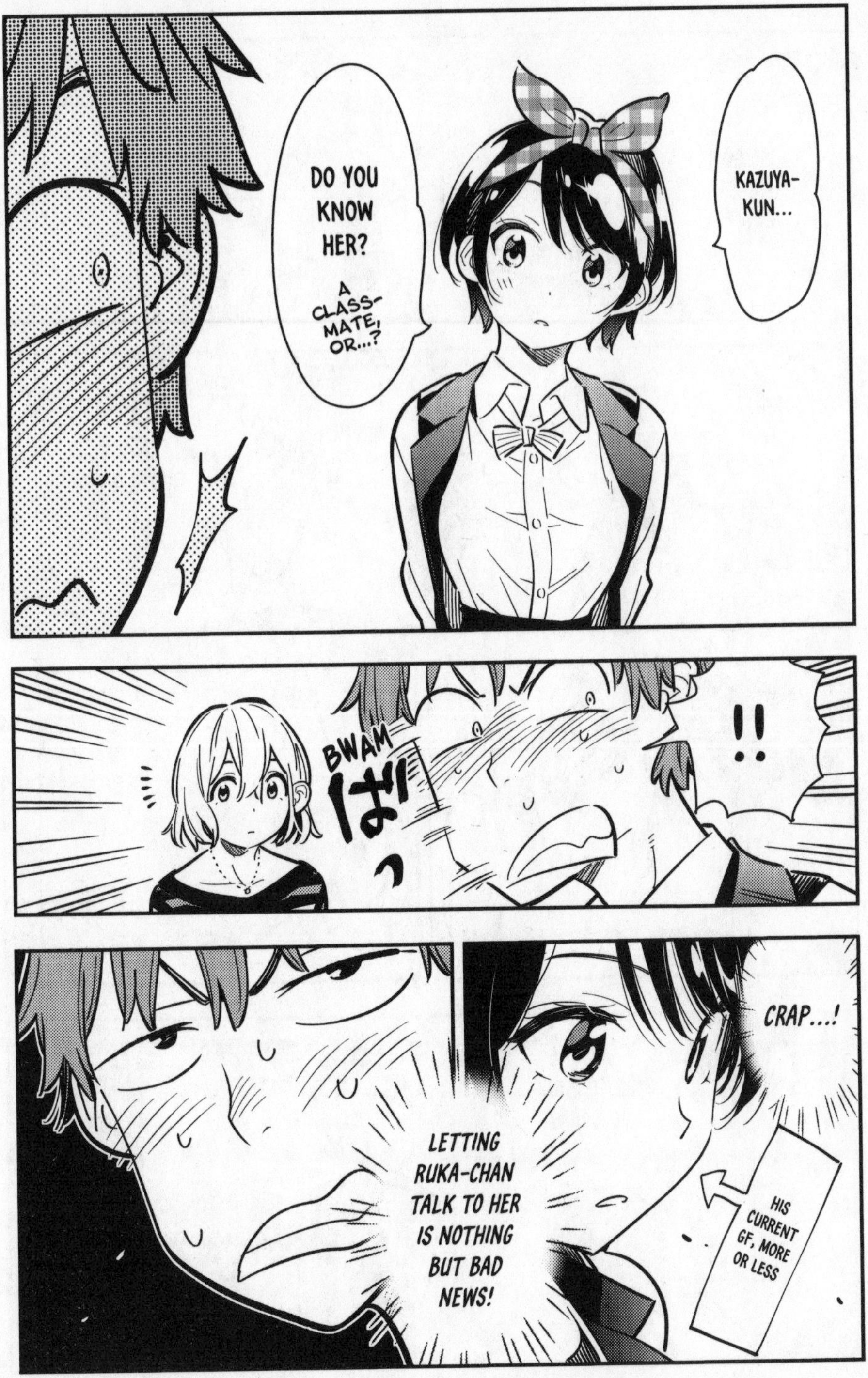
KAZUYA-KUN...
DO YOU KNOW HER? A CLASSMATE, OR...?
!!
BWAM
ぱっ
CRAP...!
HIS CURRENT GF, MORE OR LESS
LETTING RUKA-CHAN TALK TO HER IS NOTHING BUT BAD NEWS!

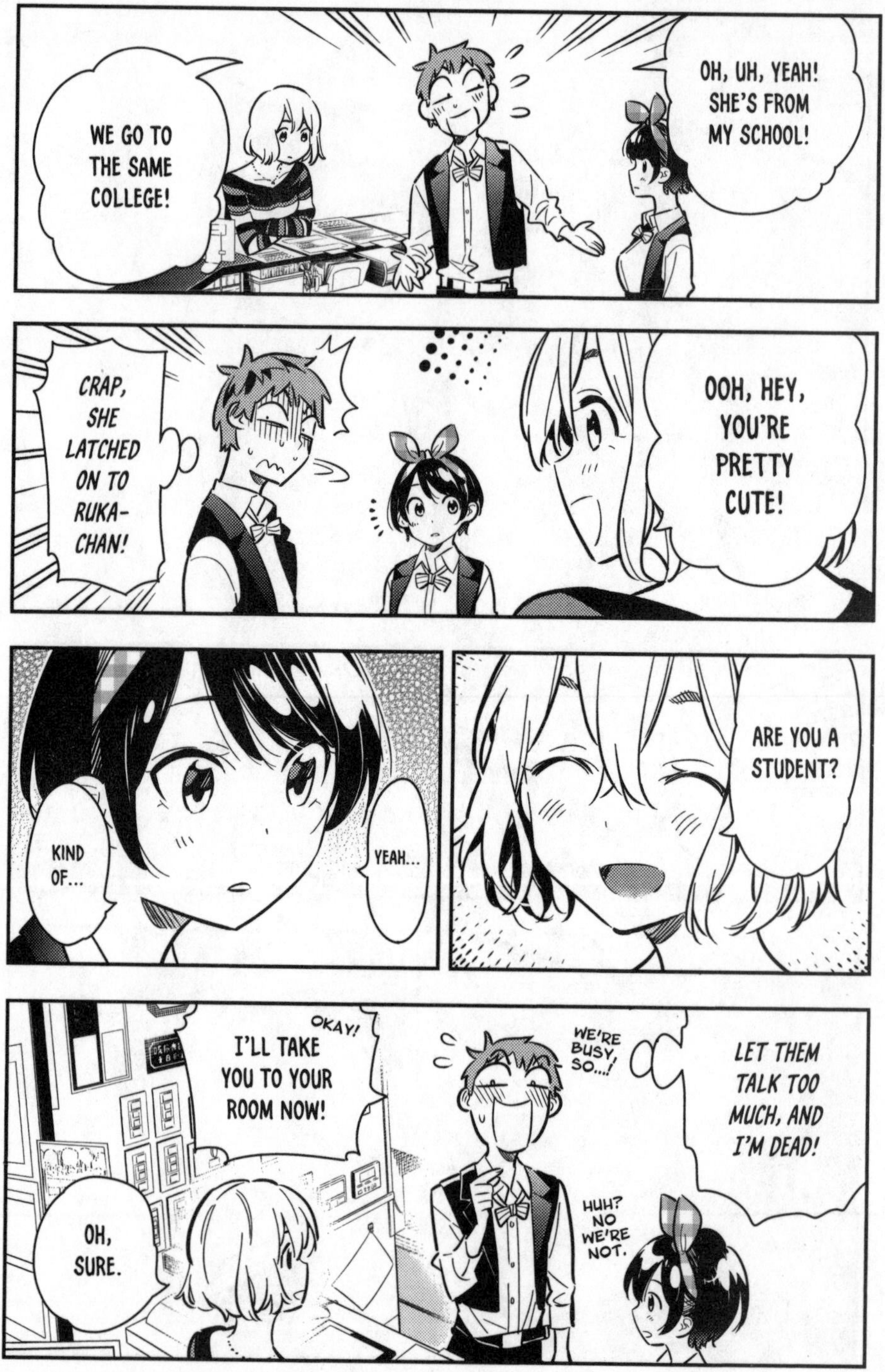
OH, UH, YEAH! SHE'S FROM MY SCHOOL!
WE GO TO THE SAME COLLEGE!
OOH, HEY, YOU'RE PRETTY CUTE!
CRAP, SHE LATCHED ON TO RUKA-CHAN!
ARE YOU A STUDENT?
YEAH...
KIND OF...
LET THEM TALK TOO MUCH, AND I'M DEAD!
WE'RE BUSY, SO...!
HUH? NO WE'RE NOT.
OKAY!
I'LL TAKE YOU TO YOUR ROOM NOW!
OH, SURE.

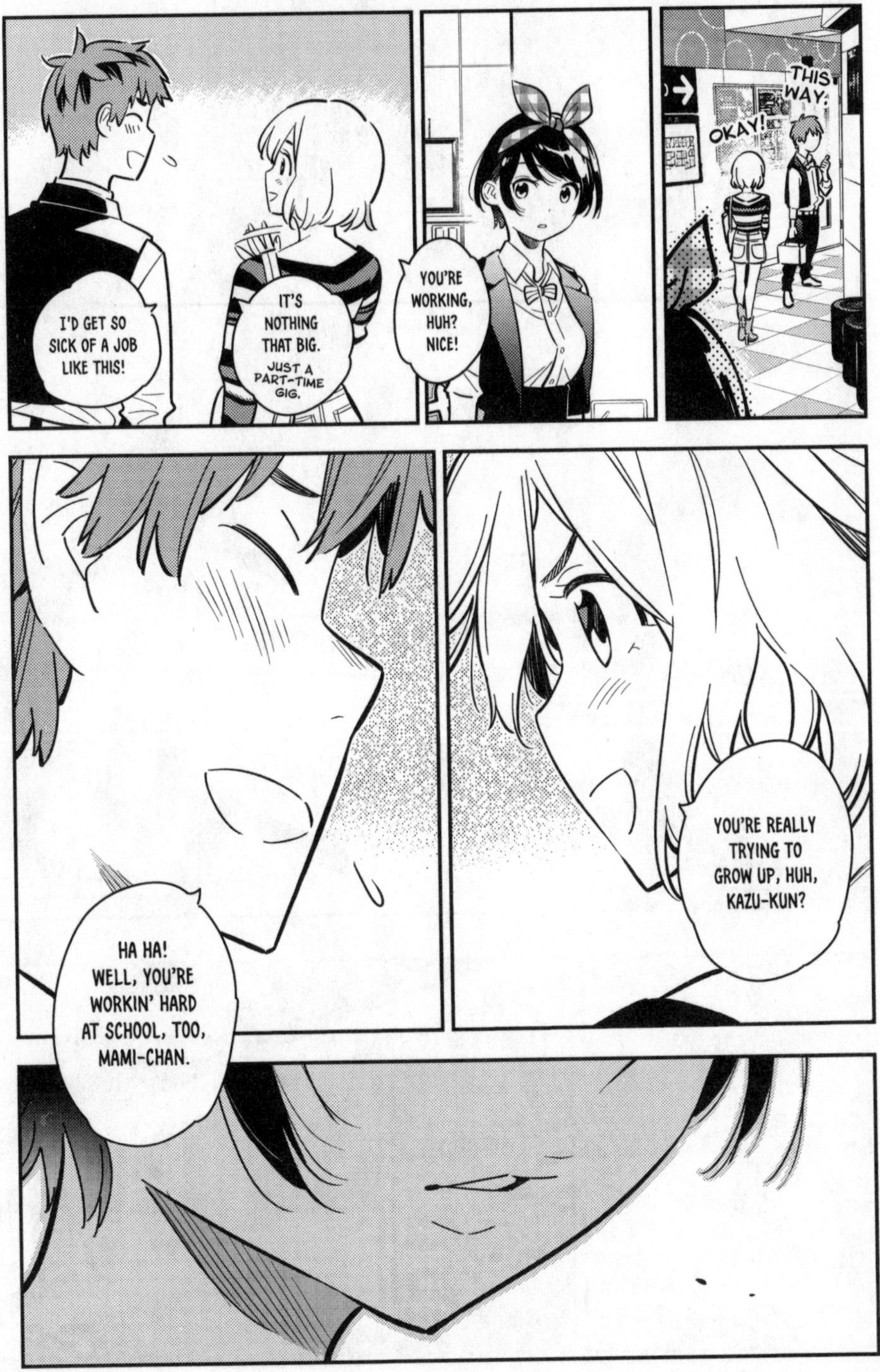
THIS WAY!
OKAY!
YOU'RE WORKING, HUH? NICE!
IT'S NOTHING THAT BIG. JUST A PART-TIME GIG.
I'D GET SO SICK OF A JOB LIKE THIS!
YOU'RE REALLY TRYING TO GROW UP, HUH, KAZU-KUN?
HA HA! WELL, YOU'RE WORKIN' HARD AT SCHOOL, TOO, MAMI-CHAN.

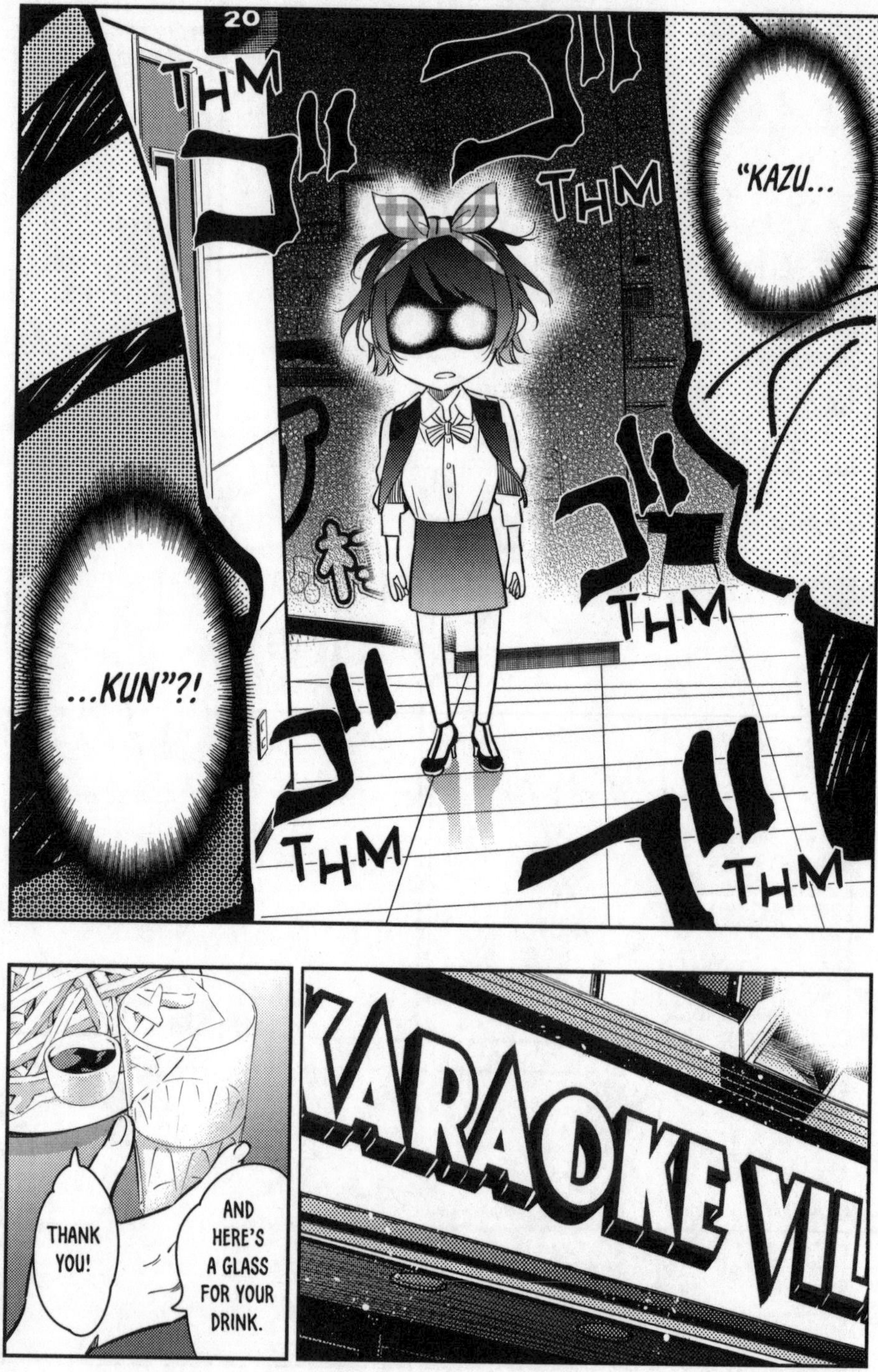
20
THM
THM
"KAZU...
THM
THM
THM
...KUN"?!
KARAOKE VIL
AND HERE'S A GLASS FOR YOUR DRINK.
THANK YOU!

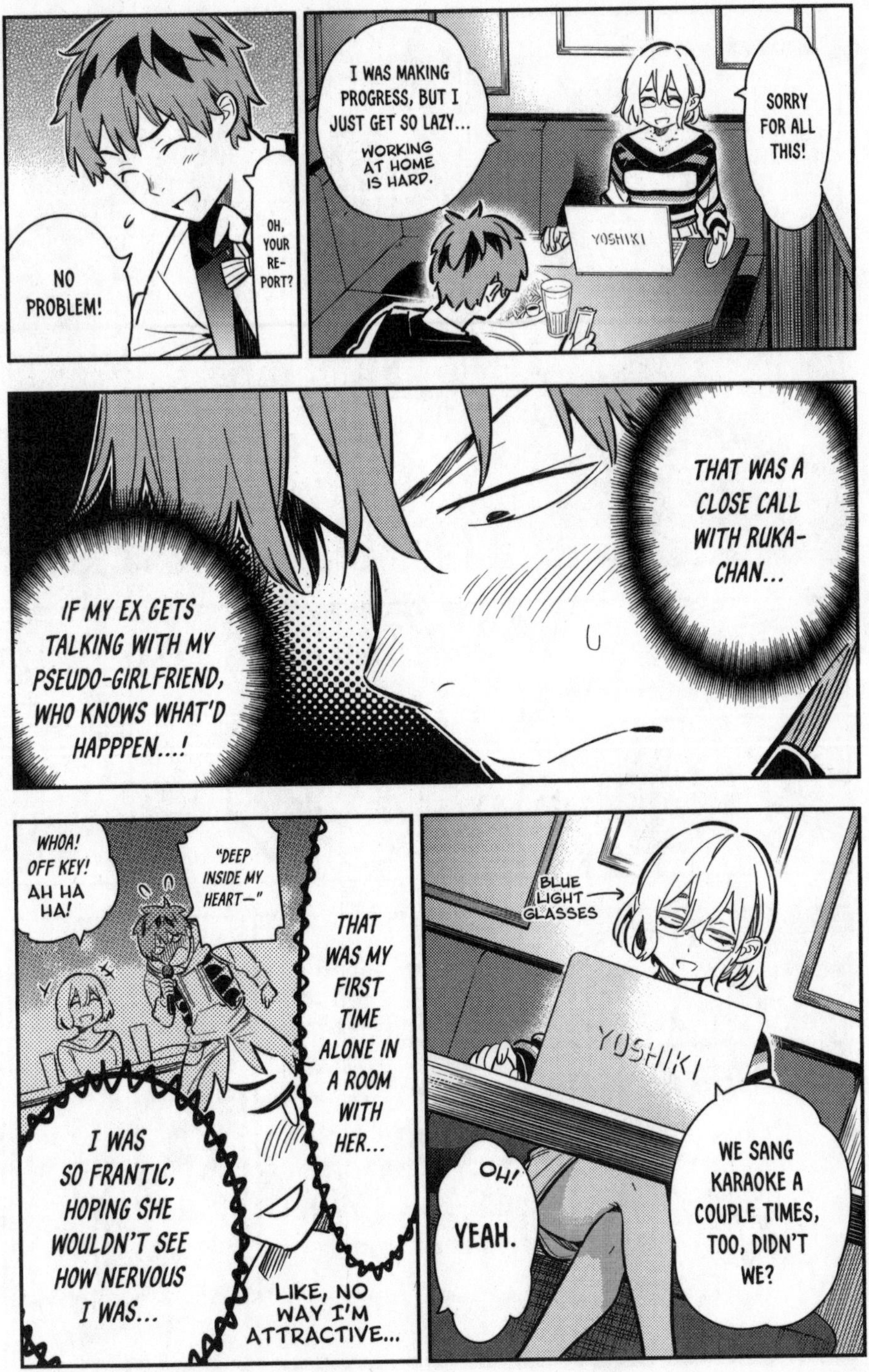
SORRY FOR ALL THIS!
I WAS MAKING PROGRESS, BUT I JUST GET SO LAZY...
WORKING AT HOME IS HARD.
YOSHIKI
OH, YOUR REPORT?
NO PROBLEM!
THAT WAS A CLOSE CALL WITH RUKA-CHAN...
IF MY EX GETS TALKING WITH MY PSEUDO-GIRLFRIEND, WHO KNOWS WHAT'D HAPPPEN...!
BLUE LIGHT GLASSES
YOSHIKI
WE SANG KARAOKE A COUPLE TIMES, TOO, DIDN'T WE?
OH!
YEAH.
THAT WAS MY FIRST TIME ALONE IN A ROOM WITH HER...
“DEEP INSIDE MY HEART—”
WHOA! OFF KEY! AH HA HA!
I WAS SO FRANTIC, HOPING SHE WOULDN'T SEE HOW NERVOUS I WAS...
LIKE, NO WAY I'M ATTRACTIVE...

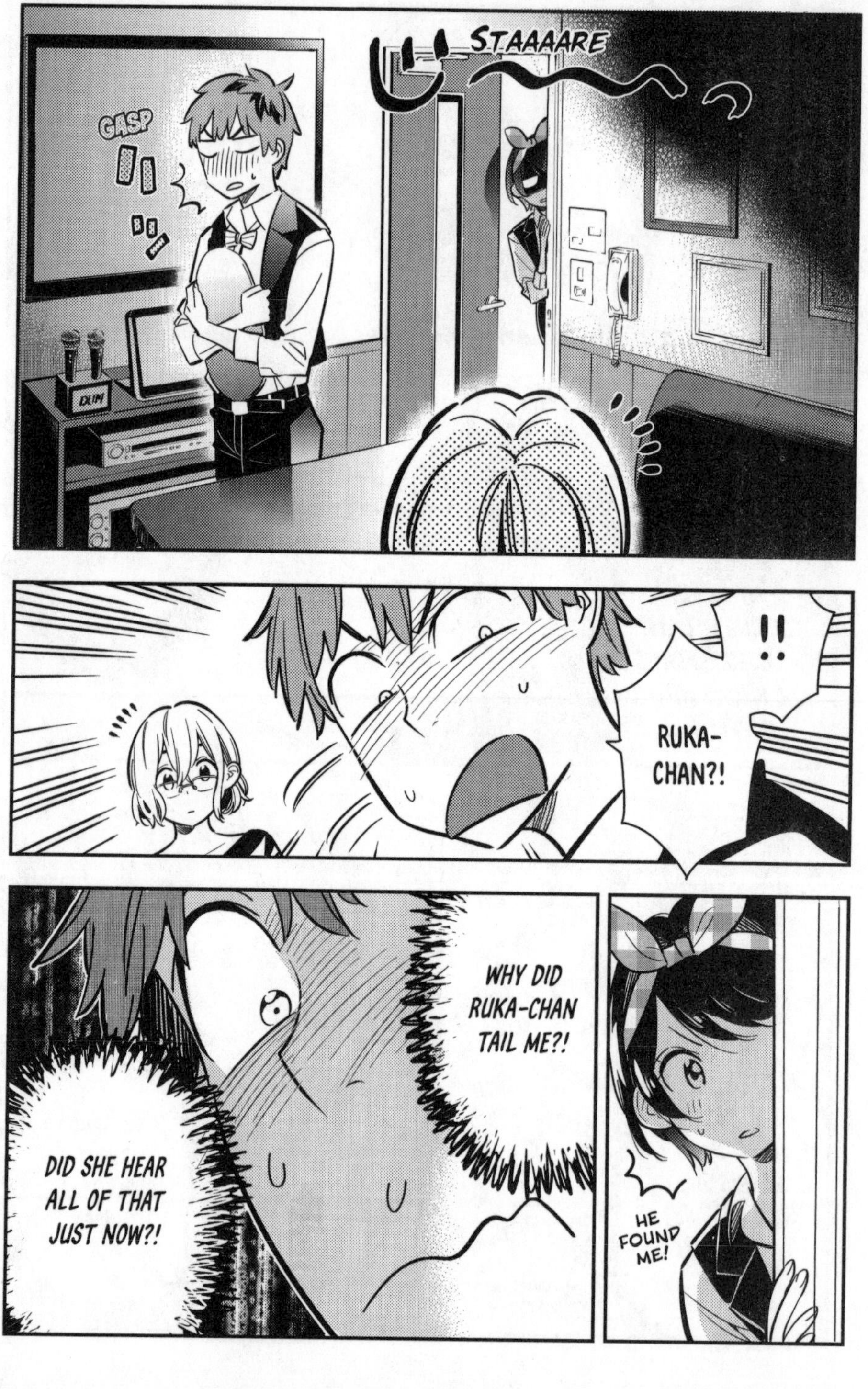
STAAAARE
GASP
!!
RUKA-CHAN?!
HE FOUND ME!
WHY DID RUKA-CHAN TAIL ME?!
DID SHE HEAR ALL OF THAT JUST NOW?!

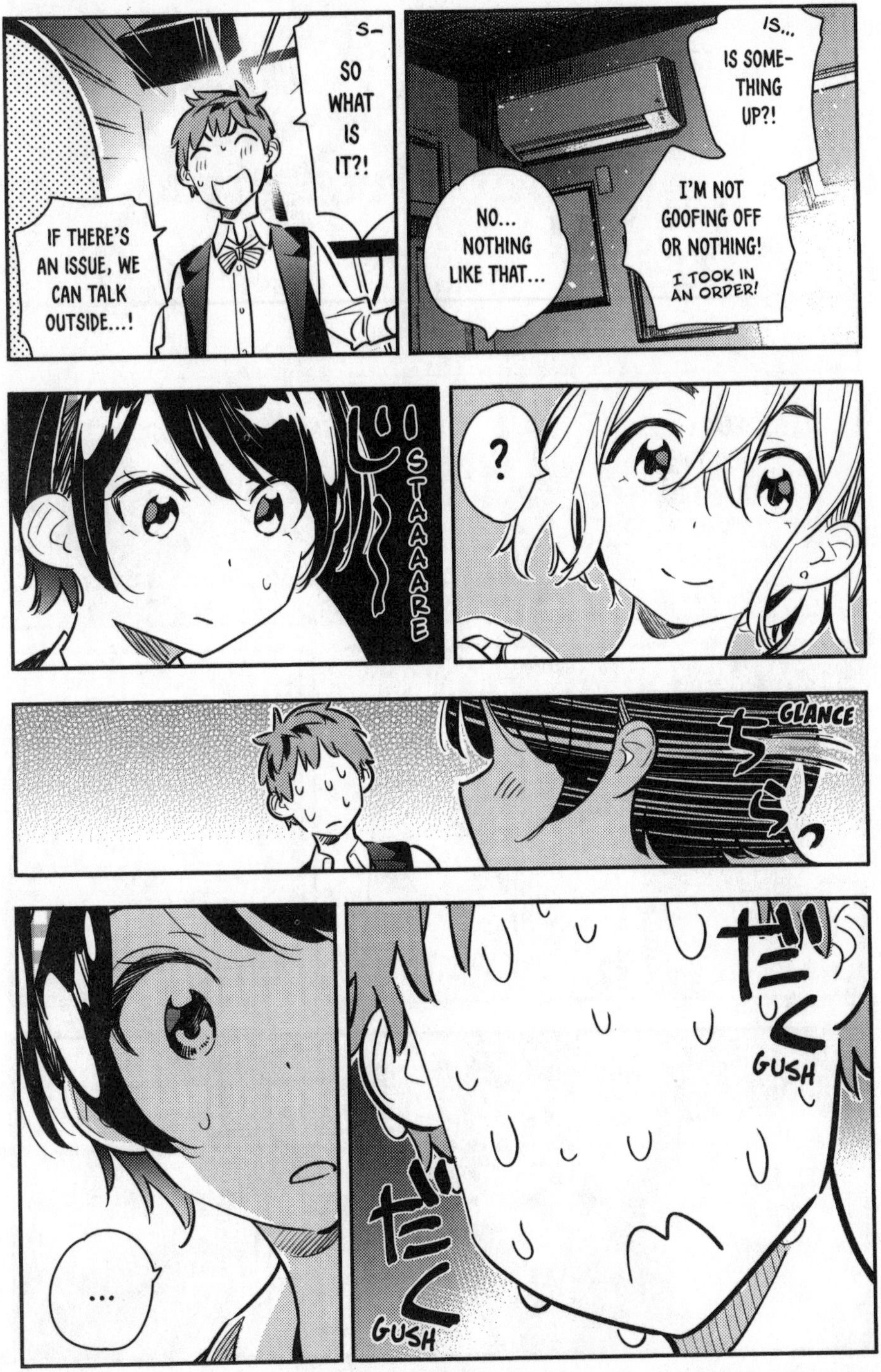
IS...
IS SOME-THING UP?!
I'M NOT GOOFING OFF OR NOTHING!
I TOOK IN AN ORDER!
NO... NOTHING LIKE THAT...
S–
SO WHAT IS IT?!
IF THERE'S AN ISSUE, WE CAN TALK OUTSIDE...!
?
じーー
STAAAAARE
ちらっ
GLANCE
だく
GUSH
だく
GUSH
...

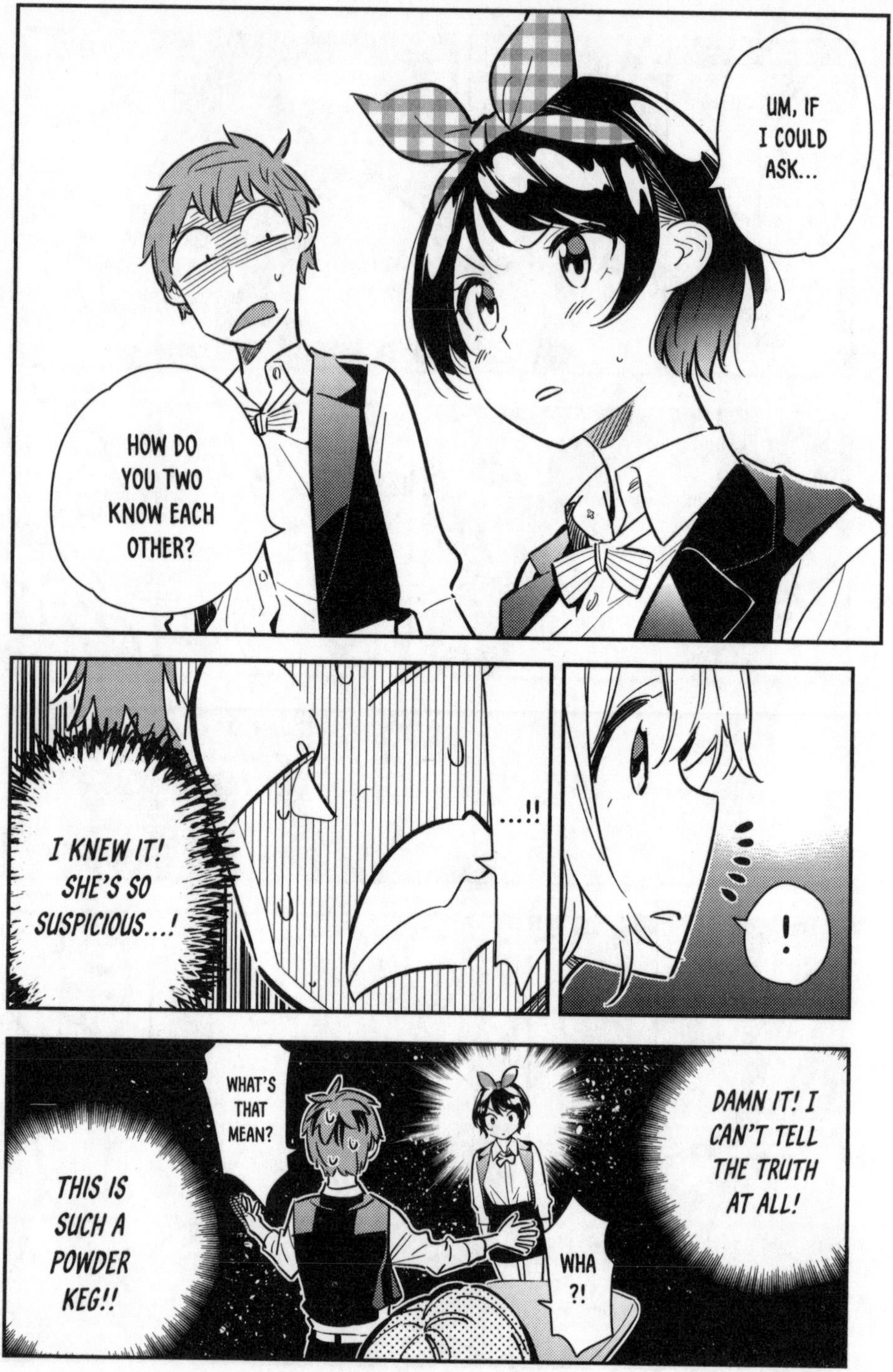
UM, IF I COULD ASK...
HOW DO YOU TWO KNOW EACH OTHER?
!
...!!
I KNEW IT! SHE'S SO SUSPICIOUS...!
DAMN IT! I CAN'T TELL THE TRUTH AT ALL!
WHA?!
WHAT'S THAT MEAN?
THIS IS SUCH A POWDER KEG!!

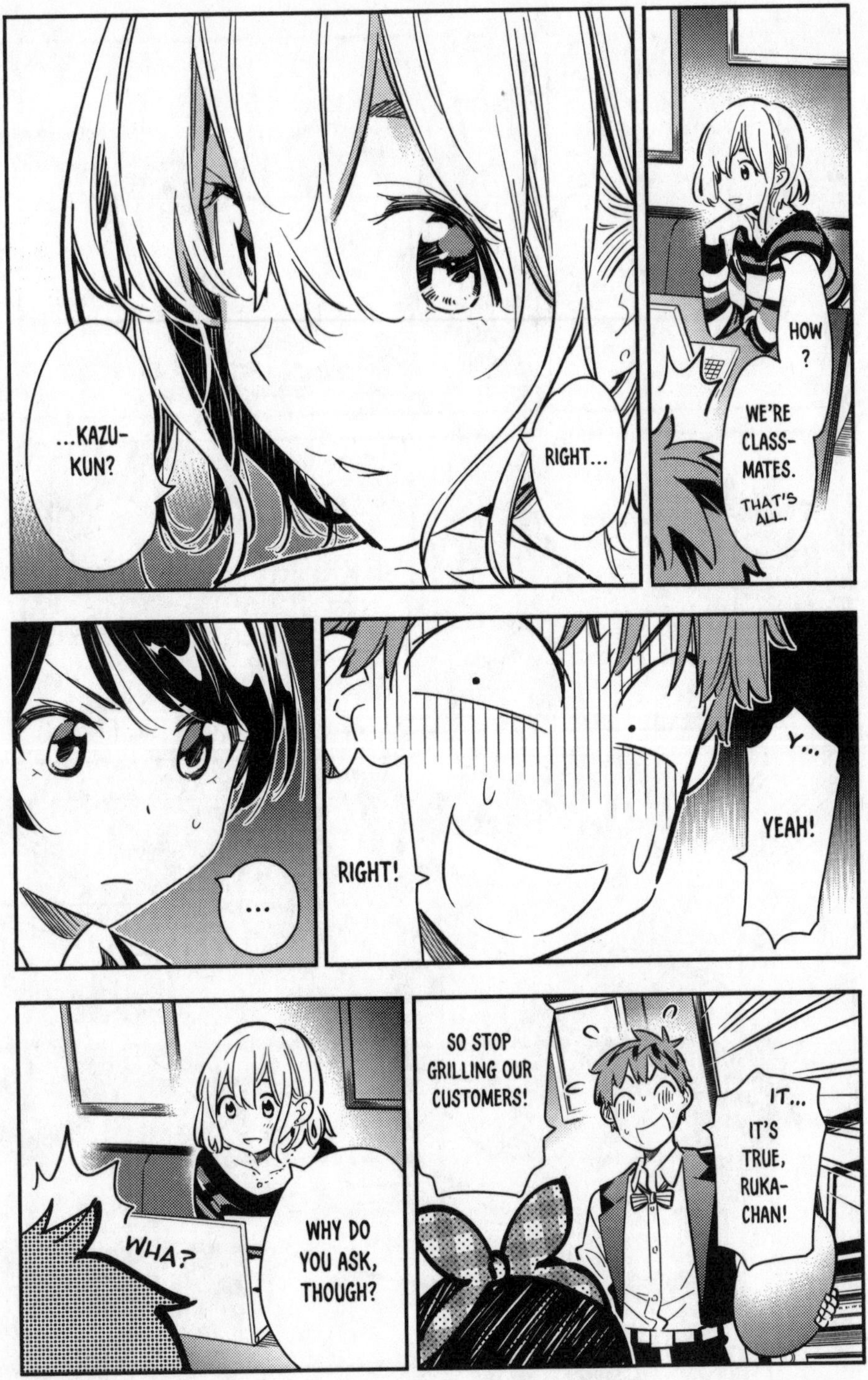
HOW?
WE'RE CLASSMATES. THAT'S ALL.
RIGHT...
...KAZU-KUN?
Y... YEAH!
RIGHT!
...
IT... IT'S TRUE, RUKA-CHAN!
SO STOP GRILLING OUR CUSTOMERS!
WHY DO YOU ASK, THOUGH?
WHA?

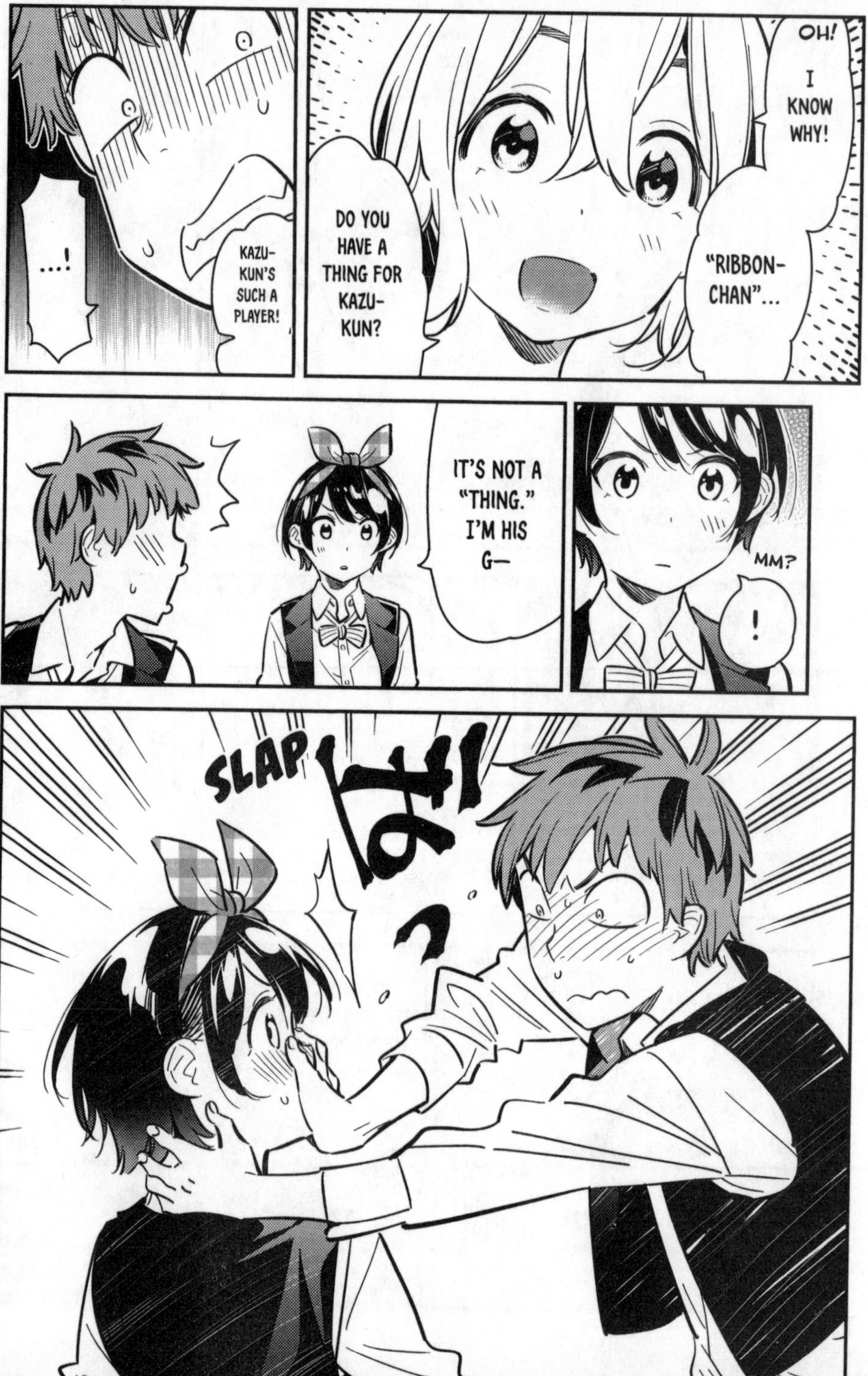
OH! I KNOW WHY!
"RIBBON-CHAN"...
DO YOU HAVE A THING FOR KAZU-KUN?
KAZU-KUN'S SUCH A PLAYER!
...!
MM?
!
IT'S NOT A "THING." I'M HIS G—
SLAP

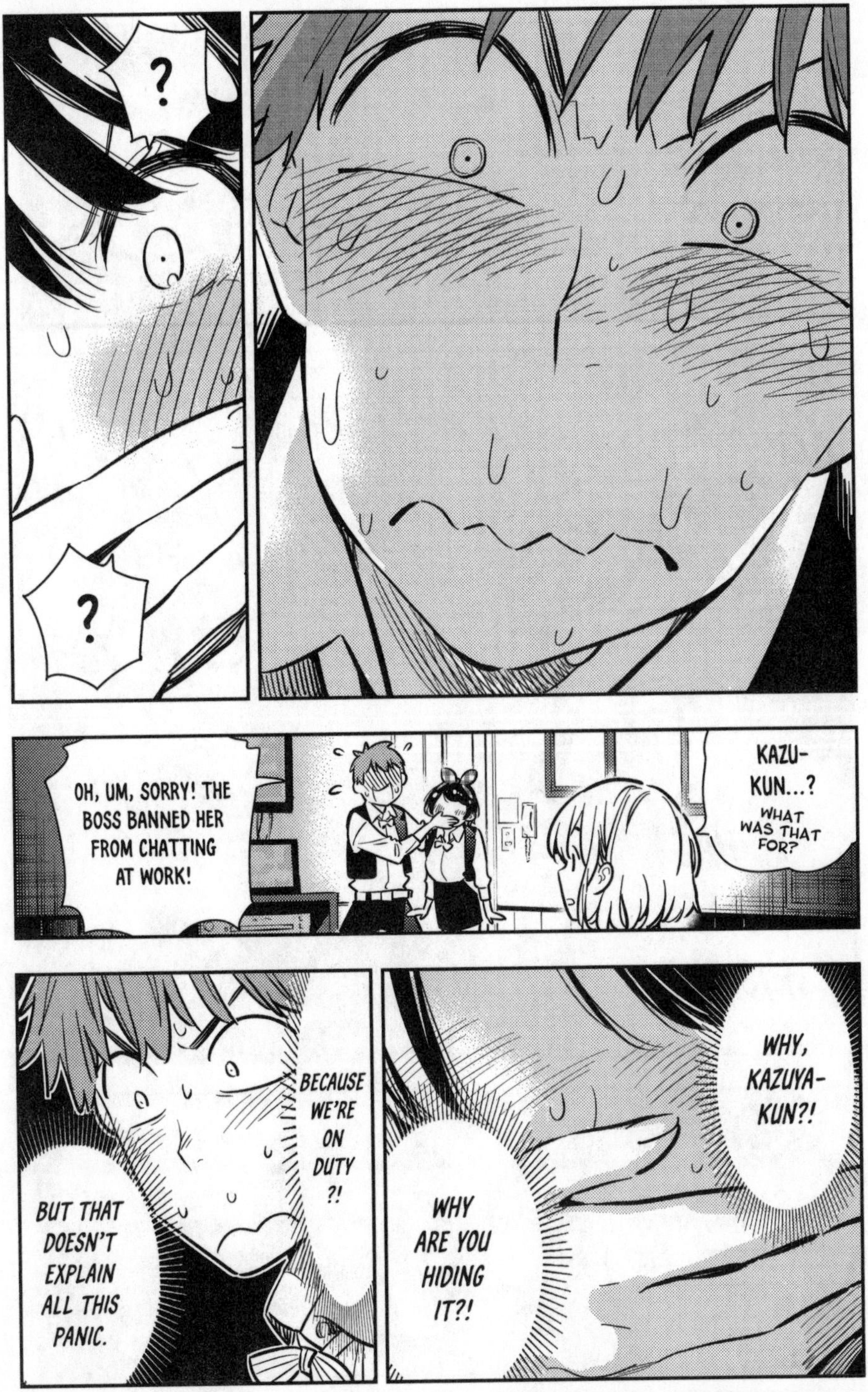
?
?
KAZU-KUN...?
WHAT WAS THAT FOR?
OH, UM, SORRY! THE BOSS BANNED HER FROM CHATTING AT WORK!
WHY, KAZUYA-KUN?!
WHY ARE YOU HIDING IT?!
BECAUSE WE'RE ON DUTY?!
BUT THAT DOESN'T EXPLAIN ALL THIS PANIC.

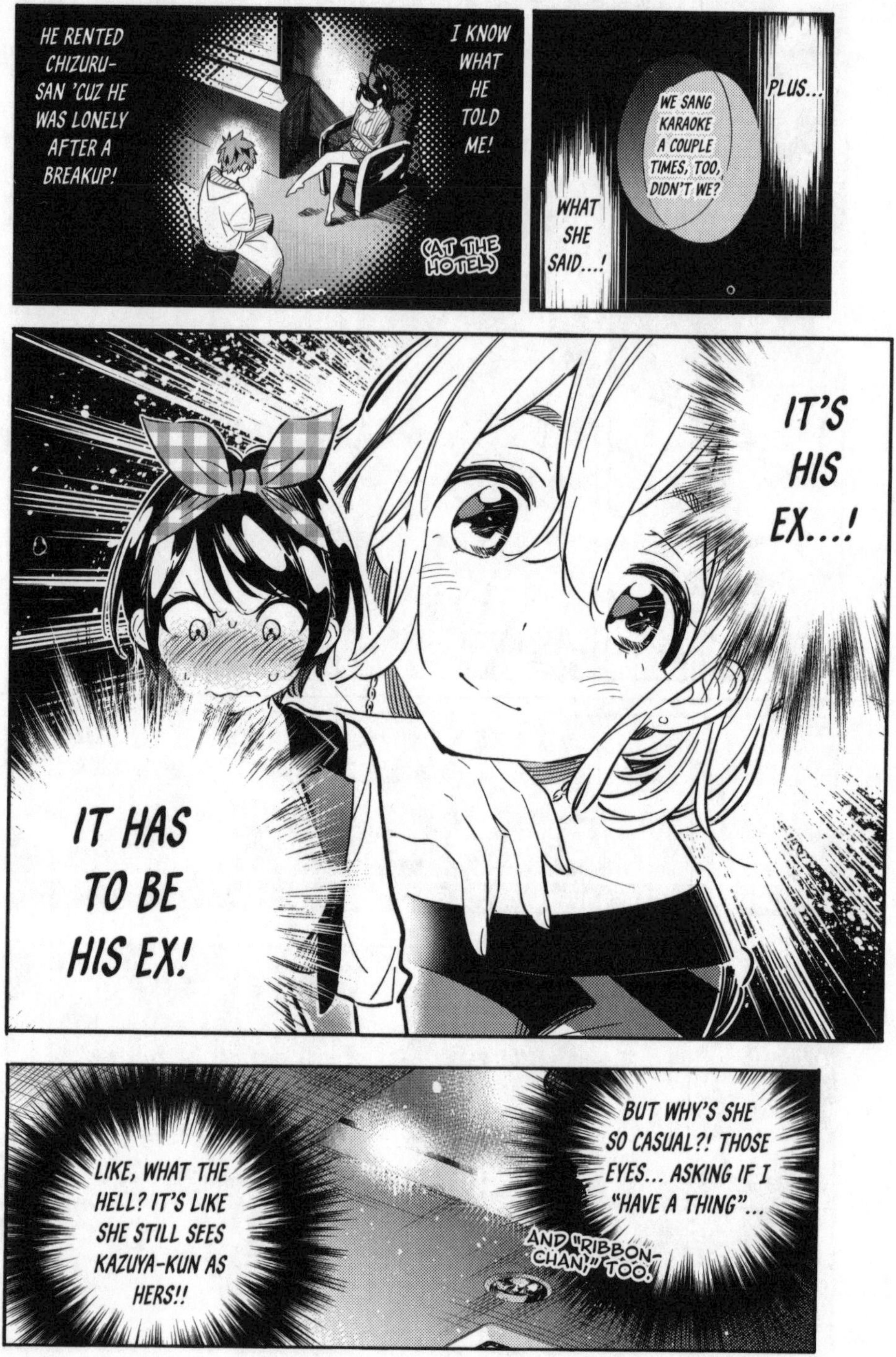
PLUS...
WE SANG KARAOKE A COUPLE TIMES, TOO, DIDN'T WE?
WHAT SHE SAID...!
I KNOW WHAT HE TOLD ME!
HE RENTED CHIZURU-SAN 'CUZ HE WAS LONELY AFTER A BREAKUP!
(AT THE HOTEL)
IT'S HIS EX...!
IT HAS TO BE HIS EX!
BUT WHY'S SHE SO CASUAL?! THOSE EYES... ASKING IF I "HAVE A THING"...
AND "RIBBON-CHAN," TOO!
LIKE, WHAT THE HELL? IT'S LIKE SHE STILL SEES KAZUYA-KUN AS HERS!!

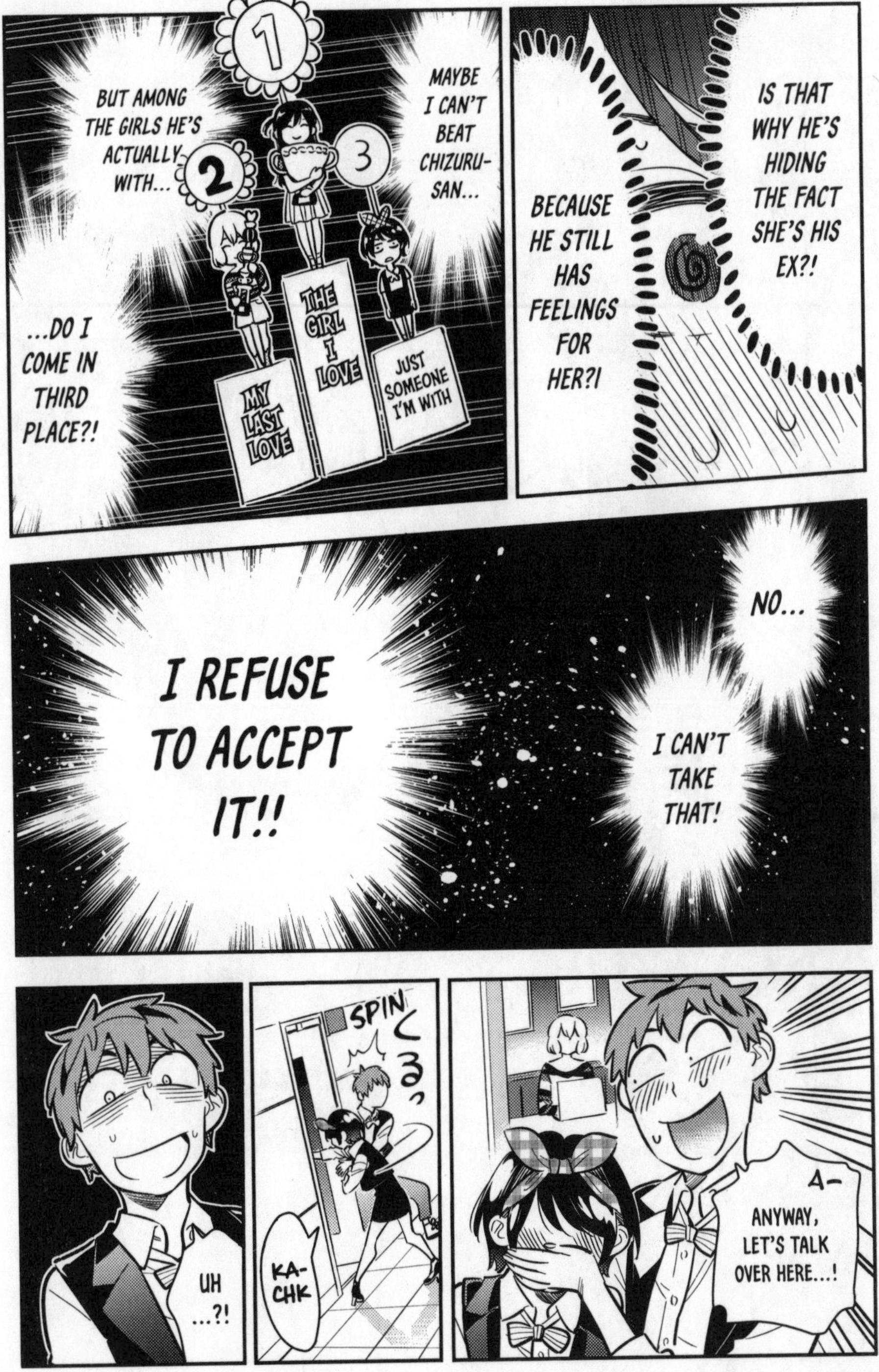
IS THAT WHY HE'S HIDING THE FACT SHE'S HIS EX?!
BECAUSE HE STILL HAS FEELINGS FOR HER?!
MAYBE I CAN'T BEAT CHIZURU-SAN...
BUT AMONG THE GIRLS HE'S ACTUALLY WITH...
1
2
3
THE GIRL I LOVE
MY LAST LOVE
JUST SOMEONE I'M WITH
...DO I COME IN THIRD PLACE?!
NO...
I CAN'T TAKE THAT!
I REFUSE TO ACCEPT IT!!
A- ANYWAY, LET'S TALK OVER HERE...!
SPIN
くるっ
KA-CHK
UH ...?!

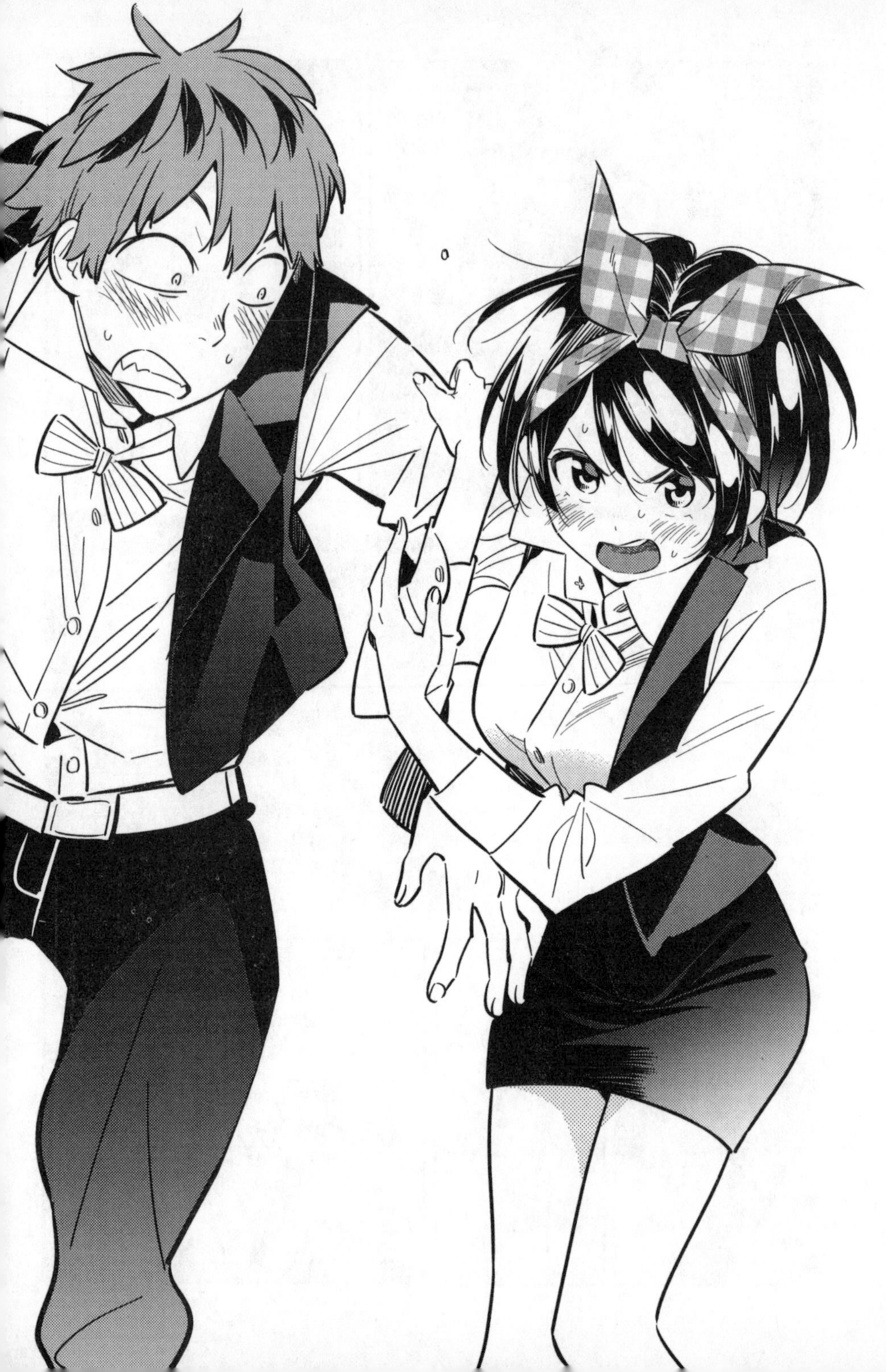

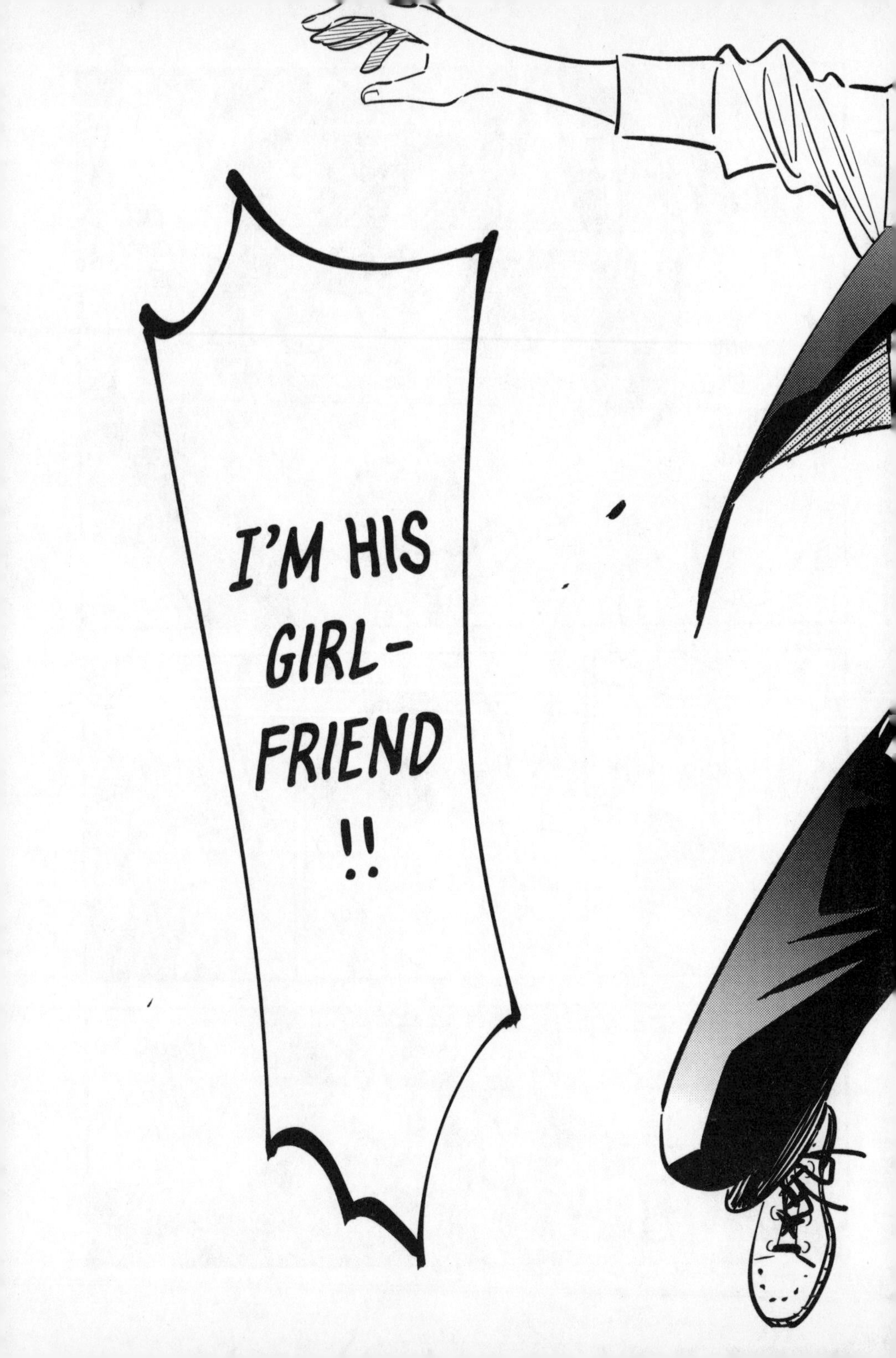
I'M HIS GIRL-FRIEND !!

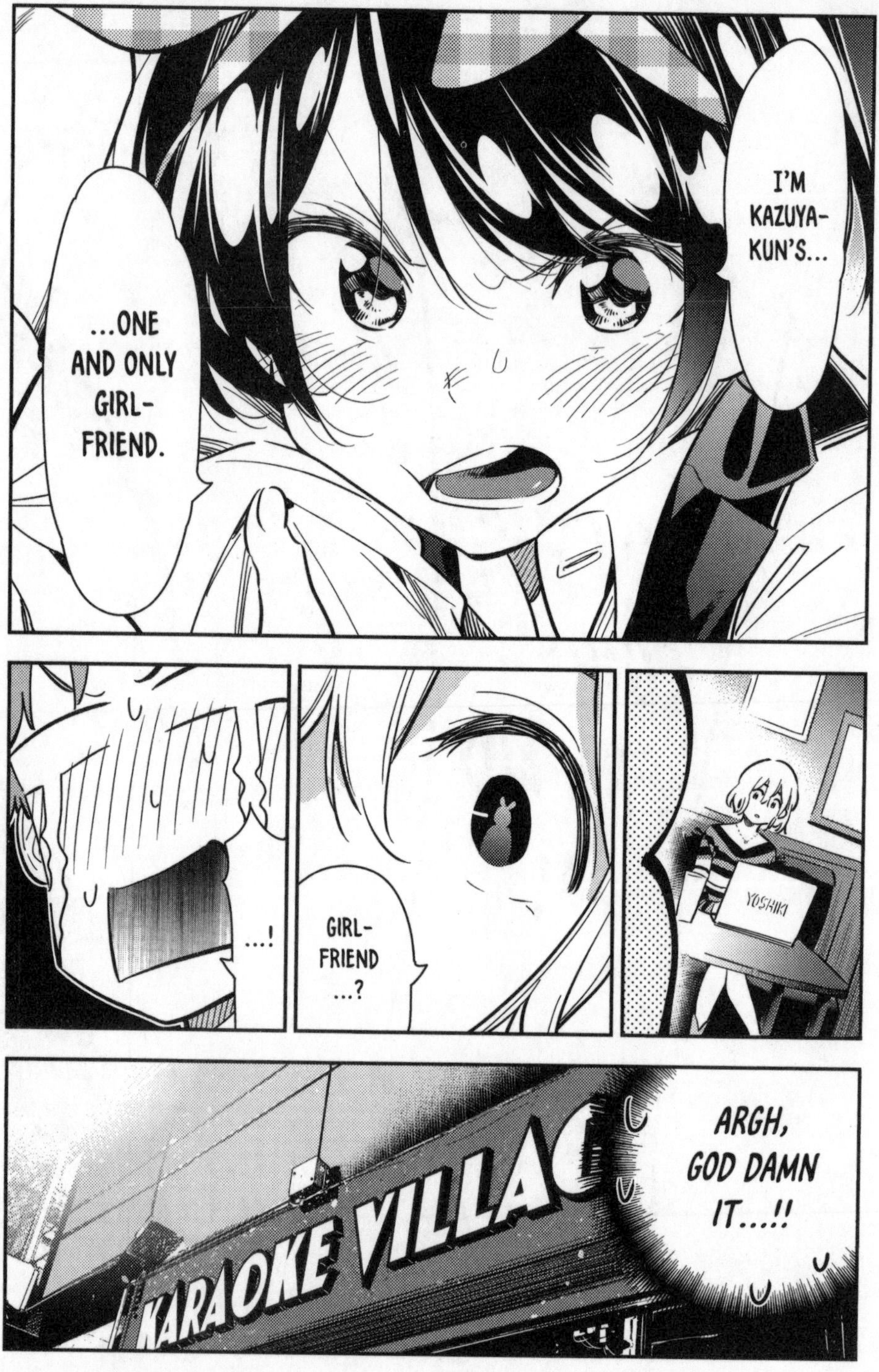
I'M KAZUYA-KUN'S...
...ONE AND ONLY GIRL-FRIEND.
YOSHIKI
GIRL-FRIEND ...?
...!
ARGH, GOD DAMN IT....!!
KARAOKE VILLA

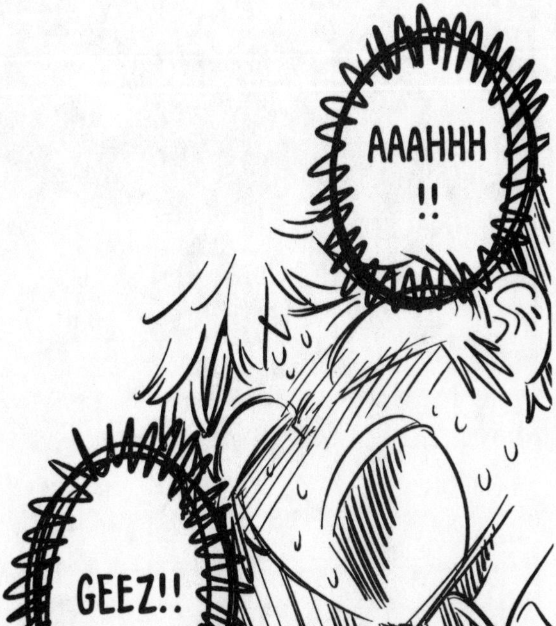
AAAHHH !!
GEEZ!!

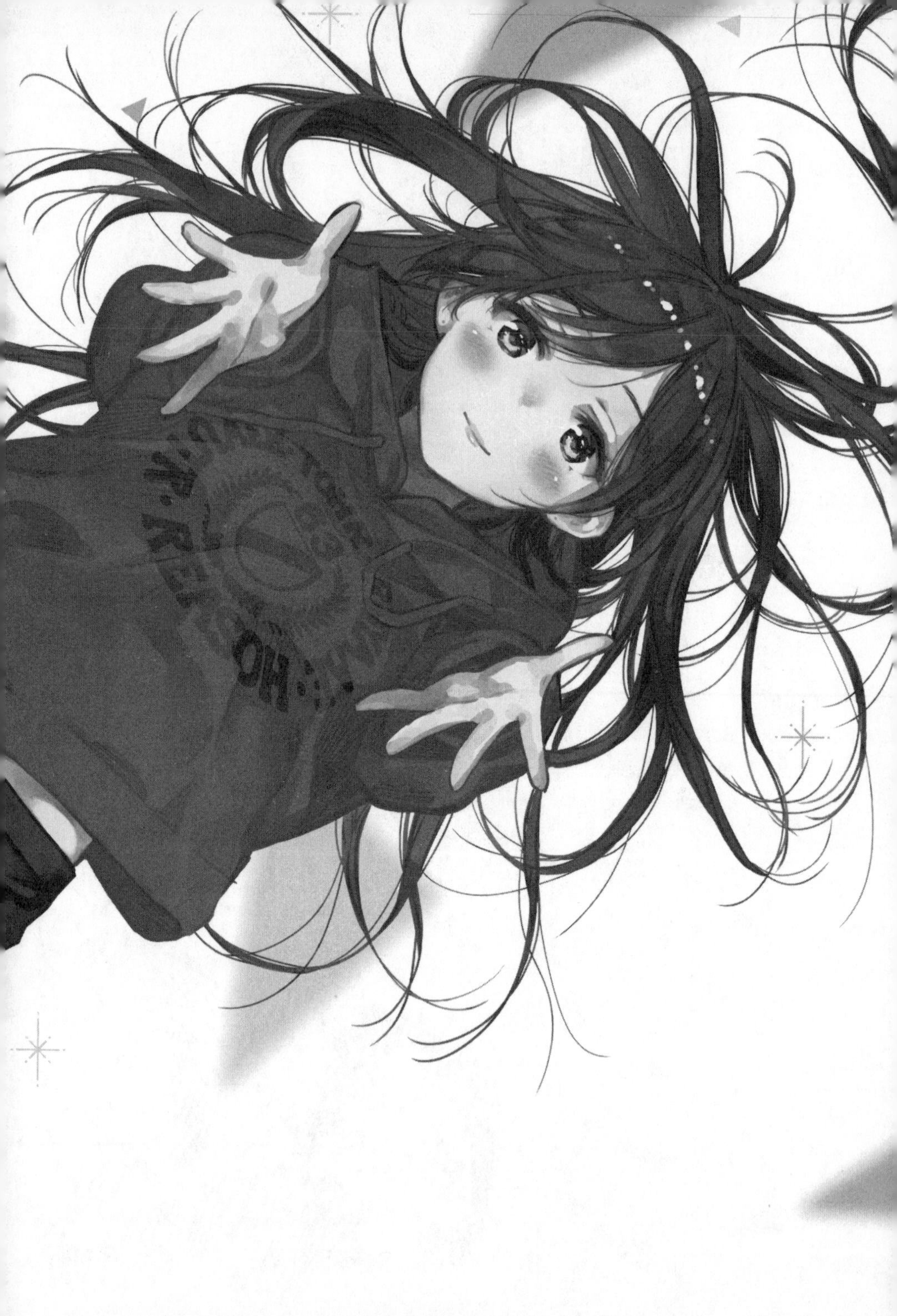

RATING 76 MY EX-GIRLFRIEND AND MY "GIRLFRIEND" 2

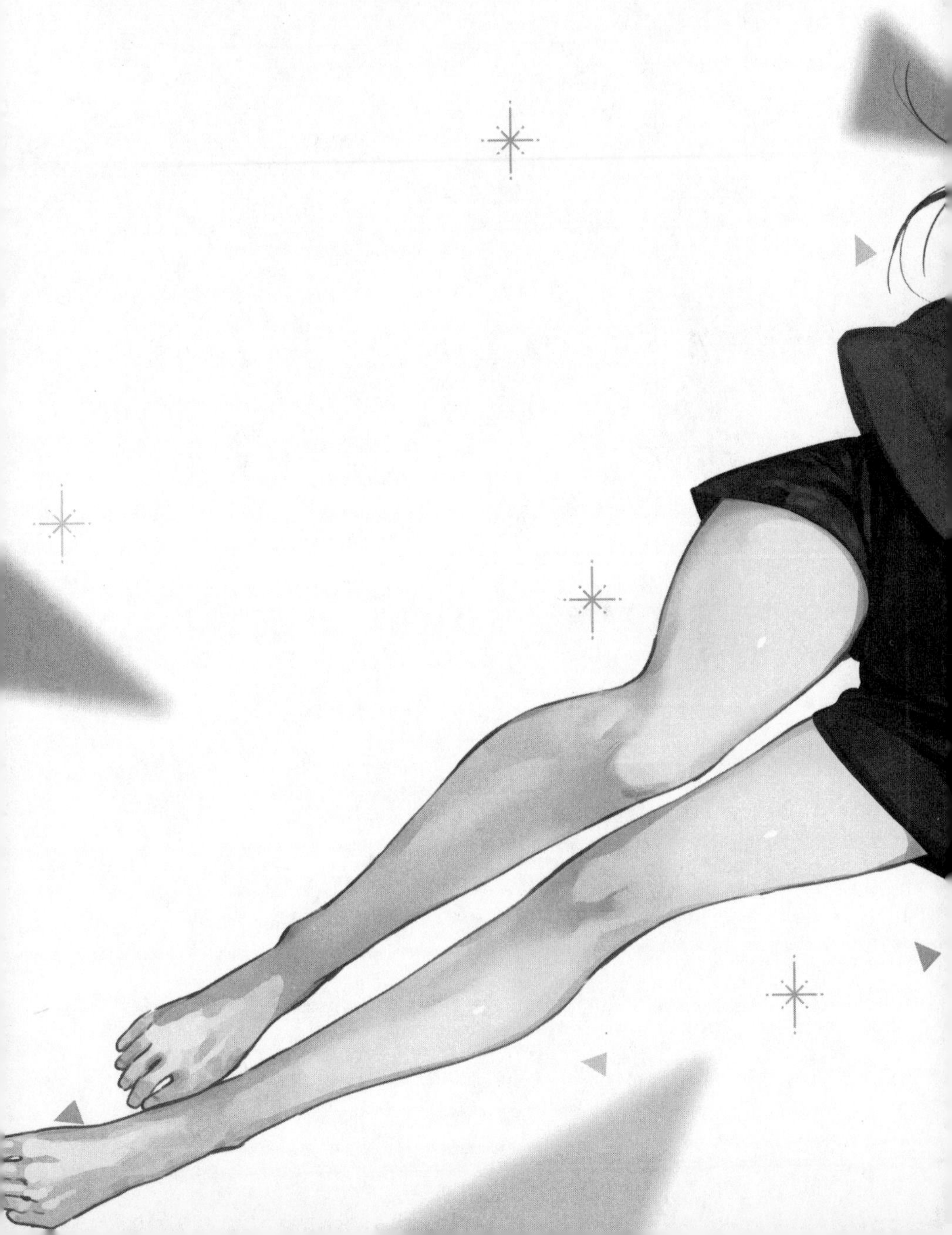

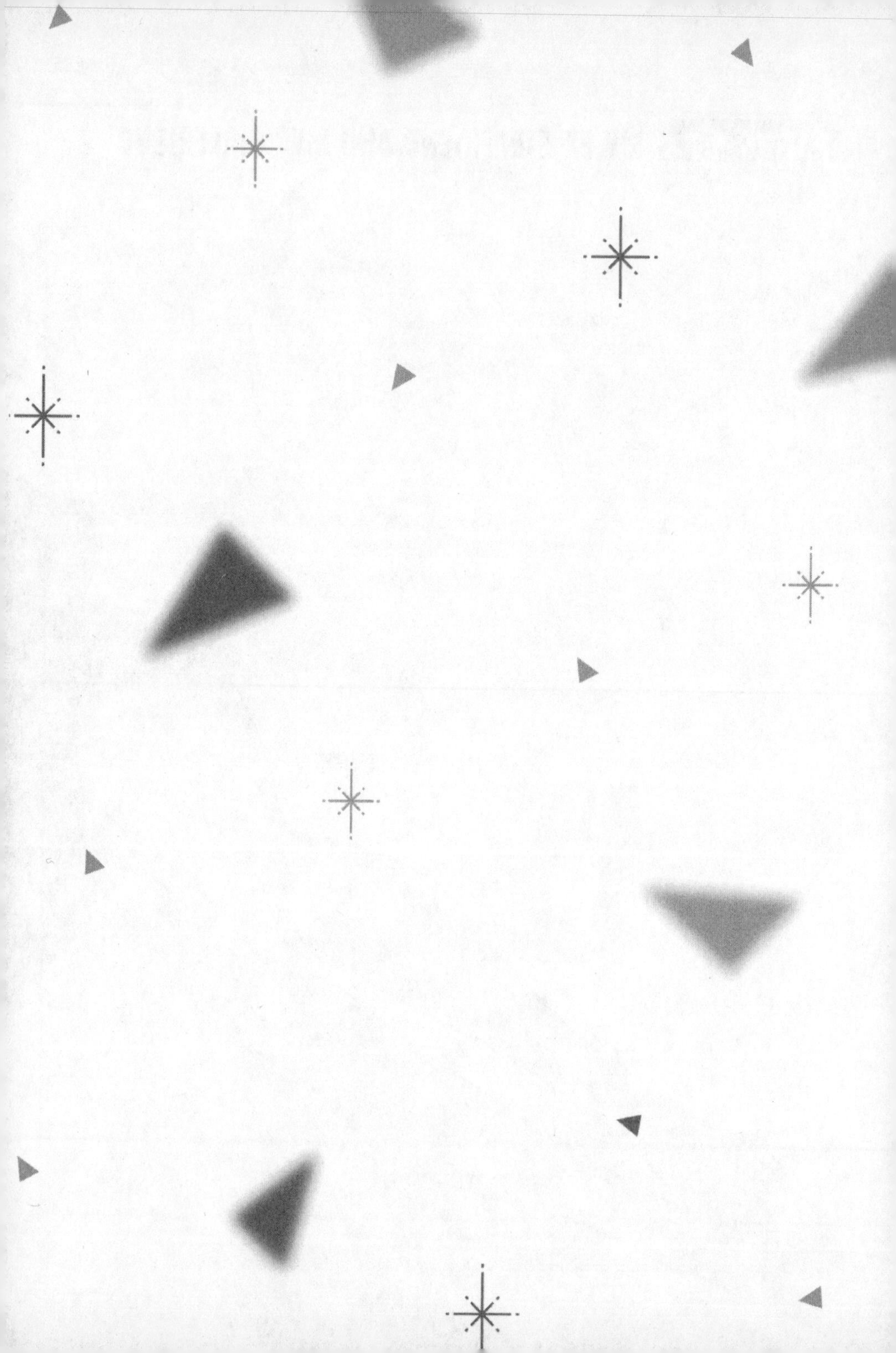

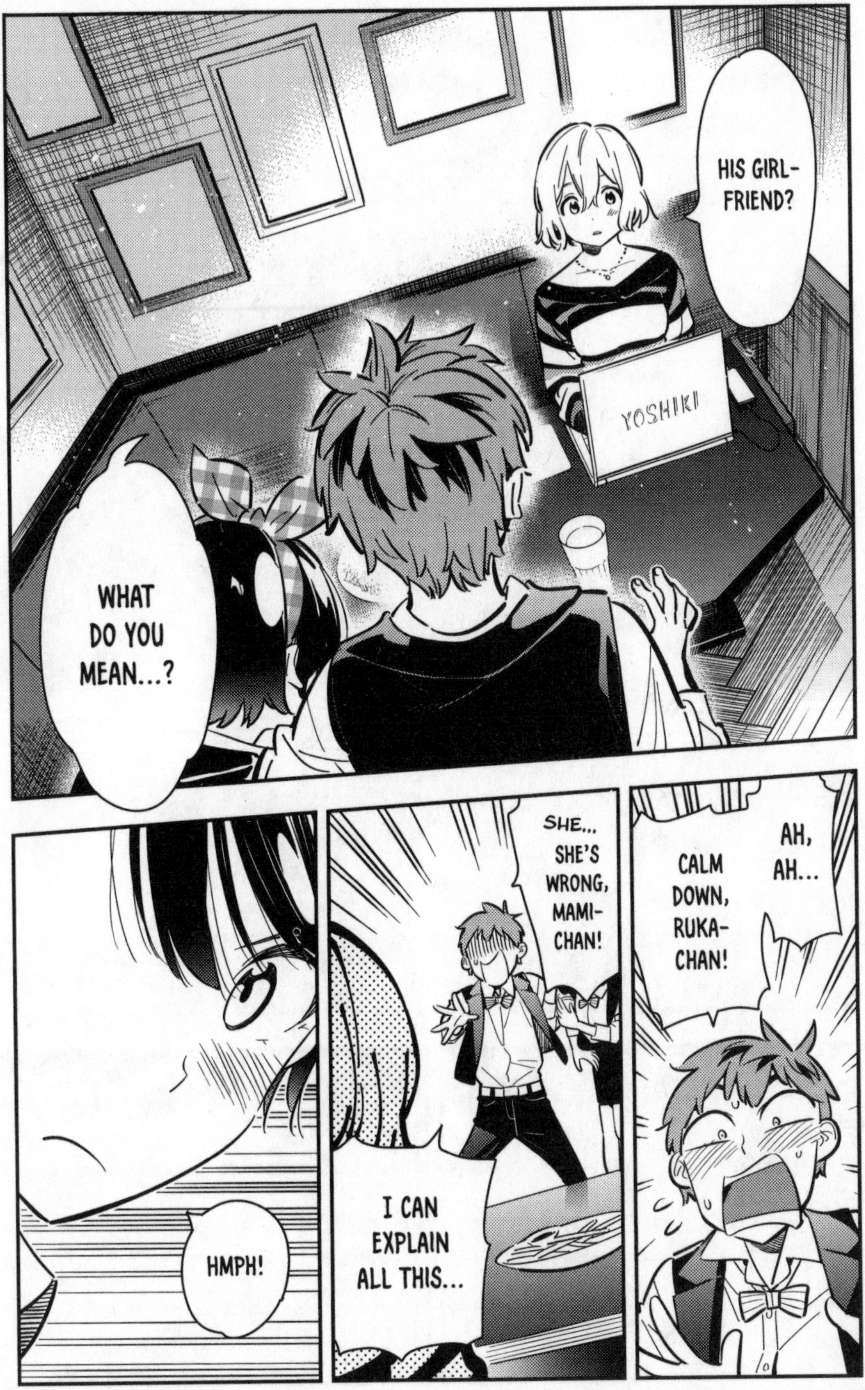
HIS GIRLFRIEND?
YOSHIKI
WHAT DO YOU MEAN...?
AH, AH...
CALM DOWN, RUKA-CHAN!
SHE... SHE'S WRONG, MAMI-CHAN!
I CAN EXPLAIN ALL THIS...
HMPH!

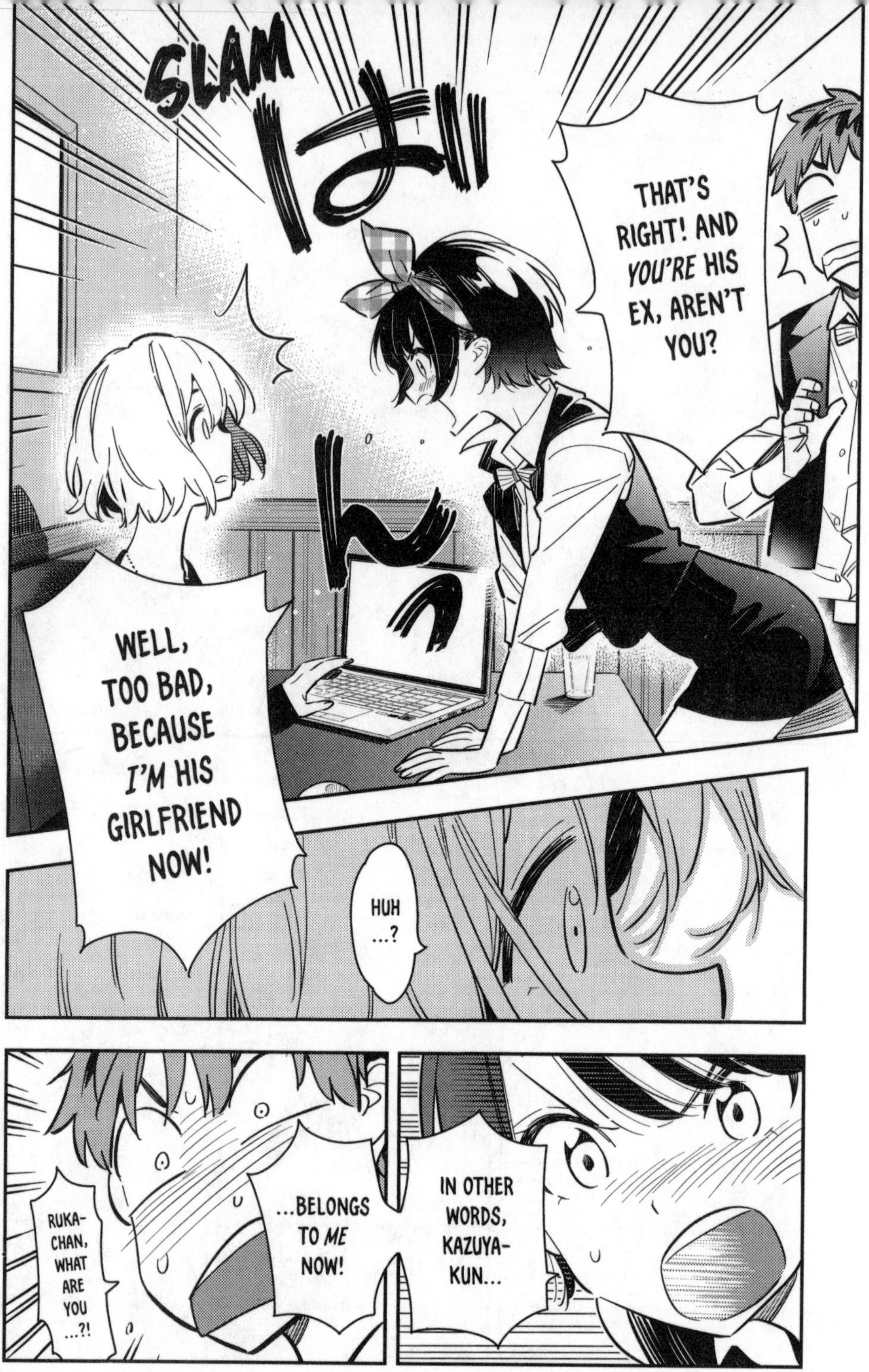
THAT'S RIGHT! AND *YOU'RE* HIS EX, AREN'T YOU?
SLAM
はんっ
WELL, TOO BAD, BECAUSE *I'M* HIS GIRLFRIEND NOW!
HUH ...?
IN OTHER WORDS, KAZUYA-KUN...
...BELONGS TO *ME* NOW!
RUKA-CHAN, WHAT ARE YOU ...?!

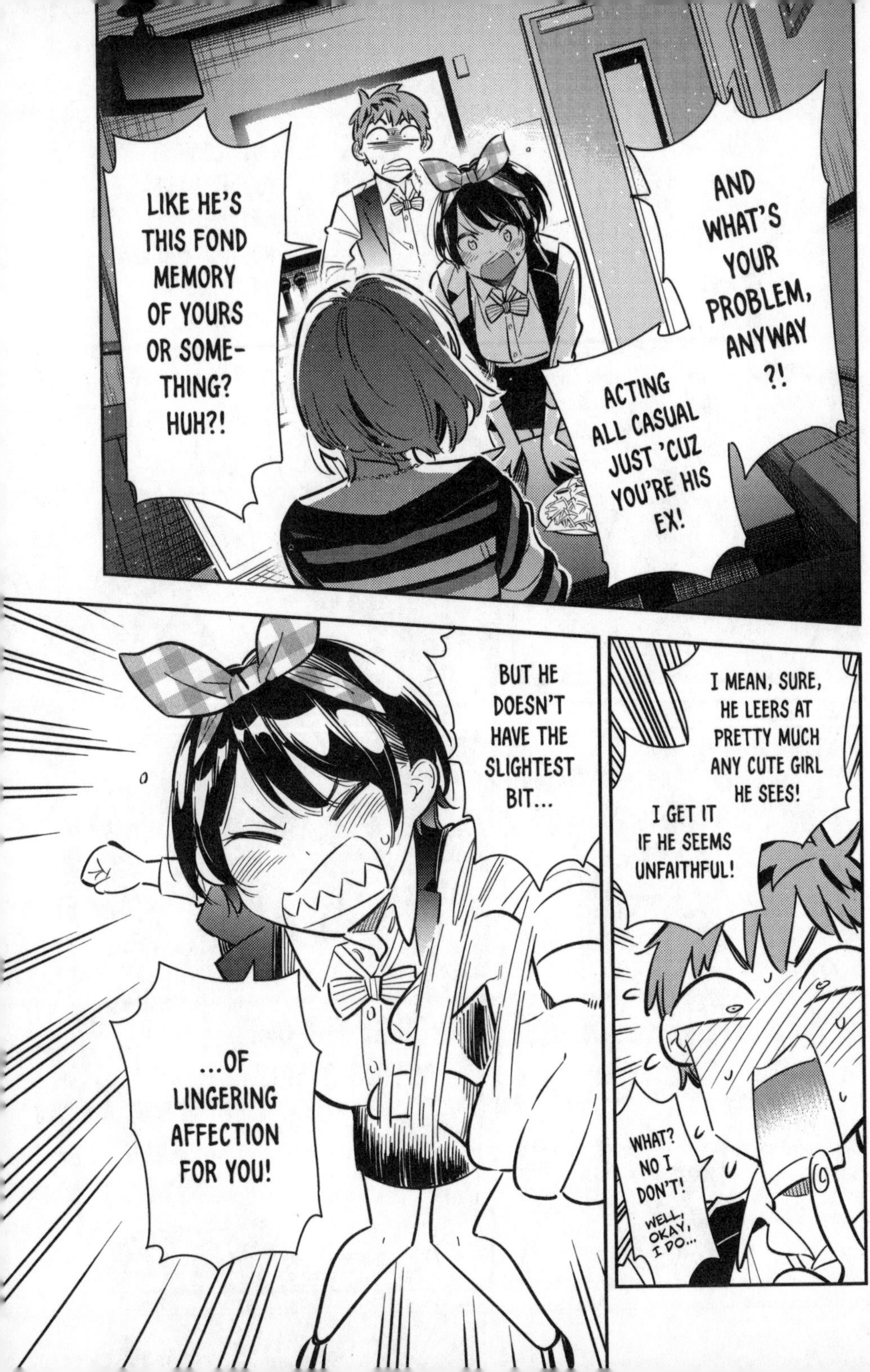
AND WHAT'S YOUR PROBLEM, ANYWAY?!
ACTING ALL CASUAL JUST 'CUZ YOU'RE HIS EX!
LIKE HE'S THIS FOND MEMORY OF YOURS OR SOME-THING? HUH?!
I MEAN, SURE, HE LEERS AT PRETTY MUCH ANY CUTE GIRL HE SEES!
I GET IT IF HE SEEMS UNFAITHFUL!
WHAT? NO I DON'T!
WELL, OKAY, I DO...
BUT HE DOESN'T HAVE THE SLIGHTEST BIT...
...OF LINGERING AFFECTION FOR YOU!

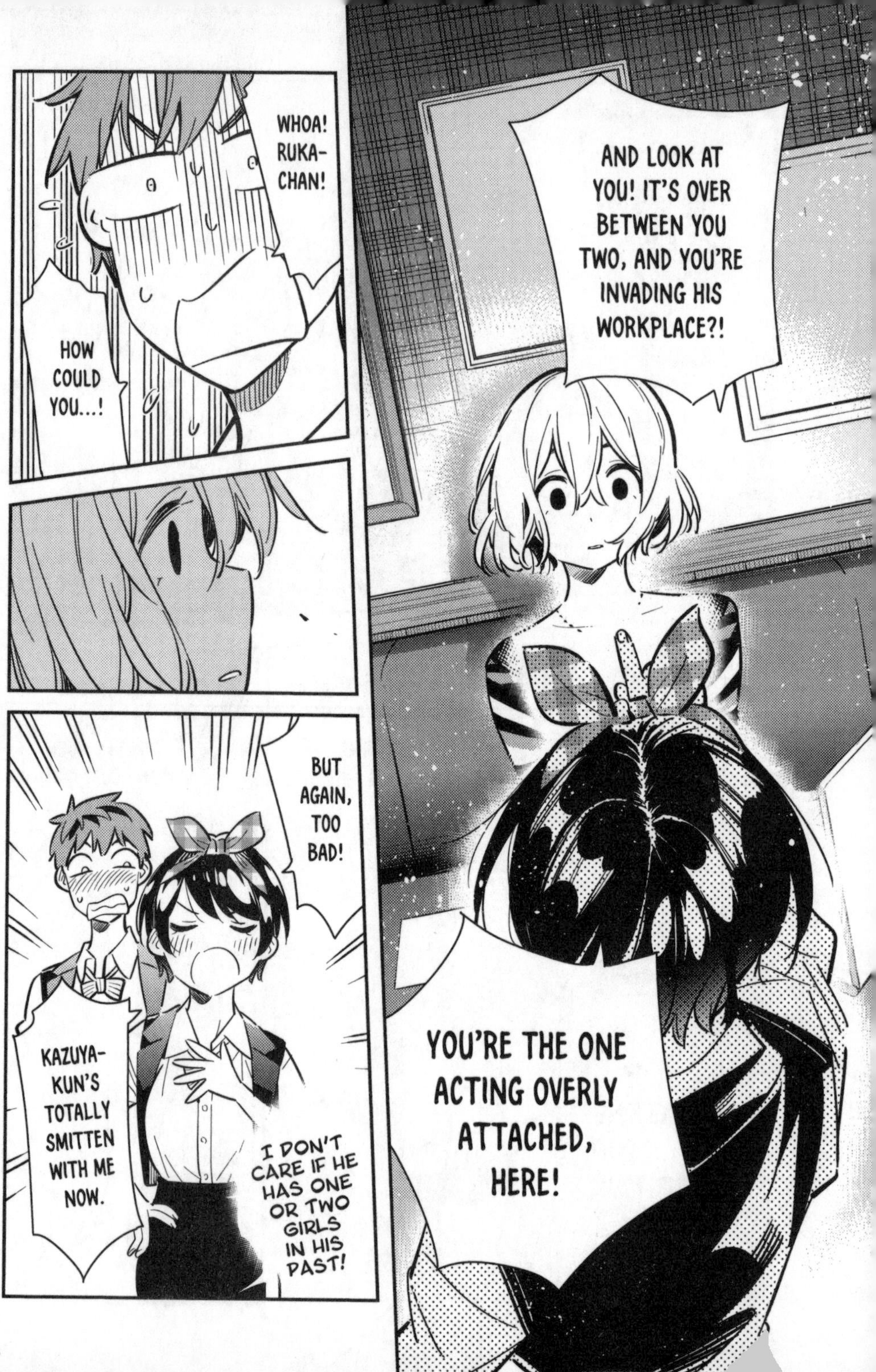
AND LOOK AT YOU! IT'S OVER BETWEEN YOU TWO, AND YOU'RE INVADING HIS WORKPLACE?!
YOU'RE THE ONE ACTING OVERLY ATTACHED, HERE!
WHOA! RUKA-CHAN!
HOW COULD YOU...!
BUT AGAIN, TOO BAD!
KAZUYA-KUN'S TOTALLY SMITTEN WITH ME NOW.
I DON'T CARE IF HE HAS ONE OR TWO GIRLS IN HIS PAST!

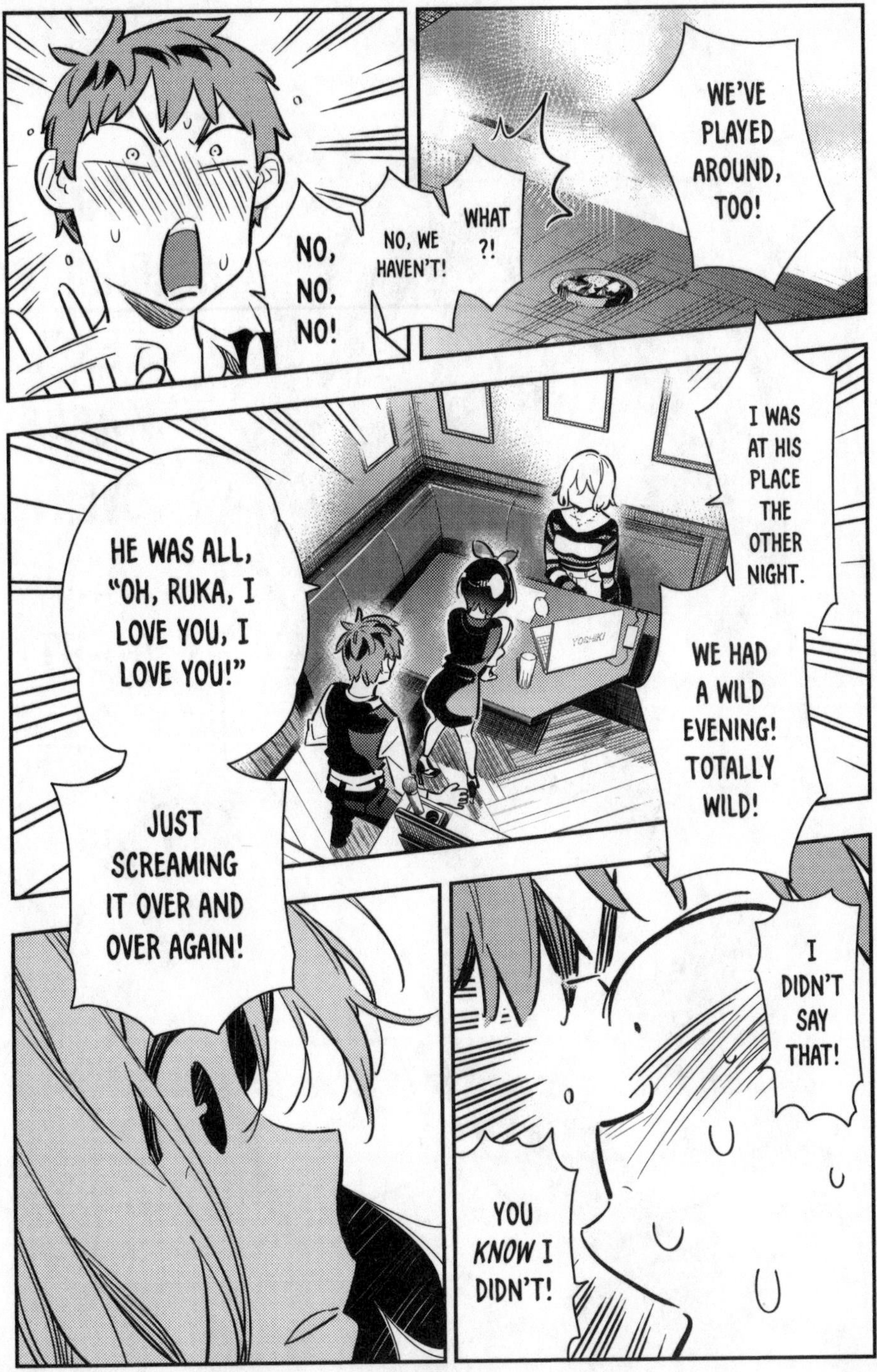
WE'VE PLAYED AROUND, TOO!
WHAT?!
NO, WE HAVEN'T!
NO, NO, NO!
I WAS AT HIS PLACE THE OTHER NIGHT.
WE HAD A WILD EVENING! TOTALLY WILD!
HE WAS ALL, "OH, RUKA, I LOVE YOU, I LOVE YOU!"
JUST SCREAMING IT OVER AND OVER AGAIN!
I DIDN'T SAY THAT!
YOU *KNOW* I DIDN'T!

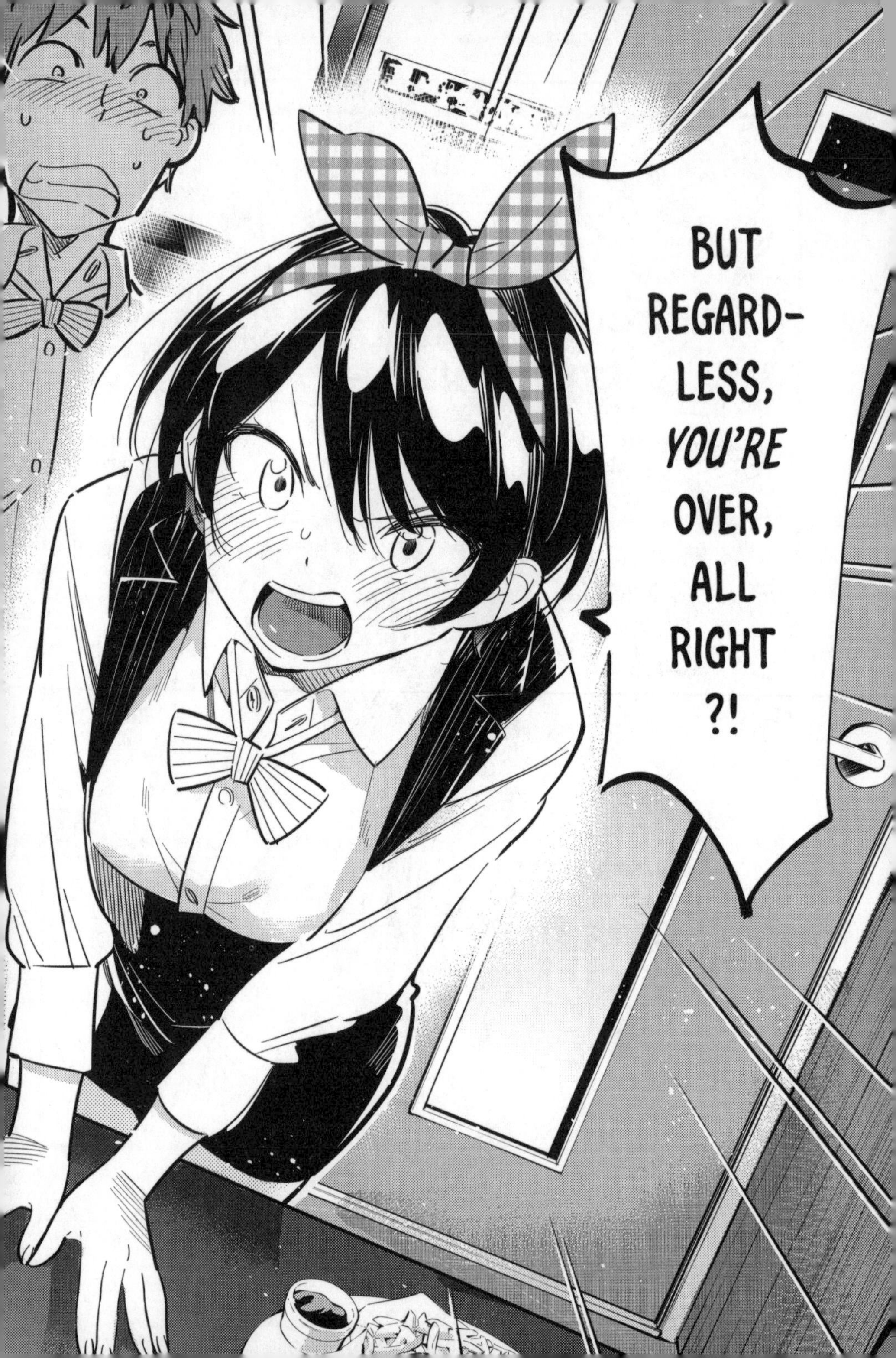
BUT REGARD-LESS, *YOU'RE* OVER, ALL RIGHT ?!

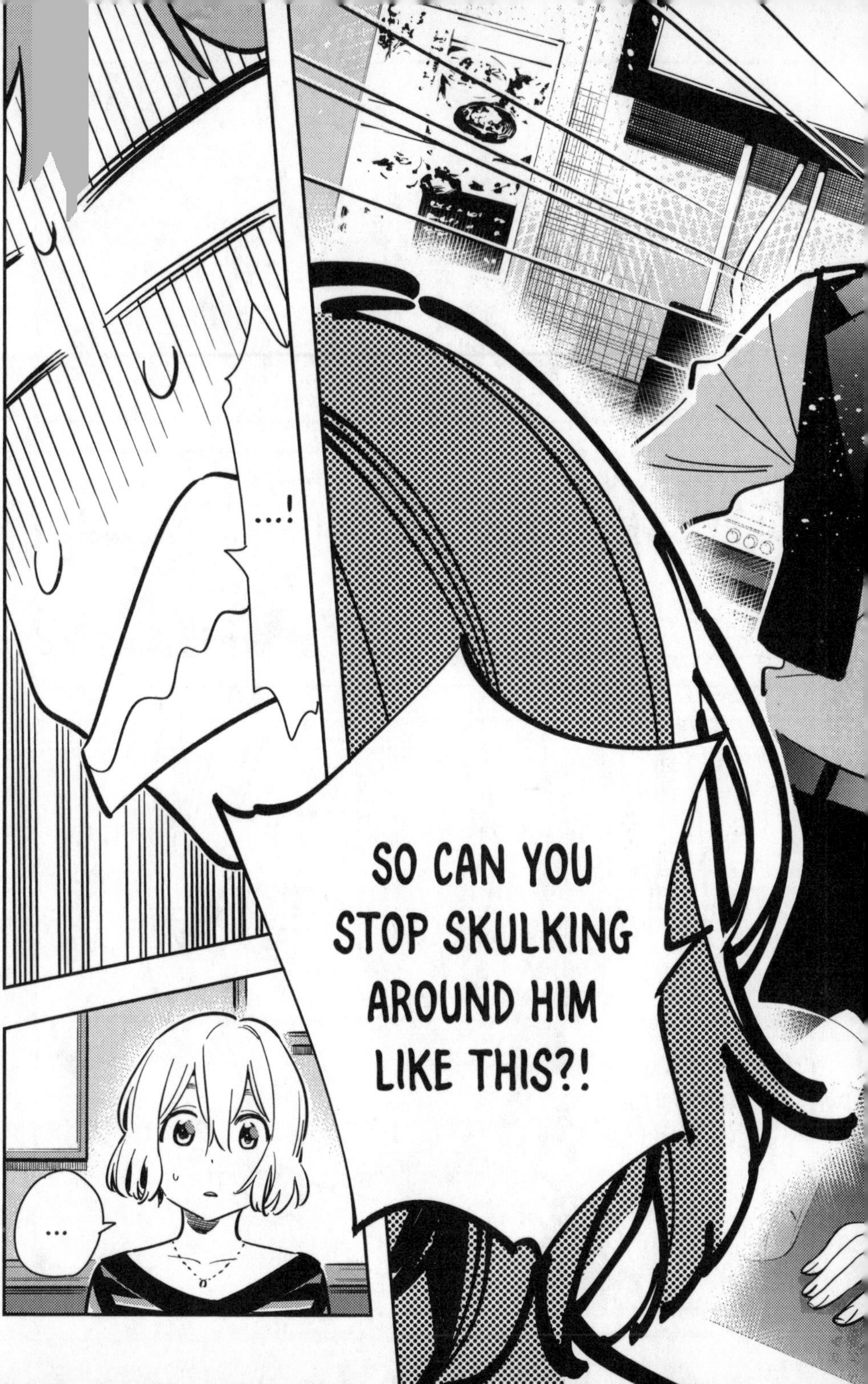
SO CAN YOU STOP SKULKING AROUND HIM LIKE THIS?!
...!
...

...

SO YOU REALLY HAVE A GIRLFRIEND, KAZU-KUN...?

OH, SURE, ACT ALL MODEST.

I'M SORRY... THAT WASN'T MY INTENTION.

IF THAT'S TRUE...

WHY'D YOU GO AND RENT A GIRLFRIEND...?

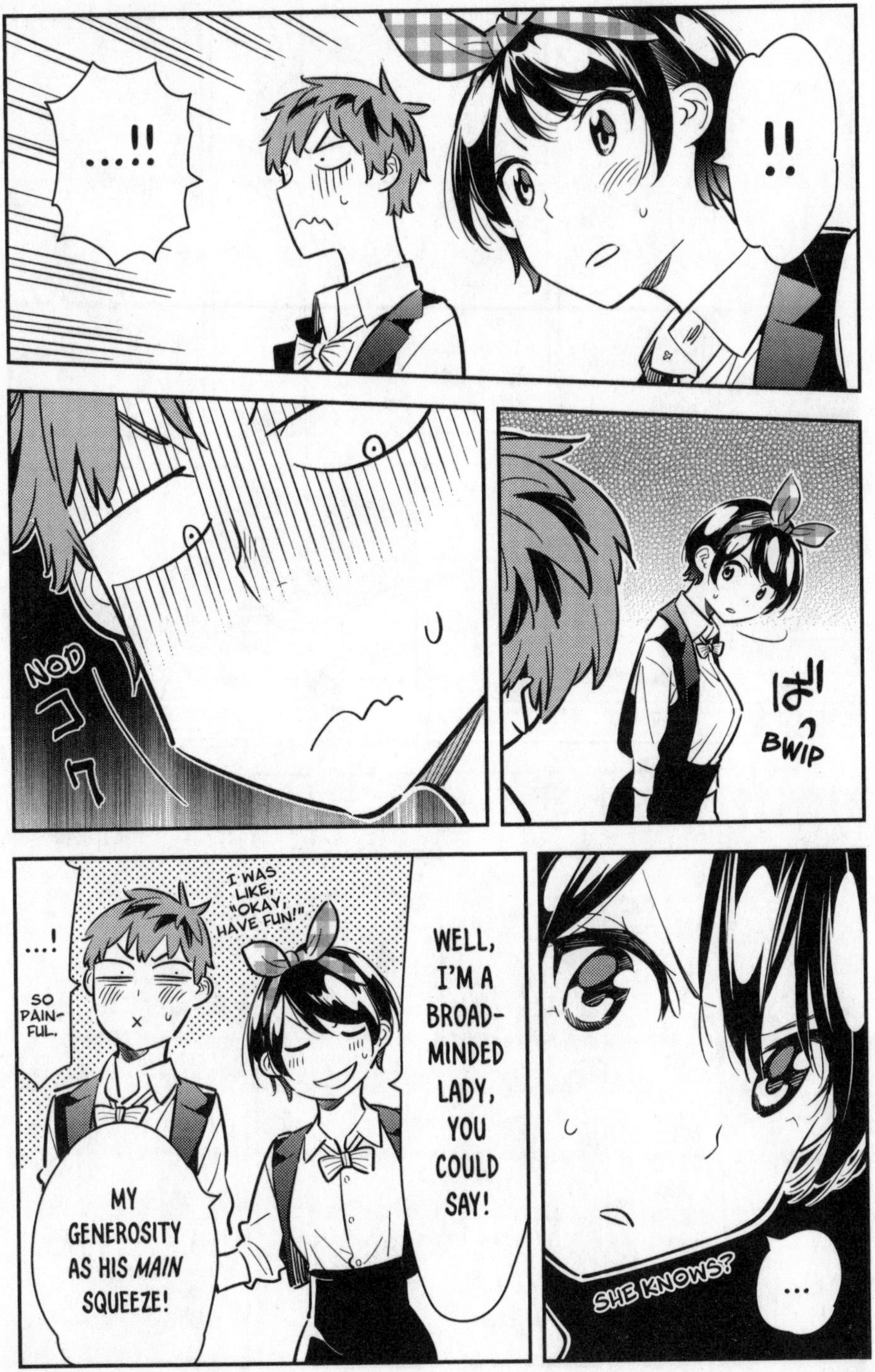
!!
...!!
ぱっ
BWIP
NOD
コク
...
SHE KNOWS?
WELL, I'M A BROAD-MINDED LADY, YOU COULD SAY!
I WAS LIKE, "OKAY, HAVE FUN!"
...!
SO PAIN-FUL.
MY GENEROSITY AS HIS *MAIN* SQUEEZE!

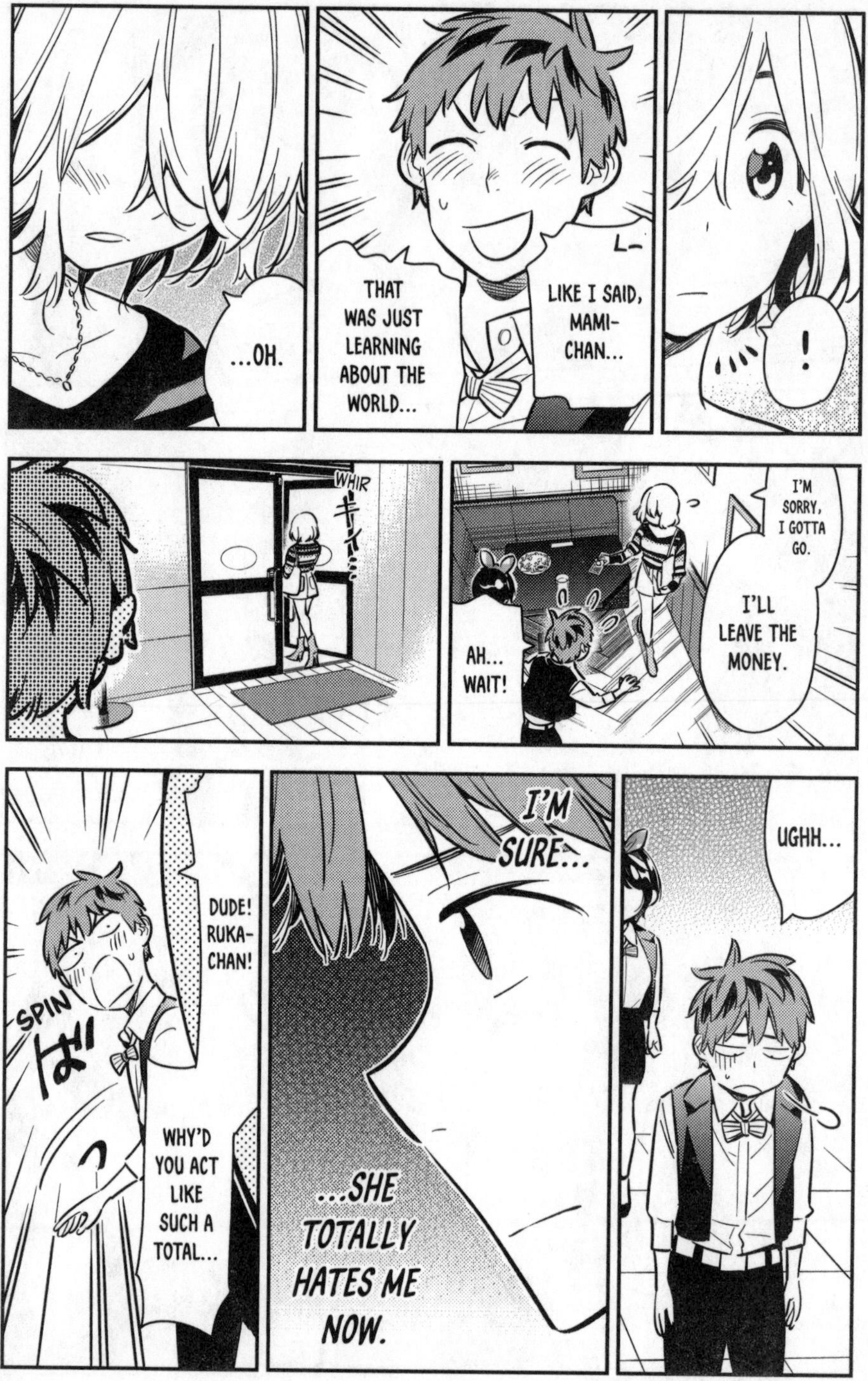
!
L–
LIKE I SAID, MAMI-CHAN...
THAT WAS JUST LEARNING ABOUT THE WORLD...
...OH.
I'M SORRY, I GOTTA GO.
I'LL LEAVE THE MONEY.
AH... WAIT!
WHIR
UGHH...
I'M SURE...
...SHE TOTALLY HATES ME NOW.
DUDE! RUKA-CHAN!
SPIN
WHY'D YOU ACT LIKE SUCH A TOTAL...

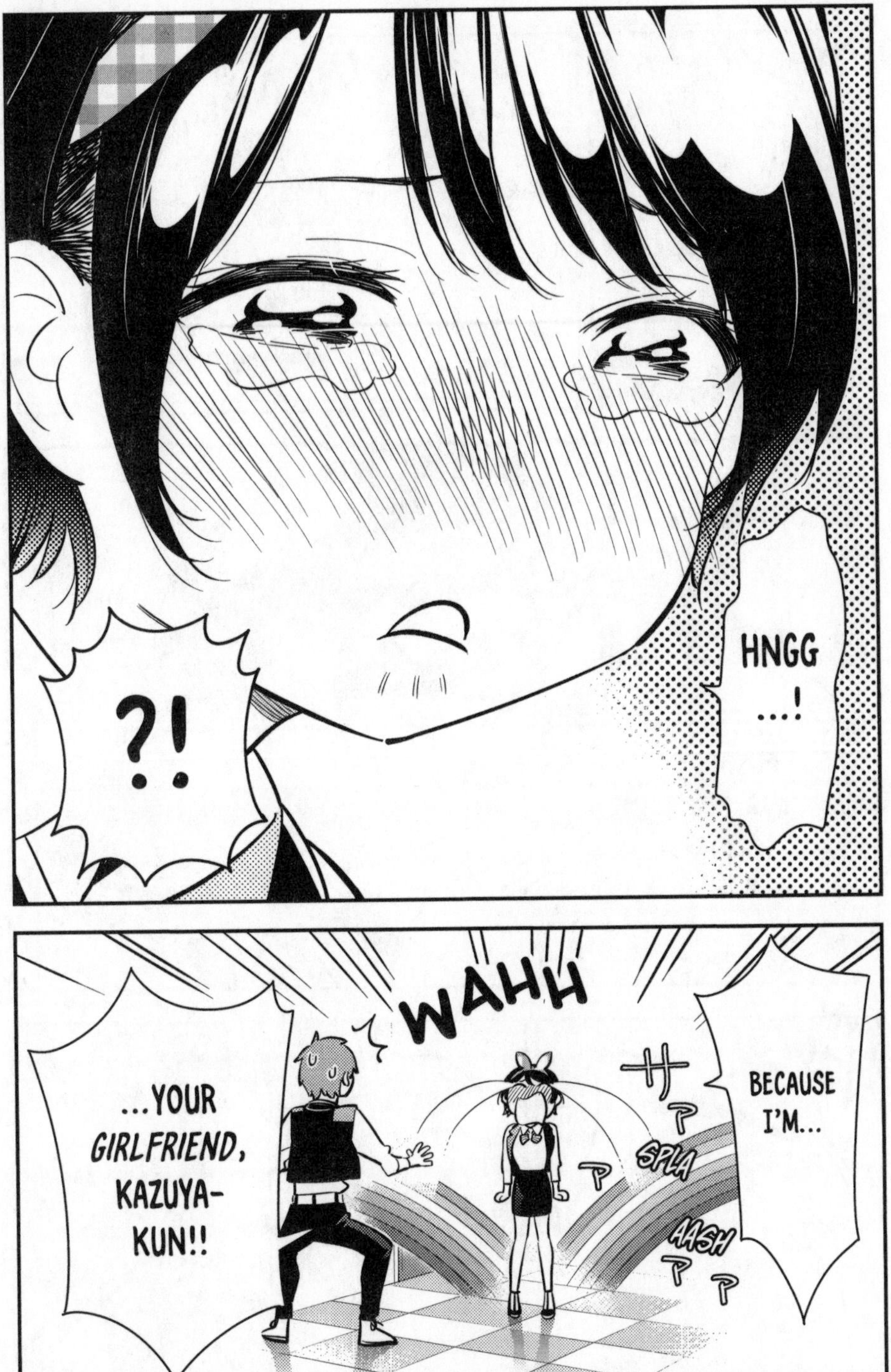
HNGG ...!
?!
BECAUSE I'M...
WAHH
SPLA
AASH
...YOUR GIRLFRIEND, KAZUYA-KUN!!

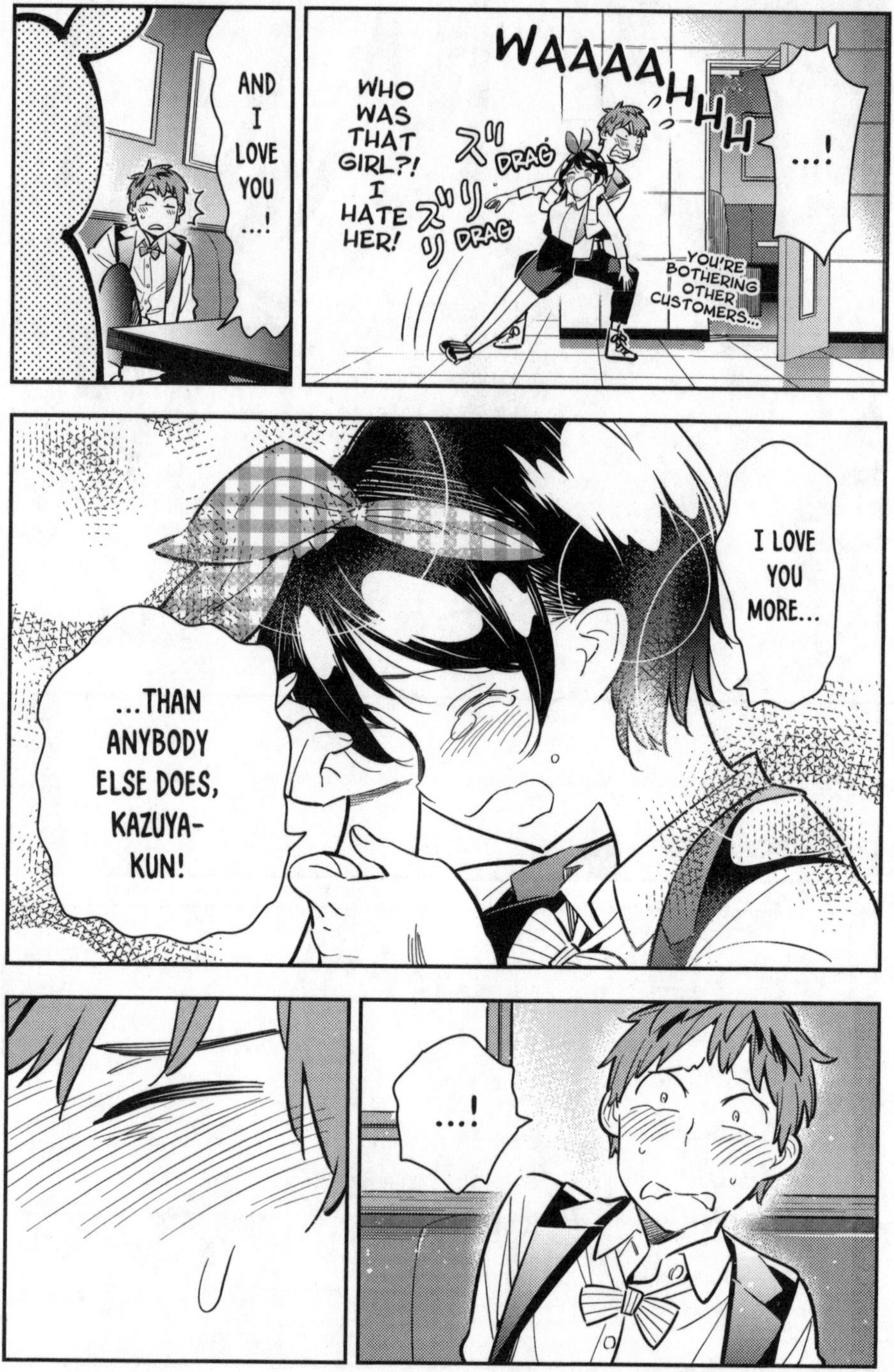
...!
WAAAAHHHH
WHO WAS THAT GIRL?! I HATE HER!
ズリ DRAG
ズリ DRAG
YOU'RE BOTHERING OTHER CUSTOMERS...
AND I LOVE YOU...!
I LOVE YOU MORE...
...THAN ANYBODY ELSE DOES, KAZUYA-KUN!
...!

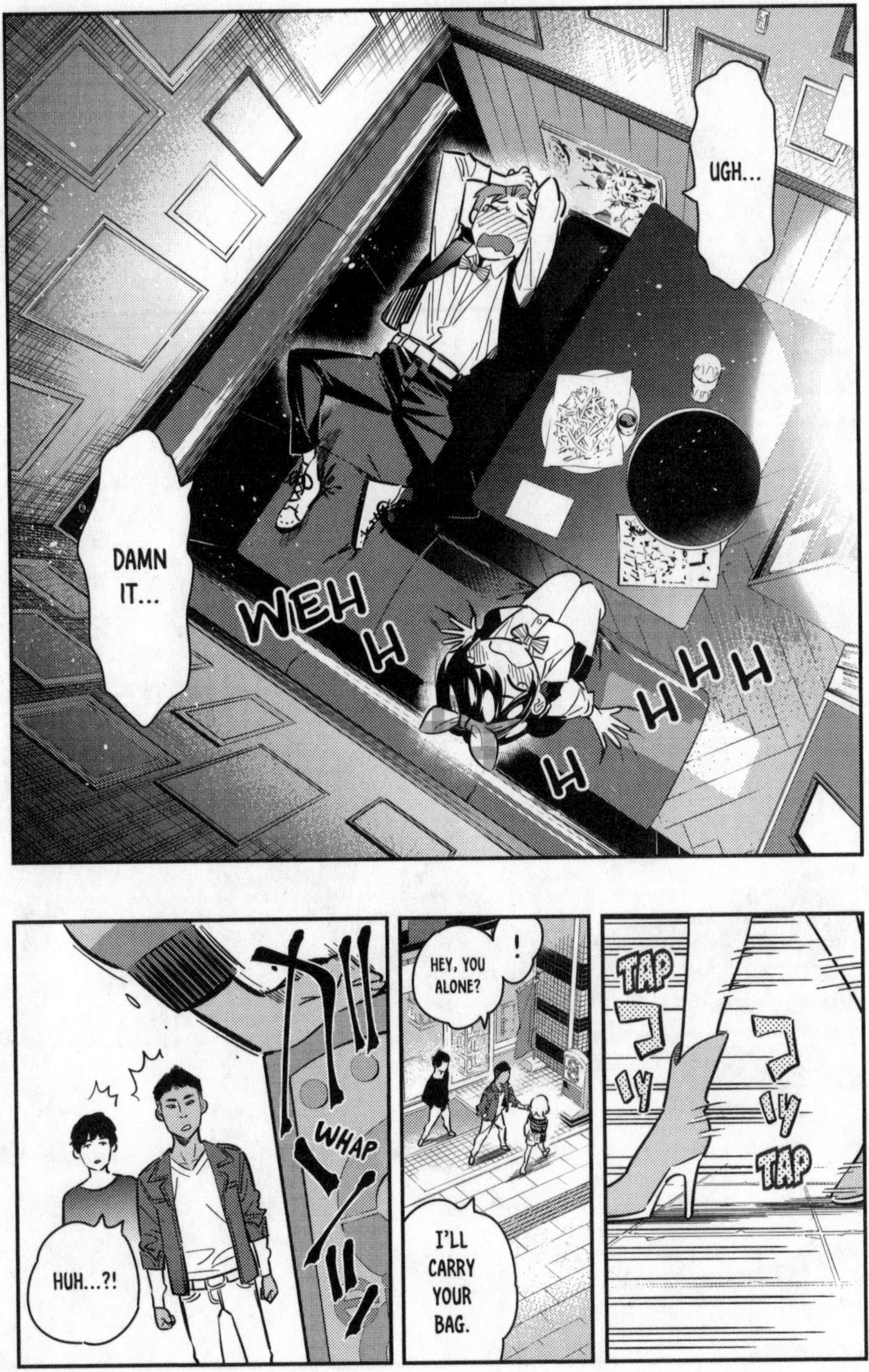
UGH...
DAMN IT...
WEHHHHHH
TAP
TAP
!
HEY, YOU ALONE?
I'LL CARRY YOUR BAG.
WHAP
HUH...?!

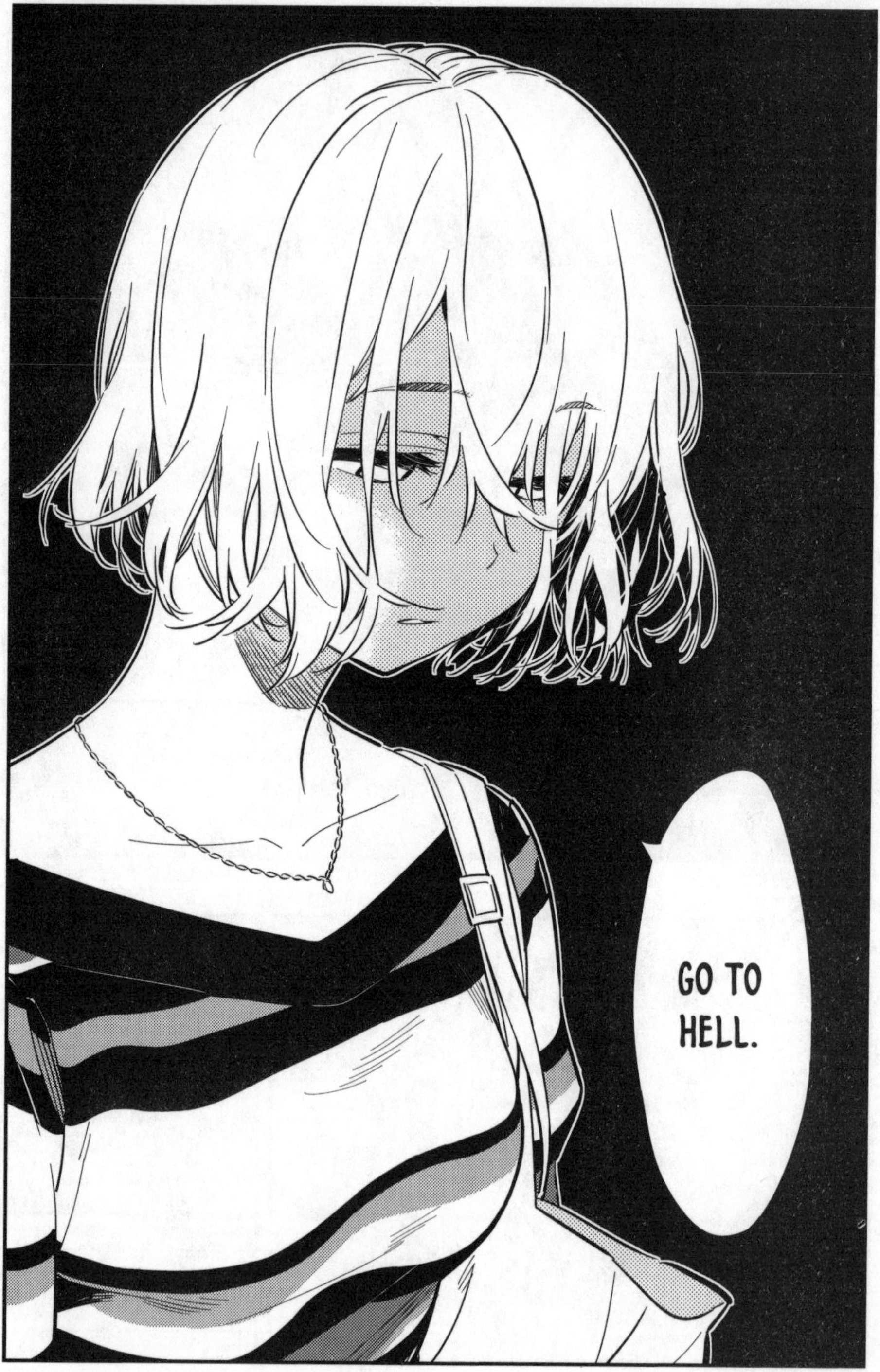
GO TO HELL.

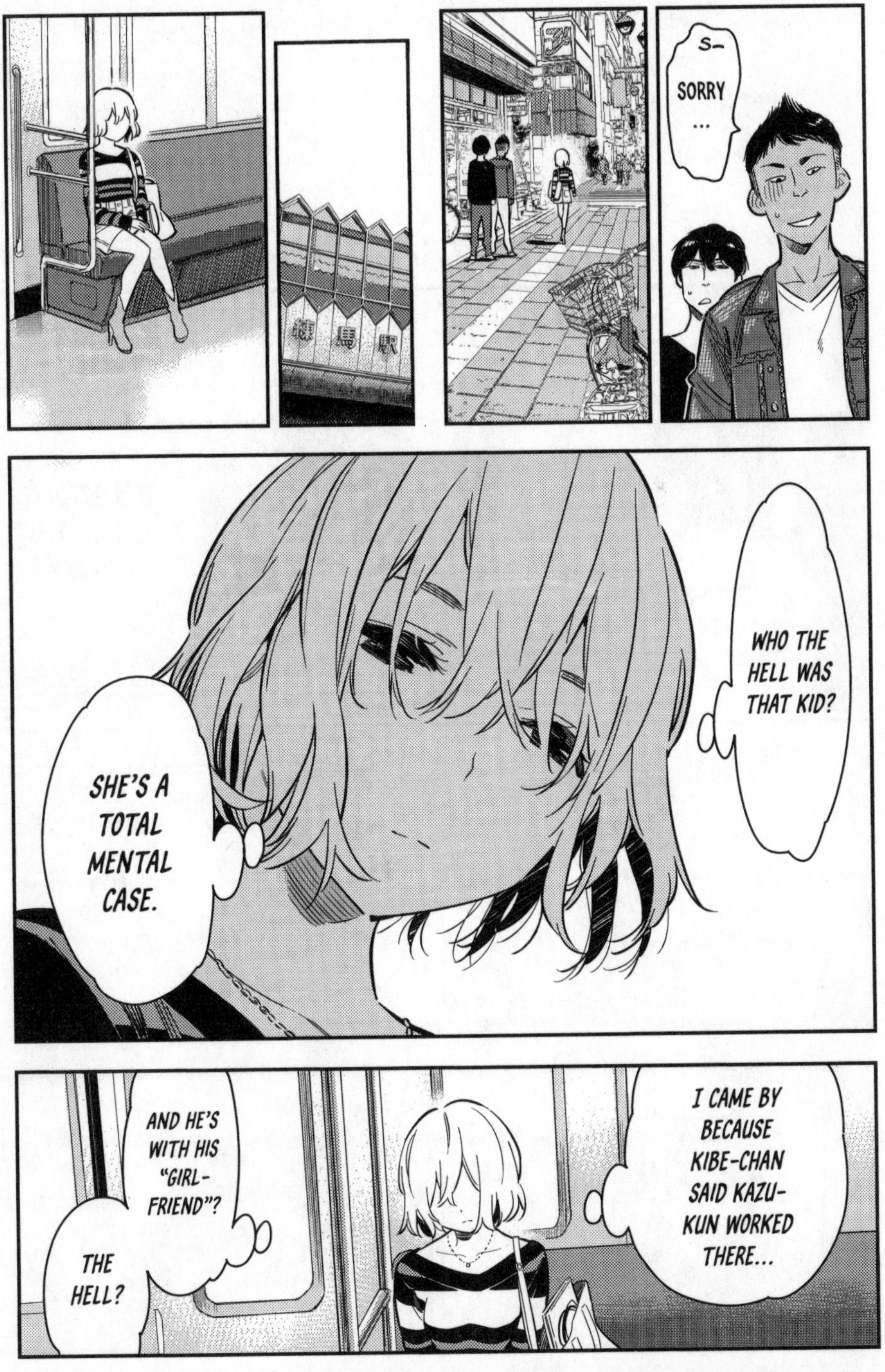
S— SORRY ...
練馬駅
WHO THE HELL WAS THAT KID?
SHE'S A TOTAL MENTAL CASE.
I CAME BY BECAUSE KIBE-CHAN SAID KAZU-KUN WORKED THERE...
AND HE'S WITH HIS "GIRL-FRIEND"?
THE HELL?

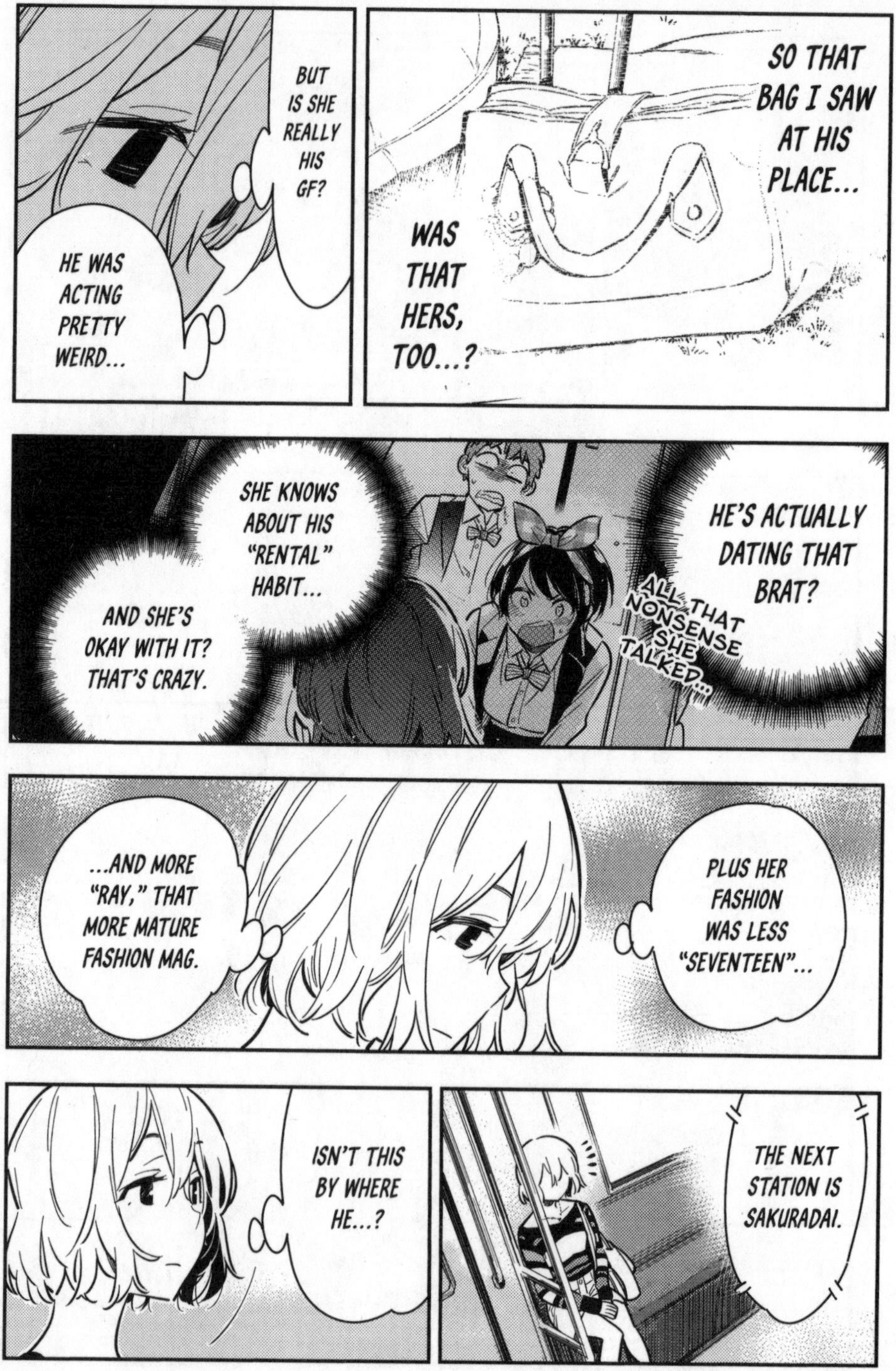
SO THAT BAG I SAW AT HIS PLACE...
WAS THAT HERS, TOO...?
BUT IS SHE REALLY HIS GF?
HE WAS ACTING PRETTY WEIRD...
HE'S ACTUALLY DATING THAT BRAT?
ALL THAT NONSENSE SHE TALKED...
SHE KNOWS ABOUT HIS "RENTAL" HABIT...
AND SHE'S OKAY WITH IT? THAT'S CRAZY.
PLUS HER FASHION WAS LESS "SEVENTEEN"...
...AND MORE "RAY," THAT MORE MATURE FASHION MAG.
THE NEXT STATION IS SAKURADAI.
ISN'T THIS BY WHERE HE...?

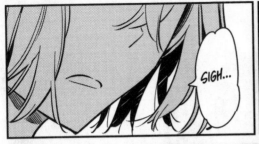

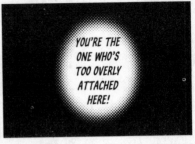

YOU'RE THE ONE WHO'S TOO OVERLY ATTACHED HERE!
SIGH...
WHY AM I EVEN THINKING...
...ABOUT ALL THIS MEAN-INGLESS CRAP?
PSSHH
TAP

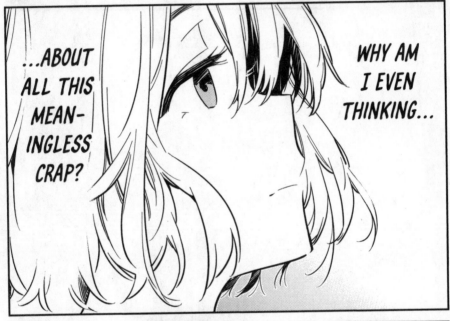

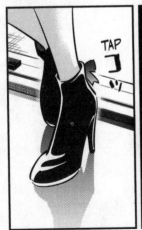

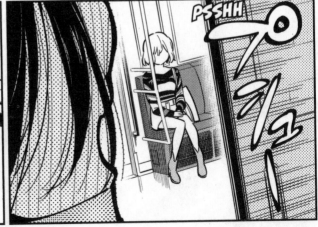

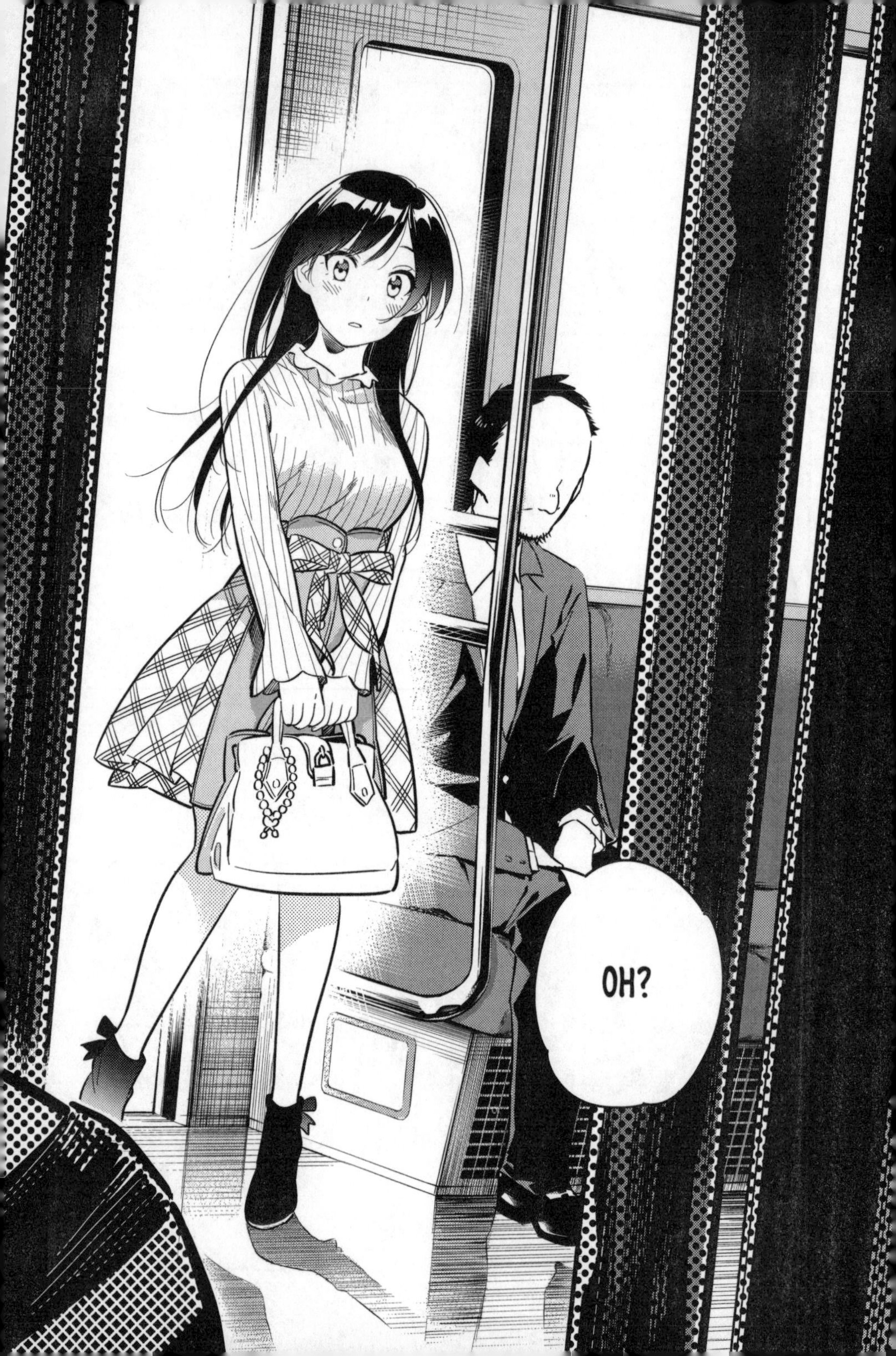
OH?

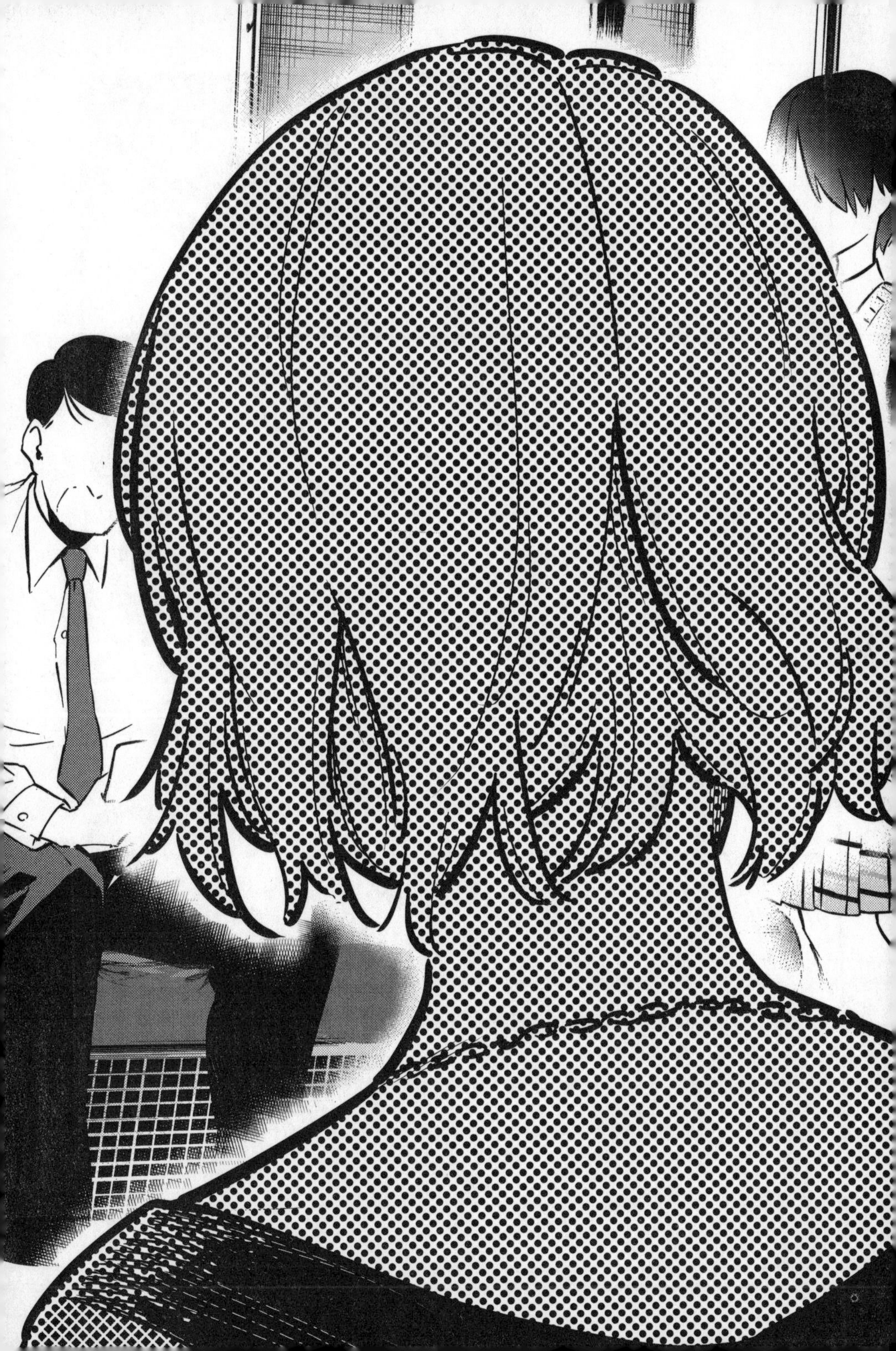

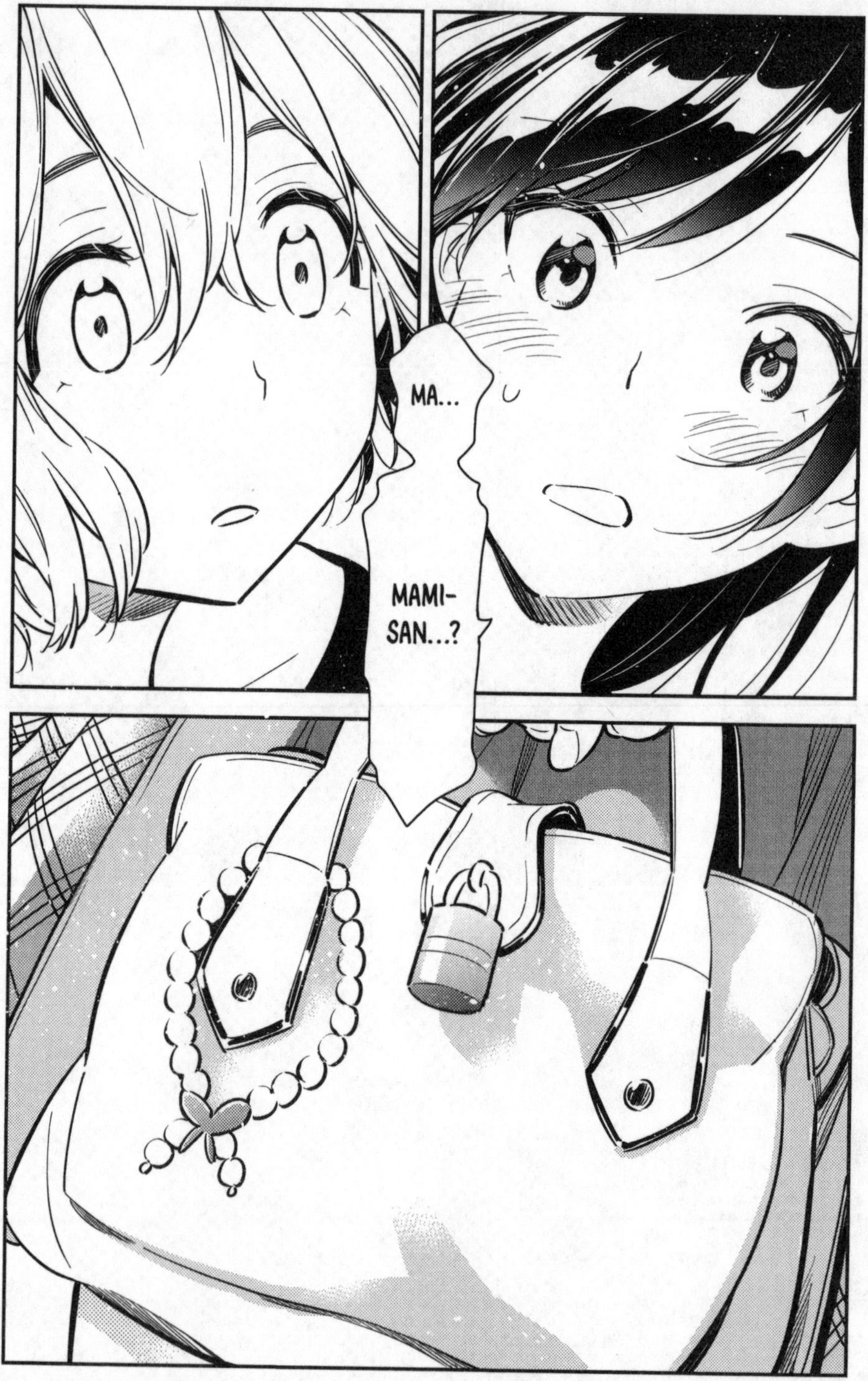
MA...
MAMI-SAN...?

MY FIRST WORK SINCE RECOVERING

DON'T ASK ME TO DRAW SUMI-CHAN →

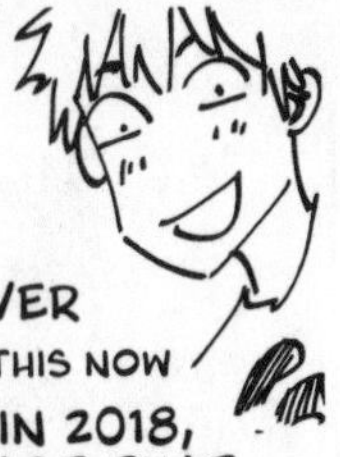

THANK YOU VERY MUCH FOR BUYING RENT-A-GIRLFRIEND VOL. 9!!!

MAN... NOW I'VE DONE IT... I'VE HAD A 102° FEVER FOR FOUR DAYS STRAIGHT. ←THE EDITOR JUST LEARNED THIS NOW

I SPENT A TOTAL OF 800 YEN* ON MEDICAL BILLS IN 2018, BUT ONE MONTH INTO 2019 AND I'M ALREADY WELL PAST THAT...

BOY, I HAVEN'T HAD IT THIS BAD IN YEARS. ←JUST GO AHEAD AND DIE

AS THE READERS KNOW, MY METHOD FOR DEALING WITH COLDS IS TO IGNORE THEM (UNLESS IT'S THE FLU). I PRETEND THEY DON'T EXIST AT ALL, LIKE I'M A PARTICULARLY CRUEL BULLY...BUT I CAN'T IGNORE THIS. IT JUST REFUSES TO BE IGNORED. ←JUST REALIZED I'LL TALK ABOUT MY COLD THE WHOLE PAGE IF THIS KEEPS UP

BUT WHATEVER. IT'S PAST ME NOW.

VOLUME 9 ENDS RIGHT AT THE CLIMAX, HUH? (VOLUME 10 COMES OUT IN MAY! ←IMMEDIATE AD MAMI APPEARED IN CHAPTER 1 ALONGSIDE KAZUYA'S FAMILY AND MIZUHARA, SO I HAVE A LOT OF ATTACHMENT TO HER. I THINK A LOT OF HER MOTIVATION AS A CHARACTER COMES DOWN TO ENVY, OR JEALOUSY, ALONG THE LINES OF "THE ONE THAT GOT AWAY" OR "THE GRASS IS GREENER"... BUT, REALLY, IT'S ***ME, MYSELF***. I REALLY DO GET JEALOUS OF OTHER PEOPLE GETTING POPULAR, DRAWING BETTER THAN ME, TELLING MORE ENGAGING STORIES. ←REPLAYED IT 200M TIMES (BY THE WAY, MY CURRENT NUMBER-ONE SONG IS "NETANDERTHAL JIN" FROM BACK NUMBER.) I HAVE TO KEEP MYSELF FROM SCREAMING ABOUT IT EVERY DAY. SO WHEN MAMI'S EX BRINGS THIS SUPER-CUTE GIRL ALONG AND ACTS ALL LIKE, "WHAT?", I TOTALLY GET THAT. ← BLAM!! I MEAN, DUDE, THAT'S SO EVIL! YOU GOTTA WORRY ABOUT YOURSELF, AND STOP FRETTING OVER OTHER PEOPLE AND RELATIVE STUFF. ← NO SALVATION

I CAN'T HELP THE WAY I THINK. STILL, AS I WROTE IN THE LAST VOLUME, I'M ABLE TO DRAW MANGA ABOUT HOW CUTE MIZUHARA IS, SO I GOT IT PRETTY GOOD.

BUT WHEN I SEE SOMEONE PAINED BY ENVY AND JEALOUSY, I JUST WANT TO EMBRACE THEM TO MAKE THEM FEEL BETTER, SO I SUPPOSE MAMI IS MY EMBODIMENT OF THOSE FEELINGS. THERE'S NO NEED TO CREATE CHARACTERS LIKE HER, BUT I HOPE YOU'LL CONTINUE TO ENJOY HAVING HER AROUND. ← I LOVE HER. SHE'S A SURPRISINGLY MUST-HAVE CHARACTER.

I FEEL LIKE I ALWAYS WRITE NEGATIVE STUFF IN HERE, EVEN THOUGH I DON'T. I THINK I'M A PRETTY POSITIVE-MINDED, OPTIMISTIC IDIOT (LIKE KAZUYA). I'M JUST ADMITTING THAT I HAVE SOME NEGATIVE EMOTIONS INSIDE OF ME, AS WELL. SO, IN THE NEXT VOLUME, I'D LIKE TO WRITE ABOUT THINGS THAT I LIKE, INSTEAD. ← NARCISSIST I BELIEVE THAT "LIKING WHAT YOU LIKE TO THE MAX IS HALF OF THE JOB," SO I THINK INTERACTING WITH WHAT YOU ENJOY, ALL BY ITSELF, ENRICHES YOUR LIFE A LOT. KAZUYA MUST HAVE SO MUCH FUN. THANKS FOR READING THIS UNREADABLE NONSENSE TO THE LAST LINE.

SEE YOU NEXT VOLUME.

REIJI MIYAJIMA

*ABOUT 155 USD

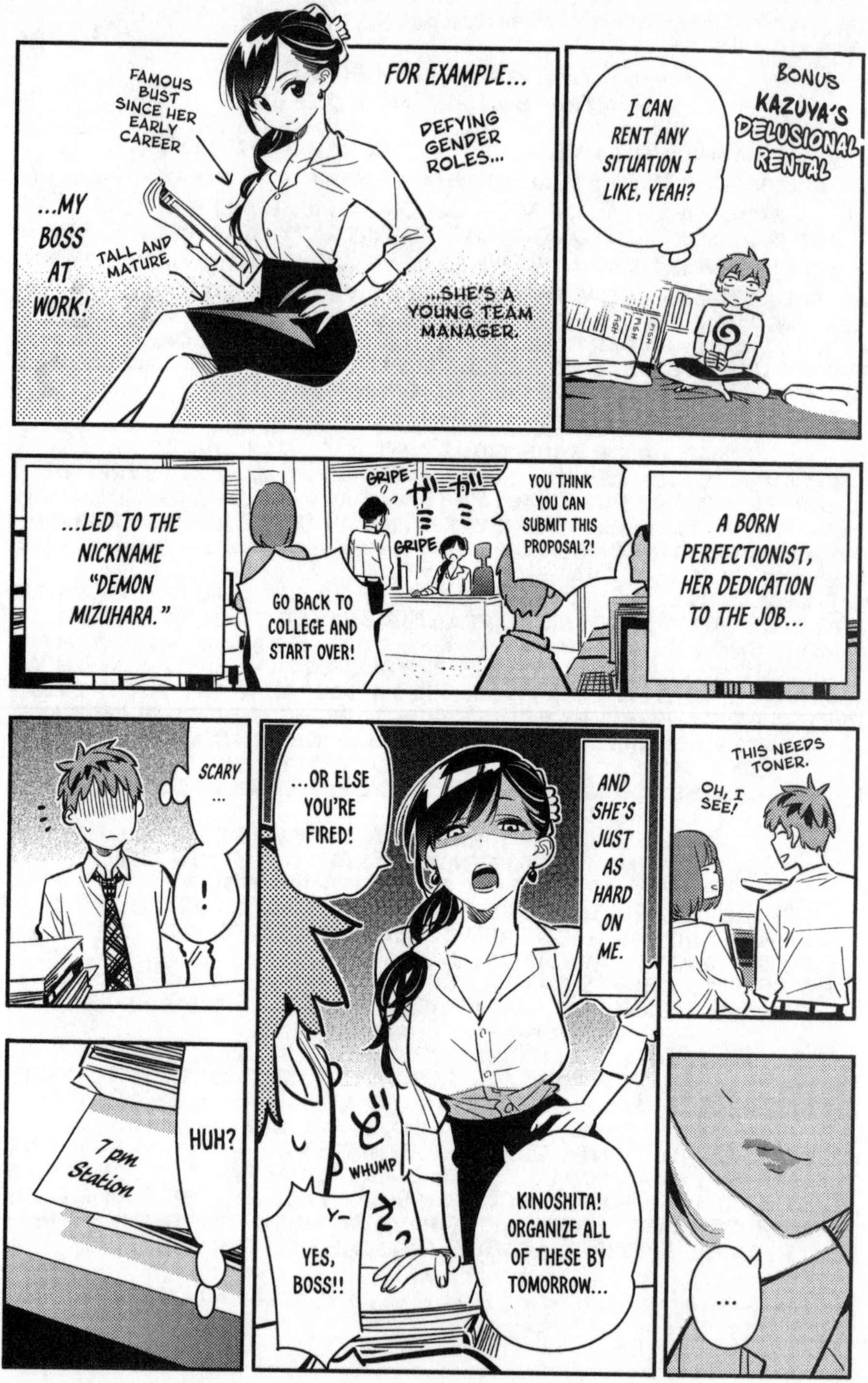
BONUS
KAZUYA'S DELUSIONAL RENTAL
I CAN RENT ANY SITUATION I LIKE, YEAH?
FISH
FISH
FISH
FOR EXAMPLE...
DEFYING GENDER ROLES...
FAMOUS BUST SINCE HER EARLY CAREER
...MY BOSS AT WORK!
TALL AND MATURE
...SHE'S A YOUNG TEAM MANAGER.
A BORN PERFECTIONIST, HER DEDICATION TO THE JOB...
YOU THINK YOU CAN SUBMIT THIS PROPOSAL?!
GRIPE
GRIPE
GO BACK TO COLLEGE AND START OVER!
...LED TO THE NICKNAME "DEMON MIZUHARA."
THIS NEEDS TONER.
OH, I SEE!
...
AND SHE'S JUST AS HARD ON ME.
KINOSHITA! ORGANIZE ALL OF THESE BY TOMORROW...
...OR ELSE YOU'RE FIRED!
WHUMP
Y–
YES, BOSS!!
SCARY...
!
HUH?
7 pm Station

RENT-A-GIRLFRIEND STAFF: A, IROHKI, TEMAENO, KUSUMI, MITSUKI, MINATO

EDITORS: HIRAOKA-SAN, HIRATSUKA-SAN, HARA-SAN, CHOKAI-SAN. ALSO THANKS TO EVERYBODY WHO PICKED UP THIS BOOK!! SEE YOU SOON! ♡

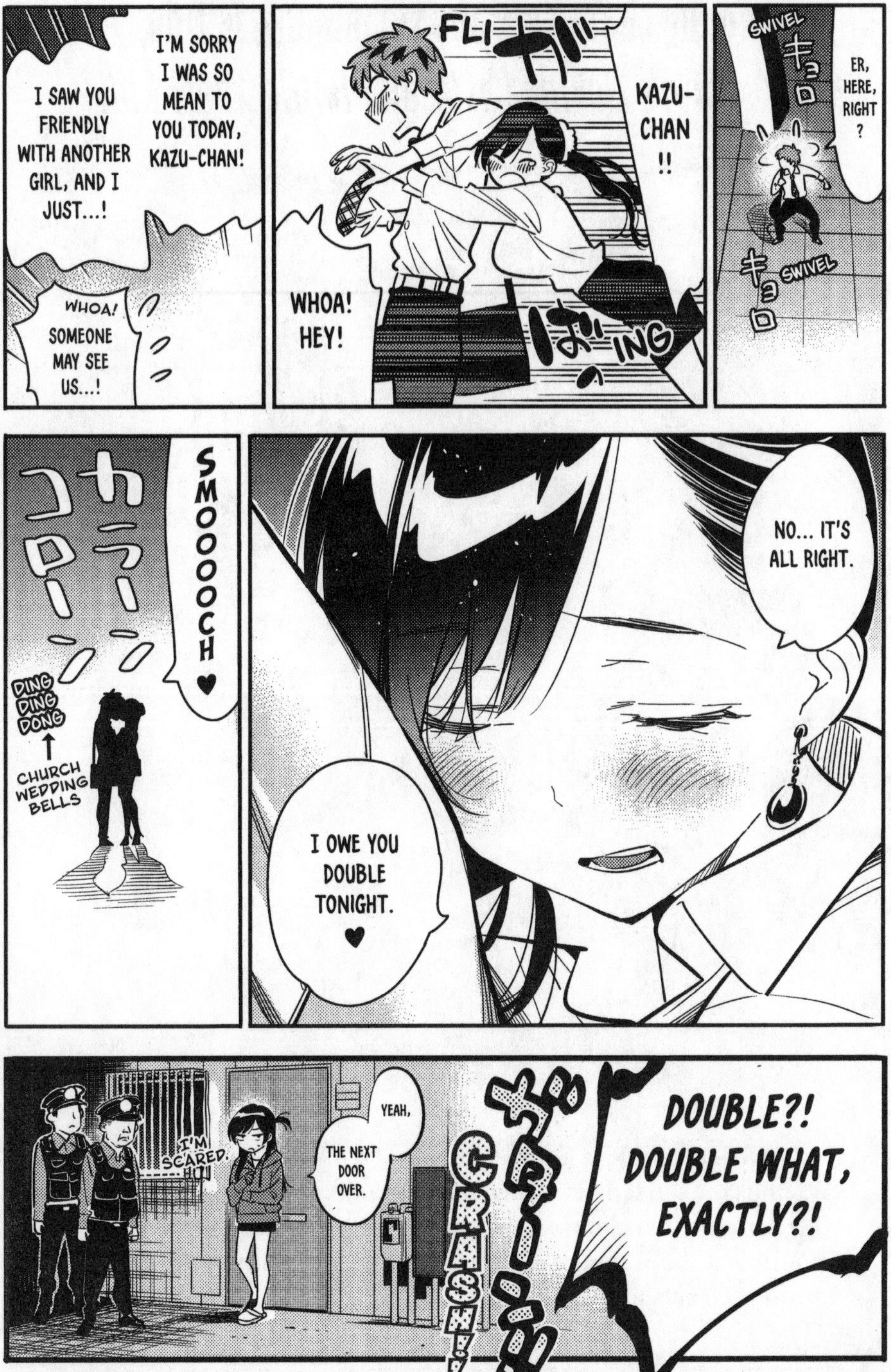

SWIVEL
キョロ
ER, HERE, RIGHT?
キョロ
SWIVEL
FLI
KAZU-CHAN!!
WHOA! HEY!
ING
I'M SORRY I WAS SO MEAN TO YOU TODAY, KAZU-CHAN!
I SAW YOU FRIENDLY WITH ANOTHER GIRL, AND I JUST...!
WHOA! SOMEONE MAY SEE US...!
NO... IT'S ALL RIGHT.
I OWE YOU DOUBLE TONIGHT. ♥
SMOOOOOCH ♥
DING DING DONG
CHURCH WEDDING BELLS
DOUBLE?! DOUBLE WHAT, EXACTLY?!
CRASH!!
YEAH, THE NEXT DOOR OVER.
I'M SCARED. HU!

Young characters and steampunk setting, like *Howl's Moving Castle* and *Battle Angel Alita*

Beyond the Clouds © 2018 Nicke / Ki-oon

A boy with a talent for machines and a mysterious girl whose wings he's fixed will take you beyond the clouds! In the tradition of the high-flying, resonant adventure stories of Studio Ghibli comes a gorgeous tale about the longing of young hearts for adventure and friendship!

One of CLAMP's biggest hits returns in this definitive, premium, hardcover 20th anniversary collector's edition!

CLAMP

Chobits 1
20TH ANNIVERSARY EDITION

"A wonderfully entertaining story that would be a great installment in anybody's manga collection."
— Anime News Network

"CLAMP is an all-female manga-creating team whose feminine touch shows in this entertaining, sci-fi soap opera."
— Publishers Weekly

Poor college student Hideki is down on his luck. All he wants is a good job, a girlfriend, and his very own "persocom"—the latest and greatest in humanoid computer technology. Hideki's luck changes one night when he finds Chi—a persocom thrown out in a pile of trash. But Hideki soon discovers that there's much more to his cute new persocom than meets the eye.

KC
KODANSHA COMICS

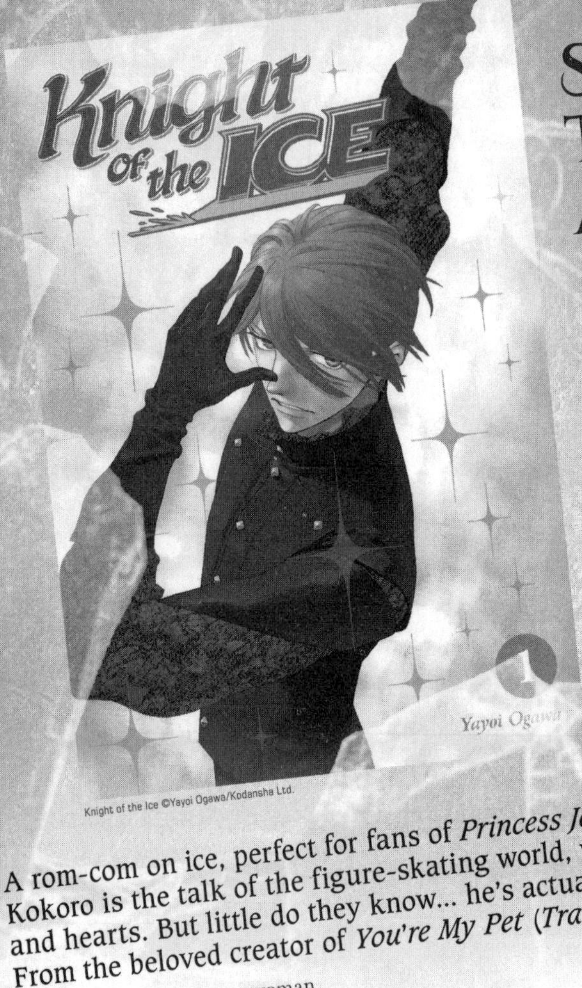
Knight of the ICE
1
Yayoi Ogawa

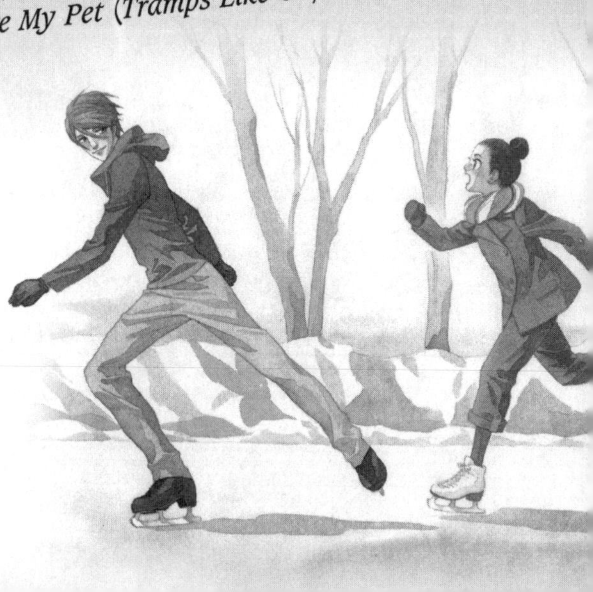

A SMART, NEW ROMANTIC COMEDY FOR FANS OF *SHORTCAKE CAKE* AND *TERRACE HOUSE*!

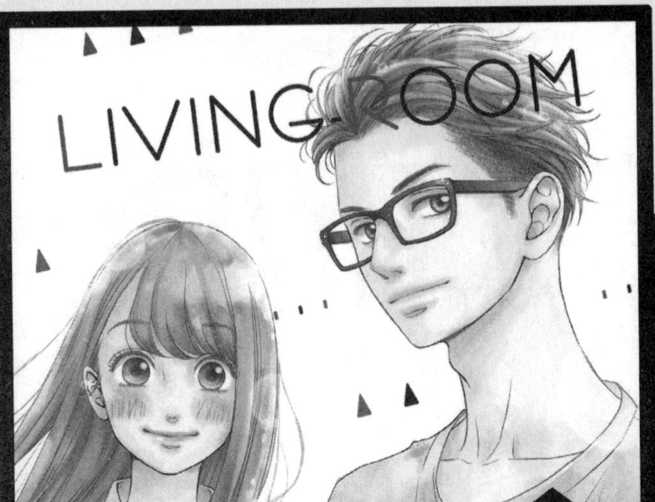
LIVING-ROOM
1
Keiko Iwashita
MATSUNAGA-SAN

KC KODANSHA COMICS

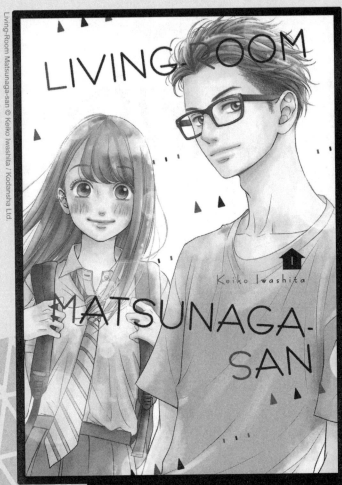

A romance manga starring high school girl Meeko, who learns to live on her own in a boarding house whose living room is home to the odd (but handsome) Matsunaga-san. She begins to adjust to her new life away from her parents, but Meeko soon learns that no matter how far away from home she is, she's still a young girl at heart — especially when she finds herself falling for Matsunaga-san.

The art-deco cyberpunk classic from the creators of *xxxHOLiC* and *Cardcaptor Sakura*!

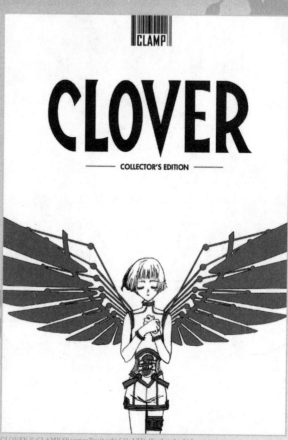

"Starred Review. This experimental sci-fi work from CLAMP reads like a romantic version of *AKIRA*."
—Publishers Weekly

CLAMP
CLOVER
COLLECTOR'S EDITION

Su was born into a bleak future, where the government keeps tight control over children with magical powers—codenamed "Clovers." With Su being the only "four-leaf" Clover in the world, she has been kept isolated nearly her whole life. Can ex-military agent Kazuhiko deliver her to the happiness she seeks? Experience the complete series in this hardcover edition, which also includes over twenty pages of ravishing color art!

KC KODANSHA COMICS

PERFECT WORLD

Rie Aruga

A TOUCHING NEW SERIES ABOUT LOVE AND COPING WITH DISABILITY

An office party reunites Tsugumi with her high school crush Itsuki. He's realized his dream of becoming an architect, but along the way, he experienced a spinal injury that put him in a wheelchair. Now Tsugumi's rekindled feelings will butt up against prejudices she never considered — and Itsuki will have to decide if he's ready to let someone into his heart...

"Depicts with great delicacy and courage the difficulties some with disabilities experience getting involved in romantic relationships... Rie Aruga refuses to romanticize, pushing her heroine to face the reality of disability. She invites her readers to the same tasks of empathy, knowledge and recognition."
—Slate.fr

"An important entry [in manga romance]... The emotional core of both plot and characters indicates thoughtfulness... [Aruga's] research is readily apparent in the text and artwork, making this feel like a real story."
—Anime News Network

KC KODANSHA COMICS

The boys are back, in 400-page hardcovers that are as pretty and badass as they are!

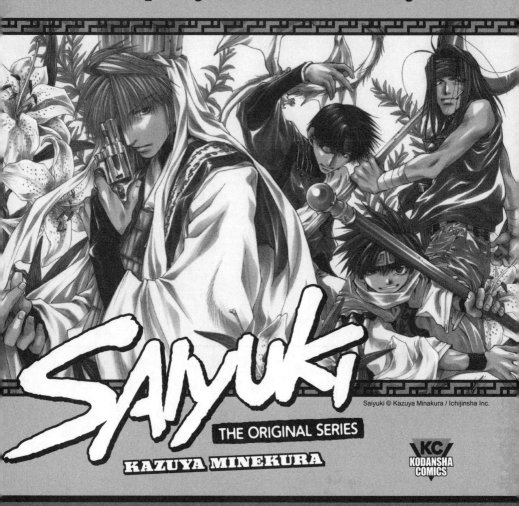

Saiyuki © Kazuya Minakura / Ichijinsha Inc.

SAIYUKI
THE ORIGINAL SERIES
KAZUYA MINEKURA

KC/ KODANSHA COMICS

"AN EDGY COMIC LOOK AT AN ANCIENT CHINESE TALE." —YALSA

Genjo Sanzo is a Buddhist priest in the city of Togenkyo, which is being ravaged by yokai spirits that have fallen out of balance with the natural order. His superiors send him on a journey far to the west to discover why this is happening and how to stop it. His companions are three yokai with human souls. But this is no day trip — the four will encounter many discoveries and horrors on the way.

FEATURES NEW TRANSLATION, COLOR PAGES, AND BEAUTIFUL WRAPAROUND COVER ART!

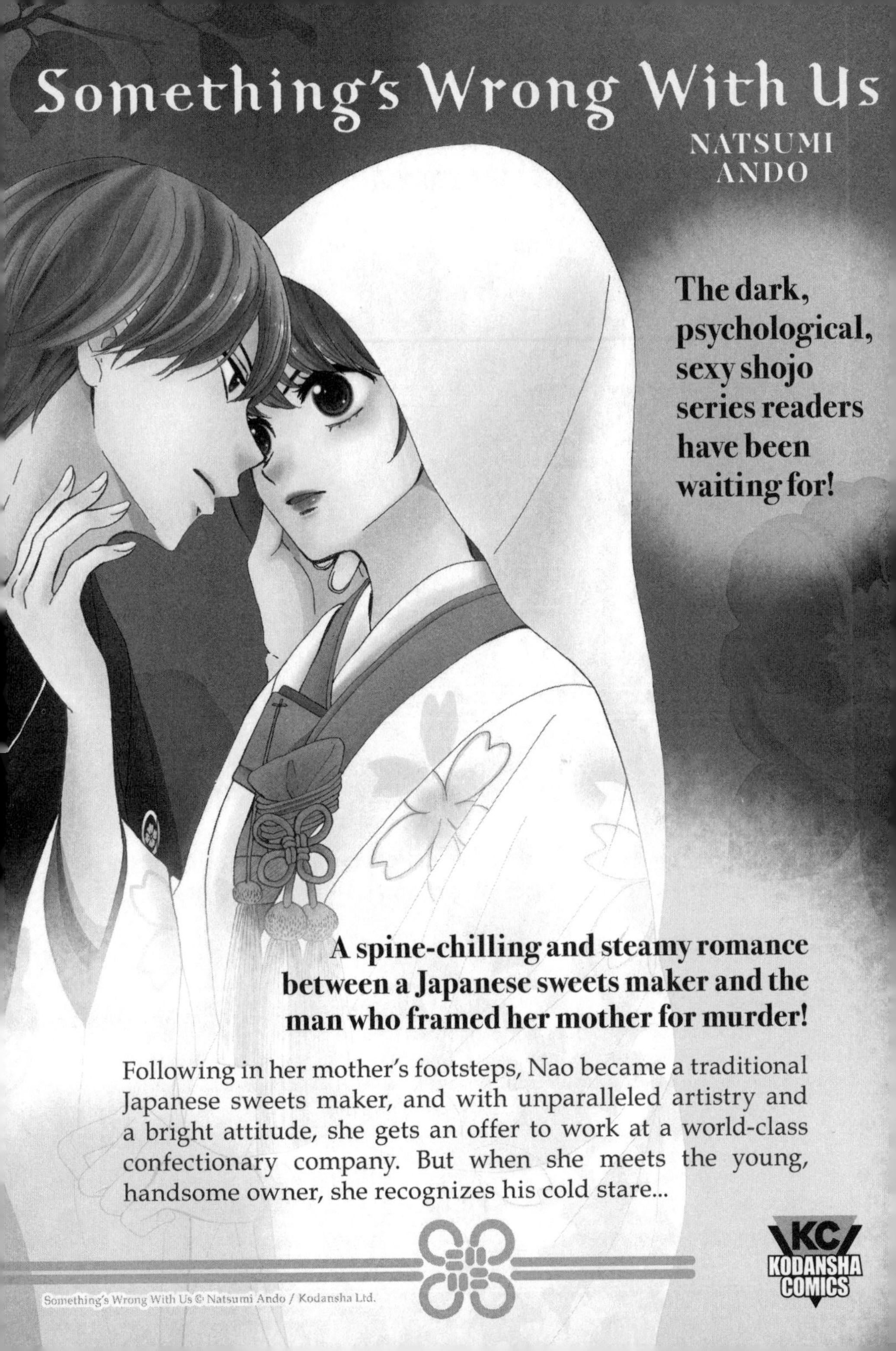
Something's Wrong With Us
NATSUMI ANDO
The dark, psychological, sexy shojo series readers have been waiting for!
A spine-chilling and steamy romance between a Japanese sweets maker and the man who framed her mother for murder!
Following in her mother's footsteps, Nao became a traditional Japanese sweets maker, and with unparalleled artistry and a bright attitude, she gets an offer to work at a world-class confectionary company. But when she meets the young, handsome owner, she recognizes his cold stare...
KC KODANSHA COMICS
Something's Wrong With Us © Natsumi Ando / Kodansha Ltd.

The beloved characters from *Cardcaptor Sakura* return in a brand new, reimagined fantasy adventure!

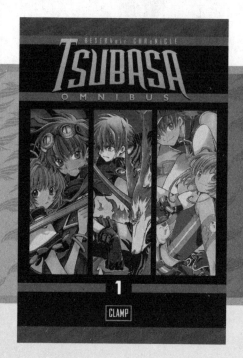

"[*Tsubasa*] takes readers on a fantastic ride that only gets more exhilarating with each successive chapter." —Anime News Network

In the Kingdom of Clow, an archaeological dig unleashes an incredible power, causing Princess Sakura to lose her memories. To save her, her childhood friend Syaoran must follow the orders of the Dimension Witch and travel alongside Kurogane, an unrivaled warrior; Fai, a powerful magician; and Mokona, a curiously strange creature, to retrieve Sakura's dispersed memories!

KODANSHA COMICS

The adorable new odd-couple cat comedy manga from the creator of the beloved *Chi's Sweet Home,* in full color!

Sue & Tai-chan

Konami Kanata

Sue is an aging housecat who's looking forward to living out her life in peace... but her plans change when the mischievous black tomcat Tai-chan enters the picture! Hey! Sue never signed up to be a catsitter! *Sue & Tai-chan* is the latest from the reigning meow-narch of cute kitty comics, Konami Kanata.

KC
KODANSHA COMICS

THE SWEET SCENT OF LOVE IS IN THE AIR! FOR FANS OF OFFBEAT ROMANCES LIKE *WOTAKOI*

Sweat and Soap © Kintetsu Yamada / Kodansha Ltd.

In an office romance, there's a fine line between sexy and awkward... and that line is where Asako — a woman who sweats copiously — meets Koutarou — a perfume developer who can't get enough of Asako's, er, scent. Don't miss a romcom manga like no other!

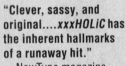

xxxHOLiC © CLAMP·ShigatsuTsuitachi CO.,LTD./Kodansha Ltd.
xxxHOLiC Rei © CLAMP·ShigatsuTsuitachi CO.,LTD./Kodansha Ltd.

Kimihiro Watanuki is haunted by visions of ghosts and spirits. He seeks help from a mysterious woman named Yuko, who claims she can help. However, Watanuki must work for Yuko in order to pay for her aid. Soon Watanuki finds himself employed in Yuko's shop, where he sees things and meets customers that are stranger than anything he could have ever imagined.

A Kodansha Comics Trade Paperback Original
Rent-A-Girlfriend 9 copyright © 2019 Reiji Miyajima
English translation copyright © 2021 Reiji Miyajima

All rights reserved.

Published in the United States by Kodansha Comics, an imprint of Kodansha USA Publishing, LLC, New York.

Publication rights for this English edition arranged through Kodansha Ltd., Tokyo.

First published in Japan in 2019 by Kodansha Ltd., Tokyo as *Kanojo, okarishimasu*, volume 9.

ISBN 978-1-64651-093-1

Original cover design by Kohei Nawata Design Office

Printed in the United States of America.

www.kodansha.us

1st Printing
Translation: Kevin Gifford
Lettering: Paige Pumphrey
Editing: Jordan Blanco
Kodansha Comics edition cover design by Phil Balsman

Publisher: Kiichiro Sugawara

Director of publishing services: Ben Applegate
Associate director of operations: Stephen Pakula
Publishing services managing editors: Madison Salters, Alanna Ruse
Production managers: Emi Lotto, Angela Zurlo
Logo and character art ©Kodansha USA Publishing, LLC